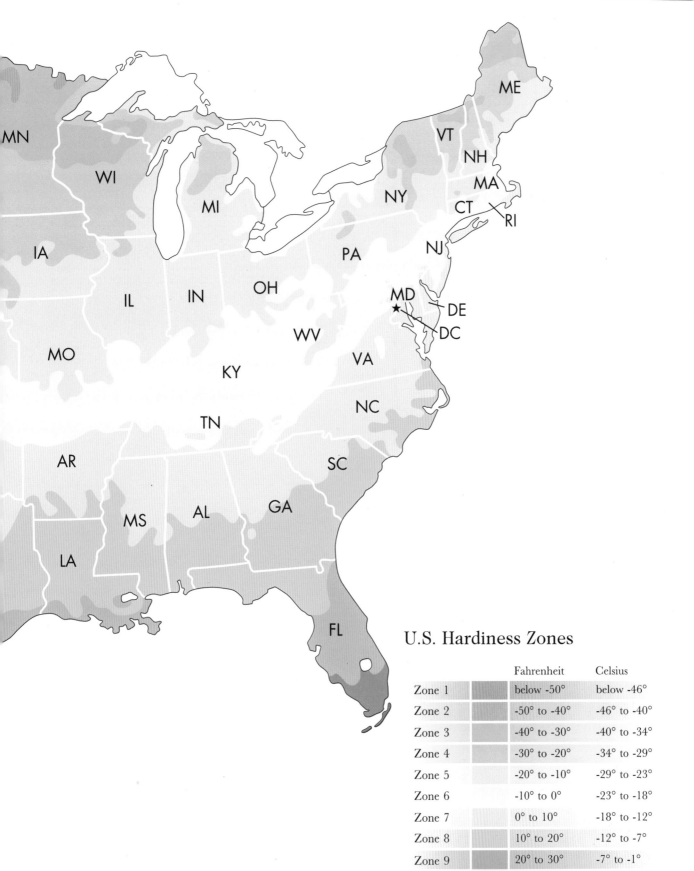

U.S. Hardiness Zones

		Fahrenheit	Celsius
Zone 1		below -50°	below -46°
Zone 2		-50° to -40°	-46° to -40°
Zone 3		-40° to -30°	-40° to -34°
Zone 4		-30° to -20°	-34° to -29°
Zone 5		-20° to -10°	-29° to -23°
Zone 6		-10° to 0°	-23° to -18°
Zone 7		0° to 10°	-18° to -12°
Zone 8		10° to 20°	-12° to -7°
Zone 9		20° to 30°	-7° to -1°
Zone 10		30° to 40°	-1° to 4°
Zone 11		above 40°	above 4°

THE COMPLETE
BOOK OF
SHRUBS

THE COMPLETE
BOOK OF
SHRUBS

Reader's Digest

The Reader's Digest Association, Inc.
Pleasantville, New York • Montreal

A Reader's Digest Book

Edited and designed by Mitchell Beazley

Executive editor: Guy Croton
Executive art editor: Ruth Hope
Editor: Michèle Byam
Art editor: Debbie Myatt
Production: Rachel Lynch
Picture research: Emily Hedges
Artwork: Martine Collings,
Anny Evason
Index: Hilary Bird

Border plans designed by Ken Rawson

The acknowledgments that appear on p.224 are hereby
made a part of this copyright page.

Library of Congress Cataloging-in-Publication Data has
been applied for

ISBN 0-7621-0014-1

Printed in Hong Kong

Contents

Foreword

The aim of this book is to describe in detail everything a gardener needs to know when choosing, planting, and growing shrubs. *The Complete Book of Shrubs* is divided into four sections. The first gives detailed information on what a shrub is and what role shrubs play in the garden. The second describes how to plant shrubs, and how to prune and propagate them, including using methods that do not need special equipment. There is also a guide to identifying the major pests and diseases of shrubs with an explanation of how to treat them. A third section describes how to select the shrubs that will grow well in your garden, how to use them effectively for different purposes, such as for hedges, ground cover, or in a border, and how to combine them with other plants.

The final section of the book is a detailed listing of the best shrubs available for your garden. There are notes on each genus, giving their uses, and any pruning requirements. Following this, the most important garden members of each genus are clearly described, giving their important ornamental characteristics and ultimate size, followed by their hardiness. Additional useful information includes a guide to which shrubs to choose, a glossary of terms, an explanation of hardiness zones with lists showing the hardiness zone range for each genus, key tips for each season, and a list of recommended nurseries from which to buy shrubs.

Camellia reticulata (above left) is a tender shrub often grown as a greenhouse or specimen plant for display.
Mahonia japonica (center) has stiff branches and fragrant yellow flowers in late fall.
Hamamelis × intermedia 'Jelena' *(above right)* is among the best of the witch hazels, with its striking winter flowers.
Hydrangea macrophylla (right, in a summer border) is among the most popular of all hydrangeas.

Shrubs are some of our most important and widely used landscape plants. They lend important structure and framework to gardens, their foliage a more permanent backdrop to the temporary displays of bulbs and annuals. Yet their variety in terms of shape, size, year-round color, and texture is astonishing, as are the decorative characteristics they can bring to the garden. From the familiar golden glow of forsythias in full bloom each spring to the profuse and long-lasting fruit display of *Cotoneaster lacteus*, shrubs are a constant delight in the garden. They happily contribute to landscapes of all sizes, from the tiniest urban pocket garden to vast expanses of parkland, and to every kind of site, from those with perfect conditions to wildly difficult rocky windswept banks.

Magnificent fall foliage
When it is planted in light shade in lime-free soil, the magnificent fall foliage colors of *Disanthus cercidifolius* are a perfect example of how a choice shrub can make an outstanding and lasting impression either in a large border or when growing at the edge of woodland.

what is a shrub?

Types of shrubs

Many trees are too large to be grown in the average garden. In those cases it is the shrubs that must provide the living framework of a garden and a sense of permanence. Shrubs can match every task performed by their taller woody counterparts except one—they will not shoot as purposefully toward the sky, as they reach a maximum of only 15–20ft (4.6–6m).

THE DEFINITION OF A SHRUB

A shrub is commonly defined as "a woody plant, smaller than a tree, with many separate stems." To expand on this, a shrub is a long-lived perennial plant that develops woody stems that with time increase in height, girth, and number. By "woody" we mean that the stems are hardened. Woody stems do not die to the ground each winter in the manner of herbaceous perennials: they remain standing above ground all year, with new growth emerging from buds arranged along the stems (except when they are grown as "dieback" shrubs, see p.78).

Trees likewise have persistent woody stems, but they are different from shrubs in that their woody branches ultimately develop into large branches, with limbs emerging from a single main trunk, or at most a very few. Shrubs, on the other hand, always have numerous primary stems emerging from a central crown, so that each individual plant creates its own individual "thicket" of growth, depending on the type of shrub.

Many woody plants straddle the line between shrub and tree. Some small trees have multiple trunks and could be technically referred to as large shrubs (e.g., some of the small deciduous magnolia hybrids or clumping birches), while some shrubs develop only five or six main stems and can be readily pruned to just one, so that they seem more treelike than shrublike. Designating such plants either "trees" or "shrubs" becomes a rather arbitrary exercise. In this volume we have relied on the natural habit of the plant and on how that plant is most often used in our gardens to dictate whether it should be considered a tree or a shrub. In brief, however, a shrub is a multiple-stemmed woody plant less than 20ft (6m) in height.

Shrubs come in an amazing number of shapes and sizes. What we refer to as the plant's *habit* is a description of the shape that the plant develops naturally (i.e., with no pruning) as it matures. Plant habit is a function of species and/or cultivar (see pp.12–13 for a discussion of these terms). The habits of shrubs range from rounded or oval in outline to narrow and upright, and from flat and ground-hugging to tall and spreading. Shrubs range in height from ground-cover plants a few inches (centimeters) tall to extensive plants such as *Heptacodium miconioides*, which reaches 15–18ft (4.6–5.5m).

Tree forms in winter
Winter reveals the true shape of these large deciduous trees. Stripped of all their leaves, the trunk and branches are exposed to create a stark silhouette in the bright sun.

Red stems in the snow
The many stems of *Cornus alba* 'Sibirica', the red-stemmed dogwood, do not die back in winter. A brilliant red thicket such as this is a truly striking sight in a frozen winter landscape.

Form and size

Shrubs are available in a variety of shapes and sizes. Small colorful shrubs such as *Genista lydia* make excellent ground cover, perfect for the gaps between larger features or awkward spaces around buildings. The dense rounded forms of varieties of *Gardenia* or *Hebe buxifolia* make for soothing displays when planted in balanced arrangements. For grander gardens, large flamboyant shrubs boasting copious flowers and foliage such as many rhododendrons are impressive sights. All shapes have their uses within the garden, and it is important to assess each plant's suitability in visual as well as practical terms.

Numerous terms are used in the description of plant habits. Deciduous plants lose all their leaves annually and nearly simultaneously, in response to seasonal patterns, remaining leafless for part of each year. Deciduous shrubs are usually spring or summer flowering. Evergreen plants appear to retain their leaves permanently. In fact, although leaves are retained for longer than a year, some of the older leaves are shed each year. Semievergreen plants are (as the term suggests) partially evergreen: they retain many leaves for more than one year, but a significant number are lost each year. More terms used in describing shrub habits are illustrated below.

Different types of habit

Coarse
Shrubs such as *Hydrangea quercifolia* can be described as "coarse." They are bold, unrefined, and often irregular in texture and/or shape.

Columnar
These shrubs have a uniformly cylindrical shape like an architectural column. An excellent example of a columnar shape is *Buxus sempervirens* 'Graham Blandy'.

Conical
Many shrubs, such as *Ligustrum vulgare* or *Pittosporum tenuifolium*, can be sheared into this shape, but very few are naturally conical (except for conifers).

Contorted
In this unusual shape, the shrub's branches and/or foliage, flowers, and fruit have twisted or corkscrewlike growth patterns, e.g., *Corylus avellana* 'Contorta'.

Ground cover
Ground-hugging and spreading shrubs such as *Hypericum calycinum* gradually increase the area they occupy in the garden by growing strongly outward.

Fastigiate
Shrubs such as *Ilex vomitoria* 'Will Fleming' have a tall and upright silhouette. The branches grow vertically, in almost parallel formation to the main stems.

Using lavender as ground cover

When considering the type of shrub that makes a good ground-cover planting, it is important to choose a species that is not only visually attractive but is also vigorous enough to fill its allotted space in the border. *Lavandula angustifolia* 'Hidcote' fulfills both criteria.

Loose/open

These shrubs have significant gaps between their branches: you can see through the plant. Individual branches are reasonably direct, as on *Poncirus trifoliata*.

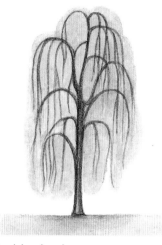

Pendulous/pendent

The entire branches, branch tips, or flower clusters of these shrubs bend weeping toward the ground. A good example is *Leucothoe fontanesiana*.

Prostrate

This term describes a low, sprawling shrub, such as *Vinca major* 'Variegata', that is not necessarily bushy but grows flat to the ground.

Pyramidal

These shrubs taper toward the top, which lends them the shape and the silhouette of a pyramid. Examples include the aptly named *Buxus sempervirens* 'Pyramidalis'.

Rounded

The height and spread of shrubs such as *Fothergilla gardenii* are roughly the same, giving these plants a dense, rounded shape or silhouette.

Upright

These shrubs have an erect shape and silhouette, their branches lifting upward. Shrubs with distinctive upright habits include *Enkianthus campanulatus*.

SHRUBS IN NATURE

Shrubs can be found growing in the wild all around the world, occupying almost every sort of habitat. Shrubs ascend high mountains into alpine areas beyond the tree line, brave salt spray at shorelines, subsist on minimal water and nutrients in the desert, anchor the waterlogged edges of swamps and floodplains, and fill important niches in the understory of both tropical and temperate woodlands. Many botanical families of higher plants have shrubby representatives. As a survival strategist, the adaptable and tolerant woody shrub is a generally successful one.

It is often useful to know the habitat of origin of a garden plant, as this can indicate the kinds of cultural practices that will give the best success when you put that plant into a garden setting. A brief note on the native region of each shrub described in the Plant Directory (pp.130–207) is included there to help you understand the diversity of origins of our garden shrubs. The following is a sampling.

● **Aucuba**, natives of China and Japan, are evergreen shrubs found growing in woodland understories at low to medium altitudes in moderately moist to drier uplands.

● **Berberis**, the familiar barberry genus, includes numerous species from China, Japan, the Himalayas, the Caucasus, and North and South America. These plants are found in a range of conditions—most usually in dry, open, scrubby areas in full sun but also on moist woodland edges.

Growing wild on plains and heaths
Erica (heath) embraces over 700 species, most of which originate from the exposed plains of South Africa.

● **Ceanothus** are North American natives found in many areas of the continent, the most popular garden species being those native to the West Coast, particularly California.

● **Corylopsis** (winter hazel) is a genus of 7–10 deciduous shrubs and small trees that is native to China, Korea, and Japan and generally grows at the edges of low vegetation underlying woodland, and in scrubby thickets.

● **Cotinus** (smokebush) is a small genus that found growing mainly across Europe, through the Himalayas, and in parts of China, where it appears on dry, alkaline upland sites and on the lower elevations of the mountains. There is also a North American species of tree, *C. obovatus*, that is only found on similar, rocky sites in a very small area of the southeastern United States.

Berberis in the wild
Berberis vulgaris grows happily in the rocky soils of mountain areas, such as the formidable slopes of the Sierra Nevada in Spain.

Cytisus (broom) are found in Europe, western Asia, parts of North Africa, and the Canary Islands, where they grow in dry sites on thin soils in full sun.

Erica (heath) is a very large genus containing hundreds of species, mostly of spreading habit. The majority are found in South Africa, but significant members of the genus also occur in the rest of Africa as well as in Europe. These plants are found in sunny, exposed sites on well-drained soils that are of low fertility and are often acidic.

Euonymus (spindletree and including the strawberry tree and wahoo) is a large genus of varied shrubs found in Asia, Europe, and North America, mostly in or near the edges of moist to moderately dry woodlands.

Forsythia, the familiar golden harbingers of spring, are native to Asia and a small region in Europe, where they grow in a range of demanding conditions in exposed sites.

Hydrangea is one of the most widely grown garden shrubs. Over 100 species are found in nature in China, Korea, Japan, the Himalayas, North and South America, and Southeast Asia. It grows in a range of conditions in the wild, from moist rich soils in lowland forest understories to dry upland bluffs and mountain woods.

Kalmia (mountain or sheep laurel) is a small genus of eastern North American flowering shrubs found growing on moist acid soils in cool areas, either in lowland pastures and marshes or at higher levels on rockier sites.

Leucophyllum (Texas ranger) is native to the southwestern United States and Mexico, where it grows in extremely dry, sandy soils and hot conditions.

Lonicera (honeysuckle) is a large genus of over 180 species, found throughout the Northern Hemisphere in many diverse habitats, from moist, coastal, low levels in California to rocky dry cliffs in China.

Nerium (oleander) is native to the Mediterranean region and is found in moist valleys on gravelly soils. It is well adapted to the dry summers and moist winters of that region.

Rhododendron, containing all our garden rhododendrons and azaleas, is a huge genus. Examples are found growing wild in China, Japan, Korea, the Himalayas, India, Southeast Asia, the Mediterranean region, the Caucasus, Europe, and North America. These shrubs are often found in understories where there are acid, well-drained but evenly moist soils, or on rocky, gravelly, well-drained sites with regularly available moisture.

Rosa (rose) is certainly among the most popular garden shrub genera around the world and is found well represented throughout the Northern Hemisphere. Over 100 species are found in a wide variety of different habitats, from lowland humid swamps to high, alkaline, dry sites.

Spiraea (bridal wreath) is another large genus and belongs to the same botanical family as the roses. They are found across a wide swath of the Northern Hemisphere: Europe, North America, and Mexico, including the cool, moist redwood forests of California and the dry, sunny hills of Asia.

Syringa (lilac) are native to Europe and East Asia, where they are usually found growing on rocky, alkaline, upland sites and in similar mountainous areas.

Viburnum is a very large genus that includes over 150 species distributed throughout the Northern Hemisphere and into South America and Malaysia (with an accompanying diversity of native habitats), although most are found in moist environments from exposed scrub to beneath trees.

Weigela is a small genus of deciduous shrubs, possessing a few species that are native to East Asia, where the plants are found growing on a wide range of soils in full sun or at the edges of scrub and woods.

Rhododendron blossoming in Sichuan, China

Discovered by the great plant hunters in some of the world's remotest regions, rhododendrons cover mountainsides with their majestic flowers in the Himalayas, China, and Korea.

SHRUBS IN THE GARDEN

Shrubs have been important garden plants for many hundreds of years. As sources of food, medicines, beverages, and beauty, they have made significant contributions, in both the past and present, to cultures worldwide. Tea, for example, is produced from the leaves of *Camellia sinensis*, while raspberries, gooseberries, currants, blueberries, and cranberries are all fruits of different shrubs. The beautiful and beguiling rose, among the most widely grown and well loved garden plants in the temperate world, is by nature a shrub.

The key difference between shrubs in the garden and shrubs in nature is that garden shrubs have been transplanted into a garden site. The statement may seem obvious, but the implications are considerable. The garden setting may be in a region with a climate and soil relatively similar to or dramatically different from that of the shrub's native habitat. How closely the setting resembles the shrub's native habitat has an impact on the plant's performance.

One might be tempted to assume that the more closely the garden site matches the climate and conditions found in the shrub's native habitat, the better the plant will perform. This principle is a reasonable general rule of thumb, but many other factors complicate any assessment of plant response, very often making it fairly difficult to predict how a given species or cultivar will grow.

Certainly it is true that attempts to grow shrubs in places that are very different from their native habitat will be likely to fail unless you offer extreme intervention. For example, if you have a heated greenhouse, trying to grow shrubs in it that are native to Siberia is surely doomed to failure. Planting flowering shrubs that are native to northern temperate areas (where they experience several months of dormancy and cold temperatures between flowering periods) in the equatorial tropics is also likely to give disappointing results—at least in terms of flowering.

Growing conditions

You can often be surprised when you include plants in your garden that come from different places. The shrub *Fothergilla major*, for example, is native to southern parts of the United States, but it happily grows in gardens a great deal farther north and south of its native range. This is because the range of conditions that a plant such as *Fothergilla major* will adapt to or tolerate is much wider than the conditions that can be found in its native habitat.

Nevertheless, the more drastically the garden conditions diverge from those of the native habitat of a particular shrub, the less likely it is that the shrub will succeed in your garden. Ultimately it is the adaptability of a given shrub to the combination of conditions in a garden that translates to vigorous growth and development over many years. Various characteristics of the garden play a part:

- **Climate** (seasonal patterns and extremes in temperature, rainfall, length of the day) as determined by latitude, height, and continental location.
- **Soil** (fertility levels, aeration, drainage).
- **Diversity of microclimate** (the many changes in the conditions in small areas that are created by garden topography, buildings, walks, lighting, etc.).

All these factors contribute to establishing the total annual package that is the growing environment for a given garden.

Selecting shrubs that provide particular desired ornamental qualities and also perform well in your garden with no significant pest or disease problems becomes a matter, then, of matching the tolerances and other aspects of the desired shrubs with the climate and characteristics of the garden. This is not as impossible or complex a task as it may seem. The key is to spend time reading and researching before you purchase your plants—in other words, you should identify desirable and appropriate shrubs for your own garden before setting out to find them. (For a further discussion of how to choose shrubs for your garden—see pp.46–47.)

There is such a wealth of selections available to gardeners, wherever they are around the world, that any garden can include numerous delightful shrubs for many kinds of plantings, from quiet and useful ground covers to dramatically large flowering specimens.

A thoughtful gardener will spend time determining which selection will perform best in their area. A northern gardener, for example, might choose *Buxus* cultivars such as 'Vardar Valley' and 'Wintergreen' with significantly improved cold hardiness and winter foliage color. Taking time to identify the best selections for your region and conditions will lead to much more beautiful and effective garden plantings with fewer disappointments and far less need to replace plants that are not performing up to expectations.

A mixed shrub border is wonderful in any garden
Correctly identifying the prevailing conditions in your garden will allow you to grow a range of shrubs successfully.

Names of shrubs

As with all plants, it is important that we know the correct names of shrubs. In order to select the shrubs we really want for our gardens, we must be able to specify their exact identities correctly. Many closely related shrubs have similar names, although their performances in the garden are quite different. Knowing the correct names of shrubs allows us to make knowledgeable observations and decisions about how to manage them.

Common and botanical names

Plants are given common names by a sort of cultural and regional tradition; let's take witch hazels as an example. Plants also have botanical names (in the case of the witch hazels, the name is *Hamamelis* spp., the abbreviation "spp." meaning the plural of "species"). If we know only the common name of a plant, we are vulnerable to confusion and the risk of misidentification. There are numerous species and varieties of witch hazels, so if we went to our favorite nursery and asked just for a witch hazel, we could receive any one of many selections—all with a distinctively different color of bloom, mature size, bloom season, hardiness, tolerance of drought, etc. However, if we know the botanical name, we can ensure that we can find the particular witch hazel that we want to grow in our garden.

Botanical names consist of at least two words in botanical Latin (which often differs from actual Latin) and sometimes a plain English name in single quotes (the cultivar epithet); sometimes there is a third "Latin" designation to indicate the botanical variety. The form of botanical names is thus *Genus species* (or possibly: *Genus species* variety) 'Cultivar', as in the name of the witch hazel *Hamamelis vernalis* 'Sandra'. In this example, the genus is *Hamamelis*, the specific epithet is *vernalis*, and the cultivar epithet is 'Sandra'. The full species name of this plant is therefore *Hamamelis vernalis*; usually, if various plants of the same genus are being discussed together, an abbreviation is used for the genus, so the name might be expressed as *H. vernalis*. The species is the basic unit of botanical naming. The genus indicates a generally related group of plants; within each genus are specific names describing even more closely related groups that are distinct from one another, even though they retain the general characteristics of the genus.

This system of using two names to identify plants (and all other living organisms) is known as binomial nomenclature—it was developed by the famous botanist and naturalist Linnaeus (Carl von Linné) in the 18th century.

There are several other species of *Hamamelis*, including *H. mollis* from China, *H. virginiana* from eastern North

Pinpointing the species
Taxonomy identifies plants clearly. The Chinese witch hazel belongs to the genus *Hamamelis*, species name *mollis*.

America, and *H. mexicana* from Mexico, to name just a few. The common names of these plants reflect their origins: *H. mollis* is Chinese witch hazel, *H. virginiana* is common witch hazel, and *H. mexicana* is Mexican witch hazel.

The cultivar designation is a more recent invention and is concerned with correct identification of cultivated varieties of plants. The word "cultivar" is a shortened form of CULTIvated VARiety. It identifies plants that have been selected for characteristics of particular value to horticulturists or agriculturists, such as disease resistance, color, or form. The cultivar is named for these characteristics (or sometimes to honor an important person), and these plants are propagated in specialized ways to ensure that their characteristics remain true to the name. The cultivar epithet is always given last in the name string. It begins with a capital letter and is set off between single quotes; it does not appear in italics.

Naming hybrids

Hybrid selections of plants present yet another sort of name for us to learn. A hybrid selection is the progeny, generally a set of seed and ultimately seedlings, resulting from a cross between two different plants. We generally refer to hybrids between two species of the same genus (although there are rare hybrids between two genera). For example, one might collect pollen from one species of holly, *Ilex serrata*, and brush it onto the flowers of another species of holly, *I. verticillata*. Any resulting seed would germinate and grow into hybrid seedlings.

These hybrid seedlings are all hollies, but they are not of pure parentage of either species, and we express their hybrid parentage slightly differently in the botanical name of these plants to indicate that fact. In our holly example here, the name of these hybrid seedlings would be *Ilex verticillata* X *serrata*. The X indicates a hybrid cross.

Because of their length, hybrid names for plants are often abbreviated, especially when a cultivar has been selected and named from a hybrid cross. If, for example, one of our *I. verticillata* X *serrata* seedlings had especially large and plentiful yellow fruit instead of the regular red color, we might wish to name this seedling as a cultivar and propagate it under that name. If we then named the cultivar 'Golden Glow', this one seedling would then have the name *I. verticillata* X *serrata* 'Golden Glow'—quite a mouthful. It is equally correct and more common to abbreviate this to *Ilex* 'Golden Glow'.

Hybrid holly
This is a shrubby hybrid of two species of *Ilex*. Its name has been abbreviated to *Ilex* x *altaclerensis*, and the distinctive stripes on its leaves have given it the cultivar name 'Golden King'.

In some cases the cross itself is given a name, e.g., *Ilex rugosa* X *I. aquifolium* is actually called *I.* X *meserveae* (after a Mrs. Meserve, who made the cross). These abbreviations are acceptable because they preserve the genus name and the correct cultivar name. There are many hybrid selections of shrubs available, and they will often be designated as *Genus* 'Cultivar', without the complete hybrid name being written out.

Initially it might seem that botanical names are just too complicated to be worth learning, but once you work through the names of a few shrubs with which you are already familiar, you will start to see certain patterns and to realize how helpful and important the taxonomic names are. For example, if you begin to take note of the botanical names of plants when visiting attractive gardens, you can investigate the cultural requirements of these plants and perhaps obtain the same plants in order to create a similar effect in your own garden. If you want your garden to look the way you want it to look, there is no substitute for being able to put the correct taxonomic name to each of its shrubs.

As with all plants, the techniques used to plant and maintain shrubs have a significant impact on their performance. The goal is to minimize the stress caused to the shrubs when they are moved during transplanting and to provide conditions as favorable as possible during their life. This is not to recommend coddling the shrubs, or spending time and energy altering the garden environment to suit an individual plant. Generally, it is best to utilize the knowledge and skills you have accumulated that will allow you to succeed with the best-chosen plants. In this way, with a reasonable degree of resources and effort, it is possible to achieve good results. The following sections offer advice on particular approaches and techniques that will help you enjoy the greatest success with shrubs, regardless of the climate in which you garden.

Growing shrubs successfully
This means choosing the right plant for your garden, creating the best conditions, and transplanting from container to bed with a minimum amount of disturbance. Shrubs such as hydrangeas *(left)* will establish more quickly if you plant them when they are small. They tolerate a range of garden sites but are best in moist, well-drained soil.

growing shrubs

Planting & aftercare

The first experience we offer our garden plants as we include them in our gardens is very stressful: we plant or transplant them in·a new home. There is no comparable process in nature—no growing plant is heaved up, transported some distance, and then replanted in a totally new environment.

Whether we are planting containerized, bare-root, or balled-and-burlapped specimens, or digging and transplanting them from one location to another in the garden, the disturbance to the roots creates a series of major stresses. The more we do to minimize these stresses and to promote recovery, the more vigorously our newly planted shrub will perform.

The main problem when planting and transplanting is the wounding of a plant and/or loss of its roots. Roots supply the plant with water and nutrients and anchor it in the ground. When we plant and transplant, excessive root damage drastically reduces the number of functional roots. This leads to water stress and dehydration of the plant, which is no longer able to supply itself with the quantity of water normally supplied by the roots. By minimizing any root damage, we can maximize regrowth. This helps the plant recover promptly while maintaining an adequate supply of water.

It is easy to make the wrong assumptions about what is actually helpful to the shrub (or any other plant) during planting and transplanting. Various approaches are more or less successful, depending on the size of the plant, how it has been grown, what type of soil you are putting it into, and what time of year you are doing so. General cases are treated below, but first consider the basic principles of planting that apply no matter what the type of plant or site.

Plant smaller rather than larger shrubs to ensure the best and fastest recovery. The smaller the plant, the easier it is to preserve a larger percentage of the root mass. Smaller plants can more easily regenerate roots that have been damaged or destroyed during the transplanting process because they have less aboveground area to support during the recovery period.

This, of course, runs counter to our first impulse, which is often to transplant the largest individual plant of the lot, representing, we think, the most vigorous and the showiest in the nursery and then the garden. Resist this impulse! The smaller plant will rebound much more quickly and robustly from transplanting than will the larger one.

Planting recommendations

Before planting in a bed, make sure you have completed all soil preparation (see pp.84–87). Always plant in moist but not wet conditions, and try to put the plant in as soon as you have dug the planting hole. Also, remember to remove any nonsoil material (for example, twine, wire, burlap, plastic tags) from around the roots and stems of the plant. The planting hole should be of the right size (see opposite).

The first stage will obviously be to remove the plants from their containers or small balled-and-burlapped plants from their burlap. (If it is a large plant, you will need to loosen pins and ties on the ball, although you should not completely remove the burlap until the plant has been positioned in the hole—see p.26.) Loosen containerized plants by tapping the bottom of the container sharply before gently sliding the plant out of the pot at a nearly upside-down angle. For stubborn containers (those that will not come away easily), use a knife

A *Buddleja* 'Lochinch' in a freshly dug and planted bed
Before planting, make sure that you have prepared the site thoroughly by removing all weeds, double-digging, and incorporating a layer of well-rotted organic matter.

to slit down one side, across the base, and up the other side (although you must take care not to slice into the root mass), then peel the pot away from the root mass.

Make sure before you begin the actual planting that you have gently loosened the outer roots of the plant so that branched ends of the roots around the root mass are clearly visible for lengths of about 4–6in (10–15cm), forming a fringe of roots around the root mass. You will also need to separate and straighten any circling or girdling roots (see below), cutting away the girdling roots if necessary.

It aids planting if you can create a raised, rounded platform of soil on which to place the plant. Simply mound the soil into a flattened cone in the center of the bottom of the planting hole (but avoid compacting or packing down the soil). Then place the plant on top of this flattened mound, which needs to lie so that the original soil line of the plant's crown matches that of the new planting hole—in poorly drained soils, ensure that the crown of the root ball is slightly raised in relation to the previous soil line.

Arrange the roots of the plant evenly around the mound, with the crown centered on the top and the roots arrayed outward and downward from the central crown toward the bottom of the hole. Larger balled-and-burlapped plants need flatter and shallower platforms; smaller containerized plants need taller, more pyramidal mounds.

Backfill the soil dug from the hole evenly around the bottom of the hole, gradually working your way up to the top. Tamp the soil lightly with your heel after every few shovels as you fill the hole; this ensures good contact between the roots and the soil. Do not stomp on the soil or roots. To help retain water, create a slightly raised lip—about 6in (15cm) high and wide—in a circle around the edges of the planting hole. After

Preparation and planting

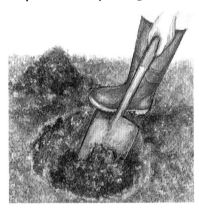

1 Dig the planting hole at least twice the diameter of and as deep as or deeper than the root ball or container.

2 Slide the shrub from its container with one hand supporting the soil mass at the base of the plant.

3 Gently loosen the outer roots to form a fringe around the root ball. Separate any girdling or circling roots (see p.24).

4 Place the shrub on a raised platform of soil in the bottom of the planting hole, its crown level with the soil line.

5 Gradually backfill the soil around the plant, mounding it slightly around the crown. Tamp it down with your heel.

6 Water the newly planted shrub thoroughly so that the surface of the soil is shiny but not puddled.

planting, water gently and thoroughly, soaking the area of the planting hole and its adjacent soil. Finally, apply a shallow, even layer of organic mulch (see p.52) to a depth of no more than 2–3in (5–8cm), and water the mulch.

A major decision you must make is whether to plant a shrub in spring or fall. In general, the decision rests on whether the plant will be able to overwinter successfully. If the plant is likely to be able to survive, fall planting is always preferable. To summarize a complicated process, the advantage of planting in fall is that during this time of the year, when the weather is turning cool and moist, there will be no additional shoot growth, and hence no increased leaf area to support with water and nutrients. Even evergreens lose some leaves toward the end of the growing season, and they do not display additional shoot growth as they go into winter.

Note, though, that if the plant is only borderline winter-hardy in your area, is slow to regenerate new roots even in the best of conditions, or is a broad-leaved evergreen, it is generally best to plant in the spring in order to avoid potential cold damage and winter dehydration.

Planting container-grown shrubs

In terms of minimizing planting stress, well-produced container-grown plants can offer the easiest option to the gardener. Because the root system of a container-grown plant is already

Container-grown shrubs

The root system of a container-grown shrub is already packaged in the container. This makes these shrubs easier to plant.

packaged in the container, there is no need to disturb the roots until the plant is ready to go directly into the ground. A well-cultivated container plant will have been shifted up from smaller to larger containers as it grew in the nursery so that there was always ample room for root development, with no restrictions on root growth. When this has been done correctly, the roots will be reasonably evenly distributed within the container, will be well branched and healthy, and will have numerous active growing points throughout the root mass, allowing further free root development later on.

There are variations on this theme, however, as the types of roots that plants develop differ dramatically among species. Some plants, such as the heaths and heathers, develop dense, fine, highly branched fibrous root masses, while others (for example, *Aucuba*) display a few large primary roots, which then form smaller knots of fine fibrous roots at their branch ends.

Problems with container-grown shrubs

You will not always be fortunate enough, however, to obtain a container plant that has been well grown. In many instances you will find that the plant has been left in a particular size of pot for too long, so that the roots have been physically restricted. In such instances the roots will have spread to the sides of the container and, having nowhere else to go, will have begun to grow in circles around its edges. Sometimes, in severe cases, these roots will even turn and grow back into the interior of the central root mass or up toward the surface of the growing medium and the plant's crown. These are called circling roots; if they have begun to grow around other roots or the crown, they are called girdling roots.

A container-grown plant whose roots have outgrown the container and are growing in circles and tangles around each other to create a nearly impenetrable root mass is said to be pot-bound or root-bound.

Circling and girdling roots are by far the most prevalent problem with container-grown plants. They rarely occur in balled-and-burlapped or bare-root plants, as these have been grown in open ground and their roots have not been restricted in any way. Circling and girdling roots must be dealt with during planting—otherwise they will continue to grow and enlarge in the directions in which they have become established. This can lead to the plant developing a very one-sided root system, weakening its structure and making it much more susceptible to being blown over in high winds. In severe cases they can eventually kill the plant.

Separating the roots of pot-bound shrubs

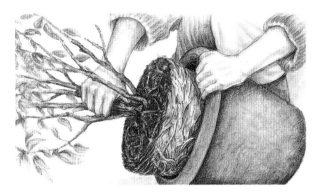

I Circling or girdling roots of pot-bound shrubs should be removed or separated before they strangle adjacent roots, or even the stem, which considerably weakens the plant's root system.

2 Carefully lay the shrub, still in its container, on its side. Tap the sides of the container sharply, grip the plant by its base and gently slide the plant's root mass out.

3 With your hands (or a spading fork if the shrub is large), tease the primary roots loose from the tangle so that you can unwind them for a good 10–12in (25–30cm).

4 Trim any dead or severely twisted ends away. Knead some of the primary central roots away from the center of the root mass and trim any dead ends from these roots, too.

Numerous methods have been recommended for dealing with circling and girdling roots, including various versions of slicing into a severely pot-bound root mass and pulling the cut sections out and away from each other. This method, sometimes called butterflying, can be effective with shrubs that regenerate new fibrous roots quickly in response to the cuts—for example, heaths and heathers, so long as the environment is favorable—but it can be a disaster when applied to species (such as most varieties of *Daphne*) that have slower-growing and less-branching root systems.

A more widely applicable method for separating the roots of pot-bound shrubs is illustrated above. This takes longer but is less risky. When you plant the shrub, use the freed roots as the skirt of roots that you lay down from the crown around the planting cone, making sure that they are in good contact with the backfilled soil.

Merely cutting into the root mass in quarters or halves generally creates many wounds and can completely isolate

pieces of root from the plant's root mass. This is the cause of considerable stress to the plant, as it has to invest more heavily in the regrowing of roots.

Planting bare-root shrubs

With bare-root plants, many of the issues that affect the way we plant container-grown or balled-and-burlapped shrubs are irrelevant because the roots have already been freed of all soil. Plants obtained bare-root have been field-grown, dug, cleaned, and then generally kept in cold storage for a period before being shipped to you. Roses are the most commonly purchased bare-root shrubs, although raspberries, blueberries, and many ornamentals are often available bare-root as well.

The primary consideration with a bare-root plant is to keep the roots moist (though not soaking wet) between the time it arrives and the time you plant it. On its arrival, unpack the plant in a cool place, avoiding both windy spots in the open and highly heated areas of a house or shed. Look for broken or bruised branches or roots. Repack the plant by placing moist sphagnum or shredded bark carefully around the roots and wrapping the whole plant loosely in plastic, then keep it in a cool dark place until planting. Try to plant as soon as possible. It is preferable to purchase bare-root plants in fall because that is the ideal time to plant them (see p.24).

On the day of planting, unwrap the plant and remove any damaged branches or roots, using a sharp pair of shears; be sure to make a clean cut close to the main shoot or root from which the damaged branch or root emerges.

It will be a bit of a challenge to determine where the original soil line was at the crown. When planting in the fall, it is best to err on the side of putting the shrub a bit too deep, to minimize the possibility of winterkill.

Planting balled-and-burlapped shrubs

A balled-and-burlapped shrub is one that has been grown in a field and is then dug up with many of the roots intact inside a ball of soil. This is wrapped in burlap and fastened with pins, clips, and twine to prevent it from coming undone.

In the past, the burlap used was an organic, biodegradable material that could be left somewhat intact in the soil, where it would gradually decay without significantly restricting the growth of the roots. This is no longer necessarily the case. Increasingly, synthetic materials are being used. These are appear to be just like natural burlap when you look at or touch them, but they do not decay (which is precisely why they are preferred by the nursery industry). For this reason, it is especially important to remove as much burlap as possible when you are planting balled-and-burlapped shrubs.

Depending on the size of the shrub, you should deal with the burlap wrapping in one of two slightly different ways. For small to medium plants, whose root balls are readily handled, it is best to remove the burlap completely before planting. For larger shrubs, leave the burlap on until the plant has been moved into the hole. (If you are working with another person, the burlap forms a natural sling in which to move the plant.) Cut the burlap away using sharp scissors or a knife (see below), trimming it as close as you can without cutting into the root ball. Remove from the planting hole all the burlap

Planting small balled-and-burlapped shrubs

1 Place the plant next to the hole. Untie the twine and remove any pins, peeling the burlap away so that it lies flat.

2 Gently lever the root ball up on a shovel blade, then slip the shovel into the hole so the plant slithers off.

3 Position the shrub so that the main stems point up. Gently separate the roots around the edges of the ball.

Planting large balled-and-burlapped shrubs

1 Again, position the shrub next to the hole and loosen the burlap so that it hangs in flaps from the top of the ball.

2 Together with a helper, grasp the burlap flaps and slide the shrub into the hole and onto the planting mound.

3 Lay the burlap flat and, using scissors or a knife, cut it away, trimming as close as possible to the root ball.

except that small, inaccessible remaining bit of fabric on which the ball now rests. Whatever the size of the shrub, make sure you thoroughly moisten the root ball the day before planting with a gentle spray of water, and then mix plenty of water into the soil when you backfill the hole.

Staking balled-and-burlapped shrubs

Large balled-and-burlapped shrubs are likely to be the only sort you will have to stake in order to keep the plant stable during its initial root growth. Staking shrubs is not as straightforward as staking trees, since you are not staking a single trunk. If the shrub has three to five main stems, position the stakes in a triad near the three largest and most evenly spaced stems. Use strong wire, commercial tree ties, or twine designed for staking (this will not stretch too much). Line the area of wire that will surround each stem with pieces of old garden hose or heavy-gauge leather scavenged from old work gloves, saddles, or the like.

A simple method is to drive a 2 x 2in (5 x 5cm) wooden stake, 4ft (1.2m) tall, into the ground to a depth of at least 1ft (30cm) and 2–3ft (60–90cm) from the shrub stem. Into both sides of the stake, about 10in (25cm) down from the top, cut a ½in (1.5cm) notch. Now cut a piece of wire two and a half times the length of the distance between the shrub stem and the stake. Pull the wire through the central hole of a length of old hose or a piece of folded-over leather some 8in (20cm) long. Center the hose/leather around the shrub stem and twist the two ends of the wire tightly around the stake. If the resulting loop proves too slack, insert a screwdriver, crowbar or similar implement between the two strands of wire and twist until you achieve the desired degree of tightness.

Transplanting deciduous shrubs

Transplanting shrubs is much like planting them, except for an additional first step. When you transplant a shrub, the first thing you have to do is carefully remove it from the ground, preserving as much of the root system as possible. Carefully dig a circle around the shrub to the extent of its branches. You can cut through woody roots but leave the fibrous ones intact. Work a piece of burlap under the root ball, tie it securely, and use this to lift the shrub out. Then replant it, following the planting recommendations detailed on pp.22–24. When transplanting a shrub, you need to make a decision about what time of year to move it. In general, follow the same guidelines as for deciding when to plant: in other words, slow-growing

and broad-leaved evergreens should be transplanted in the spring, while all other shrubs are (if at all possible) best transplanted in the fall. There is some flexibility to this rule, however. You can transplant at less ideal times of the year if you are especially careful to give the shrub winter protection, maintain adequate water, and choose a favorable new site.

Transplanting evergreen shrubs

Evergreen shrubs can be transplanted or planted in exactly the same way as other shrubs; the technique that you follow will depend on whether the evergreen shrub is container-grown, balled-and-burlapped, or bare-root. With most evergreen shrubs, however, it is very important that they are planted in spring. If your winters are either extremely cold or extremely dry, or both, evergreens will be vulnerable to dehydration and water stress—owing to the fact that they retain almost all of their foliage. However, if you ensure that you transplant evergreen shrubs during the milder, moister times of the year, you will automatically minimize the water stress that can be caused to the plant.

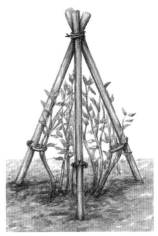

Staking using a triad

For shrubs with three to five main stems, position the stakes in a triad near the three largest, most equidistant stems. Tie with some strong wire or twine.

Tying shrubs to a single stake

Drive a 4ft (1.2m) stake in the ground about 2–3ft (60–90cm) from the shrub stem. Cut notches 10in (25cm) from the top on both sides of the stake. Use a piece of wire about two and a half times as long as the distance between the stake and the shrub.

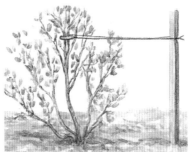

Lining the wire

Pull the wire through a piece of old hose (inset) and center the hose over the stem.

Pruning

Pruning is the process of selectively trimming and removing stems, branches, and portions of the shoots of the shrub, either to change its visual shape, to remove dead, diseased, or straggly stems or to tidy an overgrown or straggly plant. There are a number of rules and techniques for pruning various shrubs to attain these goals; indeed, there are entire volumes that explain pruning in great detail. Individual shrubs may require very specific pruning techniques; some general principles and methods are described here.

Pruning techniques

Annual pruning is by no means a required ritual for all shrubs (in the way that raking leaves or staking tomatoes may be). Specific pruning techniques should be selected to shape, invigorate, correct, thin, or renovate a particular shrub only after careful consideration. Some shrubs need no significant pruning other than a hard pruning every five years or so. Other types of shrubs do best with a light thinning every other year. Still others need an annual shearing.

Pruning, when applied correctly, is an important tool for managing shrubs. Some roses, for example, require annual pruning if they are to bloom, in the same way that these

Four basic types of shrub pruning

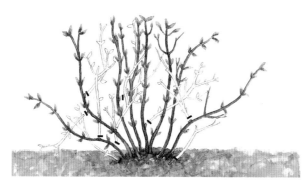

1 Corrective pruning is used to remove diseased, damaged, and dead branches, as well as to stop crossing branches from rubbing each other. Do it as soon as you see the problem.

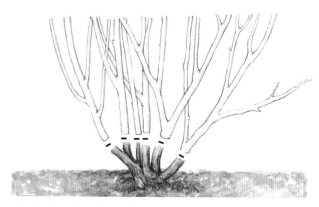

2 Hard pruning (also called renewal, rejuvenation, or renovation pruning) can be done annually or periodically. Most of the existing canopy is cut away in this process.

3 Thinning is done to improve light penetration and air circulation. Cut weak, irregular, or crossing main stems close to the soil, leaving a set of vigorous, healthy, well-spaced stems.

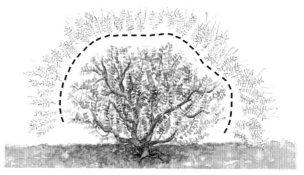

4 Shearing is used to maintain the height, shape, and silhouette of a hedge or topiary. Clip all the stems at a uniform length or distance from the ground in even planes.

particular roses require repeated treatment with pesticides if they are to survive. Most sheared hedges need at least one annual shearing to retain their shape and vigor.

The four basic types of pruning

● Corrective pruning, to remove crossed branches, damaged tissue, or diseased or dead branches. When performing corrective pruning you should cut away branches cleanly, with the cut at an angle and close to the next intersecting branch that shows no signs of damage or disease.

● Periodic or regular hard pruning, to invigorate flowering and/or to stimulate shoot growth (periodic hard pruning is sometimes called renovation, renewal, or rejuvenation pruning). In hard pruning, very significant amounts of the main stems are cut away. This form of pruning is used to renew plants that have become excessively vigorous, nonvigorous, or misshapen, or that no longer bloom well. Regular hard pruning is used to produce maximum growth of shoots on

shrubs selected for attractive, unusually colored stems and/or foliage and is done in early spring. Examples of shrubs that benefit from regular hard pruning are *Cornus alba* and purple-foliaged selections of *Cotinus coggygria*.

● Thinning, in order to improve the penetration of sunlight throughout the shrub and/or to adjust the shrub's silhouette. You should select entire main stems and cut them close to the ground, so that you leave a set of vigorous main stems evenly spaced throughout the crown.

● Shearing, to maintain the shape and height of hedges and topiary. Shearing involves trimming all of the stems and branches in a very uniform plane to produce a desired shape and silhouette. Most shrubs used in hedges perform best when sheared lightly several times during the growing season—rather than being sheared heavily only one time—if they are to maintain good shape and vigor. Frequent light shearing of hedges promotes dense growth in the same way that frequent light mowing of lawns promotes dense, vigorous

Spring pruning

1 Numerous flowering deciduous shrubs should be pruned in spring after they bloom. To remove the spent flower heads cut down to the next vigorous set of buds.

2 Spring pruning can include thinning of these shrubs by removing undesirable stems.

3 When doing seasonal pruning, it is always a good time to remove dead wood.

Summer pruning

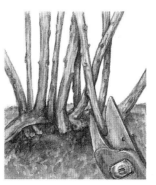

1 Summer pruning is done on plants that bloom later in the season or to thin and correct rank spring growth. Suckers, water sprouts, and the like can all be removed at this time.

2 To thin and remove poor spring growth, cut stems near the base of the plant.

3 Make all pruning cuts cleanly and at a slight angle to the stem axis.

turf growth. To maintain good light exposure throughout the hedge, shear them so that they are slightly wider at the bottom than at the top. This helps avoid uneven growth, undesirable thinning out, and dieback (see p.78) at the base of the hedge due to the top shading out the bottom branches.

To prune or not to prune?

The answer to this question relates to what you want from your garden and the biology of the shrub rather than being a matter of blind repetition. Do not take this to imply that shrubs cannot be pruned to limit their size or even that they can never be pruned at all; the point is that pruning should be undertaken selectively and with an understanding of how various types of shrubs will respond to each technique.

It is important to choose the most appropriate pruning technique for a particular shrub. It is easy to get carried away and prune plants either too hard or too often. For example, drastic pruning is not the solution to the problem if you have mistakenly selected a plant that is too large for its space. Nor is repeated pruning the solution if you have selected a plant whose shape is drastically different from the silhouette you desired in a particular space: there is no reason to shear, say, *Forsythia* annually into a perfectly round gumball when with renewal pruning every few years it will develop a graceful, arching silhouette and will bloom profusely.

As you make your decisions about how to prune a particular shrub, it is important that you know whether the shrub you wish to prune is one that flowers on new or old wood—in other words, do the buds that produce the flowers form on the current or the previous season's shoot growth? You need to prune each of these two general types of shrub at

Coppicing

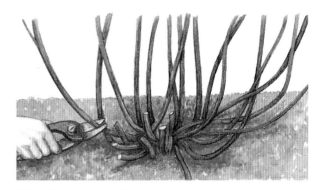

1 Coppicing is a type of hard or renewal pruning used to promote the growth of many vigorous, rapidly growing shoots. On shrubs it is often used to maximize juvenile growth of vegetative stems that offer the strongest color development.

2 When coppicing, it is important to cut stems uniformly and to make sure that all cuts have been made near a healthy set of buds. These buds are the source of renewed growth.

a different time of the year to maximize flowering. Pruning in the wrong season can mean reduced bloom, or no bloom at all—although there may be reasons why you need to prune at a time that will reduce bloom.

Pruning deciduous shrubs

1 When pruning deciduous shrubs for shape and architecture, it is especially helpful to be able to prune in late winter.

2 It is important to prune out any stems that are crossing the plant's main direction of growth.

3 Be sure to make all these sorts of cuts at the next branch point and at a slight angle to the main stem.

Pruning evergreen shrubs

1 Pruning evergreen shrubs is important for maintaining good light penetration into the center of the shrub.

2 Prune evergreen shrubs at a time of year when drought stress will be minimal and recovery from the cuts optimal.

3 Because it is more difficult to see the architecture of an evergreen shrub, be sure to cut the right stems.

Different pruning for different times

It will be helpful to look at some specific examples. *Buddleja davidii* (butterfly bush) is a commonly grown shrub that flowers on new wood. This plant can be pruned in early spring, thereby leaving sufficient time in the growing season for recovery, regrowth, and blooming. Butterfly bushes are large shrubs and can also be pruned back hard in the spring for invigoration. Lilacs and rhododendrons, on the other hand, develop flower buds at the ends of the previous year's growth. By cutting them back hard in the spring you will only ensure that they have no flowers that year.

As a very rough rule of thumb, routinely prune in early spring shrubs that flower on the current year's wood well before their time of flowering (usually these bloom in late summer/early fall). You should also shear flowering hedges in early spring. Prune shrubs that flower on the previous year's wood immediately after they bloom in spring, so that you avoid interrupting the bud-development process throughout the remainder of the growing season—and thus do not interfere with the development of next year's flower buds.

For major renewal pruning on shrubs that bloom on the current year's wood, prune in early spring; however, for those shrubs that bloom on the previous year's wood, you need to carry out your major renewal pruning in early fall, as the plants are going into their dormant season. By pruning in early fall you will inevitably have to sacrifice some flowering during the next spring, although this will not interfere with bud set during the following season.

Widely grown shrubs that bloom on the current year's wood include *Buddleja davidii, Caryopteris* species and hybrids, *Hydrangea paniculata, Perovskia,* and several *Spiraea.* Widely grown shrubs that bloom on the previous year's wood include *Deutzia, Forsythia, Hydrangea macrophylla, Kerria, Kolkwitzia, Philadelphus, Rhododendron, Syringa,* and *Weigela.* Roses are a special case—consult specialist books for detailed information on the diverse pruning routines you should employ for each of the rose groups.

When pruning a shrub, first take time to examine the entire plant to discover where all of the main stems extend and originate and where any areas of disease or damage may be, and to get a visual measure of any irregular or atypical branches you may want to thin or trim. Remember that all

The cone-shaped spikes of *Buddleja davidii*
This commonly grown species of butterfly bush responds very well to annual hard pruning with much more prolific flowering than if it is left unpruned.

dead, diseased, and seriously damaged wood should always be pruned out, no matter what other pruning goals you may have. All cuts should be made with sharp pruning shears held at a slight angle to the stem and, on large stems, as close to the joint or branch collar as possible—although you must avoid cutting into the collar. Make cuts at a branch or just above a healthy bud or pair of buds.

Tips for pruning

All pruning cuts should follow the same basic principles. Cuts should be made cleanly, without tearing any adjacent areas of bark. They should be made at a very slight angle if they are topping cuts, or should be made parallel or at a slight angle to the main stem if a side branch is being removed. When cutting a branch, cut close to any collar without actually cutting into the collar (this will not be visible on fine-stemmed shrubs). Always make cuts at the next branch point or bud or leaf node without leaving a stub. When coppicing (see p.30) or cutting the entire plant back for renewal pruning, make sure you leave enough budwood for vigorous recovery from the shrub's base. Always make cuts using the widest part of the blade. Place your pruners so that the branch to be cut is held in the base area of the pair of blades. Using the blade tips gives you less control and power, and can result in the blade snapping or turning and in so doing tearing the stem or bark.

Spring blooms of *Syringa vulgaris* 'Andenken an Ludwig Späth'
The standard pruning technique for the group of shrubs that includes lilacs *(Syringa)* is to cut out any thin and unproductive branches immediately after flowering in mid to late spring.

A general rule of thumb is that most spring-blooming shrubs should be pruned immediately after they bloom (before they begin developing their next crop of flower buds), while most late-summer-, fall-, and winter-blooming shrubs can be pruned in early spring before the next season's flower buds begin to develop and bloom.

Shrubs grown for colorful stems or foliage often give the best performance if pruned hard either annually or every other year. With these types of shrubs, you need to prune the plant very hard in either early winter or very early spring. If the shrub is being grown near the edge of its hardiness limit, it is frequently helpful to put off pruning until early spring, as the additional wood may help the shrub survive the winter. Make sure to prune sufficiently early in the spring, however, to avoid pruning as growth is resuming. As with all general rules, though, there will be some exceptions that don't fit the general rule, so you will need to make sure exactly at what time of the year the individual shrubs in your garden develop their flower buds.

The following is a quick guide for timing the pruning of some of the more popular deciduous shrubs.

Shrubs to prune immediately after they flower (those plants that bloom on the previous year's wood) include *Cytisus scoparius, Deutzia, Forsythia, Hydrangea macrophylla, Kerria,*

Fall foliage of *Cotinus coggygria* 'Royal Purple'
The group of deciduous shrubs that includes *Cotinus* should be pruned before the new season's growth, when any damaged, weak, crossed, or badly spaced branches should be removed.

Pruning an established wall shrub

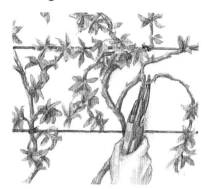

1 An established espalier or wall shrub needs regular pruning to maintain its highly trained shape.

2 Stems growing out from the wall need to be pruned back to a vigorous set of buds close to the wall.

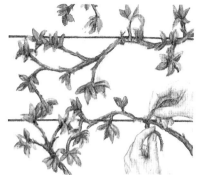

3 After pruning, vigorous stems should be tied to the wall framework and can be trained to grow into any gaps.

Kolkwitzia, Philadelphus, deciduous *Rhododendron* (including nearly all azaleas), *Ribes sanguineum, Spiraea thunbergii, Syringa, Tamarix,* and *Weigela.*

Shrubs that need pruning hard in early spring (those that bloom on the current year's wood) include *Buddleja davidii, Caryopteris, Ceanothus, Ceratostigma, Fuchsia, Hydrangea paniculata,* and *Spiraea japonica.*

Shrubs grown for colorful bark and foliage that need pruning hard in early spring include *Cornus alba* and *Cornus stolonifera, Corylus maxima, Cotinus, Rubus cockburnianus* (ghost raspberries), *Salix,* and *Sambucus.*

Pruning evergreen shrubs presents a different set of challenges. While you want to minimize water loss and exposure to disease, you obviously cannot examine these shrubs without their foliage in order to clearly see their architecture, which makes it more difficult to identify any straggly, weak, or damaged branches.

Evergreen shrubs usually fall into one of two categories—either low-growing or ground-cover types that need regular hard pruning or light shearing to maintain a dense habit, or taller plants that need minimal pruning to remove damaged, crossing, diseased, or irregular branches. Evergreen shrubs such as *Santolina,* and many heaths and heathers, benefit from a comprehensive trimming in early spring. Evergreen shrubs grown as a hedge, such as many hollies, can be trimmed in late spring or early summer; usually one pruning a year is sufficient.

Evergreen shrubs grown as specimens, such as *Camellia* and evergreen *Rhododendron,* can be lightly pruned immediately after they flower but need little pruning except for the occasional removal of crossing or dead branches.

Pruning is one of the most useful and important tasks needed to garden successfully with shrubs. Of all of the plants that you grow in your garden, shrubs are perhaps the most generally dependent on proper pruning for obtaining the best garden character and architecture. Correct pruning will ensure that these plants will provide you with many years of beautiful form, texture, and color.

A formal hedge in fall
This well-pruned shrub illustrates how regular, appropriate pruning (and, in this case, effective shearing) can be used to create elegant formal character in your garden.

Propagation

Propagation is not just a skill for nursery professionals and horticulturists—it is an essential part of good gardening practice. While there are a number of complicated systems required for some methods of propagation, there are also several straightforward techniques that home gardeners can easily enjoy and put to good use in their gardens.

A host of specific techniques are associated with both reproductive and vegetative approaches to propagation: the one that proves the most successful varies with particular species or even cultivars of species, with some plants rooting from cuttings far more easily than do their near relatives, which are better propagated by grafting, and vice versa. Likewise, seeds of a particular plant may require quite different conditions and/or pretreatments to germinate successfully than do those of another species. The details of specific propagation methods for hundreds of species and cultivars are to be found in many specialist books and if you need to know the correct propagation method for a particular shrub you should seek out one of these volumes. The general principles of propagation techniques are outlined below.

Propagation from seed

Seeds contain plant embryos. They are the products of the sexual transference of genetic information during the fertilization of the ovule by pollen. Just as a litter of puppies will contain a number of distinct individuals, plants grown from seed exhibit the characteristics of their species but will not all be the same. If, for example, you collected and planted seed from a *Berberis* shrub, the resulting crop would all look like barberries but might differ in growth rate or have variations in foliage shape or color, density of foliage cover, shade of flower color, time to ripeness of fruit, and so on. (This is why named cultivars are propagated vegetatively—propagating without involving seeds ensures retention of the special characteristics for which they were selected and named.) When propagating plants from seed, you can be in for a surprise.

When setting out to collect seed for propagation, it is important to realize that in any garden many species of a genus may be planted nearer to each other than they ever would be in the wild. As a result there may be some cross-pollination between related species, and any resulting seed may actually produce hybrids.

When collecting seed, make sure to note on the label the plant name, source, location, and date of collection. Do not collect seed from wild populations of plants that have low rates of regeneration. Once collected, different seeds need different preparation. You should store dry seed in a cool, dry place until ready to treat and sow, while fleshy fruits or

Sowing

1 Fill a medium-deep box with moist well-drained medium. Sprinkle seed evenly on the surface and cover lightly with medium.

2 Lightly moisten the seed and medium and keep it evenly moist until the seed germinates. Be sure to label the box.

3 After seedlings have emerged and developed at least 2–4 true leaves, thin the seedlings by transplanting them.

Layering

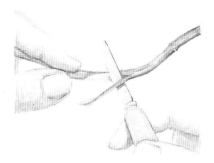

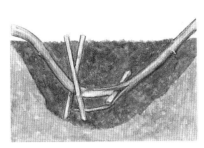

| | Remove all foliage from the stem from 20in (50cm) below the tip. Make a shallow, 2in (5cm) long, cut into the bark.

2 Prop the cut open with a toothpick, dust the cut area lightly with rooting powder, and bury that area of the stem.

3 Stake and protect the upright stem tip of the layer and water the layer well. Roots should form in several weeks.

Division

| | Division of shrubs can be achieved by severing running plants along the runner where new roots are forming.

2 Be sure to cut new divisions where some new roots have formed and where there is healthy shoot growth.

3 Plant the severed divisions directly after cutting. Water and mulch lightly after firming the soil around the division.

partially dry fruits should be stored somewhere cool and moist, although the storage should not last for more than a few days. In either event, you should clean seed of all debris, chaff, and fruit flesh. For species-specific techniques, you will need to look at books covering those particular plants.

For most cold-hardy garden shrubs, collecting seed in fall and then sowing immediately outdoors is recommended, as the winter period not only supplies the cold treatment required for germination but also gives the seed an appropriate degree of moisture. However, there are a number of cases in which seeds from some species will not germinate until they have experienced not only the initial cold season but also a warm one, so you may have to be patient for a year, or possibly even longer.

You might also choose to sow in beds lined and covered with fine-gauge hardware cloth, thereby discouraging garden pests such as rodents and birds from eating the seed.

Other forms of propagation

Vegetative propagation allows you to make exact clones of an individual plant. There are numerous methods of doing this, including layering, division, rooting cuttings, and grafting. *Layering* is a method of inducing root formation on a stem and creating a new plant by then severing the stem. *Division* is a method of separating offshoots of a parent plant that can then be planted as new individuals. *Rooting cuttings* and *grafting* are described below. Various species respond more successfully than others to particular techniques. The most widely used is the *rooting of stem cuttings*. Here, a length of stem about 3–6in (7.5–15cm) long is cut from the parent plant at a particular time of the year; the cut end is then dipped in a rooting powder (a combination of synthetic plant hormone and inert materials), inserted into a well-drained medium (for example, sand), and placed in a humid environment—either sprayed frequently by a mist head or under a plastic tent.

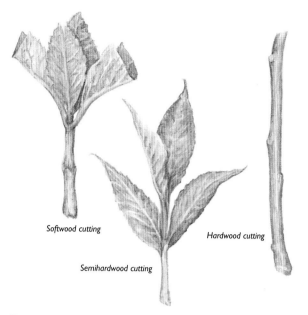

Comparison of softwood, semihardwood, and hardwood cuttings
It is important to harvest stem cuttings at the right stage of growth to ensure successful rooting of cuttings. The optimal type of cutting will depend on the individual species.

Softwood cutting

Semihardwood cutting

Hardwood cutting

Depending on the species of plant, stem cuttings should be taken at different stages of their development. Softwood cuttings should be taken in spring and early summer, when shoots are still soft and succulent; semihardwood cuttings should be taken in midsummer, when tissues have begun to harden; and hardwood cuttings should be taken in the fall and winter, after bark has formed and the stem has hardened off for the season.

An easy way to propagate from cuttings at home is to use a window box or rooting box about 5–6in (13–15cm) in depth and at least 10in (25cm) square. Fill the box with clean washed coarse sand or moistened perlite (or a mixture of both), and mound the medium slightly in the middle. Arch lengths of straightened metal coat hangers across the box, inserting both ends in the medium—you will have to use fine-gauge wire or a staple gun to secure the hanger arches to the sides of the box. You will need to rig up at least three arches—more if you are using a big box.

Taking a cutting

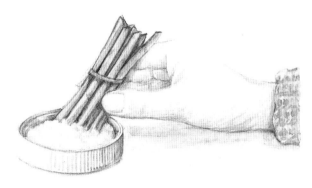

1 With garden shears or a knife cut stem cuttings at lengths of about 3–6in (7.5–15cm) and make cuts near a node *(see inset)*. Remove all leaves from the lower 2in (5cm) of the cutting.

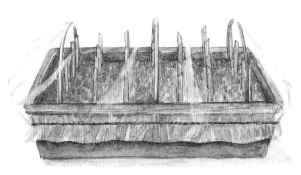

2 Dip the cut end of the cuttings in a rooting powder and tap any excess off the cuttings. Cuttings can be dipped in groups but should be stuck in the medium individually.

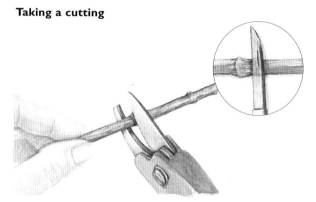

3 Stick cuttings singly in rows in the rooting box about 2in (5cm) apart. It may be helpful to use a pencil or stick to create a hole for the cutting before pressing it into the medium.

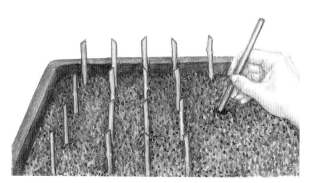

4 Cover the rooting box with clear plastic and place in a cool, low-light area. Make sure to check the medium periodically and moisten it if it has begun to dry out.

Harvest and root your stem cuttings at the appropriate season, as recommended for the given species. After harvesting, put them in a plastic bag with moist paper towels and keep them in a cooler or refrigerator (but not a freezer) until you are ready to root them. When ready, rinse the cuttings in cool water, make a fresh end cut, dip the cut ends in a rooting powder (available at most garden centers), and insert the cuttings in the rooting box to a depth of about 1½in (4cm). Sprinkle the cuttings lightly with water. Slip the entire box into a plastic bag and secure the open end. Place the box in a cool place with indirect light, checking it periodically to make sure the medium is moist (but not soggy); sprinkle more water if necessary to keep the medium moist. Depending on the species, the cuttings should root within 3–8 weeks.

While many shrubs can be rooted from cuttings, remember to allow sufficient space in the rooting boxes for root development and to give each type of shrub the right environment for rooting. For example, if you put cuttings of periwinkle (Vinca) and lavender cotton (Santolina) in the same box, the medium would either be too dry for the first or too wet for the second.

A similar technique is propagation from *root cuttings*; in this case pieces of root rather than stem are submerged in the rooting medium and kept moist until new shoots come through. The root cuttings may be treated with fungicides but not generally with a rooting powder. Far fewer species can be successfully propagated in this way.

Grafting is a traditional propagation technique. As a great deal of advanced knowledge and considerable skill is required for successful grafting, it is a difficult technique for the novice.

The principle of grafting is to take a section of stem (the scion) of the desired plant and bind it to the stem of another complete plant (called the rootstock or understock) above the soil line. A cut is first made in the stem of the rootstock and the cut edge of the scion is then lined up with this, so that the active growing internal tissues of both are aligned. The scion and the rootstock are next bound together with rubber bands and sealing wax (or plastic wrap) and left in a cool humid place. After a few days, the two cut surfaces of the graft will begin to heal and fuse together, thereby creating a continuous vascular connection—that is, the scion becomes a new shoot on the rootstock plant. You then need to gradually cut away the shoot growth of the rootstock as the scion grows, so that eventually you are left with the grafted scion's shoot growing on the roots of the rootstock.

Vinca minor 'Atropurpurea' in spring
Periwinkle (Vinca) is one of the easiest shrubs to propagate from stem cuttings. Its varied species make it a rewarding subject for propagation for the home gardener.

Rewarding projects

Rooting shrubs from cuttings is a fairly simple task if you choose shrubs that root readily and if you take a bit of time to tend to their progress during the rooting period. One of the easiest shrubs to root is one of the *Vinca* species (periwinkle). This is also one of the most rewarding and versatile shrubs to propagate yourself.

Your first project could be to try rooting directly into a hanging basket. For the hanging basket, you can use any solid basket with a detachable hanger—a wire mesh basket is not usually suitable. Fill the basket with a well-drained medium high in fiber content (for example, ⅓ peat, ⅓ perlite, ⅓ bark). Moisten the medium until it is very moist to the touch but does not drip water (alternatively, wet the medium until water runs off and then let it drain overnight). For rooting *Vinca* you need to cut the stem tips to about 6in (15cm) long from plants that are growing strongly. Cuttings can be taken almost anytime of year except during the middle of winter.

Very soft cuttings taken in early spring will root, but you must be careful not to expose them to any periods of lowered humidity; it is best just to avoid that early soft stage. You will want enough cuttings to put them about 3–4in (7.5–10cm) apart around the perimeter with 1–4 cuttings evenly spaced in the center of the basket—depending on its size. After taking the stem cuttings, trim the leaves from the lower 2in (5cm), recut the ends, dip the cuttings in a rooting powder, and insert

Side-veneer grafting

1 In grafting, the desired scion (shoot portion) is cut to match a comparable cut on the understock (root portion).

2 The scion and understock are closely matched, then bound with a grafting band and sealed with wax or plastic.

3 The completed graft is left in a cool moist environment to heal for several weeks before the graft is unwrapped.

them 2in (5cm) into the medium. Make sure to root the perimeter cuttings at least 2in (5cm) back from the rim. Put the basket in a clear plastic bag and place it in low light in a cool place. The cuttings should be rooted in about 3–4 weeks.

Check the medium periodically and sprinkle it with water if it is drying out. You may find that some spots dry out a bit more quickly than others and need more frequent attention.

The summer foliage of *Aralia elata* 'Variegata'
Often planted as a specimen shrub because of the need for space to display its splendid foliage, the variegated Japanese angelica tree is propagated only by grafting.

Check to see if cuttings have rooted by gently tugging upward on an individual cutting or two. If the cutting resists your pull, then it likely is rooted. When most of the cuttings have rooted, take the basket out of the bag and put it in a low-light, open environment. Keep the basket moist, but be careful not to overwater the plants—especially until you see active growth. Gradually move the basket into full sun or the intended final environment (keep in mind that the variegated selection of *Vinca major* will burn in full sun). Don't worry if all of the cuttings do not root. Remove any cuttings that are wilted and not rooted. Use the vigorous growth of the rooted cuttings to fill the spaces in the basket where you are missing a plant or two.

Choosing cuttings from additional pendent shrubs that root readily (such as jasmine) to combine with the *Vinca* will allow you to create unique arrangements. With a project such as this your imagination is the only limit.

Having succeeded with the rooting project, you may wish to try something a bit more ambitious but still easily accomplished. A second project could be *layering to create a mass planting or to rejuvenate an old shrub*. You may have been faced with wanting to plant a mass or grouping of plants but not wanting to purchase all the plants necessary to create the mass right away. One way to approach this dilemma is to purchase one or two plants that can be easily layered, and then propagate the rest of the mass right in place around the originally purchased plants. Shrubs that layer readily include

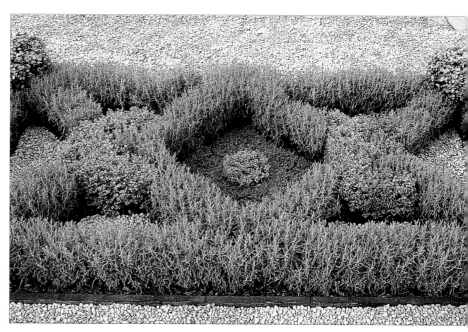

A knot garden with *Santolina*
You can propagate your own edging and herb-garden plants quite readily from stem cuttings. Plants such as *Santolina* root well if the medium is kept at the proper degree of moisture.

Salix, Rubus, Forsythia, Weigela, and *Lonicera.* Layering is a simple technique that requires a bit of digging and some patience. To layer a shrub that has been planted in place to create a mass, make sure that you site the layers where you want the plants to grow—it is possible to transplant rooted layers, but why create an extra step?

The basic concept of layering has already been illustrated on p.35. In this case, you will be burying numerous stems from the parent plant. These will form roots on the buried sections of stem and become independent new plants. To layer a shrub growing in the garden, follow the steps listed below.

First, bend down healthy, vigorous long stems from the parent shrub to the ground so that an area behind the growing point is lying on the ground. Remove all the leaves

Forsythia hedge in spring
With a minimum of equipment and experience forsythia can be propagated by taking hardwood cuttings in fall or winter, and by taking softwood cuttings in summer.

from the part in contact with the ground. Make a shallow cut in this section and treat with rooting powder. Bury the bared stem about 5–12in (13–30cm) underground. Water the buried layer in well and cover the area with a loose mulch such as straw. Then moisten the mulch. Do not mulch too deeply—a covering of 2–3in (5–7.5cm) is plenty. If the mulch is too deep, the layer will grow roots up into it rather than developing a root system in the soil. Make sure to protect the layer's buried area and upright stem so that it does not get accidentally kicked at or dug up. Stake the remaining aboveground portion of the stem loosely up and away from the soil. Depending on the species of shrub, the layer should root in 3–8 weeks.

Start the layer in spring when the shrub is in active growth. Do not disturb it until the next season, and then sever the parent plant from the layer close to the soil. You may wish to prune out the remaining stem from the parent plant. You now have a new young shrub rooted in place.

If you layer a number of stems around the parent plant, you will soon have a mass where only an individual plant grew before. If you are layering a young shrub, the branches may not be long enough for you to root the layers at a sufficient distance from the parent plant. In that case, you will have to transplant the layers once they are rooted. Make sure that you frequently water the transplanted layers in the same way that you would any new transplanted shrub.

Requiring no special tools or equipment, layering can also be used as a relatively easy method of establishing a new, vigorous plant from an old and declining favorite shrub.

Pests, diseases & hazards

Plant pests and diseases are the scourge of the garden and the gardener alike. Plagues, rampages of heretofore unheard-of insects, and bizarre afflictions appear on our plants seemingly out of nowhere—most often just as we were beginning to feel that the plants had finally begun to thrive in their new home. However, a shrub that has been well chosen for its site rarely suffers significant problems.

Shrubs are a diverse group of plants. The group includes many carefree species and cultivars but also some more sensitive plants that require relatively intensive maintenance to succeed in most gardens (for example, the large-flowered bush roses). Furthermore, even the toughest, most pest- and disease-resistant shrub will become far more susceptible if grown for prolonged periods in stressful conditions.

The best approach to reducing pest and disease problems is to choose to grow shrubs that are well adapted to your particular garden's site and conditions, rather than attempting to alter your garden conditions drastically in order to grow a plant that is basically unsuitable. It is also important to select healthy shrubs and to buy from reputable nurseries. Choose shrubs that you know do not have inherent susceptibilities to any serious diseases or common debilitating pests that are prevalent in your area. For example, if root nematodes are a widespread problem locally, avoid boxwood and choose a holly instead. Similarly, if your soil is a heavy wet clay, avoid *Daphne* and choose *Osmanthus*.

If the shrubs in your garden are well adapted to the site, well watered, given moderate fertilizer, and pruned when needed, you know you have done all that you can to prevent the development of significant pest and disease problems. Nevertheless, you will inevitably, despite all your best efforts, be troubled from time to time. In most cases there are recommended controls and techniques whereby you can attempt to cope with such problems. University agriculture departments and reliable nursery professionals are sources of regionally relevant information that can help you considerably.

One of the most important ways to deal with pest and disease problems is to spot them early. Regularly inspect your garden plants. Symptoms such as unusual changes in foliage color, outline, or the angle at which the leaves are held; signs of chewing or degradation of leaves or stems; shot holes; discolored spots or blotches; peculiar outgrowths; small piles or lines of material that look like sawdust; and disturbances at the soil line—all should be investigated and observed more closely until you can determine the cause.

A VISUAL GUIDE TO PESTS IN THE GARDEN

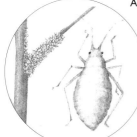

Aphids

Tiny soft-bodied sucking insects that can carry diseases. If they are present in large numbers, they can stress the plant and it will drop leaves, but otherwise they are not especially serious. *Prevention:* Encourage beneficial insects such as hoverflies, lacewings, and ladybugs. Apply a tar wash oil in winter. *Control:* Spray as soon as infestation is spotted with insecticidal soap or an aphid-specific insecticide such as pirimicarb (this will leave other pests and beneficial insects unharmed). Pay careful attention to the buds, the undersides of the leaves, and the shoot tips, as this is where the aphids congregate.

Galls

Unusual swellings and growths ranging in size from just larger than a pinhead to 3in (7.5cm) in diameter. Galls are lumps of tissue growth in reaction to chemicals or irritation from bacteria, fungi, or insects. *Prevention:* It is difficult to anticipate galls or prevent them from occurring. Some gall-causing fungi can be resident in the soil for long periods of time, so strict hygiene and careful handling of rootstock are important. *Control:* No chemical control is available. Most galls will not do fatal damage, but if the growths are very unsightly, remove and burn the worst affected leaves or shoots as soon as the attack is noticed.

Leaf miners

Larvae of flies, some moths, and some beetles that mine the foliage of some shrubs. The small white eggs hatch into grubs that chew trails through the leaf, so that the leaf blisters and becomes blotchy or marked with waxy, light brown, curving lines. An infestation is unsightly but is rarely fatal to the plant.

Prevention: Control the growth and spread of weeds in the daisy family such as sow thistle and groundsel, which host this pest.
Control: Inspect plants regularly. As soon as you spot symptoms, pick off and burn infected leaves. Chemical control is difficult; spray with systemic insecticides when eggs first appear.

Leaf-rolling caterpillars

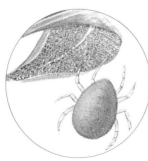

Small yellow or greenish caterpillars that feed in leaf axils, new shoots, and buds. They roll the tips of leaves over themselves as a protective layer, securing them by what looks like webbing. Plants are damaged directly by caterpillars eating the leaves; a severe infestation can cause leaf drop. Very often the leaf tying can restrict young growth.

Prevention: Examine plants regularly and crush eggs and caterpillars whenever they appear. Most eggs overwinter, so catching them before they hatch is an effective preventive measure.
Control: Spraying with contact insecticide such as malathion or more persistent insecticides such as carbaryl can be effective. Caterpillars have many natural predators, particularly birds, so encourage them into the garden by providing foliage cover.

Red spider mites

Tiny sucking arachnids that can cause severe damage: significant foliage death and major, even fatal, plant stress. Leaves become speckled with pale, stippled regions that may turn yellow or bronze-red. The mites themselves are nearly invisible.

Prevention: Avoid planting susceptible shrubs during hot dry seasons, when attacks are worse. Spider mites dislike wet places, so keep leaves damp with regular watering.
Control: For light attacks biological control is possible with the introduction of the predatory mite *Phytoseiulus*. Most chemical treatments are ineffectual, as few insecticides affect these pests.

Scale

An assault by tiny legless insects that have oval to rounded shells in shades of white, gray, or brown. Scales usually remain quite static on the plant, sucking from leaves, causing curling, discoloration, and leaf drop. Most species excrete honeydew, making plants susceptible to growth of sooty molds. Severe infestations can cause stress but are rarely fatal.

Prevention: Check all newly acquired plants carefully with a magnifying glass for signs of scale before establishing them.
Control: Treat shrubs with robust leaves by wiping scales off with a sponge and soapy water. Chemical treatment (pirimiphos-methyl or malathion) is best applied when pests are at the crawling stage.

Slugs and snails

Slugs and snails feed on foliage and stems, leaving large irregular gaps. They feed mainly at night and are most prevalent in wet weather. Their presence is indicated by the silvery trails of slime they leave behind. They can cause significant damage to leaves, but their attacks are rarely fatal.

Prevention: Slugs and snails hide in long grass and piles of stone; keep the garden tidy to reduce the amount of cover available.
Control: Traps such as saucers of beer or upturned grapefruit skins can be reasonably effective, as can laying protective trails of soot and ashes that stick to the slimy bodies, or sharp sand that cuts them as they try to cross. Beneficial nematodes can be released into the soil as biological control. Generally, pellets should be avoided, as they are poisonous to crops and domestic animals.

Tent caterpillars

You may discover these masses of caterpillars forming in a silky nest of some size. Dry, brown patches appear on the leaves. The caterpillars eat the leaves and can defoliate a plant rapidly.

Prevention: Check plants regularly, picking off and destroying tents and caterpillars wherever practical. Encourage natural predators such as insect-eating birds into the garden by providing plenty of foliage cover or nesting boxes.
Control: Physically removing the caterpillars and nests is the best control. Pick off caterpillars and crush the nests to kill the pupae. Spray with contact insecticide directly into the tents.

DISEASES AND OTHER HAZARDS

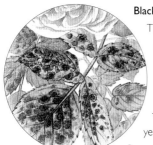

Blackspot

This is a common fungal disease of most varieties of rose. It first appears as a dark rounded spot and if left unchecked will spread rapidly to affect most of the leaf. Leaves eventually turn yellow and drop prematurely.

Prevention: The disease carries from year to year on the shoots rather than the leaves. Hard pruning in spring will considerably reduce its impact. Overall, yellow-flowered varieties are most susceptible; modern varieties have been bred to be more resilient.

Control: The best chemical spray is probably carbendazim, then bupirimate, triforine, and sulfur. Regular use could lead to the development of disease-resistant strains of blackspot.

Canker

Caused by a number of bacteria and fungi, canker is usually symptomized by a discolored irregular area on the stem; it may be sunken or weeping and in severe cases may encircle the stem. It can cause leaf drop.

Prevention: Plant shrubs carefully in well-prepared soil, feeding, mulching, and watering during dry periods. Cut out all dead and damaged wood as it occurs. Finish pruning cuts cleanly.

Control: Remove all dying and cankered shoots, and treat wounds with a fungicidal wound paint. Bushes can be sprayed at pruning time with copper fungicide. Plants can be lifted and planted more carefully. Using resistant rootstocks can reduce damage.

Chlorosis

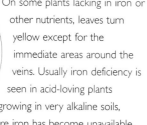

On some plants lacking in iron or other nutrients, leaves turn yellow except for the immediate areas around the veins. Usually iron deficiency is seen in acid-loving plants growing in very alkaline soils, where iron has become unavailable.

Prevention: Ensure light levels are sufficient, and do not restrict plant growth by, for example, growing in small containers. Water susceptible plants with rainwater not tap water.

Control: Improve the soil with the addition of appropriate nutrients, e.g., green manure for nitrogen deficiency, acid mulches and sequestered iron for iron deficiency.

Fireblight

This bacterial disease makes stems and foliage look as if they have been burned. The affected area often turns black and curls, and cankers develop on the stems, leaking bacterial slime in wet conditions. The whole shrub may eventually die. Plants in the *Rosaceae* family are especially susceptible.

Prevention: Keep pruning tools and cuts clean. Remove dead and damaged wood from susceptible plants as soon as it appears.

Control: No cure available. Cut out diseased wood, allowing at least 1ft (30cm) around the afflicted area. In severe cases the whole plant should be lifted and destroyed. Carefully disinfect all pruning tools after use to prevent further spread of the disease.

Leaf scorch

Leaves turn yellow, then brown from the edges inward, and can fall off altogether. This can be caused by a number of dryness-related factors, e.g., drought, intense sunlight, extreme wind, or root damage.

Prevention: Keep plants sufficiently watered; check those growing in sunny or exposed sites regularly. Shrubs growing in containers are particularly at risk from soil dehydration. Some peat-based composts are also difficult to hydrate. Mulching will aid water retention.

Control: Leaf scorch is more easily prevented than treated, as plants suffering chronic exposure are unlikely to respond when conditions improve. Take immediate steps to rectify acute water shortages.

Leaf spot

Numerous fungi, bacteria, viruses, chemical pollutants, and fertility problems may cause spots on leaves. Fungal leaf-spot diseases are often symptomized by a distinct edge and quite uniformly round spots. As the spots join together the leaf dies.

Prevention: Some bacteria are spread by wind-borne seeds or rain splash. Shelter plants to avoid soaking the foliage. Thoroughly clear away all fallen leaves.

Control: Pick off all spotted leaves. Spray plants with Bordeaux mixture, mancozeb, or thiram. If symptoms persist, the shrub may be lacking in vigor owing to a weakened root system.

Phytophthora root rot

This microscopic fungus kills roots and if unchecked will ultimately kill the entire plant. Symptoms include the yellowing and dying back of foliage following the infection of the root. Where roots are exposed, they may appear brown and diseased. Heathers and rhododendrons are particularly susceptible.

Prevention: Container-raised plants are less likely to be affected; buy only from reputable nurseries. Plant carefully, sloping soil away to avoid creating hollows at the stem base where fungi will flourish. Be very careful not to water or mulch excessively.

Control: Once it is established in garden soil, there are no chemical treatments, so careful soil preparation and hygiene are essential.

Powdery mildew

This fungus usually affects foliage in the growing season. Leaves develop a white powdery layer on their surfaces (in rhododendrons it can be buff-colored). Purple discoloration can sometimes follow. The affliction causes leaf drop and, especially if chronic, can stunt plant growth.

Prevention: Shrubs in dry conditions are more susceptible, so water and mulch as necessary. Spraying with a sulfur fungicide can be preventive. Some rose varieties are more resistant.

Control: Remove and destroy affected shoots, especially in winter when the white coating is visible. This will get rid of the primary infection. Spray with benomyl or carbendazim.

Other hazards

Air pollution Various symptoms are associated with air pollution. Ozone poisoning is one of the most common culprits: it manifests itself as whitish markings on foliage.

Prevention: When planning a garden, take location and wind direction into account. Many shrubs will tolerate polluted air, e.g., *Aucuba*, *Buddleja davidii*, *Fatsia japonica*, and *Philadelphus*.

Control: Toxins in the air are rarely potent enough to cause fatal damage to plants. Remove unsightly leaves and shoots.

Frost cracks As bark and stems expand and contract during extreme short-period temperature fluctuations (bright sunny days in winter), any areas already weakened may pop and/or tear open. The cracks usually mend during the following growing season.

Prevention: When frost is anticipated, move valuable plants under cover or shelter those in beds with woven coverings.

Control: Sprinkling plants with water the morning following a frost can slow down the thaw and reduce, if not prevent, damage.

Mower blight Repeated small wounds inflicted on plant stems by lawn mowers and trimmers can cause large damaging wounds.

Prevention: Ensure there is a reasonable margin between lawn and border, and trim back any overhanging shrubs. Avoid mowing in wet conditions, when blades may slip. Use shears for lawn edges.

Control: Remove damaged wood to prevent infection. Move and replant the affected shrub if necessary.

Salt damage Foliage browning and leaf drop, especially along roadsides and seashores, is often the result of salt toxicity.

Prevention: Avoid exposure of tender or young plants. Many shrubs will tolerate these conditions, e.g., some *Cistus*, and *Baccharis*.

Control: Plants do not grow successfully in unsuitable conditions. Remove damaged foliage and move to a new location.

Sunscald Areas of bark crack, peel, die, and enlarge into cankers on the south or southwest side of the stems in response to strong exposure to the sun. Fluctuations of temperature in winter on bright sunny days may likewise result in the bark cracking.

Prevention: Avoid growing plants near glass, which magnifies the sun's rays, as do residual beads of moisture on leaves and fruit.

Control: Shade plants in afflicted areas. Stop overhead watering.

Snow-line damage Snow cover in winter affords protection to parts of the shrub but not all of it. Exposed part may suffer foliage stress or damage, and reduced flowering the following spring.

Prevention: This is a problem only in areas that suffer particularly harsh winters. Provide winter cover where necessary.

Control: Resist the temptation to cut out affected parts.

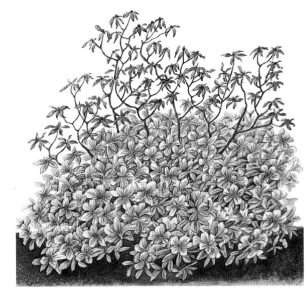

Snow-line damage
Foliar stress and damage has occurred only above the snow line, where the leaves did not have the protection of snow cover.

Using shrubs in your garden is a delightful and addictive pastime. Choosing the best selections for your site and region, with the decorative characteristics you want, and then setting out on a hunt to your favorite nurseries, is great fun. What may seem like an overwhelming task at first is made simpler by focusing on the unique combination of conditions found in your garden—and using those as the first deciding factors when determining which shrubs will be good choices for that garden. Soil type, light conditions, rainfall, and temperature will all help you identify shrubs that will grow well for you. Once you have become familiar with these conditions, you can let your imagination take over...

Where to grow roses

Among the more widely grown shrubs are roses, which are often grown as single specimens, even though they mix beautifully with other plants. Combining roses with other plants (such as the shrub *Acer palmatum*, shown growing over the garden seat) is a creative and effective way to use these popular shrubs.

using shrubs

Choosing shrubs

Every garden offers a unique set of growing conditions that changes throughout the season

of the garden's situation and prevailing climatic conditions. These growing conditions are part of

garden's regional climate and of the even greater number of microclimates (literally, "little climates")

to be found in the different parts of that particular garden.

MATCHING SHRUBS TO SITES

Key factors in determining which shrubs are the best choice for a particular garden include the combination of seasonal extremes and patterns in temperature and rainfall (or snowfall), along with the specific soil type and light conditions to be found in that garden. Every species, and even cultivar, of shrub grows best under a certain set of growing conditions. Some shrubs will perform well in a wide range of conditions, while others need very specific conditions in order to thrive.

Sun or shade?

While you can enjoy the deeply lobed leaves of *Hydrangea quercifolia* in either sun or shade, you will only get a truly glorious flowering display if it is planted in full sunlight.

There are two basic approaches to choosing plants for a garden. Either you can select plants that can easily adapt to the conditions of that particular garden and so provide the desired visual characteristics with a minimum of plantings and work, or you can select plants only for their decorative appeal, being prepared to adjust garden conditions to the specific needs of the plants. Clearly, there is a limit to just how much you can instigate and maintain any change in garden conditions no matter how much work you are willing to do.

There are some changes that can be made with a reasonable amount of work and that may be worth the effort in order to make it possible to grow certain shrubs. By annual applications of sulfur, careful selection of fertilizer, and thoughtful choice of mulch, for example, you can acidify your soil somewhat to make it possible for azaleas and rhododendrons to perform better. You can also irrigate regularly to provide ample moisture on a dry site for moisture-loving plants. You cannot, however, control either your summer high temperatures or your winter low temperatures. Nor can you turn a desert into a cool, mild rain forest. It is all a matter of degree and how much effort you want to put into maintaining your garden. A low-maintenance garden relying on plants that are naturally well adapted to a climate and site is generally a more environmentally sound garden because less water, fertilizer, and pesticide are needed for plants to succeed than for a garden using many plants that are ill adapted to the site.

The hundreds of shrubs available to today's gardeners make it possible to grow a wonderful diversity of plantings. You can find shrubs that are well adapted to just about any garden, no matter what kind of climate or site. It is critical, however, to be able to identify the shrubs that will perform reliably given the specific conditions found in your garden. There is no magical way to know which shrubs will do best in a given soil or certain light conditions. Even different cultivars of the same species can be well adapted to very different sets of conditions (in fact, many cultivars are selected because they differ from their parent species in garden adaptability, cold hardiness, drought tolerance, and so on).

Hydrangea quercifolia (oakleaf hydrangea) is an example of a shrub that will grow happily in either sun or shade, with some flowering under both conditions—but it will give its best display only in full sun. However, since this plant has beautiful foliage that develops lovely fall color, you may want to grow it to add texture and fall color to a shady area; any flowering thus becomes a bonus, rather than a focus of the plant.

Ideally, you should learn the needs and tolerances of individual shrubs. To do that, turn to reference books and periodicals, horticultural professionals, and other gardeners who have experience with a particular plant to learn under what conditions it will thrive. Of course, your own experiences will be an equally useful resource.

The best approach when you are first beginning to garden with shrubs is to use a range of tolerant plants that will give the most flexibility in your garden design. Selecting such shrubs when you are starting out also gives you the best chance of success without having to undertake extensive (or expensive) soil treatment or bed preparation.

Before selecting any plants at all, however, it is a good idea to spend time observing the various areas of your garden to become familiar with the growing conditions throughout the garden on a year-round basis.

A good rule of thumb is not to plant or move any shrubs for a year and to spend the time making careful observations and notes concerning which existing plants are thriving where, and what the conditions are in that particular part of the garden. Noting such things as which areas receive full sun and for how long, where shadows fall during the growing season or during the winter, which areas are well or poorly drained, and even (in colder regions) where snow slides off the roof and onto the ground during the early spring thaw is critical to choosing the right shrubs for each area of your garden.

The factors to consider when choosing shrubs are:

- Hardiness—the adaptability of the shrub to the climate of your area, that is, its ability to thrive given the extremes and seasonal patterns of temperature and how those patterns interact with regional rainfall (see also pp.216–218).
- Soils—the adaptability of the shrub to the particular soil types in your garden, that is, the garden's drainage, fertility, and acidity/alkalinity characteristics.

A multi-season border
Shrubs can provide superb foliage color throughout the season. Here, *Acer tataricum* subsp. *ginnala*, which provides excellent fall color, is growing behind the summer-flowering *Buddleja alternifolia*.

- Light—the suitability of the shrub to the site's light conditions, that is, will the plant be in full sun or shade and is it the intense light of the desert or the soft light of a northern forest understory (the plant growth beneath the tree canopy)?
- Moisture—the adaptability of the shrub to the site's moisture conditions, that is, how much rainfall/snowfall there is, what the seasonal patterns are, and whether the precipitation is mist or fog, light or heavy rain, or snow.

In addition, you will need to be aware of any special circumstances—both positive and negative—that your garden offers and how they affect the shrubs. Seaside gardeners, for example, need to rely heavily on salt-spray-tolerant plants unless they plant windbreak hedges of salt-tolerant evergreens. Gardeners in an urban area that has substantial air pollution or those gardening on an exposed rooftop will need to select shrubs tolerant of these conditions. There are many special circumstances under which you have to garden, and it is important to recognize them as such.

HARDINESS

A plant's hardiness usually refers to a plant's ability to survive cold temperatures. Yet a broader definition of "hardiness" is the overall adaptability to a given site and set of conditions (see also Hardiness Zones pp.216–218).

What makes a plant suitable for a particular site is the result of both its genetics and the kind of weather it is likely to encounter. A plant's basic hardiness is determined by genetics; that is, given ideal conditions and healthy growth and development, the maximum heat that a plant can tolerate is predetermined. Exactly how much heat it can tolerate each year and in each season will be influenced by local weather conditions. For example, the plant's genetic maximum capacity for heat tolerance may include temperatures in the range of 105–115°F (40–45°C) but only if those temperatures occur during a dry summer that follows a moist spring. If there was an unusually dry spring it could result in the plant being unable to tolerate what would be considered normal conditions during the summer.

Acclimation

The process that plants have developed that adjusts their metabolism to the onset of winter is called acclimation. They begin this each year in response to a series of environmental

Salix irrorata in winter
Many deciduous shrubs are planted by gardeners for their beautiful spring, summer, or fall blooms or leaves. However, this deciduous shrub also has attractive bare stems in winter.

cues such as decreasing temperature and daylength. You can influence when and how plants acclimate and thereby have a surprisingly significant impact on a plant's cold hardiness and ability to survive the winter—either for better or for worse.

When you choose shrubs for your garden, you will discover that they may be recommended as hardy in a range of hardiness zones—for example, *Hydrangea quercifolia* in Zone 4 US; 5b Can. The way in which an individual plant will perform in a garden located within that zone depends largely on the conditions prevailing in that site, including regional climate, and the way in which the plant is grown. Issues of soil, light, and moisture conditions as they affect plant health in the garden are discussed later, but it is also important to realize that these factors can have an influence on cold hardiness.

Plants that are cold–hardy to one degree or another have developed adaptations that allow them to persist through the extremes of winter (in both the Northern and Southern Hemispheres). Adaptations such as winter deciduousness (where leaves are lost at the end of the growing season), periods of dormancy, and timing of active growth and flowering to coincide with spring or favorable growing periods all improve a plant's chances of surviving the winter.

Anything that you do in the garden that mimics or influences environmental cues can affect how plants acclimate. Most shrubs acclimate to winter primarily in response to

Evergreen shrub in spring
While acting as the focal point of the border in winter, many evergreen shrubs can also make valuable spring or summer contributions. Here, *Pieris japonica* is shown in spring.

reduced temperatures, in combination with decreased water and nutrient availability. Some, however, are also very strongly influenced by the length of the day (or, more accurately, the length of the dark period within any 24-hour time span). Plants whose acclimation is induced by daylength can be severely damaged by winter conditions if they are grown where artificial light extends the daylength late in the season. You may notice that plants growing near streetlights retain their leaves longer than their neighbors in the shadows, especially on branches that are close to the light source.

It is possible to influence acclimation by continuing to water and fertilize heavily late in the growing season. Most woody plants respond best in terms of winter acclimation when fertilizer is not applied late in the season and when late-season watering is kept to a moderate level (except in cases of severe drought). This is because making copious quantities of water and nutrients available late in the growing season can prolong active growth and delay the normal hardening off that precedes acclimation. In extreme cases this can lead to serious damage to still green and growing tissue as the first frosts of winter set in.

Related to this is the issue of purchasing plants that have not been raised in your part of the country. The nursery industry is international and there are many excellent sources of plants to be found worldwide. There is no reason to restrict your plant purchases to local or even national sources. However, if new plants have come some distance, you need to be aware of their stage of development in case their seasonal "clocks" are out of synchronization with the seasonal conditions in your garden. Assuming the plant species is normally hardy in your area, this seasonal offset is usually only a temporary effect. Fall planting should be avoided, as the plants may still be growing when cold weather arrives. Spring planting gives them all summer to adjust their "clocks."

Euonymus alatus in fall
Besides its reliably brilliant red fall color, *Euonymus alatus* offers added interest for the garden during winter with the distinctive corklike wings on its shoots.

Selecting shrubs that are well adapted to your garden region and site, and optimizing general plant vigor over time through good gardening practice, are the best ways to ensure reliable plant success in both the short and long terms.

Pyracantha 'Orange Glow' in early winter
The main attraction of pyracanthas—one of the popular hybrids is shown here—is their colorful and often long-lasting berries.

SOILS

The soil in your garden is the foundation upon which everything rests. The texture, nutrient level, and degree of acidity will largely dictate what sort of shrubs will thrive. Soil is classified with a complex system of names somewhat like the botanical names applied to plants. It is important to know, however, that there are two general soil types: mineral and organic. Organic soils (for example, muck and peat) are found in just a few areas of the world and are made up mostly of decaying organic matter, with only a very little mineral material. Mineral soils are made up of mineral particles of varying sizes and composition with some organic matter. Most garden soils are mineral soils. If you garden in an area with truly organic soils, you should contact your local Cooperative Extension agency or Provincial Ministry of Agriculture for advice. Organic soils are fragile and have very specialized requirements that present a challenge to the average gardener.

Mineral soils are made of various proportions of sand and clay. Individual clay particles can only be seen through a microscope, while sand particles are much larger and can be seen with the naked eye. Gardener's refer to clay soils, sandy

Well-balanced general garden soil
The fortunate gardener will have a medium loam soil to work with. Loam soils have approximately equal proportions of sand and clay and some decayed organic matter.

soils, and loams. Clay soils have very high percentages of clay, while sandy soils have a high percentage of sand. Loams are mineral soils with close to equal proportions of sand and clay and small amounts of decayed organic matter. Clay soils tend to be fine textured, poorly drained, sticky, and easily compacted, although they can be quite fertile. Sandy soils tend to be coarse textured, very well drained, and low in fertility. Loams are, in most cases, the best general garden soils for accommodating the needs and preferences of most garden plants. There are, however, notable exceptions for plants that have special needs.

You will want to know the basic type of soil in your garden in terms of texture and mineral content (is it clay, clay loam, loam, sandy loam, or sand?), in order to identify drainage and moisture-retention characteristics. You will also want to know the nutrient content of the soil so you can make informed decisions about the use of fertilizers, and you will need to determine your soil's pH (a measure of the relative acidity of the soil). Soil analysis may be done by your county or state Cooperative Extension service or by commercial firms, who will then report back to you on the soil type, nutrient concentration, and pH value.

The characteristics of difficult soils

Sandy soil
These soils are well drained but do not retain moisture and are low in fertility.

Alkaline soil
Although difficult to manage, this type of soil is ideal for many species of shrubs.

Clay soil
These heavy soils are often fertile but are difficult to work under wet conditions.

Peaty soil
Although they may be fertile, peaty soils are often too acidic for many plants.

Soil texture

Soil texture is a function of the particle size and organic materials in the soil. A good balance of decayed organic matter, clay, and sand particles results in a soil with plenty of good-sized pores between the particles for air and water movement. Soil texture has an important influence on soil aeration and, since roots require air in the soil, on root growth. Organic matter helps the soil retain moisture and keeps it available for absorption by the roots.

Soils with good texture or "tilth" absorb moisture readily and are well drained but retain moisture in reasonable quantities after rain or irrigation. They are crumbly and easily worked and resist compaction when moist—retaining a springy texture. Loams generally have good texture. Some soils can contain large amounts of gravel or rocks—even boulders—which usually make the soil drain well but may or may not affect other qualities of the soil.

Clay soils tend to become very sticky and slick when wet. The tiny pores created by the clay particles are easily clogged and the particles are easily pushed against each other, squeezing the air from the soil and gluing these sticky particles together. When this happens to clay soil and it dries in this nearly airless state, it becomes a hard, impermeable surface that water runs off without penetrating and so is not available to roots. As the compacted clay dries and shrinks, cracks may form on the surface, which actually help improve aeration and moisture penetration, even though they appear rather devastating to the gardening eye. You should never try to work clay soils when they are wet.

Sandy soils on the other hand are almost impossible to compact because the large particles they are composed of cannot be squeezed together hard enough to eliminate the air spaces between them; also, they are not sticky and so do not adhere to each other in the same way that clay particles do. Sandy soils are not without their challenges, however. Not only are they so well drained that it is virtually impossible to keep them uniformly moist, but they generally have very low fertility and thus most plants require at least some supplementary fertilizer when grown on sandy soils (unless, of course, the plants are native to these types of soils).

Loams are the happy medium between these extremes. A mix of clay and sand particles with a healthy dose of organic matter offers not only moderate drainage and moisture retention with good aeration but also reasonable resistance to compaction because of the sand particles.

One way to improve soil texture if your garden soil is composed of sand or clay is to add composts and rotted manures. By adding organic matter to your soil, you provide the missing elements that help improve aeration and texture. It is very important, however, that you add only composted or rotted material, especially when dealing with manures and low-nitrogen-content material such as fallen leaves, or you will risk robbing your garden soil of its fertility as the organic matter decomposes.

Composts are decomposed plant material of mixed content that have been processed naturally, usually in a heap or an open-top container, by naturally occurring microbes. The microbes digest the plant matter and then conveniently die, thereby contributing some nitrogen, having converted a pile of coarse vegetable matter into a fine-textured, springy, absorbent, and crumbly material.

In order for plant material to compost completely, the pile must reach temperatures that are high enough to ensure that weed seeds and harmful microbes are killed. You can, however, leave a pile of plant matter to rot slowly untended in a corner, although you must wait for it to decompose completely before incorporating it into your soil—which can take over a year depending on the plant material in your pile (leaves, for example, can take from a few weeks to several years to decompose naturally). Increasingly, quality compost and composted manures are becoming available commercially as well, so you do not have to make compost yourself if you have neither the space nor the time.

A well-rotted compost heap

One of the best ways of improving a clay or sandy soil is by adding decomposed animal or vegetable matter in the form of compost. Here, well-rotted compost can be seen on the right of the picture.

Soil fertility

Plants need nutrients to grow and maintain good health just as much as animals do. Most nutrients that plants need are absorbed by their roots from the solution found in the soil pore spaces. As roots grow into new areas of soil, the root hairs absorb available nutrients in that area, which are then transported through the plant to supply its metabolic needs.

The most critical nutrients that plant roots absorb from the soil are nitrogen, phosphorus, and potassium, as these are used in the largest quantities by plants. Other important nutrients include sulfur, calcium, magnesium, iron, copper, zinc, manganese, molybdenum, and boron, some of which are needed only in tiny quantities. Most soils provide sufficient levels of these minor nutrients. Nitrogen (chemical symbol N), phosphorus (chemical symbol P), and potassium (chemical symbol K) are required in larger quantities, and this is why most commercial fertilizers are made up of various proportions of these three nutrients: N, P, and K. It is important to note, however, that these are not the only nutrients that plants require from the soil, which is why it is a good idea to have your soil tested in order to find out if you need to supplement nutrients besides these three.

The acidity of the soil affects the availability of soil nutrients, as does the moisture level. When soils are very dry, nutrients are less available for uptake by roots. When soils are

Feeder roots of a heather (Calluna)
The fine-textured, highly branched, light-colored roots of the root system are those that absorb most of the water and nutrients for a plant. These are often called "feeder roots."

especially acidic or alkaline, the availability of essential nutrients can change drastically. There is little iron available in alkaline soils, for example, which causes azaleas to become chlorotic because they have a high iron requirement. Neutral to slightly acidic soils are best for most plants.

Applying fertilizers is a useful way to provide ample nutrients to garden plants, but it is not always necessary to apply highly concentrated fertilizers to all plants. Vegetable crops, for example, require high nutrient concentrations in the soil to produce the abundant quantities and high quality of produce that we have come to expect. Most woody ornamental plants, on the other hand, if planted on a site to which they are reasonably well adapted, will require minimal fertilization to thrive.

Choosing the right fertilizer

There are such a great number of different commercial fertilizers available and so many different soils and plants that will benefit from additional fertilization that it becomes almost impossible to generalize when recommending which fertilizers you should use. One thing to be aware of, however, is that fertilizers come with an analysis of the percentage of the main nutrients printed on the label. Most fertilizers are composed of nitrogen, phosphorus, and potassium and are labeled as 5-10-5, 12-20-12, or some similar composition. These numbers indicate the ratio by weight of N, P, and K, respectively, in this standard order which is universally used and accepted around much of the world. Fertilizers that also include other nutrients will list those additionally.

Because there are so many formulations of fertilizer available, you may find the same concentrations of nutrients available in a variety of forms, including water-soluble salts to be applied in solution, granular forms, and slow-release fertilizers. Slow-release fertilizers are available in small, beadlike capsules that allow moisture penetration into the capsule and then a slow release of the concentrated fertilizer formula held in the beads.

A good rule of thumb for fertilizing general garden shrub plantings in temperate, nondesert, Northern Hemisphere gardens is to give one annual early-spring application to the entire area of an encapsulated slow-release fertilizer (for example, a low-nitrogen-rate formula of Osmocote). This type of fertilizer has the advantage of providing a slow, relatively steady release of nutrients to plants that lasts until the capsules are exhausted—well into the growing season—at which point it is best not to offer too high a nutrient level in any case (see also Acclimation on pp.48–49). Their other main advantage, of course, is that they require only one application.

Acidic and alkaline soils

The relative acidity of your garden soil affects the root growth and nutrient availability in the soil. The pH value of the soil is a measure of that acidity/alkalinity. pH is on a scale of 1–14, with 1 being very acidic and 14 being very basic. Because of the way that the pH value is calculated and expressed (i.e. on a logarithmic basis), small changes in pH indicate large changes in the acidity or alkalinity of the soil. A soil with a pH of 6, for instance, is 10 times more acidic than a soil with a pH of 7. As a rule, most plants perform at their best when the soil pH ranges from 6 to 7, and most soils have a pH somewhere between a range of 4 and 9.

Some plants prefer acidic or alkaline soils. Azaleas, rhododendrons, camellias, and most ericaceous plants (plants of the *Erica* family such as heaths and heathers) prefer acidic soils with a pH in the range of 4.5–5.5. You will find that plants will thrive in a wide range of soil pH but respond to the acid/alkaline balance in other ways. For example, some hydrangeas will develop blue flowers when grown in acidic soils but will develop pink flowers in alkaline soils. Alkaline soils are sometimes referred to as "chalk" soils because they have a high calcium content.

You can alter soil pH slightly by adding certain soil amendments, but it is almost impossible to alter soil pH in a significant way. Regular additions of lime (usually in the form of ground limestone) will add calcium to the soil, which can raise the pH levels to a certain extent. The lime must be thoroughly dug into the soil, however, as merely sprinkling it on the surface of beds will not allow for sufficient incorporation of the lime into the soil

Camellia 'Inspiration' grown as a border specimen.
Camellias need to be planted in well-drained, slightly acidic soil. This tender hybrid *(in foreground)* is often grown as a specimen plant. It will also grow well against a wall or in a container.

matrix, and therefore will be of little ultimate benefit. However, regular additions of sulfur and the use of nitrogen fertilizers can acidify the soil slightly (this technique is often used for growing azaleas in alkaline soils).

Mixed plantings of azaleas

Garden rhododendrons and azaleas are a group of shrubs that require slightly acidic, well-drained soil that is rich in humus. Yellowing leaves are often a sign of the presence of lime in the soil.

The stems and leaves of *Physocarpus opulifolius* 'Dart's Gold'
A chief function of a plant's leaves and stems is to provide food for the whole plant by photosynthesis.

LIGHT CONDITIONS

Green plants require light for photosynthesis—the amazing process whereby carbon dioxide and water are used to produce sugars and oxygen, thereby providing the plants with a source of food and other living creatures with the oxygen they need. Green plants also need oxygen but because they additionally use CO_2 in photosynthesis and produce O_2 as a by-product, plants do not contribute to the build-up of CO_2 in the atmosphere.

The green pigment in stems and leaves is chlorophyll—an essential light-harvesting pigment that is critical in the series of biochemical reactions that make up the process of photosynthesis. Every plant has a desirable range of light intensity within which photosynthesis, and growth and development, can occur. Some plants do best in deep shade, while others do better in dappled shade. There are other plants that require full sun to thrive, and still others that will perform well in any of those environments by producing leaves that are adapted to a shade environment when grown in the shade and to a full-sun environment in full sun.

Again, it is important to learn what light conditions are best for a particular shrub before including it in your garden. This is because regional light environments can have a major impact on plant performance. Light intensities vary around the world, so that a full-sun environment in London or Toronto will be very different from a full-sun environment in Los Angeles. Plants that require eight hours of sun in Seattle may do better with shade in Sydney.

In general, recommendations for light conditions for plants tend to be made in relation to plant performance in the Northern Hemisphere (Asia, North America, or Europe), but even so, little attention is normally paid to the fact that even differences within these geographical areas can be quite dramatic—especially to more-sensistive plants.

Many woody plants require certain light intensities throughout the growing season to enable them to maintain vigor over the course of their lifetime and to demonstrate their optimum cold hardiness, drought tolerance, flowering displays, ornamental fruit production, and disease and insect resistance. This is in large part because all of these phenomena are directly or indirectly influenced by the products of photosynthesis.

If a plant is grown where the light levels are mostly much lower than, or much higher than, those that a particular plant requires, photosynthesis will be affected (as will the resulting production of sugars, pigments, and so forth that are derived from photosynthesis). Over a period of time, this can lead to disappointing plant performance in the garden, including the absence of the ornamental traits that you would normally expect to see in a particular plant, such as prolific flowering or bright fall color.

Some plants, for example, use carbohydrates and related compounds which are derived from photosynthesis as building blocks for the biological mechanisms they use in order to survive cold winters. Their degree of winter hardiness, therefore, is readily affected by anything that influences photosynthesis over the course of the growing season. If, for example, light intensities are much lower than the desired level for a given plant for one too many seasons, its ability to survive the winter may be reduced and it will be less cold hardy in the low light area than it might be where light intensities were regularly higher during the growing season.

If certain native North American plants were grown in the United Kingdom, for example, those plants, which are adapted to higher light intensities than are found in the United Kingdom, would not survive a British winter—even though this might be milder than the winters in their native regions—because the light environment would not have allowed them normal acclimation and development of full hardiness.

Light conditions can also have a significant effect on the expression of ornamental characteristics. Many plants require full sun for optimum flowering and fruit development because higher levels of photosynthate are needed to feed the developing flowers and fruit as they mature. If light levels are not high enough, the plant is likely to respond with reduced flowering. This will not harm the plant or interfere with its general health, but it may disappoint the gardener who was looking forward to a lush display. On the other hand, a gardener may use this response to his or her advantage to reduce flowering in a plant whose blooms are only a secondary attraction to foliage, or to minimize fruit development on a plant with undesirable fruit.

Some plants flower and fruit best with some shade, either because the shade protects easily scorched or wilted petals, or because the plant is generally more vigorous in shade.

Light levels can also affect development of fall color. The reasons for fall color changes in the foliage of deciduous plants are still not fully understood. It is clear, however, that they are affected by prevailing conditions from year to year. Because, in part, fall color is due to a collection of pigments in the foliage

(as well as to a reduction of chlorophyll), insufficient light intensity during the growing season may result in reduced fall color. Again, this is why some plants renowned for fall color displays in eastern and southern North America may disappoint each fall when grown in gardens in the cloudy Pacific Northwest or in western Europe.

Variegated plants

Variegated plants—those with markings of white, cream, gold, pink, red, blue, purple, gray, yellow-green, and so forth on the leaves—are affected by light conditions in a different way. They are colored so because of their genetic makeup. The variegation itself can be more or less marked, however, depending on environmental conditions such as light and temperature. This is because the actual variegations, whatever the pattern, fall into one of two basic types.

Variegations are the result either of accumulations of pigments in the tissue that mask the green chlorophyll, or the absence of green chlorophyll, so that other pigments in the leaf become visible. In the first case, full sun usually promotes development of the variegation, while shade reduces it, since

Fall foliage of *Fothergilla major*
Although it grows well in light shade, the witch alder really needs full sun to give a truly special fall display.

The attraction of variegated foliage
Ilex cornuta 'O'Spring' is a stunning variegated holly that gives its best color when grown in full sun or very light shade.

the pigments are made from building blocks of photosynthate. In the second case, full sun usually inhibits development of variegation, while shade usually promotes it, as chlorophyll production will be reduced in the shade.

Some variegations also appear if a plant has been exposed to especially cold temperatures (this is particularly true with conifers, heaths, and heathers, many cultivars of which develop bright winter color that fades to green each spring with the onset of warmer temperatures).

MOISTURE CONDITIONS

Water is critically important for plant growth and development. It is not only used in photosynthesis, but it helps carry sugars and nutrients throughout the plant's vascular system (its circulatory system), and it keeps the plant's cells turgid (filled) and functional.

Moisture is continually lost from leaves in a process called transpiration. As air moves across the surface of a leaf, water vapor evaporates from that surface. When there is a shortage of water, plant cells shrink and the leaves visibly wilt since the cells have become flaccid and can no longer maintain the positive pressure that holds the leaves up. As water is absorbed through the roots, full rigidity is restored to the cells and the leaves right themselves again. Chronic water shortages cause stress to plants and can eventually kill them.

Too much water can be just as bad. Roots need oxygen to thrive and function. When soils are waterlogged, all of the pore spaces in the soil are taken up with water, and so little or no gas exchange can take place with the aboveground air. This means that as oxygen is used in the soil, it cannot be

Plant fluids and sugars feed the roots.

Moisture transpires through the leaves.

A plant's vascular system
Higher plants have circulatory systems that transport water, nutrients, carbohydrates, and metabolites between the roots and leaves via the conducting tissue of the vascular system.

Ideal plants for moist, sunny conditions
Heaths and heathers need a moist, humus-rich, acidic soil and lots of sun. The variety of heather shown here in all its late-summer glory is *Calluna vulgaris* 'Darkness'.

replaced from the aboveground air and the roots start to suffocate. If there is insufficient oxygen, roots will stop taking up water and nutrients. In waterlogged soil, plants can actually die from water shortages because the roots can no longer supply water to them.

As might be expected, different plants have different preferences and ranges of tolerance for moisture conditions. For example, not only can desert-adapted plants tolerate much longer periods of drought than plants adapted to the cloud forest, but they may languish if given the regular irrigation critical to the success of a cloud-forest species.

Two species may require the same total amount of moisture in a given growing season, but one may do better with frequent light watering, while another may prefer infrequent heavy watering, depending on whether the plant develops a heavily branched, shallow root system or a few deep taproots. Some plants require very moist habitats in nature but perform well in dry garden sites because the moist habitat is required for seed germination and seedling survival but is not actually necessary once the plant is established. Other plants are sensitive to overwatering because it increases their susceptibility to fungal diseases, although they will tolerate inherently damp soils as long as their foliage does not stay chronically wet.

While it is best to grow shrubs that are well suited to the conditions of your garden, all garden plants should be regularly watered during their first two growing seasons after planting (whether following an initial planting or after a subsequent transplanting). The loss of roots that accompanies planting and transplanting results in an increased need for supplemental water for all plants until they recover from the replanting with new root growth. Once most plants have been in the ground for two seasons or more, they should be sufficiently recovered to grow with very little extra water—except, of course, during periods of severe drought, when additional watering will be vital to maintain the health and vigor of both transplanted and established plants.

The effects of moisture

Moisture and its effect in the garden takes many forms. Rain, snow, sleet, hail, fog, and ice all bring water, but their effects on your garden plants vary dramatically. Rain and fog provide moisture to the garden directly by adding to soil moisture, as well as indirectly by inhibiting transpiration (see opposite page). On the other hand, frozen precipitation provides moisture but there is a delaying effect until it melts and is absorbed by the soil.

Snow acts like insulation in winter landscapes, keeping soil temperatures to a reasonable level and protecting plant crowns from extremes of wind and sun exposure. You may have noticed that, despite appearances to the contrary, portions of plants that spend much of the winter covered by snow often emerge the following spring after the snow has melted in much better condition and with far less winter damage than those parts of the same plant that were left untouched by snow for much of the winter (see also p.43 under Pests, diseases, and hazards).

Freezing rain, ice, and sleet, on the other hand, can harm plants, as well as changing their decorative structure. As ice builds up on branches, the weight can lead to breakage. Shrub trunks can also split as the branches break, sometimes causing the plant irreparable damage.

A formal English garden with snow cover
While it is easy to assume that snow adds winter stress to plants in the garden, in fact the plants may benefit from its insulating properties.

Combining shrubs

Many gardeners are content to combine different herbaceous perennials and/or annuals to provide a beautiful display of color and texture in the garden throughout the year. Far fewer gardeners realize that there is perhaps even greater potential to create an attractive garden display over time through the enormous diversity of shrub sizes, shapes, and ornamental qualities.

Gardening with shrub combinations allows scope for the same flair, spontaneity, and comprehensive designs as does gardening with herbaceous plants. The key is to understand what ornamental qualities a given shrub offers through all four seasons and to take into account the particular cultural requirements of each plant.

Shrubs can be used effectively as single specimens or massed together in groups or hedges, included with herbaceous perennials in mixed borders or in rock gardens, or combined in a showcase shrub border. There is no combination of plants, including shrubs, that is necessarily "right" or "wrong": whether or not the combinations you choose are successful depends on whether or not they achieve the effect you were hoping for, and whether or not that effect itself is pleasing to you in your garden.

Since shrubs can be relatively long lived, it is important to be aware of the changes in habit that are likely to occur throughout the life of the plant. You can take advantage of these changes to create combinations that offer a kind of living sculpture in the garden, a creation that changes not only through the seasons of one year but over the course of many years of garden development.

In a new garden, you may even include some fast-growing, bold-textured shrubs to give a rapid, temporarily planted-up effect. Within a few growing seasons you can remove these shrubs to make way for slower-growing selections. You might, for example, include the relatively slow growing contorted selections *Poncirus trifoliata* 'Flying Dragon' and *Corylus avellana* 'Contorta' for long-lived architectural effect but at the same time also plant the rapidly growing contorted *Salix udensis* 'Sekka', intending to remove it once the slower-growing plants have developed some size and presence.

The same approach can be used when renovating existing gardens and beds. If, for example, you ultimately wanted to display the beautiful evergreen variegation of *Ilex cornuta* 'O'Spring', which is quite slow growing, but wanted to emphasize the variegation effect while 'O'Spring' developed a mature habit, you could plant one of the variegated evergreen *Euonymus* selections (such as *E. fortunei* 'Canadale Gold'). If, on the other hand, you wanted even more vigor, you might try one of the variegated *Elaeagnus* selections (such as 'Gilt Edge').

Above: *Corylus avellana* 'Contorta' in winter
If left unpruned, this variety of hazel can be grown for its visual effect and will increase in character with age.

Right: *Rhododendron yakusimanum* with *Pieris* 'Bert Chandler'
Many shrubs that are striking enough to be planted as single specimens can be even more effective when planted together.

You will need to be especially careful when composing these kinds of temporary combinations not to plant the more rapidly growing "part-timer" too near the slower-growing, long-term occupant. The potential problem here is that if the slower-growing shrub is forced to compete with the faster growing shrub for light, water, and nutrients, it could take even longer to develop.

By careful positioning in relation to paths, border edges, patios, and screens, you can achieve a temporary improved visual effect without inhibiting growth of the long-term, slower plant until it is time to remove the short-term attraction and reveal the presence of the slower-growing plants in all their accumulated glory.

Factors to consider

When planning to combine different shrubs effectively in your garden there are three basic factors that you need to consider—all concerned with a plant's seasonal and long-term development. The three factors are:

- The form and habit of a particular shrub (this includes its branching characteristics, as well as its projected mature height and spread).
- The textures of its leaves, flowers, fruits, and bark.
- The colors of its leaves, flowers, fruits, and bark.

Poncirus trifoliata in spring

With attractive blossoms in spring and ornamental green shoots in winter, *Poncirus trifoliata* makes a strong show in a shrub border.

The form of shrubs changes as plants mature. Young plants are often more open and rounded than older, denser, more irregular plants. On the other hand, with some species, exactly the opposite is true and young plants are denser and more uniform in habit, only becoming spreading and informal with age.

Some ornamental characteristics do not develop until plants reach a certain age. This can be especially true of bark characteristics (one notable exception is the colored bark of the shrubby dogwoods, whose yellow or red stems show better color on younger stems).

Flowering and fruiting are usually the most prolific on mature, well-established plants, although they are often reduced on plants for the first two to three years after transplanting as

Beautiful bark characteristics

Grown chiefly for its winter display of bright yellow shoots, the dogwood *Cornus stolonifera* 'Flaviramea' will always give a better display on younger, more vigorous stem growth.

root growth recovers and plants adjust to their new situation. The plant should recover, however, unless it is stressed in its new site, in which case it will have to be relocated again.

Four-season plantings

When combining shrubs for four-season displays, be sure to think about the effect created by the combinations throughout those four seasons. For example, you may want to combine a spring-flowering viburnum that offers a prolific, fragrant spring display with lower-growing beautyberries that develop bright purple fruit in fall, but you need to remember that many viburnums develop bright red fruit, which may or may not be the color combination you want to display with the purple-fruited beautyberries in fall. If this is not the right color combination, you might choose one of the sterile-flowered viburnums to minimize any fruit development on the viburnum and keep the fruit display limited to the bright beautyberries. On the other hand, you may like the combination of red and purple and so decide to intentionally opt for a prolific, red-fruited viburnum to combine with the beautyberry.

When designing combinations of shrubs for four-season interest, remember that there are literally hundreds of shrubs that offer a vast array of visual effects. It is especially helpful to bear in mind that a plant's foliage can provide as much interest and beauty as its flower and fruit, and moreover has the advantage of often lasting far longer. *Eleutherococcus sieboldianus* 'Variegatus', for example, is a variegated form of a reliable shrub whose foliage remains dappled with white all summer long.

Variegated evergreens such as many of the cultivars of *Aucuba japonica* or *Ilex* add color interest to the gloomier days of the year. Female plants of both of these can develop showy red fruit as well, adding another dimension to their decorative characteristics.

Fruits of *Callicarpa bodinieri*
Beautyberries are extremely useful shrubs because not only do they bear brightly colored fruits profusely in fall that persist into winter, but the low-growing forms complement taller shrubs effectively.

Ornamental highlights for a winter border
Among the very best of shrub selections for interest in the winter border, *Rubus cockburnianus* has a mass of showy, blue-white stems to lighten up the gloomiest part of the year.

If, over a period of time, you deliberately arrange your shrub plantings by placing complementary or contrasting seasonal decorative traits together, you can use them to make an exceptional contribution to your garden.

Finding Shrubs

Once you have planned your garden and decided which shrubs to include in which sites, your next challenge is to find sources for the selections you have chosen. There are five general types of plant sources: botanic garden and specialty society plant sales, wholesale nurseries, retail nurseries, garden centers, and discount mass-market stores.

Availability and sources

Botanic garden and specialty plant society plant sales are often only open to members, but they are usually excellent sources of choice and rare shrubs—as well as other plants—at very good prices. These sorts of sales are frequently the only places to find unusual plants.

Wholesale nurseries sell only to retail nurseries and companies or to others in the trade. Retail nurseries sell to the general public and are the standard source of a wide range of shrubs, including less easily available selections as well as old favorites and the most commonly grown and purchased plants.

Most retail nurseries sell plants directly from their premises. Specialty retail mail-order nurseries are different in that they grow small plants (including trees and shrubs) in containers to be ordered from their catalog and shipped direct to the customer.

Specialty retail mail-order nurseries are often the first sources of new plants for the gardening public, and they perform an important service by providing unusual plants in manageable sizes for the home gardener. One advantage of this source is that smaller-size plants invariably recover better from transplanting than do larger plants, although the disadvantage is that there is no opportunity to inspect plants before they are shipped. Reputable mail-order nurseries generally offer limited guarantees on plants, so there is some recourse if plants have been damaged in shipping or are inadvertently shipped in poor condition or incorrectly named.

Garden centers cater to a very broad customer base and so usually offer the most commonly available and recognizable plants of all sorts. As well as making an array of attractive plants available to the general public, they also sell gardening tools and equipment and offer helpful advice and information all in one location.

Mass-market stores are the large retail chains that sell huge quantities of plants at very inexpensive rates. The plants are usually very common selections (which may or may not be particularly good selections of a given plant). The quality of care given these plants ranges wildly from surprisingly good to sadly neglectful, and so it is difficult to predict the quality of any plant purchased from these sources. You can occasionally find a good bargain in a mass-market store, but it often takes a keen eye and persistence to find good-quality, well-grown plants that are both beautiful and useful selections. Basically, you need to remember that when buying plants from these sources you usually get what you pay for.

Nursery professionals specialize in growing and marketing garden plants. As a result, they are usually the best source for garden plants of all sorts if you want to be sure that you have purchased a well-grown plant and have been offered reliable information with your purchase. In the end it is always worth seeking out a supplier with a good reputation.

Above: Shrubs for sale at a garden center
Many gardeners look both for inspiration on planting and for good-quality plants at their local garden center.

Right: Model borders at a botanic garden
For an overview of how their own mixed border might look, enthusiasts often travel to well-known botanic gardens.

Shrubs as garden elements

Shrubs can play a number of roles in the garden, whether it be star feature or as a complementary or even supporting player. In most gardens they are used in one of three ways: first, as a key element in a screen, barrier, or ground cover planting; second, as either an integral part or a focal point of a border or mixed ornamental planting; finally, as a key specimen—which can be either a shrub with an especially interesting form or habit, or a personal favorite.

BOUNDARIES AND DIVIDERS

Plants that either create or decorate boundaries are an unspectacular but essential aspect of most gardens. They can take the form of a screen to hide unattractive building features or views; planted as hedges they can act as a low living wall or barrier, providing either privacy or a dividing line between other parts of the garden; they can also be used as ground cover. Whatever their use, boundaries make key contributions to modern landscapes and gardens—especially in urban and suburban landscapes.

Shrubs have been used in these ways in gardens for hundreds of years. Those that are grown widely—such as the various selections of boxwood (*Buxus* species), privet (*Ligustrum* species), and barberry (*Berberis* species)—remain popular for both barriers and hedges because their size and shape make them a natural choice.

The abundance of shrubs available to the modern gardener gives you a wide choice of reliable, low-maintenance barrier plantings that are also creative and year-round attractive additions to the landscape. Their diversity means you can add color and textural interest, thereby making the most of the entire garden.

Screens and hedges

Barrier plantings are most frequently required to create a screen. In addition to their uses as a barricade against noise, traffic, or a disappointing view, screens are important devices for creating garden "rooms," or surprise elements in the landscape, as well as providing additional interest by preventing a clear open view of the entire garden at a glance. Strategically placed screen plantings can make a garden seem larger, while at the same time they can invite you and your visitors to explore around each corner and curve.

If every focal point remains completely visible, there will be no element of surprise, as it will always be in plain view for the entire length of any walk. If, on the other hand, you place a small garden sculpture or ornament in such a way that you discover it as you come out from around a hedge, it will be far more effective. Curving screens that wend their way through the garden, planted with a variety of shrubs, create spaces that are perfect for accent plants, sculptures, benches, fountains, urns, or small reflecting pools. Although your choice of ornaments is bound to be highly personal, any such feature is certain to surprise and delight garden strollers as they come upon it.

Lavender used as a low-growing living barrier
Massed plantings of low-growing shrubs such as *Lavandula angustifolia* 'Hidcote' make useful informal hedges for flanking paths or similar natural barriers within the garden.

A "window" through a tall screen
Shearing a "framed" view in a *Camellia*
hedge creates an enticing view of the
shrubs and trees beyond.

To generate a sense of both mystery and dimension as well as a feeling of space throughout a garden site, few techniques are as effective as the planting of screens. The illusion of changes in terrain can be created by planting screens using shrubs that will grow to various different heights. You might, for example, plant an irregular curve of the tall shrub *Ternstroemia gymnanthera* to define a shady bend in the path that passes below a large and evocative deciduous tree, but then ensure that the *T. gymnanthera* planting blends into a lower screen of *Rhaphiolepis indica* as the path moves into a sunny area. Both shrubs are evergreen and have attractive flowers, modestly ornamental fruit, harmonious textures and habits, and similar soil preferences and tolerances, although *T. gymnanthera* does best when grown in some shade, while *R. indica* prefers full sun.

Such differences in the preferred light conditions among plants of similar garden character can be used to advantage, even in small gardens, to add variety and interest to basic screen and hedge plantings. In this instance, the higher screen of *T. gymnathera* creates not only privacy but also a sense of suspense about what lies on the other side of the screen. The shorter *R. indica*, on the other hand, might allow a glimpse back across the garden to a specimen shrub, a seasonally attractive border, or even a view that looks outside the garden's perimeters. Judicious pruning can effect an apparently seamless blend or, if you prefer, a more dramatic change from one plant type to the other.

By pruning and shearing you can open "windows" through a tall screen to offer "framed" views or surprise vistas, but such features require more regular attention than do combinations of plants that differ in both growth rates and mature heights. If you do want a sheared "window," an effective way to achieve this is by using a shrub whose new growth emerges in a color that contrasts with that of the more mature foliage, thereby accenting and defining the sheared "window."

Shrubby screens and hedges can be especially useful on small urban properties, not only as barriers but as a way of creating the illusion of a larger garden space. They can also be an effective way of disguising views of neighboring walls, industrial complexes, or parking lots. There are many tough pollution-tolerant shrubs that can be used in small spaces. Plants such as *Rhamnus*, *Abelia*, *Aronia*, *Berberis*, *Fothergilla*, *Pittosporum*, and *Nerium* are reliable in dry, poorly drained, or cramped urban sites, where their flowers, foliage, fruit, and habit are especially welcome.

Creating living barriers

Using tall shrubs as a screen or a hedge to create an enclosed or private part of the garden often has more appeal for the urban dweller than building another wall. Even in a pastoral landscape, a living screen can be a more harmonious addition than a wall of wood or stone, particularly if you use combinations of fragrant shrubs. A screening hedge of evergreen *Osmanthus fragrans* in full bloom—with its entrancing sweet and spicy scent—surely offers a more attractive prospect than a blank stone face.

An ornamental rose hedge
While lacking the formality of a neatly trimmed coniferous hedge, a rose hedge in full bloom makes a superlative backdrop for just about any garden.

Screens and hedges in the garden are not only functional: they are hardscape and architectural features. To that end, your choice of shrubs for hedges or screens can be made from an aesthetic point of view, in the same way that you might choose materials for a stone path, wooden arbor, or carved bench. But although we think of screens and hedges in the same garden category as hardscape features, the important difference is that hedges and screens are composed of live plants whose particular cultural requirements and growth habits must be taken into account at the planning stage. A stone wall is basically unaffected by environmental conditions, light exposure, and soil type, but shrubs must be positioned in an area of the garden where they will thrive while at the same time providing the visual decoration you desire.

Virtually any shrub can be used to create or contribute to an effective screen if it is sited appropriately and if you take into account its cultural requirements as well as the prevailing microclimatic conditions. It is especially important that the plant's natural habit be appropriate for the type of screen you want to create. It is, for example, wise to choose a shrub that responds well to repeated shearing for use in a formal, sheared hedge; conversely, when planning a large, informal screen, it makes sense to choose a shrub that will develop a naturally arching, graceful habit and can consequently be left on its own for many years.

It is always difficult to predict the exact height that a particular plant will reach at maturity once it has become established. How the young plant was treated in the nursery, how well it has adapted to its new home, whether or not it has been subject to inappropriate pruning—these are just a few of the factors that can affect the ultimate size and shape of a shrub. Although their multistemmed habits make shrubs more "plastic" in both height and spread than other plants, keep in mind that each species and cultivar nonetheless has its particular range of mature sizes and shapes.

Because of the variation in shrub size, it is important to select shrubs that not only will provide the desired color and texture but whose mature size and shape will not work against the mature size and shape of the planned hedge or screen. The open, coarse-textured *Forsythia*, for example, is a poor choice if you want to create a tall, narrow formal hedge with dark green color year-round; you would do much better with evergreen holly species (*Ilex* species). Equally, tall-growing, rangy, and robust shrubs such as honeysuckle (*Lonicera*) and fall olive (*Elaeagnus*) would not be suitable for a low, narrow border around a formal brick terrace, whereas, given the right growing conditions, boxwood (*Buxus*) would make an excellent choice there.

Combination screens and hedges

While certain formal styles and plantings clearly call for a uniform hedge or screen consisting of a single type of plant—as, for example, in a maze—in many instances it is possible to add interest and vigor to the hedge simply by varying its makeup to include two or three different types of plants. Hedges and screens planted with several types of shrubs offer opportunities to include seasonal peaks in color and texture. We can, for example, plant a hedge that is composed primarily of deciduous privet but also including breaks of robust flowering shrubs such as *Weigela* or lilac *(Syringa)*. In the same way, we might include intermittent plantings of hardy camellias in a hedge of evergreen holly to add flowering interest to the hedge's quiet overall evergreen character.

Seasonal interest in hedges

Again, by combining different shrubs in a hedge, we can provide seasonal interest as well as create shifts and contrasts in texture, color, and silhouette. Hedges can consist of all evergreen or all deciduous shrubs for consistency year-round, or you can mix evergreens and deciduous plants to maximize contrasts in winter, while offering a more seamless blend in summer. Deciduous shrubs that have a special ornamental character that is attractive in winter—such as attractive-looking bark, persistent fruit, or an unusual habit—can be combined with evergreens to make an especially artistic hedge or screen. For example, an interesting combination would be a hedge that combined cinnamon-barked crape myrtle *(Lagerstroemia indica* x *fauriei)* hybrid cultivars, planted in groups of threes or fives, with clumps of evergreen cherry laurel *(Prunus laurocerasus)* and a few vigorous *Gardenia* plants. It is equally exciting to see how the multitrunked winter habit of the crape myrtle is almost completely transformed in summer, when candelabra of fleecy flowers cover these large plants. The quiet, evergreen foliage of the cherry laurel is a lovely foil for both the winter and summer characteristics of *L. indica*, while *Gardenia* offers variety with its evergreen texture and foliage color throughout the year, together with the appeal of its luscious, waxy white, uniquely fragrant blossoms during late

spring and early summer. The foliage of the cherry laurel and the foliage and flowers of *Gardenia* are a prelude to the crape myrtle's flowers in late summer and early fall.

In colder climates, a different but equally diverse and appealing hedge might combine the relatively tall cornelian cherry dogwood *(Cornus mas)*, which has pale, peeling bark and very early, canary yellow flowers, with some of the broom *(Cytisus)* cultivars, which have fountains of bright green winter stems and prolific, strikingly colored, pea-shaped flowers in late spring, together with the gracefully pendent evergreen *Leucothoe fontanesiana*, which has elegant, glossy, dark green leaves and a very distinctive zigzag pattern of branching.

A bolder combination could be made by growing *Ilex cornuta* 'O'Spring', which offers cream-and-gold variegated evergreen foliage, with yellow-twig dogwood *(Cornus stolonifera)* 'Flaviramea' , whose bright yellow winter twigs would shine in concert with the holly's foliage. Because both 'O'Spring' holly and yellow-twig dogwood tolerate

Flowering hedge with *Hypericum* species
It is the delightful contrasts of colors and textures in this scene that make the flowering hedge in the midground such a success.

difficult sites that have little high-quality topsoil, they make especially good choices for new gardens where the topsoil has been stripped by developers.

Another way to add unusual interest and dimension to a hedge is to combine climbing plants with evergreen and deciduous shrubs. When using this approach you must ensure that the climbers are not so vigorous that they will strangle the hedge plants they are clambering on. The many truly charming combinations include climbing roses that come into full bloom while draped from evergreen shrubs such as camellias or from unusual shrubs with an interesting habit, such as *Stachyurus* or *Cyrilla*. In addition, combining climbers with shrubs is often a very effective way of adding flower and fragrance interest to relatively small gardens whose limited space must be reserved first and foremost for screening hedges.

Adaptable combinations

Using a variety of different shrub species and cultivars in hedges and screens also prevents having an entire hedge planting completely destroyed by the invasion of a single pest or disease. Because individual shrub species tend to have differing susceptibilities to pests or diseases, only certain plants in the hedge are likely to be severely affected. If one species or cultivar succumbs to insects or disease, in such a case, then only that particular type of

An aromatic evergreen hedge
If plants of both sexes are grown, the female *Skimmia japonica* bears bright red fruits in fall maturing from clusters of small white flowers in spring.

shrub needs to be replaced in the hedge. Similarly, if there are pest or disease problems that can be solved by the application of a low-toxicity pesticide (which will not harm pets or garden birds) or herbicide, then only the few plants of the susceptible species or variety need be treated.

Using varied species or even cultivars of plants in a hedge or screen also gives you much more flexibility to alter parts of the hedge as the garden (or the neighboring landscape) changes over time. If, for example, you have planted a mix of evergreen and deciduous shrubs in a hedge in order to create a latticed winter view across the landscape or to let in more light in the winter months, and then find a new housing development being built next door, it is far easier to replace

Weigela, Cotoneaster, and *Syringa* by a gate.
Carefully combining deciduous and evergreen shrubs softens the outline of this wooden arch and gate and makes the "barrier" to this house attractive in all ways.

the deciduous plants with evergreens if there are a few groups interspersed throughout the hedge than if large blocks of them are planted in a row. Alternatively, if you have planted a mixed deciduous and evergreen hedge and find that the evergreens have grown too tall and your garden needs more light in winter, it is simpler and less costly to replace a few groups of evergreens from within the hedge with new deciduous selections than it is to replace the entire hedge.

Barriers

A barrier planting most often takes the form of a screen or hedge, but it also acts as a physical obstruction. Depending on whom or what you wish to bar from your garden, you can select from among a gallery of shrubs that are quite attractive yet at the same time have intimidating features.

Clearly, many thorny shrubs—such as barberry (*Berberis* species), hardy orange (*Poncirus trifoliata*), and most roses (*Rosa* species) and brambles (*Rubus* species)— make excellent barriers, although gorse (*Ulex* species) is undoubtedly the most impenetrable planting.

Thorniness, however, is not the only useful attribute. If, for example, you want your barrier to be a physical block to movement by people or animals into or out of the garden but not to be a visual obstacle, then the texture of the shrub becomes critical: a shrub with an open habit would be most appropriate. Large, coarse deciduous shrubs such as *Magnolia* 'Susan'—which has lovely rose-colored spring flowers—might be good choices here.

Barrier plantings of large, coarse deciduous shrubs also offer many opportunities to interplant the hedge with vines and climbers, in the same way as you can interplant evergreen hedges. With a deciduous hedge, a particularly effective stratagem is to use evergreen climbers such as *Clematis armandii* with deciduous spring bloomers such as forms of *Magnolia liliiflora* x *stellata*.

Shrubs used as barrier plantings are often useful for protecting delicate gardens from really severe wind and weather such as driving rain and hailstorms. In this case, reasonably dense-textured shrubs are desirable, although even a coarse, open hedge will significantly decrease the impact of the wind. Be sure that the shrubs you choose for your wind barrier are equal to the task—particularly when dealing with evergreens or any plantings intended to shield a garden from salt spray. Good choices for wind-barrier shrubs include *Weigela*, *Philadelphus*, *Forsythia*, *Nerium*, *Lagerstroemia*, *Abelia*, *Elaeagnus*, *Rhamnus*, and some species of *Viburnum*. Salt-tolerant shrub selections are also discussed on pp.96–101.

Access through barriers

You may also want a barrier that creates a visual and psychological obstacle but which also enables you to move back and forth. You may well need space to move your wheelbarrow in and out of the garden, or perhaps a footpath is needed to get to an adjacent property or a pool. In such cases you can arrange well-sited intermittent plantings of a mixture of dense shrubs in groups in such a way that the sight lines from various angles are blocked, while at the same time openings are left in the hedge that allow you access from one part of the garden to another.

For this kind of barrier you should use shrubs that are unusual or attractive enough to catch the eye. Arrange them along a curve or line that unites the entire hedge visually, thereby diverting attention away from any breaks.

An attractive thorny barrier
The flamboyant, thorny foliage of *Berberis thunbergii* 'Rose Glow' means that this shrub is not only eye-catching and handsome but is also equally effective as an obstructive garden barrier.

The hedge, as always, need not be made up of only one, not necessarily evergreen, species, Do take care, however, to choose plants that harmonize well, so that the hedge presents visual unity despite any designed breaks or gaps.

It may seem like a contradiction in terms to include eye-catching material in a hedge that you want to be visually coherent, but in fact you can achieve exactly the right effect by choosing brighter shrubs as the boldest within a palette of colors presented by the rest—as if you were a painter choosing to use, in a palette of otherwise somber reds, a touch of scarlet as opposed to a splash of bright violet or orange.

There are other possibilities. You could use mixed shrubs somewhat irregularly spaced in a loose zigzag down the line of the barrier. If you choose a unified combination that contains a few bolder individuals, you will find that the arrangement acts as a psychological barrier despite the intermittence of the clumps of plants. Maintaining this effect through all four seasons is something of a challenge, but it can be done. Common shrubs such as species of *Forsythia*, with their showstopping yellow spring-flowering display, can be set with similarly textured plantings of *Buddleja* (butterfly bush), which add bright pinks, purples, whites, or even oranges in full summer bloom. If you include a purple-fruited *Callicarpa* (beautyberry) alongside purple-flowered forms of *Buddleja davidii* (such as 'Dark Knight'), the increasing color of the beautyberry's developing fruit will overlap with the butterfly bush's strong flowering display to create a truly lovely visual arrangement.

For a coarser, bolder effect, try mixing *Pyracantha* (firethorn) into a hedge of *Hippophae rhamnoides* (sea buckthorn). The firethorn has shocking orange fall fruit; *H. rhamnoides* also has bright orange fruit but offers narrow, silvery gray foliage that makes an effective contrast with the dark green leaves of the other shrub. (However, if you want a good fruit display, be sure to plant both male and female kinds of the sea buckthorn.)

Naturalistic barriers

Another way to create visual points of interest in a non-continuous screen or barrier planting is to include a variegated cultivar in an otherwise uniform planting, or perhaps a cultivar of the same species but one that has contrasting flower or fruit color. If you would like a naturalistic barrier hedge in a wet area, you might choose one of the deciduous hollies such as *Ilex verticillata* mixed with an evergreen holly such as *I. cornuta*. Including males and red-fruited females (the most commonly available types) will give your hedge a mainly red-fruited character in fall and a lovely show as the fruits persist into winter—as well as providing food for birds and other wildlife in the garden.

If you also insert yellow-fruited forms of *Ilex* to draw the eye away from any breaks in the hedge that might occur—varieties such as *I. verticillata* 'Chrysocarpa' or *I. cornuta* 'D'Or'—you will add features of visual contrast that are still in harmony with the entire planting.

Cotoneaster lacteus hedge in fall
Running parallel to a long garden path, this high, evergreen cotoneaster hedge offers both privacy and attractive summer blooms, and bright fall and winter fruits.

GROUND COVERS

Ground covers are both a widely used and frequently underappreciated garden element. Shrubs that make good ground covers grow with a low, spreading habit and should not require much shearing. You should bear in mind, however, that ground covers may be needed in a range of heights, from plants that are completely flat and prostrate at 8–10in (20–25cm) to plants that develop into broad, irregular masses at 20–30in (50–75cm) in height. Some available ground-cover shrubs are even taller.

The particular characteristics required for your garden may call for a completely flat and uniform planting, or they may dictate an informal spread of irregular height and density either so that other plants can be planted amid the ground cover or simply to subtly vary the visual effect.

Ground cover combinations

You will almost certainly find a use for ground covers that spread horizontally, reach about 10–12in (25–30cm) in height or less, and need little attention. Ground covers can serve as neutral foils that are punctuated by flowering bulbs or herbaceous perennials, as stabilizing plantings on slopes or terraces, as visual carpets to sweep the eye along an allée or axis, or as variations of texture and color that integrate the main part of the garden with taller plantings and features. There is a ground-cover shrub to fit all these needs—as long as you remember to match the plants' cultural requirements with the site and soil conditions.

It is easy to think of low-growing evergreen conifers as the primary ground-cover plants, but the array of shrubs on the market means we can create almost any effect. Plants such as rock cotoneaster (*Cotoneaster horizontalis*) spread along the ground and rise to about 3ft (1m) to make a lovely emerald carpet of fine-textured foliage with delicate white spring flowers that mature into persistent bright red fruit. In contrast, staghorn sumac (*Rhus typhina*) can grow to over 20ft (6m) in height; it spreads to create a very open, tall, coarse mass of upright stems that are crowned with fuzzy red fruits in the fall and winter. Staghorn sumac also makes an effective bank planting on poor soils—it has the advantage of being able to grow and thrive in almost any site that has the benefit of full sun.

As with many planting plans, there is no reason to restrict your ground-cover arrangements to a single plant—unless you have a formal garden where topiary,

Climber growing through shrubby ground cover
In late fall the beautiful colors of the vigorous climber Boston ivy *(Parthenocissus tricuspidata)* combine well with the equally assertive bright red fruit of a spreading shrub such as the rock cotoneaster *(Cotoneaster horizontalis)*.

parterres, and edge plantings demand a uniformity of rows, beds, and curves. By mixing various shrubs—while at the same time keeping in mind the prevailing light and soil conditions—you can develop a four-season mosaic that brings far more interest to the garden than would be possible with any uniform ground cover.

In a small garden, there may be areas where a ground cover is required for relatively restricted areas. Many dwarf and slow-growing cultivars of otherwise large shrubs allow you to incorporate the decorative and cultural characteristics of their bigger cousins within a smaller garden space.

Heavenly bamboo (*Nandina domestica*) is a graceful evergreen shrub that can reach as much as 6½ft (2m) in height, depending on the cultivar. It produces rather inconspicuous but attractive white flowers in summer, but it is grown chiefly for its bamboo-like foliage and habit as well as for its pendent clusters of bright red fruit that mature from the flowers and persist through the winter (there are also creamy white- and yellow-fruited forms). Numerous selections have red- or burgundy-colored new growth and/or winter foliage. 'Firepower' and 'Wood's Dwarf' are two very attractive selections: they both reach about 2ft (60cm) in height but spread to make good low ground covers that take up less space than the full-size selections. 'Firepower' in particular develops bright red winter foliage—a very bold trait. *N. domestica* thrives in full sun or part shade, and so is especially useful if you have changing light conditions in a small garden or across the ground-cover area. You will, however, see more prolific flowering and fruiting when this plant is grown in full sun rather than shade.

If you have good, moist, well-drained soil in a small garden, you might consider some of the evergreen daphnes as ground covers, especially where you do not want a ground-cover plant with a spreading habit. The tight habit and dense foliage of, for example, *Daphne* x *burkwoodii* make it a beautiful low ground cover. A semievergreen hybrid that reaches about 3–4ft (1–1.2m), the Burkwood daphne grows slowly enough to be appropriate for small spaces. It flowers best in part shade or full sun. The fragrant waxy flowers, pink-blushed white in color, appear in spring and perfume a disproportionally large area of the garden. The cultivar 'Carol Mackie', which has leaves margined with

creamy white, can be planted for added interest. Daphnes as a group are difficult to transplant successfully, so take care with their initial siting.

Christmas boxwood *(Sarcococca)* will thrive in deep shade in moist soils and provides a lovely evergreen ground cover, reaching about 3–4ft (1–1.2m), with an undulating profile and narrow, dark green leaves. It produces fragrant flowers in winter that mature into glossy black berries.

Having considered a variety of attractive ground cover selections, it might be useful to think about a plan for a small hypothetical garden area. Imagine that it includes a dark corner, a partly shaded area in the curve of an informal path, and a central area with full-sun conditions all year round. You can presume that ground covers of interest are needed throughout this space in order to create an attractive garden that requires little maintenance. The shrubs mentioned above could be combined to generate a ground-cover mosaic that not only will look attractive at different times of the year but can also cope with the difference in light conditions of this garden.

For a start, you might plant a bed of *Sarcococca* in the shady corner, blending to a trio of *Daphne* 'Carol Mackie' in the semishaded curve of the path. From this area you could have *Nandina* 'Firepower' flowing out to fill in the sunny area. 'Firepower' would remain a quieter green in the part shade, harmonizing well there with the daphne; in the open it would develop winter color, while not detracting from the appeal of the shade-adapted plants.

Where space is not restricted, ground-cover shrubs can be used as alternatives to a turf lawn. Consider how eye-catching a blend of the bottlebrush buckeye *(Aesculus parviflora)* with *Rhus aromatica* 'Gro-low' would be. The buckeye, up to 13ft (4m) tall, bears upright panicles of clear white flowers in mid- to late summer, before developing lovely yellow fall leaf color. The 'Gro-low' sumac is less than 3ft (1m) in height and produces intense red-and-orange fall color. Both plants perform well in full sun, thrive on poor soils, and are virtually maintenance-free. They are better choices for the larger garden, however, as they both have a vigorous spreading habit.

Semievergreen ground cover in spring
With its dense clusters of fragrant pink flowers in spring that are occasionally repeated in fall, *Daphne* x *burkwoodii* 'Carol Mackie' is a choice selection for ground cover in small spaces.

BORDERS

The possibilities for using shrubs in borders are virtually endless. Moreover, borders come in as many shapes and sizes as the plants grown in them. And just as you can combine herbaceous perennials to create changes in color, texture, shape, and fragrance, so you can combine shrubs to create borders of great distinction.

When creating mixed borders, it is important to remember that year-round color, texture, and fragrance are important aspects of any garden. While lilacs (*Syringa* species), for example, may offer rewards of color and fragrance in the spring, they contribute little to the mixed border during the succeeding seasons. By contrast, a shrub such as the crape myrtle (*Lagerstroemia indica*) has bright summer bloom, attractive coloration in the fall, and beautiful winter bark—in other words, it is visually attractive throughout the year. This is not to say that lilacs do not belong in a border, merely that you should not restrict your borders to plants that bear interesting blooms or foliage for just one season.

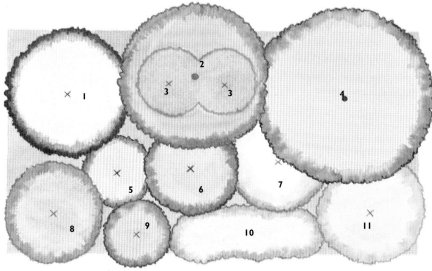

A sunny summer border

1. *Berberis thunbergii* f. *atropurpurea*
2. *Buddleja davidii* 'Black Knight'
3. *Perovskia atriplicifolia* × 2
4. *Cotinus coggygria* 'Royal Purple'
5. *Spiraea japonica* 'Shirobana'
6. *Lavandula angustifolia* 'Hidcote'
7. *Potentilla fruticosa* 'Abbotswood'
8. *Lavandula angustifolia* 'Munstead'
9. *Berberis thunbergii* 'Atropurpurea Nana'
10. *Helianthemum* 'Wisley Primrose' (out of flower during main flowering period)
11. *Cistus ladanifer* (out of flower during main flowering period)

Fall border with mixed planting
This striking border is a good example of how shrubs such as *Berberis* and *Aucuba japonica* can be used with a climber such as *Parthenocissus* to create interest.

But you must not focus your attention solely on flowering time in the garden. Remember that during the winter months, form, bark color, and persistent fruit can all be equally enticing characteristics. To take just one example, the winter color of the barks of the red- and yellow-twigged dogwoods can be used to welcome you into the garden during even the coldest months of the year.

In fact, borders afford perhaps the most scope for gardening with shrubs: in a border, plants of all sizes, shapes, colors, and forms, and with an endless variation of flower and fruit characteristics, can be combined in any way you choose. You can plan a border based on color themes, seasonal peaks of interest, textural patterns, or simply your own personal favorites.

Whatever affects your planting decisions, your planning must, as always, address not only the ornamental characteristics of the shrubs but also the limitations imposed by climate, soil, and site.

The border may be situated in full sun, semishade, or deep shade—or, indeed, it may stretch across all these conditions. It might be on a well-drained loam, a sharp sand, a heavy clay, or, in a few instances, more than one of these soil types. As to site, this could be a windswept hilltop, a frosty valley, or a sweltering urban sun spot.

Without a doubt, the primary consideration when choosing combinations of plants for a mixed border is whether they are well adapted to the site and climate. Within such constraints you can select plants whose ornamental characteristics would seem to work well in your garden. In this context, year-round interest is important. You might, for example, think about including such attractive winter-flowering selections as wintersweet (*Chimonanthus praecox*), whose yellow blooms can perfume a small garden at the bleakest time of year.

Form

The border is a wonderful place to contrast shrubs of varying heights and textures. Taller shrubs such as the various *Cotinus* and *Tamarix* (tamarisk) species offer height as well as unusual foliage color and texture. *C. coggygria* (smoke tree) reaches over 10ft (3m) in height and produces great smoky brushes of inflorescences that mature over several weeks through the summer. *Tamarix* is another tall plant but is much more feathery in texture, with threadlike blue-green foliage and racemes of pink flowers that wave above a border like a rosy haze.

Either *Cotinus* or *Tamarix* would combine well with rounded, moderate-height shrubs such as those of the genus *Fothergilla*, with their bottlebrushes of creamy flowers in late spring and their bold fall color, and *Hydrangea paniculata*, whose full pyramids of flowers gradually mature from creamy white to pink or red. All of these plants will seem even more striking if you allow a climbing rose or jasmine to clamber through them, and if you underplant them with a flowering ground cover shrub such as the aptly named blue mist shrub (*Caryopteris*) or the golden-flowered St.-John's-wort (*Hypericum*).

The great advantage of border planting is that it gives you the opportunity to intensify the contrast of form and texture. Because shrubs in borders are grown close to each other, you often get a stunning interplay of leaf, branch, stem, and bark. For example, bold-foliaged evergreen plants such as *Fatsia* and *Tetrapanax*, both of which have palmlike, incised, emerald green foliage, can be combined with other shrubs that have leaves of contrasting color. These might include such plants as lavender (*Lavandula* spp.), grown in full sun, or in part shade, with *Euonymus fortunei* 'Sunspot', the gold-variegated winter creeper, which also performs well in full sun.

While the form and habit of shrubs are of interest all year round, this is especially true in the winter or dormant season when the leaves have fallen from the deciduous plants and most flowering is over. This is the time of the year when you gain most from contorted selections and species that have a particularly attractive habit and branching patterns. One especially unusual deciduous shrub, for example, is Harry Lauder's walking stick (*Corylus avellana* 'Contorta'), a twisted-branching form of the hazel whose fascinating habit—which develops with age—is revealed only once it has lost its leaves; it makes an exceptional focal plant in an early-winter border, while in the later winter months its branches are covered with

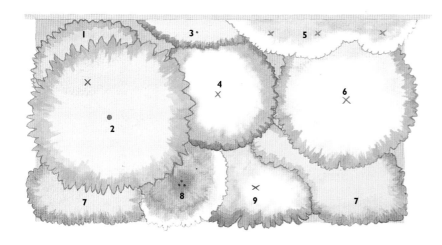

A shady foliage border

1. *Prunus laurocerasus* (good glossy leaf)
2. *Fatsia japonica*
3. *Jasminum nudiflorum*
4. *Hydrangea paniculata* 'Grandiflora'
5. *Euonymus fortunei* 'Emerald Gaiety' × 3
6. *Choisya ternata* (will have a small amount of flowers during the summer)
7. *Euphorbia amygdaloides* var. *robbiae* × 2 (as ground cover)
8. *Kerria japonica* 'Picta'
9. *Cotoneaster dammeri*

yellow catkins. Another shrub that also develops an intriguing character after its leaves have fallen is *Cyrilla racemiflora* (leatherwood)—its handsome bark combining with its curly branching and irregular stems to provide a really unusual winter effect.

Of course, form is equally important in spring and summer. Plants that offer unusual foliage or flower arrangement on the branches, plants whose interesting habit is highlighted by the presence of leaves, and many weeping selections are really at their best during the growing season. The pendent habit of the deciduous or semievergreen *Zenobia pulverulenta*, for example, is amplified when the foliage is present: this appears as a blue-gray waterfall on young plants, but the effect becomes nondescript once the leaves have fallen.

Fragrance

Fragrance is one of the most elusive yet important garden elements, and a shrub border is a wonderful way to ensure its presence throughout the year. Finding fragrant spring-blooming shrubs such as viburnums, lilacs, and magnolias, is easy enough, but it is more of a challenge to keep fragrance alive throughout the rest of the year. In addition to the fragrant roses, shrubs such as *Gardenia, Abelia*,

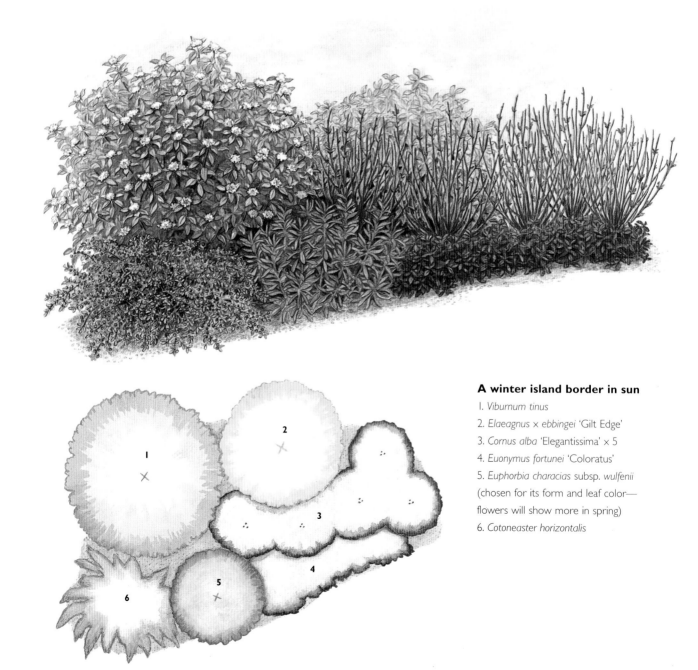

A winter island border in sun

1. *Viburnum tinus*
2. *Elaeagnus × ebbingei* 'Gilt Edge'
3. *Cornus alba* 'Elegantissima' × 5
4. *Euonymus fortunei* 'Coloratus'
5. *Euphorbia characias* subsp. *wulfenii* (chosen for its form and leaf color—flowers will show more in spring)
6. *Cotoneaster horizontalis*

Mixed spring border
A vibrant mixed spring border is one of the rewarding achievements of gardening. This brightly flowered rhododendron contrasts perfectly with the narcissus in the foreground.

Ligustrum, Enkianthus, and *Carpenteria californica* can all offer lovely summer aromas. In fall, shrubs such as *Heptacodium* and *Osmanthus* bring a summery set of scents to the air, while during the potentially dreary winter months three important genera—*Jasminum, Chimonanthus* and *Hamamelis*—can contribute an unseasonal flowery or spicy fragrance.

Aside from flowers, foliage can also add fragrance to the garden, especially when touched or when grown in strong sun. Shrubby herbs such as rosemary, lavender, and the *Santolina* species give off pungent herbal aroma as you brush by them in the border.

Fall color

The border is also an excellent place to display the often spectacular fall color of certain shrubs. Plants such as *Euonymus alatus, Aronia arbutifolia, Viburnum dilatatum,* and *Rhododendron schlippenbachii* develop bright red and burgundy-red fall coloration, while *Lindera obtusiloba, Hamamelis virginiana,* and *Aesculus parviflora* turn clear yellow-gold toward the end of the year. You will find that using shrubs such as *Lespedeza,* which has a burnished gold fall color, in combination with *Fothergilla* or *Hydrangea quercifolia,* both of which develop mixed hues of wine, red, and even some golds, will make for a dramatic show as the days become shorter.

Yet another useful example, *Corylus maxima* 'Purpurea', is a purple-leaved filbert that develops a bright red hue over the purple in the fall and makes a brilliant show; this can be dramatized even further if it is planted in front of a mass of common witch hazel *(Hamamelis virginiana).* As a general rule, when planted close to shrubs with fall coloration in golds and yellows, a contrasting evergreen with dark green leaves makes a striking foil.

A fall shrub border is also a good place for *Franklinia* to show off its burgundy-red color as a backdrop to the extremely late camellia-like white flowers overhead, while *Zenobia pulverulenta* could spread a carpet of carmine and wine foliage at your feet. The shrub border is likewise an ideal situation for highlighting *Itea virginica* or the fall color of a cut-leaf Japanese maple, combined with such herbaceous perennials as golden-foliaged *Amsonia.* Displays such as these can create a fascinating mix.

Shrubs with fruits

Shrubs that follow their spring and summer flowerings with fruit also add delightful color and texture to a mixed border in both fall and winter. Good examples of this type of shrub are the strawberry tree *(Arbutus unedo)* and the Oregon grape *(Mahonia aquifolium).* The strawberry tree is a large shrub (or small tree) that can eventually reach 30ft (9m) in height. It produces white bell-shaped flowers in early fall just as the previous year's fruits are ripening to strawberry red. The Oregon grape blooms in late winter, showing upright sprays of canary yellow flowers that mature to blue-black fruits.

Many roses have showy fruits, or hips. The fruit of species such as *Rosa rugosa* and *R. eglanteria* contribute to the border long after their blooms have finished.

Beautyberries (*Callicarpa* spp.) offer perhaps the most dramatic fruit for the border. They develop only a rather pale gold fall color, but the bright purple fruits can be dramatic. The various species have their fruits arranged differently along the stem. The showiest is the species *C. americana*, whose fruits come in large clusters wrapped at intervals along the stem—although this species is not as cold-hardy as the various Asian beautyberries such as *C. bodinieri*. Beautyberries combine to great effect with shrubs that develop deeper gold fall coloration, such as the *Lespedeza* species, which set off the persistent purple of the beautyberry fruit to advantage.

Fruits do not have to be large or brightly colored to add interest to the border. A cluster of the glossy black *Ilex crenata* fruits has quiet appeal, while the tan clusters of the dried seed heads of *Kalmia* species add a fine-textured note of interest on the top of their evergreen foliage. The mahogany fruits of some *Elaeagnus* species look very appealing set against against their stems, which are covered with a silvery waxy bloom. The fat black fruits of *Prunus laurocerasus* and *Ligustrum japonicum* are additional yet understated attractions in the fall border.

The fruits (and forms) of some shrubs may be more than purely visual attractions. If the plants are relatively dense and/or evergreen, they make excellent winter shelter for certain types of birds and small animals. Moreover, the persistent fruits of some species such as those of *Aronia* can provide vital food for a number of garden residents during the months when harsh winter weather leaves them with little else to eat.

Shrubs can supply food for people as well as for birds and other animals. Pawpaw (*Asimina triloba*), raspberries (*Rubus* spp.), shadbush (*Amelanchier* spp.), beach plum (*Prunus maritima*), and the cornelian cherry dogwood (*Cornus mas*) are just a few examples of those shrubs that, when included in a mixed border, offer the gardener not only attractive plants to look at but edible fruit as well.

DIEBACK SHRUBS

Shrubs are versatile and can function in the border in various ways. Many of the half-hardy vigorous plants can be grown as dieback shrubs, effectively behaving as herbaceous perennials but offering their shrubby characteristics during the growing season. One useful technique is to use the purple-foliaged selections of a smoke tree such as *Cotinus coggygria* 'Royal Purple'. Cut the plants back hard in late winter and each spring they will give you deeply colored new growth that will eventually develop significant height and mass without flowering.

Vitex is another genus that makes good dieback plants for colder climates. If pruned to the ground each year, in spring these shrubs will send up vigorous shoots, with flowers forming on the new growth. This is a good reason to include in your border the handsome *Vitex negundo* var. *heterophylla*, which has toothed foliage and spires of lavender-blue flowers.

Border with shrub, perennial, and climber
For a completely different effect in a mixed border, *Rosa rugosa*, *Sedum* 'Autumn Joy', and *Vitis vinifera* are ideal.

A choice specimen shrub

One of the most unusual specimen shrubs is *Enkianthus campanulatus* 'Red Bells', which always makes an intriguing statement in the garden.

SHRUBS AS SPECIMENS

You have probably heard of specimen trees—special individual trees that are rare or unusual in some way, or that may be challenging to grow. It is more unusual to hear of specimen shrubs, even though there are many shrubs that fit the same criteria as those for specimen trees and that can become useful specimen plants in any sort of garden.

A specimen may be a single plant sited either at a visual focal point in the garden—such as in a corner that you regularly pass—or in an area where you like to sit and appreciate the plant's shade or the movement of its branches. A specimen may also be a plant with a particularly interesting habit that is placed in a raised bed or at the top of a rise in order to highlight it. Or it may be a plant that produces large and colorful blooms at the time of year when you are most likely to be out in the garden to enjoy the display. There may be other, more personal reasons why you may come to regard individual plants in your garden as specimens: they may, for example, have an emotional association for you.

A specimen shrub need not require a great deal of maintenance or special treatment, but it should offer a particular characteristic or "presence." Remember, as always in planning your garden, that no plant is there in isolation. Just as with other plants, specimens should be chosen not just individually but in the context of your overall planting scheme. Although you may want to select the specimens in your garden because they represent a combined expression or a color theme, because of their similarity in form, or because they provide multiple identical focal elements throughout the garden, keep in mind that each plant nevertheless needs to retain its prominence or key role in its particular location.

One way of selecting your specimen shrubs is to opt for the unusual. You might choose an uncommon cultivar, such as *Enkianthus campanulatus* 'Red Bells', which unlike other plants in the species has red flowers, or shrubs from a genus that is rarely deployed in the garden, such as *Callistemon*, the bottlebrush, whose species have long, brightly colored and distinctive inflorescences. Then there are unusual forms of species to choose among—for example, the magenta-flowered selections of the otherwise white-flowered *Loropetalum chinense*. You might also consider the variegated *Aralia* cultivars, which, although difficult to propagate, make excellent specimens. A further option might be to plant slow-growing, extremely valuable individual plants, such as the red-foliaged Japanese maples.

At this point it is worth taking a closer look at some specimen shrubs and the ways in which they can be used. *Leptospermum scoparium*, the tea tree, is a tall evergreen shrub that reaches as much as 16ft (5m) in height and bears white flowers in summer. The small narrow leaves exude a spicy scent if you brush against them. Some unusual cultivars have deeply colored flowers and make very reliable specimens, or focal plants in a border. *L. scoparium* 'Ruby Glow' is one such cultivar: it has double, deep magenta-red blooms and bronze-red foliage. This is a truly striking plant that commands attention; it makes an excellent specimen wherever it is well adapted (it is hardy only in relatively mild climates).

Another sort of specimen shrub might be an individual that is of great age even though it has no other distinctive characteristics. You might, for example, find when you take over a garden a mature *Pieris japonica* in a moist, well-drained corner. *P. japonica* may grow to nearly 6ft (2m) or more, have many stout main stems and an extensive leaf area, and bloom quite prolifically each year. Its habit is interesting and unusual, with numerous bends and twists in the main stems (the flowers are the usual miniature white lanterns), and the plant provides a light sweet fragrance when in bloom. Such a plant, the gardening equivalent of an objet trouvé, can bring great character to your garden: it warrants specimen status merely because of its "presence."

Another sort of specimen planting is the "gardener's challenge"; that is, a shrub that by rights should not be thriving in your garden. Usually you will look for plants that require little care, but many gardeners are unable to resist a challenge. Succumbing to this temptation is not a sound overall approach when creating your garden, although it can be interesting to take on a few individual specimens.

Dramatic specimen shrubs include plants such as California lilac *(Ceanothus thyrsiflorus)*. This is a tall, rounded evergreen shrub that can reach a height of 20ft (6m) and bears great frothy clusters of blue flowers. It does best in very well drained soils and in full sun.

Another eye-catcher is *Desfontainia spinosa*, a tall evergreen shrub native to Chile. This reaches over 6ft (1.8m) in height and has fine-textured, hollylike spiny leaves and extraordinary flowers whose tubular blooms are bright red with a yellow interior. In favorable areas and with cool moist conditions, the flowering period lasts from late spring or early summer into early fall.

A final showstopping specimen is *Grevillea* 'Canberra Gem'. As with all members of this genus, the flowers appear as a cluster; each bloom is long, slender, and tubular, then later in the season they split and curl. The pink-red flowers are very showy against the gray-green foliage. This vigorous shrub reaches upward of 6½ft (2m) and makes a dramatic statement when in bloom. The unique texture of its foliage alone can earn it specimen status.

The prime rule when choosing specimens—as it should be in all other aspects of your gardening—is that you should use your imagination and rely on your own taste.

Left: Early summer fragrance
Although the pure white lantern-like flowers of *Zenobia pulverulenta* offer a more understated specimen shrub effect, it nevertheless contrasts well with many other plants.

Right: Maple in fall woodland
A specimen shrub will always stand out, whatever the reason for its planting. Here there is a bright fall contrast between *Acer palmatum* 'Chitoseyama' and the nearby golden tree foliage.

Shrubs in garden styles

The individual style of a garden dictates the types of plants that you can grow there. Formal walled gardens, for example, suggest a range of plant possibilities very different from that suggested by sweeping seashore landscapes. When choosing a plant palette for a garden, the challenge is to narrow down the choice from the endlessly inspiring range of shrubs whose colors, textures, shapes, and fragrances can be combined and contrasted in an infinite number of ways.

WALLED AND COURTYARD GARDENS

Walled and courtyard gardens can be very grand and formal areas or small intimate spaces where gardener and plants can escape from the wider world. Above all, irrespective of its size, the walled garden can also offer useful shelter from extreme weather conditions.

A fragrant shrub for an enclosed space
This containerized fragrant tea olive *(Osmanthus fragrans)* is a good example of a shrub whose extremely fragrant white flowers make it a special pleasure in a walled garden.

This protection can have surprising effects on the plants, however, depending on how the garden is managed. For example, the increased protection and warmth of a walled garden can push early-spring bloomers into flowering prematurely: in late winter, day temperatures may be quite warm in the walled space but night temperatures will still dip below a cold threshold the flowers cannot tolerate.

The protection afforded by an enclosed environment can also lead to increased humidity and decreased air flow, and thus to a higher incidence of fungal diseases. Again, an excessive buildup of heat in the summer can accelerate soil drying and cause plant stress. In short, managing walled gardens is not as simple as it might seem.

That said, a walled garden does offer opportunities for the creation of some very special effects: training as espaliers, training climbers, and coaxing into bloom plants that would not normally overwinter successfully, let alone flower reliably. The walls minimize air flow in and around the garden, which is clearly a boon in a windy area; walls can also work to your advantage if you plan a fragrant garden, especially if the plants' fragrance is subtle.

Fragrance in a walled garden

Imagine entering a walled garden perfumed with fragrant tea olive *(Osmanthus fragrans)* warming in the sun; you can add to this selections from the genera *Gardenia*, *Magnolia*, *Daphne*, *Rosa*, *Hamamelis*, and *Jasminum* and you find yourself in a heady paradise.

Lady of the night *(Cestrum nocturnum)* is an evergreen native to Central America; its flowers, which appear in late summer and fall, are an inconspicuous green-white but are very fragrant at night. This relatively tender shrub makes a perfect candidate for a walled garden.

Rosa, *Euphorbia*, *Taxus*, and *Yucca* in a walled garden
It is the shrubs in this densely planted wall garden that provide all the key visual points of interest, contributing fine form, strong colors, and vibrant textures.

There are myriad ways of creating special fragrances in walled gardens, but careful planning is needed to guard against the possibility of cultivating shrubs that bloom at the same time and whose fragrances in combination might fight with each other or become cloying. If a gardenia and a butterfly bush (*Buddleja davidii),* for example, were grown in the same walled garden, neither would appear at its best precisely because the two plants flower at about the same time. The gardenia's fragrance, being much the stronger, would easily overpower that of the butterfly bush. With a careful choice of partner, however, both of these shrubs would make appropriate plants: either of them could be included alongside the summer-flowering blue mist shrub (*Caryopteris*), as its fragrance is less strong.

Planting against walls

Walled gardens and courtyards always offer wonderful opportunities for the use of climbers and ramblers as well as any shrub that responds well to training or pruning—particularly espaliered specimens.

You may have often seen fruit and nut trees espaliered against a stone wall, but numerous ornamental shrubs also make beautiful espaliered material. A good example of this is *Pyracantha*, which throughout both spring and summer can create a pleasing green tracery sprinkled with white bloom that matures into bright orange or red fruit—a stunning display in the fall within the structure of the walled garden. Flowering quince (*Chaenomeles*), when grown as an espaliered specimen, will make a dramatic show of its early-spring blooms.

Striking effects can also be created by growing shrubs against a wall whose own color contrasts with that of the flowers, foliage, or variegations: the wall highlights unusual flower form, brightly colored foliage, or variegation.

Yucca flaccida 'Golden Sword' in a cottage garden
The striking foliage of this yucca underlines why this popular shrub is the durable, striking mainstay of so many different gardens.

For example, the golden spikes of *Yucca flaccida* 'Golden Sword' seem even brighter and bolder when grown against a dark background. The showy ornamental catkins of *Garrya elliptica* also look especially attractive when set against the comparatively neutral hues of a stone wall.

Because of the protecting walls, you may be able to grow plants that are only marginally hardy in your area or to grow sensitive evergreens successfully. A walled garden filled with evergreens of contrasting foliage shapes and textures—including some that bloom in late winter—can make a delightful retreat. You could combine the narrow foliage whorls of a *Pieris* shrub, interspersed by its tan seed capsules, with the zigzag, low-spreading branches of a *Leucothoe*, and the bold foliage ladders of a *Mahonia*, whose long sprays are topped with bright yellow flower clusters.

The effect of walls on adjacent soil

Drainage is often reduced because of the buried portions of walls and walks, so there are likely to be wet pockets in parts of the walled garden, and fertilizer salts may build up. You should therefore, before you undertake any major planting scheme, observe a walled garden for at least a year in order to identify areas of drainage problems or poor growth. To determine the specific soil makeup, it can also be useful to send off samples from several areas to be tested for pH and nutrient content. The results will identify any areas where fertilizer salts may have built up and reveal whether any unusual materials are present.

All sorts of shrubs perform well in walled gardens and courtyards. A chief consideration is the size of the shrub, both in relation to the scale of the garden and in terms of the available rooting area. It is easy to forget that a shrub's root system usually occupies at least as much volume underground as the shoot system does above ground. This factor becomes particularly important in enclosed gardens where the below-ground space is limited. If your walled garden cannot afford this much rooting space, you can either plant the shrub as a temporary addition to the garden, knowing it may have to be replaced if it runs out of rooting area, or choose instead a plant that will require less rooting area.

Walled garden with hydrangea
When planning a walled garden, consider plant sizes and be sure that the different elements will not "fight" with each other.

A fragrant foliage plant
The bold, dense evergreen shrub *Santolina chamaecyparissus* is not only visually attractive but releases scent as you walk by.

Steps and paths

Steps and paths, like walls, also influence the microclimate immediately adjacent to them, though to a lesser extent and depending on the materials used in their construction. Paths and steps can act as storage heaters, absorbing heat during the day and radiating it at night, thereby extending the growing season in fall and making it start earlier in spring. In addition, steps and paths can hasten water flow away from an area and prevent absorption of water directly beneath. Nearby areas may also become compacted if they are well trodden.

The influence exerted on the microclimate by steps or paths can cause an adjacent mass of early-spring-flowering shrubs to bloom at staggered intervals. Those plants that are nearest to the feature would tend to bloom first, followed by those situated farther away, which would have received less residual heat. One way around this problem near paths and steps is to use plants that bloom sporadically over an extended period. Alternatively, use plants that bloom fairly late in the season and offer other ornamental characteristics throughout the rest of the year—such as fragrant foliage that releases scent as you brush by. Suitable fragrant shrubs to plant alongside paths or steps include *Santolina* (lavender cotton), *Lavandula* (lavender), *Rosmarinus* (rosemary), *Salvia*, and *Comptonia* (sweet fern).

Sweet fern is an unusual deciduous shrub that grows to about 3 ft (1m). It does not produce showy flowers, but its lovely divided ferny foliage develops into a spreading mass (it is not a good choice for very small gardens) whose fragrance is delightful. For centuries this foliage has, in dried form, been made into pillows, mattresses, and pomanders. One of the few nonvegetable woody plants that can fix nitrogen in the same way that soybeans and peas do, the shrub performs well on poorer soils, although it does not tolerate high-pH soils.

Shrubs with graceful forms that drape themselves over, around, and partially across steps and paths are particularly apt choices. Plants can be used to soften any hard edges, hide a newly replaced section of an older structure, or fill in a difficult corner in a path where little else can be done.

Steps overhung by a mixed planting
The design of these garden steps are complemented by plantings that include shrubs, ferns, conifers, and perennials.

Container-grown shrubs in a summer garden
Many container shrubs— such as the *Hydrangea* and *Fuchsia* shown here—need to spend the winter months in a greenhouse to protect them from frost.

Plants such as winter jasmine (*Jasminum nudiflorum*), which has a naturally curving drape to its branches, offer interesting possibilities: the curve of the stems following the progress of the steps can appear to integrate the plant into the slope. When winter jasmine blooms, it covers itself with sprightly yellow flowers, adding character and interest to the stems as well as a light, sweet fragrance at a time of year when there is little else in bloom.

Other good choices for planting near steps and paths include *Abelia*, fragrant *Viburnum*, *Genista*, *Illicium*, *Leucothoe*, and *Hypericum* x *moserianum*. The abelias generally grow quite large, but the cultivar 'Edward Goucher' is more compact than most, reaching 4–5ft (1.2–1.5m) in height; with its arching branches, semievergreen foliage, and mauve-pink flowers that are borne throughout much of the spring and summer, it adds a graceful note to a garden path for most of the season.

There are numerous fragrant *Viburnum* selections (such as 'Eskimo') that, when placed near a path or steps, will provide great pleasure as you walk by and catch a whiff of their sweet scent. Most of the brooms (*Genista* species) have long arching branches that drape pleasingly over a path or steps and offer lovely yellow, pea-shaped flowers.

The anise trees (*Illicium* species) are evergreen shrubs. They have a rounded habit, and their very unusual spring flowers have star-shaped outlines and straplike petals; these are the type of really unusual garden plants that are best appreciated at close range, perhaps when you pass by them on a leisurely stroll.

Leucothoe racemosa is a pendent evergreen shrub. Far from overpowering, it makes a perfect waterfall of dark green foliage over a slope, set of steps, or cracked path. It does best with some shade. *Hypericum* x *moserianum*, on the other hand, is a deciduous, low-growing shrub that becomes covered with yellow flowers in summer and flows attractively around paths and steps in full sun.

GREENHOUSE AND CONTAINER GARDENS

There are two basic approaches to using a greenhouse. One is to grow the plants as a permanent collection under glass. Another is to use the milder environment to house long-term container-grown shrubs during the winter.

If a glasshouse is to be used to fulfill both these functions at the same time, it is important to find out the needs of both types of plant, and to be sure that these requirements can be met in your greenhouse. Temperate shrubs that are borderline hardy in your climate, for example, may need a chilling period if they are to grow, develop, and/or flower well. If you want to grow tropical palms alongside such plants, you will need to be able to divide your greenhouse and maintain appropriate conditions in both areas. If this is not possible, you may have to choose between your shrubs and your palms.

A conservatory or greenhouse garden is in effect an unusual walled garden. The space is enclosed and defined, and the environment protected. Gardeners tend to pay closer attention to the features of plants grown under glass because it is easier to examine them at close range in a leisurely manner and—as they are protected from wind, mud spattter, slugs, and so on—the specimens themselves are likely to be better presented. A plant such as beautyberry (*Callicarpa*), with its striking, bright purple fruit, is reasonably hardy and can be grown outdoors, but it becomes a showstopper when viewed at close quarters in a large container that has also been planted with the late-blooming lavender-flowered *Abelia* 'Edward Goucher'.

Greenhouse and container gardens allow gardeners to bring plants into showy bloom well out of season. Almost any of the camellias make excellent long-term container plants when grown in large containers under glass. *Camellia japonica* 'Tricolor' is an impressive sight in full bloom; its dramatic double streaked-pink-and-white 4in (10cm) flowers appear in the depths of winter while the outdoor garden may be covered in snow and ice.

Cut blooms out of season

Container and greenhouse gardens also allow you to have cut material—foliage, flowers, fruits, and stems—for decoration all year round. Even common shrubs such as flowering quince and the deciduous hollies can seem exotic when grown under glass and cut for flower arrangements before or after there is any hint of color on their outdoor counterparts. Plants with colored or contorted stems are good choices for cut arrangements, as are shrubs that are easily forced. Rosegold pussy willow (*Salix gracilistyla*) can easily be forced to produce branches of silky catkins.

Other plants that can be grown under glass offer lush, exotic character in a greenhouse setting. Glory bush (*Tibouchina urvilleana*), for example, with its large violet velvet-textured flowers, is a tender shrub that makes an excellent container plant under glass; to thrive it needs lots of light as well as cool roots.

Tetrapanax papyrifer, which originates from China and Taiwan has bold, almost palmlike, evergreen foliage. Although it can be grown in a border in full sun in regions

with hot summers, it also adds a decidedly tropical flavor to the indoor garden, where it is sure to thrive even in unpredictably severe winters.

Indoor gardens give you the opportunity to grow plants whose natural habitats have vastly different climates and completely different rainfall patterns, precisely because you control the elements. Almost all the water, for example, will have to be provided through irrigation. You can control periods of dry and wet, and so be able to grow desert shrubs such as those of the genus *Leucophyllum*, which require extended dry periods.

Container gardens

Displays and plantings made up entirely of container plants are becoming increasingly popular. They offer a great deal of flexibility: you can change your plantings at any time in response to changed needs for space. Container gardens are more mobile than any other kind: favorite plants are

Forms of *Camellia sasanqua* in terra-cotta pots
There are many kinds of plants that lend themselves to the convenience of container gardening, but none so spectacularly as a large-flowered shrub, such as the outstandingly beautiful camellia, *Camellia sasanqua*.

Spiraea japonica 'Golden Princess'
With its wide range of forms, all noted for their striking blooms and foliage, *Spiraea* can make a key contribution to any garden. Here, 'Golden Princess' is a bright star in this combination of container plants.

also to freeze and thaw more readily as temperatures swing back and forth. The root systems of container plants are vulnerable to frost damage, as containers do not provide the good insulating qualities of inground planting. Use the largest containers you can, and choose your plants carefully for tough and reliable root growth.

In cold climates, containers need winter shelter. Packing them tightly together under deciduous shade, insulating them with leaves or straw, and covering them with plastic will work in areas with moderately cold winters—but remember to check the containers for moisture content throughout the winter. If your winters are harsh, you will need to bring your containers into an unheated cellar or cold frame to avoid irreparable damage to the plants' roots.

Plant scale and soils

Another important consideration for growing shrubs in containers, both outdoors and in a greenhouse, is whether or not your selected plants will tolerate root restriction. Since long-term container-grown shrubs should be transplanted or moved to larger pots only infrequently, they must be able to tolerate restricted root growth for extended periods.

It is also necessary to bear in mind the mature height and habit of the plants you are considering. If you want to include plants that will become especially tall or bushy, you need to know whether they will tolerate or even be invigorated by a hard pruning, so that you can periodically

easily moved and resited if you move. It is also simpler to replace a container plant if it fails to thrive or does not work well in a particular combination than would be the case in the open garden: replanting a single container is much easier than reworking an entire bed.

Before deciding whether to plant a container garden, consider your site carefully. If it is very exposed and/or windy, the containers are likely to dry out more quickly and

Mixed container arrangement
Combining shrubs with distinctively different foliage and flowers such as *Skimmia*, *Hebe*, *Gaultheria*, and *Leucothoe* with pots containing perennials and a dwarf conifer creates an attractive display.

reduce their size by half or more and therefore keep them growing in the same container for a prolonged period. Shrubs such as *Weigela*, *Forsythia*, *Abelia*, *Deutzia*, and *Pyracantha* will tolerate regular heavy pruning. Other shrubs, such as *Ternstroemia* and *Loropetalum,* do not benefit from being heavily pruned.

The growing medium you use in the containers is also important. It is always best to use a highly aerated and well drained soilless mix rather than soil from the ground. The commercial soilless mix will be sterilized and so free of disease; it will also drain readily in a container and provide the shrub with a good rooting environment. Some mixes include low concentrations of fertilizers, but even so you will need to fertilize the plants regularly. Frequent watering leaches stored nutrients out of the soil in containers and plants can quickly become starved. To avoid this, it is best to use a granular slow-release fertilizer rather than a liquid feed.

In some ways containers require more work from you than standard plantings in the ground, but selecting a diverse range of shrubs that will tolerate long-term container culture can be a fascinating challenge.

HEATHER GARDENS

Heathers and heaths are in a class by themselves as garden shrubs. The genera *Calluna*, *Erica,* and the latter's close relative *Daboecia* are the most familiar heathers and heaths grown in the garden. Aside from a few tree heaths, all are low-growing, fine-textured shrubs with tiny leaves and small bell- and urn-shaped flowers.

Trained *Pyracantha* 'Orange Glow'
Selections of *Pyracantha* such as this container-grown 'Orange Glow' are easy to train against a trellis, as they respond well to regular pruning.

Erica, the heaths, is a large genus found in diverse natural habitats, but the hardy garden forms of both heathers and heaths thrive on moist, well-drained, acidic sandy or peaty soils in full sun. These plants do best when transplanted from containers. Their root systems tend to be fibrous, their fine roots tangled and knotted together. When transplanting, it is important to separate the tangled root mass out around the edges to ensure direct contact between the individual roots and the new soil.

Many gardeners recommend cutting a cross in the bottom of the root mass as it comes from the container, then spreading the quarters across (or "butterflying" them) in the planting hole. However, the effect is primarily to cut roots away from the main root mass rather than to separate them to allow new root growth. A much better alternative is to tease out as many individual roots as possible from the primary tangle without cutting any roots (as described on p.23).

Once established, most heaths and heathers do best with an annual light to moderate shearing to keep them tidy and vigorous. Trim heaths and heathers right after flowering has finished; or, if you are growing the plant for its colored foliage rather than its flowers, trim in the spring.

Erica species can bloom from late winter to very early in spring and can be among the earliest shrubs to flower in temperate gardens. These shrubs have tiny fine-textured foliage and a demure flowing habit.

A close cousin of *Erica*, *Calluna vulgaris* (the sole species of heather), tends to blooms much later—in late summer, fall, and even early winter in some areas. As a consequence, when you plant heaths and heathers together you can achieve a remarkably long period of bloom.

There are many species of heath, and they have diverse native habitats and a range of sizes and ornamental traits. There are hundreds of named selections of both heaths and heather; they may have variegated or contrastingly colored winter foliage, various bloom colors and times, and some variation in mature heights and spread.

Heaths that add character to a heather garden include *Erica arborea* (tree heath), the summer-blooming *E. cinerea* (bell heather), and *E. vagans* (Cornish heath). *E. arborea* is a

Above: *Calluna vulgaris* in late fall
This variety of *Calluna vulgaris* is 'Wickwar Flame', and the ground indeed seems on fire when it is widespread and growing rampantly, as in this picture.

Above: Blooms of *Erica carnea* 'Vivellii'
This shrub can bring real elegance to the late-winter or early-spring garden, with its fine foliage and discreet flowering habit.

Right: *Erica carnea* 'Springwood White' in a woodland setting
In a naturalistic setting, white-flowering heaths can form contrasts that are as striking and beautiful as any to be found in the most painstakingly planned garden.

tall shrub—it reaches 20ft (6m)—and has dark green foliage and white flowers. When offset against the low-growing species, it can be especially attractive. *E. cinerea* flowers in summer, when many of the other heaths and heathers are out of bloom. The flowers of the species itself are a warm purple, but cultivars offer a range from white to red to pale pink and lavender. *E. vagans*, with white or rose-pink flowers, has an especially low and thick habit: it reaches only about 2ft (60cm) in height and makes a very dense ground cover.

Heaths and heathers are frequently planted in drifts of various selections with a range of bloom times and foliage colors, thus creating a fascinating carpet of colors and textures. They are especially effective on somewhat rolling terrain, but by choosing selections that have different mature heights, you can create the effect of rolling terrain even on a flat piece of land.

These plants are often grown in combination with conifers and with shrubs that have colored bark or twigs. Perhaps because their foliage seems needlelike, they blend especially well with needled evergreen conifers. Dwarf or weeping conifers are particularly effective alongside heaths and heathers. Conifers such as the Norway spruce (*Picea abies* 'Pendula') and *Abies koreana* 'Horstmann's Silberlocke', a dwarf Korean fir—which has silver-white needles—make dramatic specimens when planted with white-flowered forms of *Erica carnea* such as 'Springwood White'.

A combination with more contrast might include *Cornus stolonifera* 'Flaviramea' (yellow-twig dogwood), used for a bold vertical line, planted in a small mass with three plants of the winter plum-colored, soft-needled cultivar of Japanese cedar, *Cryptomeria japonica* 'Elegans', amid a rolling carpet of yellow-foliaged *Calluna vulgaris* 'Beoley Gold', and *Erica carnea* 'Ann Sparkes', punctuated by a few well-placed plants of *E. carnea* 'December Red'.

The white-barked ghost bramble (*Rubus cockburnianus*), a deciduous arching shrub whose prickly shoots are brilliant blue-white in winter, can be underplanted with a mix of white-flowered *Calluna vulgaris*—the silver-foliaged 'Anthony Davis', for example—and a white-flowered spring heath such as the vigorous *Erica carnea* 'Cecilia M. Beale'. The blooms of the heaths and heathers provide an interesting echo of the bark of the ghost bramble.

KNOT GARDENS

Knot and herb arrangements are most often associated with formal and historical gardens and landscapes, yet they can also make an attractive contribution to modern horticultural styles. Many of the plants most widely used in knot gardens are true shrubs.

A knot garden comprises an intricate arrangement of lines and beds of herbs and flowers of contrasting colors and/or textures so as to give the appearance of a garden-wide knot or weave. The plants should really be kept low enough for the intricate design—and the knot effect—to be clearly visible to those standing or walking nearby.

As it is easy to maintain, many kinds of shrubs lend themselves to this sort of garden. Because a knot garden is best appreciated from above, any plant that can be cultivated into a handsome and reliable low hedge is a good choice. These include the various species of boxwood

A knot garden
A knot garden can be comprised of any number of different low-growing shrubs; its elaborate loops and knots will bring an old-fashioned feel to any garden.

Parterre of *Buxus* hedge with *Santolina* inside

A formal garden design of level geometrical beds, parterres are often laid out in squares edged with hedging of dwarf box. This type of garden design is usually best viewed from above so that the low growing plants inside the squares can be easily seen.

(*Buxus*), for example, which can be grown as low hedges and borders in such a way that their lines contrast with silver-foliaged shrubs, such as a clipped *Santolina chamaecyparissus*. A curve of boxwood, broken by a curve of the *Santolina*, with both being intercepted by yet a third line—say, of a purple-foliaged plant (such as *Berberis thunbergii* 'Atropurpurea')—can be used to create the appearance of systematic knots.

The shrubs you choose for a knot garden do not have to be evergreen. Plants such as *Ribes alpinum* 'Green Mound'—a dwarf mounding form of the alpine currant—make beautiful neat hedges in the right proportion for a knot garden. 'Green Mound' reaches only about 3ft (1m) and grows into a dense mound. In winter, a deciduous line of dense uniform mounds of light tan twigs makes an effective contrast with an evergreen shrub line, and in spring, the new growth on the deciduous shrub emerges to clothe the plant in bright lime green.

No matter what plants you choose for your knot garden, or how carefully you water and fertilize them, occasional light shearing may be needed—to balance growth, to even out irregular growth patterns between plants, and to enhance full branching and foliage cover.

Most knot gardens consist of plants that thrive best in full sun and reasonably well drained soils, so any inconsistencies in light, water, and nutrients within the area will result in slight unevenness of growth along the line of the knot. One solution may be to supplement the water and fertilizer allowance of the slower plants. Even so, if they receive just a little less light than their neighbors, it is unlikely that they will be able to match their growth rate. The shade of a garden post, birdhouse, or tree, for example, may seem inconsequential, but over a few seasons it can significantly affect growth rates.

If growth rates are uneven among the plants in your knot garden, an occasional light shearing of the more forward plants is one relatively simple solution. If the growth rates are affected on only a few of the plants, you may consider growing "replacement" plants elsewhere in the garden that can be "patched in" when necessary.

PARTERRES

A related type of planting to a knot garden is a parterre, a pattern of straight or curved lines created by a uniform, clipped planting. Parterres are particularly vulnerable to uneven growth. Such gardens can be on any scale, from vast (such as Versailles in France) to much more modest (and manageable) arrangements.

The essence of a parterre is control and perfect depiction of the desired pattern. A parterre shrub planting needs to remain as uniform as possible: you have to clip the plants to maintain the formal character. If the growth rate differs too much from one part of the planting to the other, it can be difficult or impossible to clip back the precocious shrubs enough without harming or even killing them. Choose shrubs that will tolerate repeated shearing and will respond readily to changes in water and fertilizer.

Useful shrub choices for parterres include *Ilex crenata* (Japanese holly), *Buxus* (boxwood), *Santolina*, *Myrtus communis* (common myrtle), and many *Ligustrum* species (privets).

HERB GARDENS

Herbs are plants that can be used for culinary and/or medicinal purposes, and many of them are shrubs. Herb gardens are the modern form of the ancient physic (or medicinal) garden, which would be in a protected area near a house or the cloister area within a monastery or convent so that the plants would be readily accessible for use.

Old herb gardens were usually arranged in well-ordered patterns for various symbolic, practical, and visually attractive reasons. But they need not be designed in such a rigid fashion: they can be developed in any garden style that suits the site and landscape. With a very few exceptions, herbs perform best in full sun and well-drained soils.

Shrubs such as the beautiful and very fragrant lemon verbena *(Aloysia triphylla)*, lavender *(Lavandula)*, rosemary *(Rosmarinus officinalis)*, and sage *(Salvia officinalis)* not only offer handsome aromatic foliage but also produce lovely flowers. The flowers of lavender and rosemary are found in distinctive shades of cool colors, while the various species and cultivars of sage bear flowers in a much broader range of colors, from white to cool blues, violets, reds, and pinks.

A popular aromatic herb
The silvery green, upright strands of *Rosmarinus officinalis* (common rosemary) will offer a distinctive fragrance and a fine contrast when it is grown against a warm wall.

Knot garden with *Berberis*, *Buxus*, and *Santolina*
This informal, sprawling knot garden has a good contrast of colors and textures provided by the chief constituents, *Berberis*, *Santolina*, and *Buxus*.

Less well known as herb-garden plants are shrubs such as *Prunus spinosa*, whose blue-black fruits are used to make sloe gin, and any number of roses grown for their petals (used for perfumes and confections) or fruit, the hips being used medicinally in tisanes as a source of vitamin C. Shrubs such as St.-John's-wort (*Hypericum* spp.) and germander (*Teucrium* spp.) make surprising and interesting additions to a modern herb garden. *Teucrium chamaedrys* is a low-growing, mounding shrub that reaches only about 1ft (30cm); it has fragrant foliage and delicate pink flowers.

Ornamental combinations

In a modern herb garden there is no need to restrict your choice of plants too rigidly. Try mixing shrubby herbs with other ornamental shrubs and perennials; you can include annual flowers for seasonal accent and color. A combination of, for example, variegated 'Tricolor' sage, rosemary, and a low-growing selection of heath or heather with an interesting flowering annual can create an unusually dramatic blend of foliage color, fragrance, texture, and bright bloom, which also has a long season of interest.

An unusual ornamental combination
This combination of *Buxus sempervirens* (boxwood) with burgeoning rue (*Ruta graveolens*) creates powerful contrasts of foliage color and texture.

leaves turn pale yellow in fall. Carolina allspice's colors, fragrance, and textures blend well with those of shrubby herbs. Again, it offers a taller focus for an herb garden without overshadowing the other plants.

Their fragrance makes herb gardens a natural home for garden furniture such as benches, tables and stools. A wooden or stone bench set at the end of a path defines the space in front of it and draws attention to the plants in its immediate vicinity. The evergreen shrub *Solanum pseudocapsicum* (winter cherry), when covered with its cheery round red-and-orange fruit in various stages of ripeness, seems even more like a firecracker when planted near a sand-hued stone bench.

Shrubby perennial herbs can be used to create the foundations and primary elements in an herb garden that is annually supplemented with other culinary plants. An assortment of tender basils with burgundy, curly, and marbled foliage would be handsomely offset by a lavender edge or by a common myrtle (*Myrtus communis*) hedge.

You could choose an unusual specimen shrub as the centerpiece. For example, the dwarf elm *Ulmus* 'Jacqueline Hillier' offers bright yellow fall color and, during the summer, an intriguing fine-textured crown that gives special interest without overshadowing the ornamental features of the herbs. Another good choice would be Carolina allspice (*Calycanthus floridus*), which has large leathery leaves and intriguing dark maroon flowers with a spicy fragrance. The

Many shrubby herbs can be grown in containers. Grown this way, herbs such as rosemary and lemon verbena can be placed on a table or near a bench to be brushed for fragrance or snipped to be dried for sachets.

A useful evergreen herb
The lavender cultivar *Lavandula angustifolia* 'Hidcote' is an extraordinarily versatile plant with a wonderful scent, brightly-colored flowers, and an unparalleled ability to withstand drought.

SEASHORE GARDENS

A seashore garden can be a challenge, but it can also be a triumph. A site blessed with spectacular vistas, glorious backdrops, perfect drainage, and lots of light can change suddenly to one assaulted by winds, storms, and salt spray, and at season's end the garden can face severe drought.

There are many ways to approach gardening with shrubs at the seashore. Many shrubs can be grown as natural windbreaks; salt-tolerant shrubs can be used to create a sheltered area that can still enjoy plenty of light as well as a view out of the garden. Salt tolerance is a paramount consideration. Salt acts as a dehydrating agent, even to the underground portions of the plant, and many plants cannot tolerate even minimal exposure to it.

Seashore plants face two sorts of chronic salt exposure: first the spray, which acts constantly to leave a thin layer of drying salt on foliage and branches, and second the salt solution, which splashes onto the ground and thus finds its way to the roots of the plants. Fortunately, a number of shrubs offer protection to less salt-tough selections. Gorse (*Ulex* spp.), for example, makes an excellent barrier plant by the shore. Plant it in a mass some distance upwind from the area where you want to garden more intensively. *Cytisus scoparius* offers prolific, brightly colored flowers in diverse

Above: Fruits of sea buckthorn
The dense, salt-tolerant thickets and long-lasting, bright orange fruits of *Hippophae rhamnoides* make it an excellent choice for growing as a screen or hedge near the shore.

forms, while *Rosa rugosa* is a quintessential shore shrub: its pink and white flowers, tossed among the crinkled lawn green leaves, are an attractive sight along many coastlines.

Shrubs whose native habitats are the seashore are obviously good choices for seaside gardens. *Baccharis halimifolia* is found growing along the shores of eastern North America; its salt tolerance, gray-green fine-textured foliage, and silver gossamer hairs combine to give the plant an arresting presence. *Prunus maritima* (beach plum) offers sweet white flowers followed by small red or purple plumlike fruits that make tasty jelly; the shrubs develop an appealing character as they age. Make sure that you avoid planting potentially invasive species such as gorse near sensitive natural areas or less vigorous plants.

Sandy soils

When growing shrubs on the sandy soils generally found in seashore gardens, be aware of some particular cultural concerns. Young shrubs transplanted into this sort of soil need regular, generous watering for at least the first three growing seasons: sandy soil retains very little moisture between waterings. Most sandy soils are poor in nutrients and tend to be acidic, so it is usually helpful to provide a newly transplanted plant with supplemental fertilizer for the first three springs—more for heavy feeders.

The special light and expansiveness found in most seashore gardens means that gardeners can experiment with bold combinations that would be overwhelming elsewhere. Just because you have to use salt-tolerant shrubs in a salt-spray screen does not mean that the hedge has to be dull. Sea buckthorn (*Hippophäe rhamnoides*) is a natural choice for screens and hedges by the shore. It is a tall, dense deciduous shrub that eventually reaches over 15ft (4.5m) and has a fairly narrow spread. A relative of the fall olives (*Elaeagnus* species), it has similar silvery waxy foliage, although the sea buckthorn's leaves are narrower. It is thorny and makes a good barrier as well as a salt-tolerant screen. The lovely silver hues of the foliage make an excellent foil for the bright orange berries produced on female plants. Sea buckthorn is dioecious (that is, the male

Right: A seaside garden
The main consideration when designing a seaside garden is choosing plants that are not only salt tolerant but that can withstand high winds.

Baccharis halimifolia beside a path
The large clusters of white flowers and robust, spreading habit of *Baccharis halimifolia* can make a dramatic effect along seaside paths.

and female flowers are borne on different individuals), so that a male plant is needed to ensure prolific fruit production. The cultivar 'Sprite' is a compact narrow male selection that fits in well with an otherwise female or mixed hedge as a pollinator.

Of similar character but smaller in scale are the salt-tolerant *Shepherdia* species, native to North America. Buffaloberry (*S. argentea*) has silvery foliage, inconspicuous flowers, bright red fruits and thorny stems; it grows to about 10ft (3m) and has a somewhat more rounded habit than sea buckthorn. *S. canadensis* is a smaller relative of *S. argentea* reaching only 6½ft (2m); it has gray-green foliage that is less conspicuously covered with the waxy scales that give *S. argentea* and sea buckthorn their silvery appearance. As *Shepherdia* species are also dioecious, a male plant is needed to ensure fertilization of the tiny yellowish flowers and development of the cherry red fruit.

Combinations for seashore gardens

For a truly bold combination, *Nerium oleander* can be used with either of these two silver-foliaged plants. Oleander is a very popular seashore shrub because it is both salt and drought tolerant. There are numerous selections available in a range of mature sizes and flower colors. Oleander is by nature a large, vigorous, medium-coarse shrub, reaching over 16ft (5m). It has dark green, leathery, strap-shaped leaves and candy pink flowers. The many cultivars have been selected for their more compact habit, smaller size, and different flower colors, which range from deep red to white, apricot, and lavender, including double forms.

When you combine silver-foliaged plants with oleander, the silver brings out the intensity of the flower colors of single-flowered red selections such as 'Calypso'—which, in return, work well with the red-berried *Shepherdia* species. If you would rather have a less bold combination, a vigorous, single, white-flowered oleander such as 'Sister Agnes' or a pale pink, single-flowered one like 'Tangier' presents a softer picture. White-flowered oleander cultivars can be used if there is a danger of a color clash between the red-flowered oleander and the orange-fruited sea buckthorn. *As all parts of the oleander are highly poisonous, it should never be planted anywhere where young children might pick the leaves or flowers.*

Other good shrubs to combine with silver-foliaged seashore plants such as sea buckthorn are the Australasian daisy bushes (*Olearia* species). These dark-green-foliaged evergreens produce clusters of fragrant white daisylike flowers. The species vary in mature height and bloom time, with flowers from late spring to early fall. One especially

Ulex europaeus blooms in close-up
In many respects, gorse is the archetypal seaside plant. It is tough, is salt- and wind-resistant, and likes sandy soils. It also has attractive yellow flowers, although it is often invasive.

Plant combination for a seaside garden
Here, seashells of various shapes and colors have been carefully
placed to contrast pleasingly with the surrounding flowers and shrubs.

hardy species is the hybrid *Olearia* x *haastii*, which grows
into a dense mound about 6½ft (2m) tall and blooms in
summer with heads of sweetly fragrant flowers.

Olearia species also combine well with another widely
grown shrub, *Escallonia rubra* and its hybrid selections. Red
escallonia, which comes from Chile, is a medium-height,
upright arching evergreen that generally reaches 10ft (3m)
in height. The small, neat, finely toothed dark green foliage
enhances the colorful flowers, which are borne in summer.
A number of hybrid cultivars have been selected, most
with flowers in the pink to rose-red range, although
there are one or two white-flowered selections. There are

also several with variegated foliage forms. Escallonia
cultivars such as the gold-variegated, red-flowered
'Gold Ellen' make stunning combinations when grown
with red-flowered oleander cultivars.

If you have only limited space in your seaside garden, or
if you are gardening in containers on a seaside patio, it is
well worth considering the many species and cultivars of
Hebe, the shrubby veronicas. The wide array of differing
mature heights, flower colors, and foliage colors makes
gardening with hebes particularly rewarding. All the species
of this genus, most of which are native to New Zealand, are
full, mounding shrubs that range from dwarf buns and
ground-covering mats to species 5ft (1.5m) tall that are
especially good for hedges. The leaves are small, evergreen,
and densely arranged. Hebes produce spikes of pastel-
colored flowers from white to baby blue, lavender, pink,

Hebe cupressoides near a path
Although shown here growing alongside the path of a seaside garden, this slow-growing evergreen is an equally good selection for a seaside container plant.

but is fairly slow-growing. Another very distinctive whipcord hebe that always combines beautifully with *H. cupressoides* is *H. ochracea*. Similar in appearance to *H. cupressoides*, *H. ochracea* has bronze-gold foliage, bears white flowers, and develops a more irregular habit with age; it reaches about 4ft (1.2m) in height, although a dwarf form, 'James Stirling', grows only to about 1ft (30cm), which makes it an excellent choice for a container or miniature garden.

Another dwarf hebe is 'Red Edge', which reaches about 1ft (30cm) in height. Its blue-gray foliage is edged in a thin red margin (most prominent during the winter). Lavender-colored flowers, which fade to white, appear from early to midsummer.

Evergreen combinations

The hebes combine beautifully not only with each other but with any number of other seashore plants. An underplanting of low, mounding *Hebe pinguifolia* 'Pagei'—with its distinctive slender blue-gray leaves and spikes of white flowers—makes a colorful carpet for the beach plum (*Prunus maritima*), which also produces white flowers in late spring. In winter, the hebe's evergreen foliage is an attractive foundation for the irregular tracery of the bare beach plum stems. If you prefer a little more color, interplant the *Hebe pimeleoides* cultivar 'Quicksilver', which has demure silvery leaves and delicate lilac flowers.

Two evergreen genera that provide handsome foliage as well as fragrant flowers are *Pittosporum* and *Rhaphiolepis*. *P. tobira* is a large shrub, eventually reaching 16ft (5m); its glossy dark green foliage, arranged in whorls, gives it a

rose, and purple, and some have foliage in a contrasting burgundy-red color or with purple-tinged undersides. All of these hebes are good choices for seaside gardens.

Container plants

In seaside containers and small gardens, selections such as *Hebe cupressoides* mimic the effect of a dwarf cypress but require less maintenance. *H. cupressoides* is a whipcord hebe, having compressed foliage reminiscent of many conifers. The tiny, almost needlelike blue-gray leaves are visually very similar to those of cypress and offer a lovely setting for the spikes of lilac-colored flowers the shrub bears in summer. This species eventually reaches 5ft (1.5m)

Mixed planting in a shoreside garden
The beautiful foliage from this mixed planting includes *Pittosporum tenuifolium* 'Irene Paterson' and *Fothergilla major*, together with trees and perennials.

distinctive dense cover and somewhat undulating silhouette, and its white, intensely fragrant flowers—borne in rounded clusters in spring—mature to unusual fruits. A much lower-growing dwarf cultivar, 'Wheeler's Dwarf', reaches only about 3ft (1m) in height and makes an excellent long-term container plant for shoreside gardens. The handsomely variegated *P. tobira* cultivar 'Variegatum' has silver-gray leaves with white blotches on the leaf margins. Because 'Variegatum' is a slower-growing plant than the species, it combines to great effect with 'Wheeler's Dwarf' in containers or in the border, where the latter's dark green foliage sets off the tricolor leaves of 'Variegatum'. Another useful trait of *P. tobira* is that it thrives in either sun or shade by the shore, which makes it a good choice for a massed bed or low hedge that has changing light conditions.

A natural companion to *P. tobira* is *Rhaphiolepis indica* (Indian hawthorn). Another mounding, evergreen shrub, this reaches about 3ft (1m) in height. Its foliage is more pointed and leathery than that of *P. tobira,* and it produces very showy clusters of white, sweetly fragrant flowers that are heavily tinged with pink. Some selections of *R. indica* have deep pink flowers and especially dark, almost black, foliage. Hybrids with the more cold-hardy *R. umbellata* have been produced to improve flowering in areas that have colder winters. These include the vigorous 'Majestic Beauty', which reaches 6½ft (2m) in height, with large clusters of pale pink flowers. All the hybrids and forms of *R. umbellata* produce clusters of delicate-looking, fragrant white or pink flowers in summer and rounded, leathery dark green leaves. Like the pittosporum, both *R. indica* and *R. umbellata* make good candidates for a container planting by the shore as well as in the seaside garden bed.

A useful seaside planting
The shrub *Rhaphiolepis* x *delacourii* is a good choice for a seaside or a dry garden, as its beautiful summer blooms can be seen to equally good effect in a container or a garden bed.

WINTER GARDENS

There is something magical about strolling through a winter garden filled with plants bearing colorful bark, evergreen foliage, fascinating branching, bright fruit, or, where the climate permits it, fragrant flowers.

Almost any shrub can contribute to a winter garden, but many shrubs go further: their particular winter characteristics offer extraordinary features, which can be persistent fruit, evergreen foliage in varied hues, prolific bloom, unusual bark color or texture, a dramatic habit, or interesting branching patterns. Often shrubs have more than one of these characteristics, making them especially suitable for winter gardens.

Shrubs such as species of *Aronia*, many *Viburnum* species, *Ilex*, *Hedera*, *Nandina domestica*, *Pyracantha*, and *Rosa*—not to mention various hybrids and cultivars—hold their fruit well into winter. Evergreens such as *Ilex* species and *Nandina domestica* also provide color and texture with their foliage. *Chimonanthus praecox* (wintersweet) produces waxy cream-colored flowers of subtle visual appeal that perfume the garden with an amazing scent. The pussy willow catkins that come into bloom at the end of winter on *Salix* species are familiar harbingers of spring.

Many shrubs have bright stems or bark that can be used to great effect in a winter garden. Yellow-twig dogwood (*Cornus stolonifera* 'Flaviramea'), for example, has upright masses of bright yellow stems that provide a bold spot of cheerful color on many difficult sites. There are also many selections of red-twig dogwood. The white-barked ghost brambles, such as *Rubus cockburnianus*, are excellent winter-garden plants.

Weeping and contorted selections of otherwise upright shrubs (such as *Poncirus trifoliata* 'Flying Dragon') add visual interest to winter gardens, as do coarse deciduous shrubs with prominent thorns or spurs (such as *Aralia*).

One way to enhance a winter garden is to use plants whose winter features are not visible or appreciated during the rest of the year. A deciduous shrub with a seemingly unremarkable habit may become a focal point in your garden when covered by a sharp frost or a blanket of snow; the irregular branching of *Magnolia stellata* (star magnolia) is a good example of this.

Another shrub that comes into its own in winter is *Kerria japonica*. During most of the growing season, this is an unassuming multistemmed mounding shrub of medium texture—not dissimilar to *Forsythia* in habit but somewhat more demure; it produces a lovely crop of bright orange-yellow spring flowers but then becomes a quiet background plant. The cultivar 'Kinkan' becomes quite showy during the winter months. Its slender stems have narrow, yellow-gold stripes that contrast with the grass green base color of the stems to create a beautiful winter effect. One additional trait of 'Kinkan'—and of Japanese kerria in general—is that it thrives in

Left: Attractive shrub stems in winter
The ghostly white stems of *Rubus cockburnianus* perfectly reflect the still, calm atmosphere of a winter garden.

Right: Frost-bound evergreen foliage
This striking winter scene includes *Viburnum*, *Rhododendron*, *Euonymus*, and *Lavandula* growing beside a yew hedge. *Buxus* can be seen through the arch.

The winter-flowering *Hamamelis*
The extraordinary, spiderlike flowers of *Hamamelis*
x *intermedia* 'Ruby Glow' (witch hazel) come into their
full glory in late winter.

mahonias reach 4–5ft (1.2–1.5m) or more, with long ever-green leaves composed of many hollylike leaflets in rows. A number of hybrid cultivars of *M. japonica* and *M. lomariifolia* (known as *M.* x *media*) have improved cold-hardiness. 'Lionel Fortescue', 'Charity', and 'Buckland' offer reliable and prolific winter bloom in partly shaded settings.

These mahonias make very effective companions to the deciduous hybrid witch hazel *Hamamelis* x *intermedia*. In late winter this produces fragrant unusual flowers in various warm shades, depending on the cultivar. The fragrance is distinctively spicy; the petals are crinkled and straplike. The hybrid witch hazels are open upright shrubs that can eventually reach 15ft (4.5m) or more. Their irregular branching has great appeal, and for this reason they should be left unpruned. Bright yellow cultivars such as 'Arnold Promise' are among the most readily available, but there are beautiful red forms, such as 'Ruby Glow', and

shade or sun, so the plant can be an excellent way of brightening up a shaded corner of a winter garden without becoming overblown or gaudy.

Winter-blooming shrubs

Few shrubs bloom in deep midwinter, but many do in late winter when we need their color and fragrance most. A favorite is *Stachyurus praecox*, a 10ft- (3m-) tall, irregular branching-to-arching deciduous shrub, that has ordinary foliage but whose long chains of tiny yellow, lightly scented, urn-shaped flowers are borne in late winter and are quite long-lasting. Although *S. praecox* prefers full sun, it also blooms in light high shade (in winter it makes a good planting under trees). It is marvelous when underplanted with very early bulbs that bloom while the flowers are still on the shrub. The cultivar 'Magpie' is dressed in the growing season with white-and-pink variegated foliage. All *S. praecox* develop some pleasing yellow-red fall color.

A relative of the daphnes, *Edgeworthia chrysantha*, is an unusual winter bloomer. This deciduous shrub reaches about 6ft (1.8m) tall and has a relatively open branching habit. It needs moist, fertile, well-drained soil and a sunny or lightly shaded site. In late winter, *E. chrysantha* is covered in white, glossy, slightly fragrant tubular flowers with distinctive yellow throats. The plant makes a wonderful specimen in winter, especially if underplanted with early-blooming, white-flowered spring heath or snowdrops.

Another fragrant combination for winter bloom is *Mahonia* and *Hamamelis* shrubs. Mahonia's upright sprays of sweet-scented canary yellow flowers appear in late winter atop the plants' bold evergreen foliage. The showiest

Unusual winter blooms
Easy to grow either in a border or trained against a wall, *Stachyurus praecox* is an especially useful shrub offering drooping spikes of tiny yellow flowers that open in late winter.

Winter border with *Mahonia* x *media* 'Winter Sun'
The tall, striking flowers and ladderlike evergreen foliage of
Mahonia combine well with witch hazels and many other shrubs,
particularly when deployed as a backdrop.

even orange-flowered selections, such as 'Jelena'. These
cultivars are marvelous when planted together, the red,
orange, and yellow flowers playing off one another,
especially when emerging from a mass of mahonia.

Mahonias and witch hazel hybrids perform well in the
light shade of a wooded area. Neither requires pruning and
both will provide unique winter features in such a setting.

Winter gardens are good places to display sculpture.
Dark evergreen ground covers may seem natural choices
for backgrounds, and indeed serve well in many cases. But
the whole range of shrubby ground covers can be used to
set off artwork in a winter garden—depending on the
color, texture, and intended effect of the piece. Plants with
colored foliage, such as *Euonymus japonicus* 'Silver King',
may be good choices for dark places, while a mixed planting of contrasting colors and textures—perhaps a combination of different heather cultivars—may be better for a tall,
intricate, light-colored piece.

WOODLAND GARDENS

Woodland gardens may be:

- open pools of space surrounded by overarching trees;
- shaded glades and paths under the canopies of trees;
- intermittent plantings of unusual shrubs, flowers, bulbs,
and small understory trees scattered throughout a larger
woodland landscape.

The appeal of a woodland garden is that of the forest
itself, but enhanced by a range of plants grown to please the
gardener's personal tastes. There are widely differing types
of woodland garden—this is not just a matter of choosing
plants but also depends on the climatic and site conditions.
Is the woodland that of old forest with a deep humus soil
and large trees offering dappled shade? Is it a wood where
the trees are relatively young, closely spaced, and struggling
for water and light on thin, eroded soil, and form a low,
heavy canopy? Or is it something in between the two?

Tree types and shade

The nature of woodland shade is important. Dappled shade
contains a surprising amount of light. This means that, since
all plants (except for fungi) require light for photosynthesis
(see pp.54–55), you are able to grow a completely different

selection of shrubs in dappled shade than you would be able to if you were planting in a far denser, more heavily shaded section of woodland.

Also important is the sort of tree in any woodland area. Are the trees mostly conifers (which over the years will have shed numerous needles, thereby creating a particular kind of soil)? Or is this a mixed deciduous hardwood forest (with broadleaf litter each fall)? Factors such as soil acidity, nutrient levels, tilth, and moisture retention can be deeply affected by which kinds of trees are growing there.

Shade-tolerant, spring-flowering shrubs—such as *Corylopsis*, with its butter-gold chains of flowers; *Rhododendron calendulaceum*, which has yellow to bright orange or red flowers; and *Lindera*, with its spicy-scented flowers—are natural choices for the woodland garden. *Rhodotypos scandens* thrives in woodland shade and produces bold bright white flowers in spring, when few woodland shrubs offer a show. *Viburnum tinus* is an evergreen with lovely clusters of pink-white bloom that mature into small fruits in the light shade under tall trees.

Broad-leaved evergreens are always useful in woodland gardens because they add distinction throughout the year. If the soil is moderately well drained, moist, and slightly acid, there are a number of evergreen rhododendrons that are suitable. *Osmanthus*, *Illicium*, some *Ilex* species, *Daphne*, *Pittosporum*, *Sarcococca*, *Vinca minor*, and *Ternstroemia gymnanthera* are all evergreen shrubs that can look lovely in a woodland setting. Try combining these shrubs with spring annuals and wildflowers and bulbs.

A winding path can be highlighted by irregular pools of *Skimmia*, with its deep evergreen foliage, creamy white flowers (borne in spring), and bright berries. *Skimmia japonica* grows with a variable habit, from a low ground cover to an upright shrub reaching 6½ft (2m). Its sharply oval, glossy deep green leaves show off the white flowers very well. This is a dioecious species: female plants produce upright clusters of scarlet fruit that persist well into the winter, and male plants are needed for good fruit set and development. Red-pink buds held in tight clusters are set in fall and are showy through the winter. The foliage is fragrant when you brush it in passing. If you prefer a lower ground cover than the species itself offers, you could try the selection 'Bowles Dwarf', which reaches only 10in (25cm) tall. Other selections have been produced for their very large and showy fruit and flower buds. 'Rubella' is a male type worth including because it will ensure good fruit production.

A woodland setting

Deciduous and evergreen shrubs can be interplanted, creating a woodland ambience, but you need to determine the kind of woodland you are working with.

A shade-tolerant spring-flowering shrub

Corylopsis pauciflora works well in most woodland-style settings, being both shade-tolerant and an attractive, adaptable "mixer" that has pale yellow flowers throughout the spring.

Woodland ground cover

An excellent ground cover for a woodland garden—especially in cold climates—is yellowroot (*Xanthorhiza simplicissima*). This spreading, suckering deciduous shrub reaches about 2ft (60cm) and has a somewhat open, coarse texture. It has beautiful lacy divided leaves that emerge tinged deep burgundy and later develop red-burgundy fall color. The flowers are rather inconspicuous from afar, but the small lavender-colored stars hung from very slender threads are lovely when observed at close range. A great advantage of yellowroot is that it performs well in either shade or sun. It prefers moist, well-drained soil but will tolerate dry spells, so it is a good choice for planting under large trees with extensive root systems. Even so, you must provide it with ample moisture while it establishes itself.

Two favorite evergreen ground covers for the woodland garden are the slow-growing Alexandrian laurel (*Danae racemosa*) and the closely related and equally patience-provoking *Ruscus*. Both are arching low shrubs that eventually reach 2–3ft (60–90cm). The apparently evergreen leaves are actually flattened areas of stems. (The true leaves are almost invisible.) These leaflike areas, like leaves, perform photosynthesis and transpiration.

The Alexandrian laurel makes a very graceful ground cover, as its inconspicuous greenish flowers eventually mature into translucent orange-red fruits. Flowers and fruits are rarely prolific, so the few fruits that develop seem like precious jewels—their bright hues make a significant show against the green stems. This shrub performs best in a moist woodland understory.

The soil in woodland gardens can be very dry, the extensive root systems of trees easily outcompeting those of any newly introduced plants for moisture. *Ruscus*, which is a much larger and more robust plant than *Danae*, will grow to 3ft (90cm) high, even in very dry shade. It bears sharp-pointed hollylike "leaves" that, as with *D. racemosa*, are actually flattened areas of stem, and—if both male and female plants are present (*Ruscus* is dioecious)—it produces scarlet berries in showy bunches. This plant makes a wonderful ground cover for those difficult areas in the woodland garden where little else will grow. It also combines well with *Xanthorhiza simplicissima*, adding evergreen interest after *X. simplicissima* has lost all of its leaves.

Another good evergreen for dry woodland shade is *Aucuba japonica*; this is relatively slow-growing, but its gold-variegated selections—such as 'Crotonifolia' and 'Variegata'—are useful for brightening dark corners and adding a splash of color to an otherwise quietly green area. The females produce bright red cherrylike fruit, although not usually in great numbers. The gold-variegated selections make beautiful companions to shade-loving ferns.

Aromatic blooms in late winter

Grown in a range of forms from sprawling to upright, *Skimmia japonica* is tolerant of shade and neglect. The compact form *S. japonica* 'Fragrans' (*above*) flowers profusely.

combines beautifully with shade-tolerant shrubs such as *Hydrangea paniculata*, which produces pyramids of creamy white flowers in late summer after the dipelta's have finished flowering and adds its own inflorescences as part of the post-bloom display.

Fall color

Achieving good fall color in woodland gardens can be quite a challenge, as most plants need full sun to develop bright color at that time of year. However, there are a few shrubs that are suitable, notably *Lindera obtusiloba* and *Disanthus cercidifolius*.

L. obtusiloba is an Asian lindera that reaches about 16ft (5m) in height; its blue-green foliage turns bright butter yellow in fall, even in shade. Its small yellowish flowers mature into shiny black fruits that contrast well with its fall foliage. *L. obtusiloba* thrives in both damp and dry conditions, and it gives good fall color in all but the darkest shade.

D. cercidifolius, an interesting relative of the witch hazels, is an open, coarse shrub that reaches 8ft (2.5m) tall. In summer it has heart-shaped blue-green foliage; in fall this turns to striking shades of beet red, purple, and scarlet. In fall, the plant bears purplish red strap-shaped flowers, much like those of *Hamamelis* (see pp.104–105), but these are rarely noticed among the colorful foliage. It provides good fall color when grown in partial shade. Combining *L.obtusiloba* with *D. cercidifolius* makes a fine fall color display for a woodland garden.

WATER GARDENS

Woodland gardens are quite often areas with streams, bogs, pools, and ponds—that is, places with a significant amount of moisture. But there are other types of gardens

Spring and summer interest

Many shrubs can be used to add spring and summer interest to a dry shaded area. A good example is *Sinocalycanthus*, which tolerates dry periods once it is established. This large shrub, reaching 10ft (3m) tall, has broad glossy green leaves that turn light yellow in fall. In spring its beautiful flowers, a waxy pink-blushed white with yellow centers, reach 3–4in (7.5–10cm) across and have a pleasant light fragrance. *Sinocalycanthus* will flower lightly even when grown in shade (the more light, the more prolific the blooming) and offers delightful spring character in a woodland area.

Similarly, you can plant *Dipelta floribunda* around the edges of a woodland where there is part (not full) shade. This fascinating shrub can reach 16ft (5m). Its foliage is large and grass green in spring and summer, pale yellow in fall. It blooms relatively prolifically in spring; the lovely flowers are long, pink, and tubular with a yellow throat, and they mature into curious winged capsules that have a subtle ornamental character. The plant is a year-round attraction, as its light, peeling bark is quite showy and can brighten a woodland garden in winter. *D. floribunda*

that feature water, either through the workings of nature or because you have planned a form of water garden. Watery areas can become the highlights of your garden.

The source of the water may be:

- periodic flooding;
- continual flow from a spring, stream, or river;
- a natural or constructed pond or dam;
- seasonal seep.

As with any area of the garden, you will need to consider which shrubs will be most successful growing in these wet or very damp conditions.

Pond gardens

Gardens that include a pond can generally depend on its contents to supply moisture for most of the year. Some natural ponds and pools dry up in the summer and reappear in the winter or spring, creating a distinct gardening challenge. Ponds that are permanent features of the garden are another matter.

Pond edges provide a very distinct microenvironment. The soil at the edge of a pond is permanently damp, and it may gather a great deal of organic matter that has not been broken down. The increased humidity also means that any plants prone to fungal diseases should be avoided. The positive aspect about gardening near ponds is that the plants are likelt to have sufficient water all year round so that there is no need to haul around hoses or sprinklers.

Sometimes you may wish to camouflage or disguise the edges of either a constructed or a natural pond. Pendent shrubs that hang down to the water or suckering shrubs that spread a little way into the water can make effective plantings.

Special considerations for water gardens

As with all specialized areas of the garden, there are general and specific rules for successful water gardening. For example, if you live in a rural area, you need to watch out in case ducks or geese trample on your favorite plants and graze on (for them) particularly delicious species.

Light conditions are as important as ever. The pond may be in full sun, part shade, or full shade. It is important to be aware of your pond's situation, as well as of the damp soils and increased humidity, taking these properly into account when considering appropriate plantings.

Ponds are often found at the bottom of a small slope, and for roughly the same reasons that water has pooled there, so will cold air. This means that you have to take extra care when selecting plants for the site: you need to ensure that any plant you choose is reliably frost-hardy, since the cold air may well damage tender plants that can grow successfully in other parts of your garden.

A water-garden setting
Assorted perennials here vie for attention with various trees and shrubs in this superb streamside garden, but it is the shrubs that provide much of the form.

Country garden with pool
The blue decking over the pool at the heart of this country garden creates an unusual effect but blends well with the sumptuous mixed planting around it.

Although there can be difficulties involved in pondside gardening, there is something appealing about having a patch of water in your garden. The pond's size and depth clearly affects your choice of plants. Note the scale of the plants you see in the wild growing around ponds that are about the same size as yours. In general, position low-growing plants near the water's edge, progressing to taller ones farther away, but don't let this principle stop you from putting a tall, willowy plant near the pond, so that you can see its reflection on the surface on a calm day, or planting a sprawl of low, handsome evergreens at the waterside.

Most naturalistic ponds call for quiet compositions with varied textures and soft flowering displays, but a formal, constructed pool may need a bolder hand; in such a case you may want to use bright colors and dramatic forms.

Many shrubs make good pondside specimens and combinations. For obvious reasons, you should put plants that tolerate considerable moisture immediately adjacent to the pond and others that like regular but not excessive moisture farther away. For example, use *Ilex glabra* (inkberry) near the pond's edge. This reliable, medium-sized evergreen shrub has fine-textured, black-green foliage and small glossy black fruit. To create contrasting texture and color, you might also plant the deciduous *Rhamnus frangula*. The alder buckthorn is an

indestructible shrub that can eventually reach 6ft (5m) in height; it has glossy green leaves and a rather coarse habit. The cultivar 'Aspleniifolia' has narrow, deeply incised foliage that curls and twists and is covered with a light gray pubescence; this misty, woven texture makes its appearance totally different from that of its parent species.

Another good choice of pondside plant is the unusual gold-foliaged form of the American elder, *Sambucus canadensis* 'Aurea'. This shrub reaches 6–8ft (1.8–2.5m) in height and has large interesting leaves together with white flowers that develop into dark red berries (the species proper has purple-black berries). If the strong-growing 'Aurea' gets too large, you will need to cut it hard to the ground. It will still send up new shoots, and by cutting the plant down you will get the benefit of having brighter-colored foliage on the gold selection.

Good shrubs of shorter stature for use near the pond's edge include the hybrid of *Fatsia* and *Hedera* called x *Fatshedera lizei*. This low-growing plant reaches up to 5ft (1.5m) high with palm-shaped leaves. It produces clusters of small cream-colored flowers in early fall, but its main appeal is its bold-textured "tropical" foliage. Of the various showy variegated selections, 'Annemieke', with

Showy foliage for a pool edge
The low-growing x *Fatshedera lizei* 'Annemieke' offers an attractive surround for pools and other water features, particularly in a woodlike setting.

Aralia elata in a mixed border
For imperious height and spread in any mixed border,
Aralia elata 'Variegata'—the Japanese angelica tree—is
always hard to beat.

cream-yellow blotches in the middle of its leaves, is a good choice for underplanting a larger pondside shrub such as *Exochorda* x *macrantha* 'The Bride', a selection of pearlbush that has a more compact habit and more prolific bloom than its parent. 'The Bride' is covered with pure white flowers in spring, and these blanket gracefully arching branches that fall in lovely cascades; the effect is especially beautiful if the shrub is close enough to the water for the flowers and branches to be reflected on the surface. Pearlbushes will always give some flowering in light shade but bloom more prolifically in full sun.

Subtler than *E.* x *macrantha* 'The Bride' is *Cephalanthus occidentalis* (buttonbush). This deciduous shrub reaches at least 6ft (1.8m), with a lax spread and nondescript grass green foliage. In summer it bears dense spherical clusters of white buttonlike flowers. In flower, it is an interesting plant, and it adds a note of unassuming detail to the border. *C. occidentalis* can be combined effectively with shrubs that

are more notable for their form, such as *Cyrilla racemiflora* (leatherwood) and *Corylus avellana* 'Contorta' (Harry Lauder's walking stick), both of which have the kind of twisted branching that is shown to best effect in winter.

If you wish to create a display of bold foliage at the pond's edge, you will find very few plants that can compete with *Aralia elata* (Japanese angelica tree). This shrub develops tall, upright, spiny main stems that are clothed with very large, divided leaves. The plant can attain a height and spread of 20ft (6m). The variegated selections are often quite costly, because they are difficult to propagate, but they are well worth the investment. The leaflets of the slower-growing 'Variegata' are splashed with creamy white around the edges and contrast well with the dark green foliage of other shrubs.

A flowering shrub well suited to pondside conditions is *Styrax americana* (American snowbell), which has a delicate yet decidedly ornamental character. This reaches about 8ft (2.5m) tall and has small oval leaves. Its slender branches are covered with enchanting, dangling, clear white, bell-shaped flowers in spring. This plant is complemented by *Enkianthus campanulatus* (red-vein enkianthus). The latter is also a somewhat slender-stemmed shrub but is

A water and rock garden
In this superb landscape, shrubs of varied colors are all perfectly integrated with the stone and water at the heart of the garden.

If you want a rather less demure flowering shrub for the pond's edge, you could try *Rubus odoratus* (flowering raspberry). This woodland shrub has large light green leaves, as well as an open rambling habit with virtually thornless stems, and surprisingly showy flowers that are about 2–3in (5–7.5cm) across. The flowers mostly face upward, so the plants make a beautiful display if grown where the stems can cascade down a bank or slope, possibly dangling in the edge of the water. The flowering color of *R. odoratus* is somewhere between violet and pink. Borne in summer, blooms mature into the type of berries characteristic of the whole *Rubus* (bramble) genus.

Another gracefully pendant shrub with a showy flowering display is *Spiraea thunbergii*. This slender-stemmed arching plant reaches about 4–5ft (1.2–1.5m) in height and has small, fine-textured, medium-green leaves. In early spring, flat clusters of snowy white blooms are borne along the branches, making the shrub look as if it is covered in veils or ribbons of white. *S. thunbergii* is a lovely addition to a pond's edge alongside *Rubus*

taller and more upright, reaching 10–13ft (3–4m) in time. Its tufts of small neat leaves turn red, yellow, and orange in fall; they create an attractive effect when they fall on the pond surface. In the spring, *E. campanulatus* bears weeping clusters of small urn-shaped flowers that are pink-tinged white with red-pink veins. A white-flowered form, *E. campanulatus* f. *albiflorus*, is especially attractive when paired with the American snowbell.

odoratus: it provides early bloom, while the *Rubus* flowers later in the season, yet their habits create a harmonious effect as they trail down toward the water.

Classic shrubs associated with pond and pool edges are the cutleaf and weeping forms of Japanese maple *(Acer palmatum),* such as 'Dissectum', with finely cut leaves that turn deep gold in fall, and the burgundy-foliaged 'Dissectum Atropurpureum'. The striking habit of the latter echoes the water's fluidity, and its foliage appears as a waterfall of green or wine red. *A. palmatum* offers fall color in shades of scarlet, bright red, burgundy, and maroon.

Stream and bog gardens

Streams and boggy areas offer a different set of gardening challenges. Streams may overflow their banks in winter or dry to a dribble in summer after flooding in spring; the environment around them can be in a state of constant change. Bogs, by contrast, are sites that are permanently damp and therefore require plants that can tolerate wet feet all the time, as well as low soil fertility.

For streamside plantings, you need to choose plants that will grow well in constantly changing moisture conditions. Two such shrubs that also make agreeable companions are *Clethra alnifolia* (summersweet) and *Itea virginica* (Virginia sweetspire).

C. alnifolia is a deciduous massing shrub that reaches to at least 6ft (1.8m) in height and has an equal spread. Its upright branches bear spikes of very fragrant, clear white flowers between midsummer and early fall; the flowers have a very spicy scent. The leaves turn an attractive bright yellow in fall.

I. virginica is another massing deciduous shrub. It grows to about the same size as the summersweet, but not only is it not as vigorous or dense in habit, its branches and flowers are less upright. Virginia sweetspire blooms in midsummer, producing clusters of creamy white flowers, and its foliage develops burgundy-red fall color before the leaves drop. Combining these shrubs extends the period of bloom and offers a wonderfully vibrant mixture of fall colors. Since these two plants tolerate alternatively wet and dry conditions, they can thrive alongside a stream whether it is in full flood or reduced

A streamside shrub
The delicate and very fragrant summersweet *(Clethra alnifolia)* thrives in changing moisture conditions, alongside streams, pools, ponds, and bogs.

to only a trickle. By planting these shrubs intermittently along the side of the stream, you are able to catch sight of the water through their branches.

A bog garden affords many opportunities to use beautiful and interesting varieties of shrubs. In addition, many delightful herbaceous plants either are well adapted

Shrubs and perennials in a bog garden
Bog gardens offer a unique environment for many different plants, resulting in verdant foliage and color.

Colorful shrubs at a pool's edge
At this richly planted water's edge, a swath of good flowering plants shoots across the path running down to the water's edge, giving the large pool beyond a powerful central focus.

to boggy areas or have been specialized for growth in this type of environment; in many cases these bloom with showy displays in early spring. Select plants that require or tolerate damp roots for much of the year for the central, boggiest areas; farther away, put in plants that prefer more regular moisture. Boggy soil is often very acidic, so you need to choose plants that either prefer or tolerate such conditions.

Year-round interest in bog gardens

In the very wettest section of the bog garden, deciduous shrubby dogwoods (*Cornus* spp.) can provide you with year-round interest, as these shrubs can be grown either for their attractive flowers or often variegated leaves, or for their bright winter stems. These dogwood species include *C. alba* (red-twig dogwood), *C. mas* (cornelian cherry), *C. racemosa* (gray dogwood), *C. sanguinea* (common dogwood), and *C. stolonifera* 'Flaviramea' (yellow-twig dogwood). A planting that includes a combination of other dogwoods works extremely effectively in creating changing patterns of color and texture through damp areas of the garden.

A showy plant for multi-season interest
The tall-growing deciduous chokeberry *(Aronia arbutifolia)* is highly valued for its spring flowers and red fall color and fruits. Best results are obtained from mass planting in full sun.

C. alba is a medium sized deciduous shrub that can reach 8ft (2.5m) in height and that produces suckers to form a thicket as it grows. Most selections have showy red twig color in winter, and some display contrasting foliage color during the growing season. *C. alba* 'Elegantissima', for example, has green leaves edged in bright white that contrast beautifully with the red stems, while *C. alba* 'Aurea' has light yellow leaves that keep their color throughout the growing season and add an unusual note against the red stems. *C. alba* 'Sibirica' is a selection known for its especially deep red stems. *C. stolonifera* 'Flaviramea' has brightly colored yellow stems and

Ornamental stems in winter
Among the best winter-interest shrubs, these shrubby dogwoods are grown for their bright winter stems. Shown here are *Cornus alba* 'Sibirica' and *C. stolonifera* 'Flaviramea'.

forms short thickets reaching about 3–4ft (1–1.2m). *C. mas* has deep green leaves that give good fall color in shades of orange-red and purple. It produces small, star-shaped, yellow flowers that are borne on the bare shoots before the leaves open in late winter to early spring; in areas with warm summers these mature into edible bright red fruits. *C. racemosa* is a larger shrubby dogwood, reaching a height of 10ft (3m) or more. Its fruits are porcelain white. Mixed plantings of red-twig and yellow-twig dogwood can create breathtaking sweeps of color in a large bog garden. Alternatively, you can use individual plants as bright specimens at the edges of a smaller garden. *C. mas* and *C. racemosa* especially can be good specimen plants because of their interesting fruit displays.

A shrub worth combining with the colored-twig dogwoods is *Aronia arbutifolia* (chokeberry). This tall deciduous plant reaches 6–10ft (1.8–3m) in height and has an open rounded habit. Its white flowers, although individually small, are showy together in spring; they mature into glossy red fruits about the size of small cherries. The beautiful fruits attract birds and small mammals. In fall this plant is very showy, offering a red-orange hue; the fruits persist well into winter.

For greater variety in texture and form, and subtler color, try combining *Myrica gale* with *Ilex verticillata*. *M. gale* (bog myrtle) is a thicket-forming deciduous shrub that reaches about 5ft (1.5m) in height and has very aromatic

dark green leaves. It makes an interesting combination with the deciduous holly, *I. verticillata* (winterberry). This charcoal-barked, multistemmed shrub forms vigorous masses reaching between 8ft (2.5m) in height, with a broad spread and stiffly arching branches that create a dense canopy. In summer the branches are cloaked in small, fresh green leaves. Winterberry bears small clusters of creamy white flowers that are always very attractive to bees. These flowers mature into fire-engine red berries that glow against the green late-summer foliage. In fall the red berries become more prominent, and they make a beautiful winter ornament.

Shrub combinations for bog gardens

When looking for interesting plant combinations for bog gardens, it is worth considering *Salix gracilistyla* (Japanese pussy willow), which makes an effective companion for the two shrubs, *Myrica gale* and *Ilex verticillata*, discussed above. *S. gracilistyla* is a large deciduous shrub reaching 8ft (2.5m) or more in height. In spring its catkins, silvery with pink tones, cover the stems and combine handsomely with the red fruits of the winterberry. A cultivar of this pussy willow, 'Melanostachys' (black pussy willow), has wine red stems and black catkins with anthers that emerge with a red cap. All these shrubs perform well in a wet situation but also tolerate periodic drying. Together they make a display that changes through the year.

Large shrubby plants near a bog edge
Amelanchier alnifolia var. *cusickii* offers multiseason interest. The changing colors of its foliage, bark, flowers, and fruit ensure its interest throughout the year.

Another combination that would be suitable nearer the edges of a bog, where the ground is not so permanently saturated but remains evenly moist, is shrubby serviceberry (*Amelanchier alnifolia*) underplanted with bog rosemary (*Andromeda*) species and cranberry (*Vaccinium macrocarpon*). Shrubby serviceberry is a large, multistemmed deciduous shrub, reaching 10ft (3m) in height and suckering to form thickets. It has pure white flowers and neat oval blue-green foliage that turns a brilliant red and orange-yellow in fall. Its bark is a handsome light silvery gray. In early spring the shrub is covered with

Salix gracilistyla with catkins
Japanese pussy willow can grow to a great height—more than 8ft (2.5m)—but in this picture it is the plant's spread that is most impressive.

Mixed planting for a dry garden
Despite their label, dry gardens can give a fresh appearance in a rain-starved landscape. Here, a mixed planting of shrubs, bulbs, and perennials borders a "stream" of gravel that has replaced the natural stream that would be found in wetter regions.

snow-white flowers that mature into bloomy blue-black fruit enjoyed by both birds and gardeners. Shrubby serviceberry is truly a bog-garden ornament for each of the four seasons.

Bog rosemary is a demure little dwarf evergreen. It has dark blue-green oval leaves. In late spring it produces sprightly pink urn-shaped flowers in downturned clusters; these are beautiful against the silvery bark of the shrubby serviceberry. Cranberry is another low-growing evergreen shrub; the mat form reaches only 6in (15cm) in height. The plant bears small pink flowers that in summer mature into red fruits.

DRY GARDENS

Any garden that receives little or no supplemental moisture for much of the year is a dry garden. It may literally be in a desert, or it may be designed to evoke a desert landscape through the use of plants native to desert or very dry, hot habitats. A similar effect can be created by using plants with ornamental characteristics similar to those of desert plants.

Dry gardens can be either simple or rich in texture, fragrance, form, and color. We think of them as being positioned in full sun, but you can create a dry garden in the shadow of a building, in a courtyard, or even under large drought-tolerant trees. The key aspect when designing a dry garden is to select shrubs with a minimal need for water; some dry-garden plants suffer diseases and root rot if given amounts of water comparable to that needed by many other plants in order just to survive.

Dry-garden plants can be combined in many different styles. The foliage of dry-garden plants is often as beautiful and interesting as their flowers and fruits. Frequently the leaves and/or stems of dry-adapted plants are covered with waxy or hairy coatings, and are thorny, or have an unusual structure to help the plant cope with the lack of moisture.

Arctostaphylos uva-ursi (bearberry) is a creeping evergreen shrub that reaches only 10–12in (25–30cm) in height. Its small leaves are a bright glossy green and keep their color very well throughout the summer, acquiring bronzy hues in winter. This plant flowers in spring to produce delicate, urn-shaped, pink-tinged white flowers that are less than a quarter of an inch (6.5mm) across but are borne in clusters at the end of the shoots and so are quite showy despite their size. In late summer the flowers mature into cherry red fruits that are equally attractive and persist into winter. Bearberry will grow as a prostrate mat to cover uneven ground or the edges of a walkway or steps, making a pleasing mounding carpet of bright green.

If you use bearberry as a base and interplant its ground cover with *Spartium junceum* (Spanish broom), you can add height and color without taking up much more space. This is a multistemmed shrub with nearly leafless bright green shoots; it reaches about 10ft (3m) and has a fountainlike habit. Its stems are bright green all year round, and they are covered with canary yellow pealike flowers for much of the summer. The flowers have a sweet scent and mature into dry-tan leguminous pods. This shrub is similar to some species of *Cytisus* and *Genista*. If you want it to remain dense and compact, cut it back lightly each year in spring. If it has become leggy or too large, it can be cut back quite hard periodically, although its bloom will be reduced in those years.

To add a further exotic element, consider including an individual specimen plant of *Grevillea rosmarinifolia* (rosemary grevillea). Its rosemary-like leaves, with silvery undersides, appear to emerge directly from the shoots. It is a medium-sized shrub, reaching about 5ft (1.5m), and has a rather loose and open habit. In summer it produces clusters of tubular deep red flowers that split and curl as they open. The blooming period lasts several weeks. The narrow foliage reflects the rushlike green stems of Spanish broom, but the combination of its deep red flowers with the canary yellow of the broom is gloriously bold.

An equally striking planting combination can be achieved by using *Myrtus communis* 'Compacta' as a tall ground cover. Common myrtle is an evergreen that can reach heights of

Left: Useful ground cover
Spanish broom *(Spartium junceum)* is a good choice for dry gardens, especially when planted with other ground-cover dry-garden shrubs such as bearberry.

Right: Soft and bright colors
This brighter *Lavandula stoechas, Cistus x purpureus,* and *Fremontodendron* 'California Glory', blend with the softer hues of *Perovskia atriplicifolia,* thyme, and borage.

A mixed dry-garden planting

The mixed planting in this French Mediterranean garden includes the shrub *Hypericum*, growing alongside such perennials as *Pelargonium* and *Erigeron*, and olive trees.

over 10ft (3m). 'Compacta' grows to only about 2ft (60cm) in height. The foliage, as with other varieties of common myrtle, is a glossy dark green and gives off a pungent fragrance when brushed or crushed. 'Compacta' grows with a rounded, mounding silhouette and has a relatively dense habit. In late summer the plant bears small starry white flowers that have a sweet scent.

Perovskia atriplicifolia (Russian sage) creates a pleasing contrast with the myrtle. This deciduous, fine-textured, upright shrub has very slender stems that can reach 5ft (1.5m) in height. It performs best if cut back almost to the ground each year in early spring. Its stems and foliage are a lovely silvery green and are covered with fine gray hairs. In late summer this shrub produces tall spikes of dusty lavender-blue flowers that contrast appealingly with the color of the foliage. The cultivar 'Blue Spire' has particularly large flower spikes.

A dry-garden shrub that makes a good choice for combining with the Russian sage and myrtle could be any of the genus *Acacia* (wattles). These tend to be among the taller shrubs—they can reach as much as 15–20ft (4.5–6m). One of the most striking (and a good choice for combining with Russian sage and/or myrtle) is the evergreen *A. pravissima* (Oven's wattle). This grows upright with an arching habit. As with many other wattles, its apparent leaves are actually modified areas of flattened leafstalk; on this plant they are a beautiful blue-gray color and are armed with spines. The "leaves" go well with the silvery foliage and lavender flowers of the Russian sage above the dark green myrtle foliage. In spring this plant produces clusters of little round heads of bright yellow flowers that tuck in and around the "leaves."

In order to add variety or to pick up a color reflection of the Russian sage or wattle, try mixing in a few small pools of *Myrtus communis* 'Variegata'. This myrtle cultivar has gray-green leaves edged in creamy white that tie in nicely with the silver-gray foliage of the other plants.

Cool dry-garden colors

Silver and lavender-blue are colors widespread among dry-garden shrubs. Another combination using these tones relies on a tall ground cover that is a mix of two silvery shrubs. *Artemisia arborescens*, an evergreen, has silvery white leaves densely covered in wooly white hairs and deeply incised into fine lobes. It eventually reaches about 4ft (1.2m) and has an irregular, slightly open habit and inconspicuous flowers. It combines effectively with another, taller shrub, *Leucophyllum frutescens* (Texas ranger). This rounded, mounding evergreen shrub reaches at least 5–6ft (1.5–1.8m) and has a dense habit. The covering of fine hairs on its leaves and stems gives it an overall silvery appearance; clouds of violet-blue flowers cover the plant for several weeks in summer.

A choice large specimen to combine with *A. arborescens* and *L. frutescens* is something from the genus *Ceanothus* (California lilac). There are a vast number of species, hybrids, and cultivars: they range from tall and treelike to dwarf and prostrate in size, and from deciduous to evergreen. One of the evergreens, *C. thyrsiflorus,* provides a mass of color; this species can become quite tall, reaching 15–20ft (4.5–6m) in height. It has fine-textured, glossy medium-green leaves that set off the large clusters of various shades of blue flowers that are borne in spring.

Ceanothus 'Concha' in spring
The cool, lavender-blue color of this outstandingly beautiful California lilac evergreen hybrid makes it a perfect large specimen for the warmer garden.

As their flowering periods overlap, the *Ceanothus* and *Leucophyllum* offer continuous lavender-blue tones. Note that both these and the *Artemisia* are sensitive to root rot, and so can be grown successfully only in well-drained soils.

A cool-colored shrub for a dry garden
Its aromatic foliage makes *Artemisia arborescens* a useful shrub for planting in a dry sunny border or against a wall.

Warmer colors

If these cool colors are not for you, a hot sunny bed is also an excellent place to grow a riot of oranges, yellows, and burnt umbers. *Potentilla fruticosa* is a reliable deciduous shrub that reaches heights varying from 2 to 5ft (60cm to 1.5m), depending on the cultivar. It flowers over a very long period from spring through early fall. The flowers are single, about 1½in (4cm) across, and are scattered throughout the fine, upright, densely arranged stems. The leaves, which are quite small, often have blue-green tints. The branches tend to arch gracefully as the shrub ages, so that the flowers are presented in an ever more appealing manner. Flower color can be pink, red, yellow, orange, or white.

A combination of the *Potentilla* cultivar 'Red Ace', which has orange-red flowers, with 'Sunset', which bears orange-yellow flowers, and 'Tangerine', which has yellow flowers infused with tangerine, will ensure that the garden is lit up with a blaze of color.

Caragana frutex reaches 8ft (2.5m) or more in height and offers divided, fresh green stems and bright canary yellow, pealike flowers in late spring. 'Globosa' is a very compact selection, reaching 2ft (60cm) in height, that combines nicely with hot-colored perennials.

A bright colored evergreen or semievergreen
The tall, vigorous *Fremontodendron californicum* has beautiful, olive green leaves that complement the striking yellow blooms that flower from late spring to early fall.

A reliably long-flowering deciduous shrub
With their bright-colored and long-lasting blooms, potentillas are an especially attractive summer planting for dry beds. This cultivar is the striking *Potentilla fruticosa* 'Red Ace'.

You can top off these shrubs with a tall plant such as *Fremontodendron* (common flannel bush). This evergreen shrub from the southwestern United States and Mexico reaches 20ft (6m) and has a pyramidal habit, making it look like a large flame. Its leaves, which are divided into three lobes, are a burnished olive green color. In summer the plant is covered with stunning yellow flowers about 2in (5cm) wide. Beware of touching them, however: the foliage and stems are covered with prominent hairs that often cause an allergic reaction. The two species most commonly grown in gardens are *F. californicum* and *F. mexicanum*. Some of the most ornamental selections are hybrids between the two and have vigorous growth and large flowers. 'California Glory', for example, has large, orange-tinged flowers that glow like embers against its evergreen foliage.

For a subtler picture, try *Arbutus unedo* (strawberry tree). Another tall shrub, it can reach 33ft (10m) or more in the wild, although it generally has more shrublike proportions in the garden. Its beautiful peeling mahogany bark provides a perfect foil for its demure evergreen leaves and the small clusters of urn-shaped pinkish white flowers that are borne in fall while the previous year's round, bright strawberry red fruits are still in the process of ripening.

Succulent dry garden
In this exotic dry garden on the West Coast of the United States, bird statues peck and forage among an eclectic mix of succulents and shrubs.

A truly charming combination of shrubs can be achieved by underplanting *Arbutus unedo* with a bed of *Phlomis fruticosa* (Jerusalem sage). This relaxed-looking, vigorous, deciduous subshrub reaches about 4ft (1.2m) tall. It has light gray downy leaves that curl and wave slightly around the margins, and in summer it bears prominent whorls of yellow-lipped flowers.

Plants native to dryland regions

For authentic character, you might choose to turn to shrubs native to the dryland regions of the world. *Holodiscus discolor* (ocean spray) is a large lax deciduous shrub reaching 10ft (3m) in height and offering tall vaselike shoots. It bears pendent clusters of frothy cream-colored flowers (hence its common name) in summer. This shrub is foolproof in the dry garden. Another dryland native is *Acacia pravissima*, an evergreen that reaches about 16ft (5m) tall and has blue-gray, spine-tipped "leaves" that are really modified leafstalks. The leaves are sprinkled with small, rounded, soft yellow flowers that open in clusters in spring. Both shrubs are very handsome when combined with cacti such as those of the genus *Opuntia*, which produce large yellow flowers.

For spiky textures without the actual thorns of a cactus, the evergreen *Callistemon* (bottlebrush) species are excellent choices. These are, in general, medium-sized arching shrubs, reaching 6–10ft (1.8–3m), with relaxed habits and short, narrow, spiky-looking leaves arranged around the stems. They produce very exciting flower heads, usually in bright shades of red or yellow: cylindrical clusters of blooms are borne on the ends of the stems, and protruding stamens give the flowers their bottlebrush look. *C. citrinus* is both extremely popular and reliable; it has crimson flowers and narrow leaves. For added spiky texture, plant a low-growing stemless yucca at its base.

Yucca filamentosa (Adam's needle) reaches 6½ft (2m) in height and produces sword-shaped leaves in whorls. The species' foliage is a dull gray-green, but some of the brightly variegated selections can be dramatic. With the broad gold edges on its leaves, 'Bright Edge' makes a very strong statement.

Dendromecon rigida (tree poppy) is a less domineering plant. This evergreen reaches to 13ft (4m) and has upright shoots that bear blue-green bloomy leaves. The flowers, which look like poppy flowers, bloom sporadically throughout the year. *Cistus* x *purpureus* (rock rose) makes an excellent companion. It is a low shrub, about 3ft (90cm) tall, with a rounded irregular habit. It has narrow gray-green leaves, and in late spring and early summer it produces magenta-pink, poppylike flowers, marked with deeper spots of color at the base of each petal.

A slightly more unusual suggestion would be to try *Robinia hispida* (rose acacia or bristly locust). This is a spreading deciduous shrub, reaching up to 10ft (3m) in height. It spreads vigorously by suckering and so should not be grown where it can run. The divided leaves are an attractive medium green, and in late spring and early summer the plant is festooned with a prolific array of rose-pink pea-shaped flowers that pleasingly match those of *C.* x *purpureus*. Together, these three shrubs present a soft-textured and extremely attractive arrangement.

MINIATURE GARDENS

The appeal of dwarf and miniature plants is universal. Whether grown in rock gardens, troughs, containers, or tiny planting beds, these miniaturized cousins of familiar garden shrubs offer a charming, elvish charm.

Lithodora diffusa 'Heavenly Blue' in a rock garden
With its profusion of deep blue flowers borne in early summer, the evergreen, prostrate shrub *Lithodora diffusa* becomes an ideal planting for a rock garden.

Rock gardens usually include significant plantings of alpine species. Although a miniature garden may include some of the more normal-sized alpines, it is usually primarily a garden of miniature plants. The number of dwarf, compact, and miniature selections of otherwise normal-sized shrubs seems to multiply daily. You can derive great pleasure from creating a miniature garden, either as part of a larger garden scheme or as the focus of a small, specialized landscape.

The cultural considerations you face when planning gardens and landscapes with full-sized plants remain unchanged with miniatures. The variation in mature size of a dwarf cultivar does not necessarily alter its preferred conditions: it will probably require roughly the same degree of sun or shade and the same sort of soil as its full-sized relatives. The one difference may be a decrease in the need for water: because the canopy and leaf area of a dwarf plant are much smaller, it will probably require less water than a full-sized version of that species.

It is possible to create a miniature garden in any landscape setting. While we tend to think of shrubs as being medium or even large plants, many dwarf selections are equally healthy and vigorous. These offer you some very interesting opportunities. The challenge of combining miniature selections is to create the same diversity of texture and color as in larger plantings.

Tough evergreen ground covers such as *Baccharis pilularis* (coyote brush) are a good place to begin when planting a miniature garden. This creeping evergreen does not grow much taller than 1ft (30cm), but it spreads much farther along the ground. Tiny glossy green leaves are a delicate foil for the miniature heads of white flowers that appear in late fall and early winter. Its delicate appearance belies its tough nature: it will thrive on the worst of poor exposed sites, including shoreside sites.

Another good evergreen ground-covering miniature is *Lithodora diffusa*, which grows into a dense mat of deep green foliage, again under 1ft (30cm) tall, and produces masses of funnel-shaped, deep blue flowers in late spring and early summer. Although the flowers are very small,

Right: A rock and water garden
This bold combination of water tumbling over stark, sloping rock faces, and the mixed planting of alpines, mixed shrubs, and conifers makes for a dramatic landscape.

they are extremely striking. Several cultivars have been selected for variation on the flower color. 'Alba' has white flowers and looks extremely pretty in combination with the blue forms. Related to *L. diffusa* is a comparatively rare plant with similar characteristics that grows on an even smaller scale. *L. oleifolia* reaches only 6in (15cm) in height. It too becomes a dark green mat and produces striking light blue flowers, opening from pink-tinted buds, in late spring and early summer.

Cool and sunny sites

For cool sunny sites, several of the dwarf and low growing willows offer unusual character and charm in a miniature garden. *Salix* x *boydii* is a slow-growing hybrid species with an upright habit, 1ft (30cm) in height. It has beautiful rounded foliage with a distinctive, dark gray-green color. *Salix helvetica* is among the most beautiful of the small willows. It grows into a small mound, 2ft (60cm) in height, and the new growth emerges covered with bright silver hair. In addition, male catkins emerge, also covered with silvery "fuzz", that eventually develop showy red anthers that contrast beautifully with the silvery leaves. The wooly willow, *Salix lanata*, is larger than either *S.* x *boydii* and *S. helvetica*, reaching about 3ft (1m) in height, but its irregular branching, silver wooly new leaves, and gray catkins add structural interest to the miniature garden.

Rock garden with miniature rose, *Hydrangea,* and *Vinca*
Shrubs can look especially effective in sloping gardens, where their varied foliage, heights, and spreads provide a strong contrast to miniature alpine plants.

Other low growing plants which develop mounding habits can add diverse character to miniature gardens in the full sun as well. There are some lovely species to choose from, including the evergreen *Ozothamnus selago*—a dwarf species from a genus with members often reaching 5ft (1.5m) tall. *O. selago* reaches only about 12in (30cm) and has arching stems densely layered with tiny dark green leaves. In some years, in early summer, little pale yellow to creamy white flower heads are produced at the ends of the stems. This plant always combines very effectively with the dwarf *Leptospermum* cultivar 'Kiwi'; this shrub reaches only 12in (30cm), unlike its parent species, *L. scoparium*, which can grow to 10ft (3m) or more. 'Kiwi' has bronze-tinged evergreen foliage that contrasts nicely with the dark green foliage of *O. selago*; in early

Genista scrambling over rocks
The charming *Genista sagittalis* has creeping green-winged stems and golden yellow flowers in early summer.

summer it produces deep pink flowers that, despite their small size, make a striking impression when combined with the yellow to creamy-white flowers produced by *O. selago*.

If you want to add even bolder color, there are three dwarf broom or broomlike shrubs that turn into tiny fountains of gold when in flower. *Cytisus* x *beanii*, a dwarf broom with a sprawling deciduous habit, reaches about 18in (45cm) in height. In late spring and early summer its curved stems are covered with sprays of bright yellow pea-shaped blooms.

Even smaller is the deciduous *Genista sagittalis*, which has green-winged stems and grows only about 6in (15cm). From these creeping stems tiny upright shoots develop, on the end of which bright yellow flowers appear in early summer. The largest of the three broomlike shrubs is *Caragana pygmaea;* this is not a true miniature, as it can grow up to 3ft (90cm) in height. It has an arching, pendent deciduous habit and produces yellow pealike flowers in early summer. This makes a wonderful specimen plant, adding height and scale to a miniature garden. In winter the branching habit is very attractive.

You may want an even more assertive deciduous flowering display. For a carpet of bright white flowers, *Deutzia crenata* 'Nikko' is unbeatable if grown in full sun. This little shrub reaches about 24in (60cm) in height, forming a rounded mound with many fine stems. In late

Helianthemum in a rock-garden setting
Rock roses such as the popular variety *H.* 'Raspberry Ripple' offer an unparalleled range of choices for natural color in any garden that enjoys full sun.

spring it produces starry white flowers that blanket the plant. 'Nikko' can also develop quite handsome red color in the fall. Another dwarf shrub with fine white flowers and good fall color is the sand cherry (*Prunus pumila* var. *depressa*). This deciduous creeping cherry sends long silvery shoots along the ground and in spring produces delicate white flowers that mature into little fruits; it develops a quiet but arresting orange-red fall color if grown in full sun. This is also a good shrub for seaside gardens.

Bold-colored miniatures

For more colorful flowers, it is worth trying *Forsythia viridissima* 'Bronxensis', which reaches about 1ft (30cm) in height and in early spring is covered with sprightly yellow flowers: it is wonderful when combined with dwarf daffodils or the smallest of species tulips. For bolder summery golds in full sun, use the dwarf deciduous St.-John's-wort (*Hypericum olympicum*); this reaches about 18in (45cm) and has quite large, bright gold flowers in summer. *Halimium* 'Susan' is an evergreen that produces a spreading mound some 18in (45cm) in height; in early summer its warm golden flowers appear. The petal bases of the flowers are blotched with deep red-purple—making 'Susan' an excellent companion for any purple-flowered plants you might be growing in the vicinity.

Bold color in the summer rock garden
The joyously colored, bold flowers of the dwarf St.-John's-wort (*Hypericum olympicum*) make this dense shrub a useful plant for adding brightness to a miniature garden.

The genus *Helianthemum* (rock roses) offers a huge group of sun-loving plants with bold-colored flowers. These are natural choices if you wish to bring vibrant color to a miniature garden that enjoys full-sun conditions. Clambering evergreen shrubs, they reach only about 1ft (30cm) in height. In summer they are covered with buttercup-like flowers about 1in (2.5cm) across. Named selections afford nearly every flower color you can think of—orange, yellow, pink, rose, red, white, and burnt umber—and some selections have contrasting centers or edges.

Miniatures in shade

A miniature garden can take on extra charm when grown in shade. The special considerations that affect general gardening in the shade apply also to miniatures. You have to allow for reduced growth and flowering and fruiting rates, the potentially increased susceptibility to fungal diseases, and more open, rangy habits.

In lighter shade, the *Hydrangea macrophylla* 'Pia' makes a bold and attractive mound of medium textured stems that are topped with cheery, pink flower heads with white centers in summer. 'Pia' combines a small size with a bold floral display—an unusual and effective set of traits, that is a surprising and delightful way to bring color to a miniature garden situated in the shade.

Another good combination is to plant the dwarf *Cotoneaster congestus* with *Leucothoe fontanesiana* 'Rainbow', *C. congestus* is a creeping evergreen that never reaches heights above 8in (20cm) or so. Its neat little dark green leaves are the backdrop for demure white flowers that mature into sparsely borne red fruit. The slow growing but larger evergreen, *L. fontanesiana* 'Rainbow', makes a low, graceful mound that forms a thicket of arching shoots up to 6½ft (2m) in height. Its handsome foliage is splashed with tones of pink, cream, and pale to dark green. It adds some height and winter interest, and the pink tones in the foliage harmonize well with the red fruits on the cotoneaster.

In yet deeper shade, *Paxistima canbyi* is a naturally small and compact evergreen shrub; although its flowers are inconspicuous, the glossy green leaves turn a handsome bronzy hue in winter. The shrub reaches about 12in (30cm) tall and spreads by rooting where the stems touch the ground. It makes a lovely combination with the dwarf *Pieris japonica* 'Little Heath', whose small evergreen leaves have thin white margins—a nice echo of this cultivar's tiny white urn-shaped flowers, which come in spring. These white flowers blend well with the showier soft mauve-pink blooms of *Rhododendron* 'Pink Drift', which reaches about 18in (45cm) in height and blooms quite prolifically.

For hotter colors, try combining two other dwarf rhododendrons with *Gaultheria procumbens* (checkerberry). This prostrate-growing evergreen has mats of dark green leaves that turn bronze-red in winter. Its pinkish blooms mature into red fruit. *Rhododendron forrestii*, a mat-forming shrub that can reach 1ft (30cm), bears bell-like scarlet flowers that are even more dramatic when seen against the orange-red blooms of the evergreen *R. nakaharae*—a dwarf rhododendron of about the same height.

Whether grown as a specimen or with other plants, miniature shrubs are especially good for container plantings; not only do they have great visual appeal, but they can be easily transported if you move or wish to redesign an area of your garden.

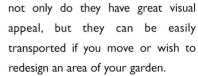

Left: An ideal summer miniature
Its beautiful blooms makes *Hydrangea macrophylla* 'Pia', a dwarf hortensia, a good choice for a miniature garden, especially when complemented by other shade-loving miniatures.

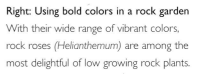

Right: Using bold colors in a rock garden
With their wide range of vibrant colors, rock roses *(Helianthemum)* are among the most delightful of low growing rock plants.

The following section catalogs a wide range of popular garden shrubs. Although many more shrubs are available, particularly from specialized nurseries, those included are among the most useful and ornamental for garden use. A general introduction for each genus gives information on the number of species and where they occur in the world, as well as important details on cultivation and suggestions on where to plant shrubs in the garden. Each species and selected cultivars are then described with information specific to that plant, such as its ultimate size and hardiness. Size is important for determining which shrubs are suitable for which position, while hardiness will help you indentify which shrubs it is possible to grow in your region.

The glory of shrub foliage
Although shrubs with attractive foliage are often used merely as a bed, their long and variable seasons of display make them arguably the most useful of all garden plantings. The garden on the far left includes the beautiful *Salix lanata* (with blue-gray foliage) with Japanese maples (*Acer palmatum*); the outstanding fall foliage of the maple is also shown in close-up (*left*).

plant
directory

Abelia x *grandiflora* 'Francis Mason'

Abeliophyllum distichum 'Roseum'

Abutilon megapotamicum

Abelia

The 30 or so species in this genus of deciduous and evergreen shrubs are native from the Himalayas to China and Japan, and to Mexico. Grown for their profuse, sometimes fragrant bell-shaped to tubular flowers, they are well suited to a sunny position or for training against a wall. Most are valuable for their late-summer and fall flowering, and even when the flowers have finished, persistent sepals continue the ornamental effect. Little pruning is required except to cut back in spring if needed to restrict the size.

A. 'Edward Goucher'. A semievergreen hybrid of *A.* x *grandiflora* with bronze leaves when young and lilac-pink funnel-shaped flowers borne continuously from summer to fall. It reaches 5ft (1.5m) tall and across. Zone 6 US; 7 Can.

A. x *grandiflora.* The most popular shrub in the genus, making a vigorous, evergreen or semievergreen plant 6ft (1.8m) tall and across or more, with glossy dark green leaves on arching shoots. The whole bush is smothered in fragrant, pink-tinged, white flowers from summer to fall. 'Francis Mason' has yellow-variegated leaves. 'Prostrata' is a low, spreading form reaching a height of 3ft (1m). Zone 5 US; 6 Can.

A. schumannii. A rounded deciduous shrub to 6ft (1.8m) tall with arching branches producing its fragrant, funnelshaped pink flowers, which are white inside blotched with orange, over a long period during summer and fall. It will take considerable exposure. Zone 7 US; 6 Can.

Abeliophyllum

The single species in this genus comes from Korea and is sometimes known as the white forsythia. It grows best in full sun and is excellent for training against a wall. Little pruning is needed, but old specimens can be improved if cut back hard after flowering.

A. distichum. A rather straggly deciduous shrub, reaching about 5ft (1.5m) tall and across, with green leaves that will often turn purple in the fall. The beauty and usefulness of this plant lies in the white flowers borne on bare, purple shoots in late winter to early spring. 'Roseum' has flowers that start off pink and fade to white. Zone 4 US; 5b Can.

Abutilon

This large genus of more than 100 species is found mainly in tropical regions, and while it provides us with many showy greenhouse plants, some are hardy enough to be grown outside in a sunny position, except in colder regions. The striking flowers come in a range of colors and vary from saucer- to bell-shaped.

A. x *hybridum.* A group of striking hybrids, with large flowers that will reach a height of 13ft (4m) or more. Where not hardy they are suitable for the greenhouse. The many forms include those with white flowers such as 'Album' and with red such as 'Nabob' and 'Vesuvius Red'. Zone 8 US; 9 Can.

A. megapotamicum. This fast-growing evergreen shrub is ideally trained against a wall to provide support for its arching shoots and can reach 10ft (3m) tall and across. The conspicuous, pendulous flowers, with bright red sepals and yellow petals, are borne continuously during the growing season. 'Variegatum' has yellowblotched leaves. Zone 7 US; 8 Can.

A. vitifolium. A fast-growing upright deciduous shrub reaching 10ft (3m) or more tall and ideally sited amongst other large shrubs or near a wall to give it protection from winds. The large, normally mauve, saucer-shaped flowers are set against, bold, vinelike, gray-green leaves in summer. Zone 8 US and Can.

Acacia

The wattles make an enormous genus of more than 1,000 species, mainly trees, and found largely in Africa and Australia. The apparent "leaves" of many of them are really modified leaf stalks, the normal, finely cut leaves appearing only in seedlings. Dense, rounded or cylindrical heads of usually yellow flowers are composed of numerous stamens. They all require sun, and the only pruning needed is after flowering to restrict growth.

A. longifolia. The Sydney golden wattle is a vigorous evergreen shrub growing to 20ft (6m) or more, with dark green "leaves." The yellow flowers are borne in long spikes in spring. Zone 8 US and Can.

A. pravissima. This evergreen shrub can reach 16ft (5m) tall and across and has long, arching shoots densely clothed with blue-gray, spine-tipped "leaves." The small, rounded, yellow flowers open in clusters during spring. Zone 8 US and Can.

A. verticillata. The prickly Moses is a treelike shrub that can grow to 20ft (6m) tall and across, with slender, spine-tipped, dark green "leaves." The bright yellow flowers are borne in cylindrical clusters in spring. Zone 8 US and Can.

Acca

Only one species of this South American genus of evergreen shrubs and trees is commonly cultivated. Planted in a sunny location, it is grown for its showy flowers and can also be used for hedging.

A. sellowiana. Also known as *Feijoa sellowiana*, the pineapple guava can reach 8ft (2.5m) tall and across or more. The leathery, dark green leaves have a white felt beneath. Showy flowers with four white, red-centered petals and a center of crimson stamens open in midsummer. Reliable fruiting forms include 'Coolidge' and 'Pineapple Gem'. Zone 8 US and Can.

Acer

Maple

The maples, a genus of mainly deciduous trees, are widely distributed mostly in north temperate regions. Several of them are useful garden shrubs, grown for their foliage, which often colors attractively in autumn. Most prefer full sun or light shade, with the best color being developed in good light. They do not grow well on shallow, dry, alkaline soils, and the forms of *A. palmatum* should not be planted in exposed positions.

A. palmatum. The Japanese maple will normally make a picturesque, spreading tree to 25ft (8m), the leaves deeply cut into five to nine taper-pointed lobes, turning orange, yellow, or red in fall.

There are a very large number of selected forms of this species with variously cut and colored foliage. The following normally reach about 5ft (1.5m). 'Butterfly' is an upright form, the small leaves narrowly edged with white, although pink when young. The form 'Chitoseyama' makes a mound of arching branches, with deeply cut bronze-tinged leaves brilliant orange-red in fall. Zone 5 US and Can.

Dissectum Group. This name covers forms of *A. palmatum* with deeply cut leaves. They are normally of arching habit with drooping branches. 'Crimson Queen' has slender and finely cut deep purple lobes. 'Dissectum' has green foliage. 'Dissectum Atropurpureum' has purple leaves. 'Dissectum Nigrum', also known as 'Ever Red', has bronze-purple leaves, red in the fall. 'Garnet' has garnet red foliage. 'Seiryu' is like 'Dissectum' but with upright branches. Zone 6 US and Can.

A. tataricum subsp. *ginnala*. The very hardy deciduous Amur maple will normally make a small tree to 25ft (8m). It has fragrant white flowers in spring, while the glossy green, three-lobed leaves can turn yellow and red in the fall. The following reach about 10ft (3m) tall. 'Compactum' is a compact shrubby form that colors red-purple in the fall. 'Flame' is dense, with red fall color. Zone 2 US and Can.

Aesculus

Horsechestnut, Buckeye

This genus of some 13 species of deciduous trees and shrubs, natives largely of north temperate regions, provides gardens with some striking flowering trees. The shrubby species described here is an excellent specimen plant that can make a large clump.

A. parviflora. The bottlebrush buckeye is a deciduous open shrub that spreads by suckers, forming thickets up to 13ft (4m) tall or more. Its large leaves change from bronze to dark green, turning yellow in the fall. The bottlebrush-like spikes of white flowers open in mid- to late summer. var. *serotina* is a late-flowering form, and 'Rogers' flowers very late with long flower spikes. Zone 4 US and Can.

Acca sellowiana

Acer palmatum 'Chitoseyama'

Aesculus parviflora

Aloysia triphylla

Andromeda polifolia

Aralia elata

Aloysia

Of the 35 or so species of shrubs in this genus, natives of the U.S. Southwest to South America, only one is at all common in gardens. Grown for its aromatic foliage, it needs a well-drained soil in sun. As it is not very hardy, it is often grown in a container and moved indoors during the winter. The leaves can be used to make tea or in potpourri.

A. triphylla. Also known as *Lippia citriodora*, the lemon verbena is a deciduous shrub reaching 8ft (2.5m) tall or more in areas with little frost. The lemon-scented leaves are borne in whorls of three, and tiny, lilac-tinged white flowers open in summer. Zone 8 US; 9 Can.

Amelanchier

Serviceberry, Shadbush

The serviceberries are a genus of some 10 species of deciduous shrubs and trees, found in the wild in North America, Europe, and Asia. They contribute to the garden their spring flowers, colorful fall foliage, and small but edible fruits that ripen in summer. They mainly prefer a well-drained soil in sun or light shade.

A. alnifolia. The Saskatoon berry makes a spreading shrub that grows to between 5ft (1.5m) and 10ft (3m) tall. The pure white flowers open in late spring and are followed by purple-black fruits. Many forms selected for their fruit are also cultivated. In the fall, the leaves turn shades of red and yellow. var. *cusickii* has larger flowers with fewer in each cluster. Zone 3 US; 2b Can.

A. canadensis. Similar to *A. alnifolia* but makes a thicket of upright shoots. Zone 3 US; 3b Can.

Andromeda

Natives of Europe, northern Asia, and North America, the two species in this genus are small evergreen shrubs that require a moist, peaty soil in sun or shade. Pruning is not required except in spring to remove any dead wood.

A. polifolia. The bog rosemary is an attractive dwarf shrub for the peat garden, with slender shoots and narrow blue-green leaves that are white beneath. Small, usually pink, urn-shaped flowers are borne in small clusters at the ends of the shoots in late spring and early summer. 'Macrophylla' has rather broad leaves and bright pink flowers. Zone 2 US and Can.

Aralia

Deciduous shrubs, sometimes trees, and perennial herbs make up this genus of some 35 species, found mainly in North America and eastern Asia. Their attraction lies in their bold leaves, which are divided into many leaflets, and their stout, spiny stems.

A. elata. Sometimes a tree, the Japanese angelica tree is more often a shrub spreading by suckers; it can reach 20ft (6m) tall. The huge leaves are found mainly at the tips of the spiny stems and turn orange and yellow in the fall. In early fall the tops are crowned by clusters of white flowers, followed by black fruits. 'Variegata' is a slower-growing form, the leaflets edged with creamy white. Zone 4 US; 5 Can.

A. spinosa. Similar to *A. elata*, this flowers earlier, each flower cluster with a single main stem. Zone 4 US and Can.

Arbutus

The 15 species of evergreens in this distinguished genus are mainly trees and are natives of the Mediterranean region, western North America, and Mexico. The species listed here is grown for its attractive, glossy foliage as well as its flowers and fruits. It will grow in most soils in sun or light shade and is among the few heather relatives that will thrive on limy soils. To maintain as a shrub, prune in spring before growth starts.

A. unedo. The strawberry tree is normally a tree reaching 30ft (9m) or more in height but is often a shrub in gardens or can be maintained as one. The small white flowers open in late fall as the red, strawberry-like fruits from the previous year are ripening. Pruning prevents fruiting, but selected compact, shrubby forms such as 'Compacta' are also available. Zone 7 US and Can.

Arctostaphylos uva-ursi 'Point Reyes'

Aronia arbutifolia

Artemisia arborescens

Arctostaphylos

Most of the 50 or so species that make up this genus of evergreen shrubs and trees are natives of California and Mexico, but the one most commonly grown and useful in gardens is found around cooler regions of the Northern Hemisphere. Best in a sunny position, it makes a vigorous ground cover and only needs pruning when necessary to restrict its spread.

A. uva-ursi. A creeping evergreen shrub to 1ft (30cm) tall, the bearberry has long shoots densely covered with bright green leaves. Small, white or pink, urn-shaped flowers open in nodding clusters in spring, followed by bright red fruits. 'Massachusetts' is vigorous and has small, dark green leaves and pink-tinged white flowers. 'Point Reyes' has arching, peeling shoots; rounded leaves; and pink flowers. 'Vancouver Jade' has glossy bright green leaves that bronze in cold weather. Zone 3 US; 1 Can.

Aronia

Chokeberry

The two species in this genus are deciduous shrubs, native to eastern North America. They are valued in gardens for their fall color and their fruits and are most effective when mass-planted. They will grow in most soils but do not do well on dry, shallow alkaline ones. No pruning is usually necessary.

A. arbutifolia. Upright in habit and reaching 6–10ft (1.8–3m) tall, the red chokeberry has oval leaves that are downy beneath and turn red in the fall. Heads of small white flowers in spring develop into clusters of small red berries. 'Brilliant', also known as 'Brilliantissima', is a form with especially bright red fruits. Zone 4 US; 4b Can.

A. melanocarpa. The black chokeberry, is similar to *A arbutifolia* but with larger black fruits, while *A.* x *prunifolia* has purple-black fruits. Zone 4 US and Can.

Artemisia

The 300 or so species in this genus of herbaceous perennials and shrubs are widely distributed throughout the world.

Often with gray, aromatic foliage, they are good subjects for a dry, sunny border or wall and are best in a well-drained, not too rich soil. Pruning consists of cutting back hard in spring.

A. arborescens. The stout, upright shoots of this evergreen shrub reach 4ft (1.2m) tall and bear finely-cut, gray-white leaves. Tiny yellow flowers open in summer. Zone 7 US; 8 Can.

A. californica. The California or coastal sagebrush, is taller, to 6ft (1.8m), the gray leaves cut into very narrow lobes. Zone 8 US; not hardy Can.

Asimina

The eight species that make up this genus of deciduous and evergreen trees and shrubs are native to the southeastern United States. The following species is cultivated for its foliage, unusual flowers, and its fruits, which are edible. It prefers a good soil in full sun or light shade. No pruning is usually necessary.

A. triloba. The pawpaw is a large deciduous shrub, sometimes a tree, that can reach 16ft (5m) tall and across or more. The bold, rather drooping leaves turn yellow in the fall. Large, purple-brown flowers open as the young leaves emerge and are followed by yellow-green, edible fruits up to 5in (13cm) long, which taste of bananas. Some forms selected for their fruits are grown. Zone 4 US; 6 Can.

Atriplex

This genus of some 100 species consists of annual and perennial herbs and shrubs widely distributed throughout the world, with several species common garden weeds. The two shrubby species are grown for their ornamental evergreen foliage and grow well in salty soils and in coastal areas. They should be planted in full sun and can be pruned in spring to remove any dead wood or to restrict size.

A. canescens. A bushy, mound-forming shrub to 5ft (1.5m) tall and more across, with gray-white leaves. The yellow flowers are borne in slender spikes in midsummer. Zone 7 US; 8 Can.

Aucuba

Of these three species of evergreen shrubs from East Asia, only one is commonly cultivated. Grown for its foliage and red berries, it is useful in shady positions and will grow in dry soil.

A. japonica. This dense, upright bush is ideal for making a bold splash in shady places. It can reach 6–10ft (1.8–3m) tall and bears tiny flowers in spring, which are followed on female plants by bright red berries. Many different forms are cultivated, varying in leaf shape and color. 'Crotonifolia' is female with leaves strikingly spotted with gold. f. *longifolia* is female with long, narrow leaves. 'Picturata' is female; the leaves have a central golden blotch but tend to revert to green. 'Rozannie' is compact and very free-fruiting. 'Serratifolia' has coarsely toothed leaves. Zone 7 US; 8 Can.

Azara

Of the 10 species in this genus of South American shrubs and trees, a few are grown in gardens. Their yellow flowers consist of masses of stamens and are effective against the green foliage. They prefer a position sheltered from cold winds. Little pruning is needed except to cut out any dead wood in spring.

A. lanceolata. An evergreen, bushy shrub to 10ft (3m) or more, with arching branches and slender, sharply toothed, glossy green leaves. The small clusters of fragrant, pale yellow flowers open along the shoots in summer. Zone 8 US; 9 Can.

Baccharis

Relatively few species of this genus of about 350 species of trees and shrubs, natives of North and South America, are grown in gardens.

B. halimifolia. The bush groundsel is a vigorous deciduous shrub reaching 13ft (4m) tall, with gray-green leaves. The small white flower heads are borne in large open clusters in the fall. A useful plant in coastal positions and for its late flowering. The ornamental display is created by clusters of silvery hairs that are attached to the tiny flowers, persisting as seed develops. Zone 5 US; 6 Can.

B. pilularis. Frequently used for ground cover, the coyote brush is a creeping evergreen growing to about 12in (30cm) tall and more across. It has small glossy green leaves and tiny white flowers in the fall and early winter. 'Centennial' is a hybrid making a mound 3ft (1m) tall and twice as much across, with very narrow leaves. Zone 8 US; not hardy Can.

Berberis

With about 500 species, all widely distributed, the barberries are a diverse genus of deciduous and evergreen spiny shrubs. The larger ones make splendid specimen plants, while others can be used for hedging or in the rock garden. Grown for their relatively small spring flowers, which range from yellow to orange-red, and their fruits, which can be red or blue-black, they are of easy cultivation in sun or partial shade.

B. calliantha. The species name of this evergreen shrub means "beautiful flowers", and the pale yellow flowers are lovely as well as being among the largest in the genus. It makes a compact shrub about 3ft (1m) tall with glossy green spiny leaves, white beneath, and bears blue-black fruits covered in a white bloom. Zone 7 US; 6 Can.

B. darwinii. One of the most popular evergreen barberries, this dense shrub can reach 10ft (3m) or more tall and has small, glossy green, hollylike leaves. The orange flowers open early in spring and are followed by blue-black berries. Zone 7 US and Can.

B. julianae. One of the hardiest evergreen barberries, this species makes a dense mass of upright shoots to 10ft (3m) tall, bearing glossy green leaves. Clusters of yellow flowers are followed by blue-black berries. Zone 5 US; 6 Can.

B. koreana. This vigorous deciduous species is of upright habit and can reach 8ft (2.5m) tall. It is extremely hardy and can be used for hedging in cold areas. The drooping clusters of yellow flowers are followed by long-persistent red berries. It is excellent for providing color in the fall, the particularly large leaves turning red-purple. Zone 3 US; 5 Can.

B. x mentorensis. Popular as a hedging plant this semievergreen shrub has a dense, rounded habit, reaching 5ft (1.5m) tall and across. The nearly spineless leaves persist long into winter, when they turn orange-red. It bears clusters of yellow flowers but fruits only occasionally. Zone 5 US; 6 Can.

B. x ottawensis. This vigorous deciduous shrub is best known in gardens in its purple-leaved form 'Superba' (syn. 'Purpurea'), which reaches 6ft (1.8m) or more tall and across. Zone 4 US; 5 Can.

B. x stenophylla. A popular evergreen making a mass of arching shoots to 10ft (3m) tall and more across, clothed in dark green, spine-tipped leaves. Yellow flowers are profusely borne, followed by blue-black berries. 'Corallina Compacta' is very dense, to 12in (30cm) tall, with flowers orange-red in bud. Zone 6 US and Can.

Aucuba japonica f. longifolia

Berberis verruculosa

B. thunbergii. A compact, mound-forming shrub to 6ft (1.8m) or more tall and across, with small leaves that turn bright red in the fall. The small flowers are pale yellow tinged red and are relatively inconspicuous but are followed by bright red berries. f. *atropurpurea* has deep purple foliage. 'Atropurpurea Nana' ('Crimson Pygmy', 'Little Favourite') is dwarf and compact, to 2ft (60cm) tall, with red-purple foliage. 'Aurea' has bright yellow foliage. 'Bagatelle' is similar to 'Atropurpurea Nana' but more compact, with deep purple foliage. 'Erecta' is a form with upright shoots. 'Golden Ring' has purple leaves edged with a narrow gold band. 'Helmond Pillar' is narrowly upright, with red-purple foliage. 'Kobold' is dwarf and compact, with freely produced berries but no fall color. 'Pink Queen' has red-purple leaves marbled with pink and white. 'Red Chief' has bright red shoots and narrow red-purple leaves. 'Rose Glow' is similar to 'Pink Queen' but not quite as effective. Zone 4 US and Can.

B. verruculosa. This attractive evergreen shrub makes a compact bush to about 5ft (1.5m) tall with arching, warty shoots. The small, glossy dark green leaves are blue-white beneath, and it bears yellow flowers followed by blue-black berries. Zone 5 US; 4 Can.

B. wilsoniae. The true plant of this name is a gem for the front of the border or a large rock garden. Unfortunately, it can often be raised from garden seed and the resulting hybrids are vigorous, larger plants. A dwarf deciduous shrub, it grows 3ft (1m) or less tall and more across with small, blue-green leaves turning orange and red in the fall. The yellow flowers are followed by profuse and showy coral-red berries. Zone 6 US; 7 Can.

Buddleja

Invaluable in gardens for their showy, usually summer flowers, the buddlejas make up a genus of some 100 species, widely distributed. Although they are easy to grow in a sunny position, forms of *B. davidii* can quickly become leggy and will benefit from hard pruning just before

Buddleja davidii 'Pink Delight'

growth commences in spring. The following species are deciduous unless otherwise stated.

B. alternifolia. This very distinctive species has slender, willowlike leaves and arching shoots. It will grow to 10ft (3m) or more tall, and with time it can be trained into a small tree that develops attractive peeling bark. The fragrant lilac-purple flowers are borne in dense clusters along the shoots in early summer. 'Argentea' is a form with particularly silver-gray foliage. Zone 4 US and Can.

B. davidii. The butterfly bush is the most popular of the buddlejas. Reaching 10ft (3m), it is well known for its dense, conical spikes of fragrant flowers, very attractive to butterflies, borne at the ends of the shoots over a long period during summer. Many forms have been selected with flowers ranging in color from white to pink, red, blue, and purple.

'Black Knight' has very deep purple flowers. 'Charming' bears pink flowers. 'Dartmoor' has magenta flowers. 'Empire Blue' has violet-blue flowers with an orange eye. 'Harlequin' offers red-purple flowers and leaves margined with creamy white. 'Nanho Blue' has narrow leaves and pale blue flowers. 'Nanho Purple', also known as 'Petite Plum', has narrow leaves and violet-blue flowers.

'Pink Delight' is a compact, upright hybrid, with gray-green leaves and dense panicles of bright pink flowers. 'Royal Red' bears large panicles of red-purple flowers. 'White Harlequin' has white flowers and

Buxus sempervirens

leaves margined with white. 'White Profusion' carries its pure white flowers in large panicles. Zone 5 US; 5b Can.

B. globosa. Sometimes known as the orange ball tree, this vigorous semi-evergreen shrub can reach a height of 10ft (3m) or more. The angled shoots bear glossy green leaves, and in summer compact heads of orange flowers appear. It is best not pruned. Zone 7 US; 8 Can.

B. 'Lochinch'. A beautiful shrub, it reaches about 7½ft (2.5m) tall and has gray-downy leaves, later dark green. The fragrant violet-blue flowers are borne in clusters in summer. Zone 7 US; 6 Can.

Buxus
Boxwood

Only a few of the 30 or so species in this genus of evergreen shrubs and trees, found in Europe, Asia, Africa, and Central America, are commonly cultivated. Boxes are of easy cultivation in sun or shade and respond very well to pruning.

B. microphylla. A dense, mound-forming shrub to about 3ft (1m) tall and across, with small, oblong, dark green leaves. It is excellent for formal gardens, the front of borders, and low edging. 'Compacta' is even more compact, to about 1ft (30cm) tall. var. *koreana* is much hardier, with an open, spreading habit. 'Wintergreen' is recommended for low hedges in cold areas. Zone 4 US; 5b Can.

B. sempervirens. The common boxwood makes a large shrub or small tree most frequently used for hedging or

Callicarpa bodinieri 'Profusion'

Callistemon citrinus 'Splendens'

Calluna vulgaris 'Wickwar Flame'

topiary. 'Argentea' has leaves margined with white. 'Aureovariegata' has leaves striped and blotched with yellow. 'Elegantissima' is very compact, with small leaves edged with white. 'Graham Blandy' is a narrow form with upright branches. 'Marginata' is vigorous and upright, with leaves edged with yellow. 'Suffruticosa', the edging box, is a dwarf shrub reaching about 3ft (1m) tall that is commonly used in formal gardens for a low edging. 'Vardar Valley' is low and wide spreading. Zone 5 US; 6 Can.

Callicarpa
Beautyberry
This genus of some 140 species of shrubs and trees contributes some hardy species grown particularly for their strikingly small, colored fruits, borne most prolifically in long hot summers and when planted in groups. The following are deciduous.

C. americana. The American beautyberry makes an open spreading shrub to 8ft (2.5m) tall, bearing small, pale pink flowers during summer. Clusters of pink fruits are borne along the shoots in fall. It is a beautiful shrub that needs hot summers to thrive. Zone 7 US; 8 Can.

C. bodinieri. An upright shrub reaching up to 8ft (2.5m) tall with hairy leaves turning purple in the fall. The small lilac-pink flowers are borne during summer, followed by small but very conspicuous lilac fruits. 'Profusion' is a selection that fruits freely and has purple young foliage. Zone 6 US; 5b Can.

C. japonica. A hardy, spreading species with long pointed leaves and pink flowers followed by violet berries. 'Leucocarpa' is a form with white flowers and berries. Zone 5 US; 7 Can.

Callistemon
Bottlebrush
This genus of about 25 species of evergreen Australasian shrubs derives its common name from the flowers, the showy part of which is the long, colored stamens. The flowers are borne in dense cylindrical clusters on the end of shoots, followed by the attractive young foliage. Bottlebrushes need a warm climate but are otherwise easy to grow and will take well to training against a sunny wall.

C. citrinus. A popular but rather tender species reaching 10ft (3m) or more tall and across. It bears willowlike, lemon-scented leaves and dense clusters of red flowers. 'Splendens' has bright crimson flowers with very long stamens. Zone 9 US; not hardy Can.

C. salignus. The willow bottlebrush, although a tree in its native habitat, is usually shrubby in cultivation, growing to 10ft (3m) or more, with leathery leaves, pink when young. The flowers are white, but some forms are grown with pink or red flowers. Zone 9 US; not hardy Can.

C. sieberi, syn. *C. pithyoides.* The alpine bottlebrush is of dense habit to 6ft (1.8m) or more, with narrow leaves, it bears small spikes of yellow flowers. Zone 9 US; not hardy Can.

Calluna
This genus of a single species from Europe and northern Asia, is represented in gardens by more than 500 cultivars. These vary in the color of their foliage and their flowers, which can be single or double, as well as in time of flowering and habit. Evergreen shrubs with slender shoots densely clothed in tiny leaves, they bear small but profuse flowers in racemes from summer to fall. Ideally planted in full sun in a humus-rich, acidic soil, they are excellent mass-planted and associate well with the heaths (*Erica*), dwarf conifers, and white-stemmed birches.

C. vulgaris. Common heather, Ling. Unless otherwise stated the following forms reach about 18in (45cm) tall. All except the dwarfest benefit from cutting back lightly either after flowering or in spring for those with colored winter foliage. 'Allegro' has deep red flowers. 'Anthony Davis' has white flowers and gray foliage. 'Beoley Gold' is vigorous, with yellow foliage and white flowers. 'County Wicklow' is dwarf and spreading, to 10in (25cm) tall, with double pink flowers. 'Darkness' is compact, to 12in (30cm), with purple-pink flowers. 'Elsie Purnell' has double silver-pink flowers and gray-green foliage. 'Firefly' has bronze foliage, orange-red in winter, and lilac flowers. 'Gold Haze' has bright yellow foliage and white flowers. 'J.H. Hamilton' is dwarf, to 8in (20cm), with double pink flowers. 'Joy Vanstone' has yellow foliage, orange in winter, and pink flowers.

'Kinlochruel' has double white flowers and bright green foliage. 'Peter Sparkes' has double pink flowers. 'Robert Chapman' has golden young foliage, turning orange and then red in winter, and soft purple flowers. 'Silver Queen' has silvery gray leaves and pale mauve flowers. 'Sir John Charrington' is vigorous, with yellow young foliage, turning red in winter and lilac-pink flowers. 'Spring Cream' is vigorous, with dark green foliage, contrasting cream young shoots, and white flowers. 'Sunset' has yellow, gold, and orange foliage, red in winter, and pink flowers. 'Tib' has long racemes of double rose-red flowers. 'Wickwar Flame' has golden foliage, deep red in winter, and mauve-pink flowers. Zone 4 US; 3 Can.

Calycanthus

Allspice

With four species growing wild in North American woodlands, the allspices give us some unusual summer-flowering shrubs for the garden. Grown for their quite distinctive, aromatically fragrant flowers with numerous petals, they like a sunny position in a good, not too dry soil and will flower over a long period.

C. floridus. The Carolina allspice is a deciduous shrub that can reach 8ft (2.5m) tall and more across, with aromatic, dark green, slightly rough leaves. The purple-red, spicily fragrant flowers, with numerous straplike petals, open during summer. 'Athens' has yellow flowers. Zone 4 US; 5 Can.

C. occidentalis. The California allspice is similar but more vigorous, to at least 13ft (4m), with more strongly aromatic leaves and larger, paler, but less fragrant flowers. Zone 7 US and Can.

Camellia

The popular, hardy camellias are derived from relatively few of the 200 or more species of this genus of evergreen trees and shrubs, which are native to East Asia. They are best in a well-drained slightly acidic soil, in sun or light shade. Those that flower early may be damaged by frost, especially if exposed to early morning sun. No pruning is usually needed except to remove any dead wood in spring. Size can be restricted by cutting back, hard if necessary, before young growth emerges in spring. They can be grown successfully in containers, which is extremely useful in areas with alkaline soil.

C. 'Cornish Snow'. This rounded bush about 6ft (1.8m) tall has arching shoots and glossy green leaves. The single flowers are profusely borne in early spring and are white tinged pink. Zone 7 US; 8 Can.

C. 'Inspiration'. A vigorous and upright hybrid to 13ft (4m) tall bearing large, semidouble, pink flowers very abundantly in early spring. Zone 7 US; 8 Can.

C. japonica. The most popular species in gardens has given rise to numerous forms differing in shape and color of their flowers. They are generally dense, rounded bushes 6–10ft (1.8–3m) or more tall, flowering in early to midspring.

'Adolphe Audusson' is vigorous and has semidouble, deep red flowers. 'Alba Plena' bears large double white flowers. 'Elegans' has double pink flowers, sometimes marked with white in the center. 'Guilio Nuccio' has coral-red, wavy-edged, semidouble flowers with a conspicuous golden center. 'Lady Vansittart' has semidouble white flowers, the petals often blotched with pink. 'Mrs. D.W. Davis' is semidouble and pale pink, nearly white, with golden stamens in the center. 'R.L. Wheeler' bears large, rose-pink, semidouble to nearly double flowers with twisted petals. 'Tricolor', also known as 'Sieboldii', is a compact form with semidouble cupped flowers strongly flushed and streaked with pink and red. Zone 7 US; 8 Can.

C. 'Leonard Messel'. This showy hybrid has large semidouble flowers with pink petals and golden anthers in the center. It is of spreading habit and about 10ft (3m) or more tall. Zone 7 US; 8 Can.

C. reticulata. A vigorous species that can attain 16ft (5m) or more tall. It is generally rather tender and suitable for areas that are frost-free or nearly so, but it is often grown as a greenhouse plant or as a specimen plant. Zone 8 US and Can.

C. sasanqua. The forms of this species will reach about 10–13ft (3–4m) tall and are very useful in gardens as their fragrant flowers open in the fall and can continue through winter. 'Crimson King' has deep red flowers with golden stamens.

C. hiemalis grows to 8ft (2.5m) tall, with fragrant white flowers in early spring. Zone 8 US and Can.

C. sinensis. The tea plant makes a dense bush in gardens to about 8ft (2.5m) or more tall, with bright glossy green, sharply toothed leaves. Small, nodding white flowers open late in the fall and early winter. Zone 8 US and Can.

Caragana

This genus of some 80 species of often spiny deciduous shrubs and trees contains some of the hardiest of all woody plants, native to eastern Europe and Asia. The attractively divided leaves have four or more leaflets, and the pealike flowers are

Calycanthus floridus

Camellia sasanqua **'Crimson King'**

normally yellow. Tolerant of harsh conditions, they are valuable in cold, dry situations. Pruning is not usually needed.

C. arborescens. The pea tree is more often a shrub than a tree, with upright shoots bearing leaves with 8–12 leaflets. The small yellow flowers open in late spring. 'Lorbergii' is an attractive and graceful form with leaves cut into very narrow leaflets and with smaller flowers. 'Pendula' has stiffly arching branches. Zone 2 US and Can.

C. frutex. Of upright habit, this species reaches 8ft (2.5m) or more and bears leaves with four leaflets. Bright yellow flowers open in late spring. 'Globosa' is a very compact dwarf form reaching about 2ft (60cm). Zone 2 US and Can.

C. pygmaea. This small shrub will reach only about 3ft (1m) tall and has long branches bearing leaves with four narrow spine-tipped leaflets. Small yellow flowers are borne along the shoots in late spring and early summer. Zone 2 US; 2b Can.

Carpenteria

This genus contains a single species, native to California, that is grown for its white fragrant flowers. It prefers a sunny

Carpenteria californica

position in a well-drained soil, and although not fully hardy in the open in many areas, it can also be grown against a sunny wall.

C. californica. Often known as the tree anemone, this upright evergreen shrub has glossy dark green leaves. In summer they provide the perfect foil for the white, fragrant flowers, which have a center of yellow stamens. It grows to about 6ft (1.8m) tall but can reach much more when grown on a sunny wall. Zone 8 US and Can.

Caryopteris

This genus of about six species of deciduous shrubs and perennials from East Asia is represented in gardens mainly by the hybrid described below. A valuable plant for the bloom time and color of its flowers, it is effective planted in groups in the front of a sunny border. It requires a well-drained soil in full sun. Cutting it back hard to the base in spring will both restrict its size and improve its flowering display.

C. x clandonensis. A deciduous shrub forming a dense mound to about 3ft (1m) tall, with aromatic, usually gray-green, lobed leaves. Clusters of small blue flowers are borne over a long period during late summer and early fall. 'Arthur Simmonds' has bright blue flowers. 'Blue Mist' has powder blue flowers. 'Dark Knight' has deep purple-blue flowers and silvery leaves. 'Kew Blue' bears deep blue flowers. 'Longwood Blue' has blue-violet flowers. 'Worcester Gold' offers yellow foliage. Zone 5 US; 6 Can.

Ceanothus

Commonly known as the California lilacs, the 50 or so species in this genus of evergreen and deciduous shrubs and trees, as well as their numerous hybrids, have given gardens a wealth of flowering shrubs. Native mainly to California, they range from prostrate to treelike. They are suitable for many garden situations, from a scree or bank to shrub borders or for training against a wall. All like a well-drained soil in sun. The evergreen

Caryopteris x *clandonensis* 'Kew Blue'

sorts do not respond well to hard pruning, while the deciduous ones can be cut back in spring.

C. americanus. The New Jersey tea, or redroot, is the hardiest species in the genus. It is deciduous and makes a small shrub about 3ft (1m) tall and a little more across. White flowers are produced in dense clusters during summer. Zone 4 US; 5b Can.

C. arboreus. Although not very hardy, this fast-growing evergreen shrub will quickly make a bold display. Reaching 20ft (6m) or more tall with dense branches and almost treelike proportions, it has large leaves and large clusters of blue flowers in spring. Zone 8 US; 9 Can.

C. dentatus. The cropleaf ceanothus makes a dense mound of spreading shoots to 5ft (1.5m) tall bearing small, glossy leaves. The clusters of bright blue flowers open in late spring. Zone 8 US; 9 Can.

C. gloriosus. Ideally sited on a rock garden or bank or where the branches can drape over a wall, this prostrate evergreen to 1ft (30cm) has hollylike leaves. The lavender-blue flowers open in dense clusters in late spring. *C. prostratus* is similar but with smaller leaves and darker blue flowers. Zone 8 US and Can.

C. griseus var. *horizontalis.* Known as the Carmel creeper, this evergreen shrub makes low, spreading mounds with glossy green leaves and clusters of blue flowers. 'Yankee Point' grows to 2ft (60cm) tall and is wide spreading, with profuse bright blue flowers. Zone 8 US; 9 Can.

Ceanothus arboreus 'Trewithen Blue'

Ceratostigma willmottianum

C. impressus. This very hardy evergreen shrub to 6ft (1.8m) tall is a parent of many hybrids and is distinct in its small, deeply veined leaves. The deep blue flowers are borne in small clusters in late spring. *C.* 'Puget Blue' reaching 10ft (3m) tall and across or more. The dark green leaves are deeply veined, and clusters of deep blue flowers are profusely borne over a long period in late spring. Zone 7 US; 8 Can.

C. thyrsiflorus. In its typical form, the blueblossom makes a large evergreen shrub, reaching 20ft (6m) or more tall. It has glossy green leaves and bears clusters of flowers in various shades of blue in late spring. More popular is var. *repens*, the creeping blueblossom, which is similar but makes a dense mound of arching shoots 3–5ft (1–1.5m) tall and more across. It is particularly hardy and makes an excellent ground cover. Zone 8 US and Can.

Chaenomeles x *superba* 'Pink Lady'

C. x *veitchianus.* This vigorous and hardy hybrid can grow to 10ft (3m) or more. It has glossy green leaves and bears clusters of blue flowers in late spring and early summer. Zone 8 US; 9 Can.

Of the other evergreen hybrids, 'Concha' is fast growing, to 10ft (3m), with glossy leaves and clusters of blue flowers in late spring. Zone 7 US; 8 Can.

Cephalanthus

Of the six species in this genus, natives of North and Central America, Africa, and Asia, only one is occasionally seen in gardens. Though easy to grow in any not-too-dry soil in full sun, it requires abundant summer heat to thrive.

C. occidentalis. The buttonbush is a deciduous shrub that can reach 6ft (1.8m) tall or more. The glossy green leaves emerge late in spring, and in late summer, or earlier given abundant heat, the dense, spherical heads of small fragrant white flowers appear. Zone 4 US and Can.

Ceratostigma

The cultivated members of this small genus of about eight species of deciduous and evergreen shrubs and perennials from East Asia and Africa are invaluable garden plants for their striking blue flowers borne late in the year. They thrive in a sunny position in a well-drained soil. In areas where they are cut to the ground in winter, they can be treated as perennials. Pruning consists of cutting any remaining shoots to the ground in spring.

C. griffithii. This attractive evergreen or semievergreen shrub can reach 3ft (1m) tall but is usually smaller. The dark green leaves are edged with purple and turn red during the fall. The blue flowers open in clusters during late summer and in the fall. Zone 8 US; not hardy Can.

C. willmottianum. Similar to *C. griffithii* but hardier, this has larger leaves and masses of blue flowers. Zone 6 US; 8 Can.

Cestrum

Suitable only for areas with little frost, the cultivated members of this genus of some 200 species of deciduous and evergreen shrubs from Central and South America have tubular to bell-shaped, often fragrant flowers. They should be grown in a good soil and a sunny position.

C. nocturnum. Known as the lady of the night or night jessamine, this evergreen shrub will reach 13ft (4m) or more and has long, narrow leaves. The greenish white flowers open during summer and in the fall and are fragrant at night. Zone 9 US; not hardy Can.

Chaenomeles

The flowering quinces are valued in gardens not only for their bright flowers borne early in the year but also for their hardiness and their ability to grow in tough situations. The aromatic fruits, usually yellow when ripe, are edible when cooked, similar to those of the common quince tree (*Cydonia oblonga*). With three species from mountain woodlands in East Asia, they are deciduous, spiny shrubs, generally growing to about 5–6ft (1.5–1.8m) or more tall, making excellent shrub border subjects, and are also suitable for training against a wall. Any pruning should be carried out immediately after flowering, when they can be cut back hard if necessary to restrict size.

C. japonica. Usually seen as a low, spreading bush about 3ft (1m) tall and more across, this species bears orange flowers in early spring, followed by yellow fruits. Zone 5 US and Can.

C. speciosa. This species is similar to *C. japonica* but is more vigorous, with larger leaves, flowers, and fruits. A number of selections have been made in various flower colors. 'Moorloosei' has beautiful white flowers delicately flushed with pink. Zone 4 US; 5b Can.

C. x superba. This group of hybrids generally combines the vigor of *C. speciosa* with the habit of *C. japonica*, making dense, spiny, usually spreading bushes with glossy ovate leaves. Many selections have been made for their flower color. 'Cameo' has double peach-pink flowers. 'Crimson & Gold' is very dense and wider than tall, with crimson flowers and contrasting golden stamens. 'Jet Trail' is low and spreading, with white flowers. 'Knap Hill Scarlet' has orange-red flowers. 'Pink Lady' is bushy and rounded and bears deep pink flowers. 'Texas Scarlet' has large scarlet flowers and few thorns. 'Toyo Nishiki' bears a mixture of pink, red, and white flowers. Zone 4 US; 5b Can.

Chimonanthus

The wintersweets are among the best loved of winter-flowering shrubs and, like many, have delightfully fragrant flowers. The following is the only one of six species, natives of China, that is commonly grown. It is easy to grow and flowers best in a sunny position. The wintersweet takes well to growing against a sunny wall, where its size can be controlled by cutting back after flowering.

C. praecox. Reaching 10ft (3m) or more tall without pruning, this deciduous shrub can, in winter, often be found by its scent alone. The small yellow flowers are purple inside and are deliciously fragrant, opening on the bare shoots in late winter to early spring. 'Grandiflorus' is a form with particularly large flowers, while 'Luteus' has pure yellow flowers with no purple markings. Zone 6 US; 7 Can.

Chionanthus

This genus of some 120 mainly tropical species is represented in temperate gardens by only two of them, of which the following is the best known. It is easy to grow and requires only adequate sun to flower well. In areas with cool summers it

may not flower well or at all; given regular hot summers it will make a small tree.

C. virginicus. The fringe tree is a deciduous shrub or sometimes a tree, reaching up to 16ft (5m) or more tall. The small fragrant white flowers are borne in large drooping clusters that contrast well with the bold, dark green leaves in early to midsummer. Zone 3 US; 5 Can.

Choisya

This genus of seven species of evergreen shrubs, from the southwestern United States and Mexico, is related to *Citrus* and,

Chimonanthus praecox

Choisya ternata 'Sundance'

like many other members of the same family, has aromatic foliage. They are cultivated for their flowers and foliage and make excellent shrub border plants. Being naturally compact in habit, they need little pruning, but if it is necessary to restrict size, they can be cut back lightly after flowering.

C. ternata. The Mexican orange blossom is a popular evergreen shrub with dark green, aromatic leaves. The white, fragrant flowers open in clusters in late spring and again in early fall. It can reach 5ft (1.5m) tall, if grown against a wall. 'Sundance' has yellow young foliage but is less free-flowering. Zone 7 US; 8 Can.

Cistus

Rock rose

With a mainly Mediterranean distribution, the 20 or so species of evergreen shrubs in this genus thrive in sunny positions. They prefer a rather poor, well-drained soil, tending to become too leggy on rich soils, and flower in early to midsummer. While the larger ones are suited to a border, the smaller sorts are excellent in a rock garden. They tend to be rather short-lived and should not be pruned.

C. albidus. A compact species normally up to 3ft (1m) tall, the leaves densely covered in white hairs. A profusion of lilac-pink flowers is borne in summer. Zone 8 US; 6b Can.

C. 'Elma'. One of a group of several similar hybrids, this vigorous shrub is compact and upright in habit, reaching

Cistus x purpureus

5ft (1.5m) tall or more. It has bright green. very sticky leaves and very large, pure white flowers. Zone 8 US; 7 Can.

C. x *hybridus.* Also known as *C.* x *corbariensis*, this rounded bush, 4ft (1.2m) tall, has dark green, hairy leaves with wavy edges, and profuse small white, yellow-blotched flowers with yellow centers and stamens open from the red-colored buds. Zone 7 US and Can.

C. ladanifer. Although not as hardy as some, this species is, in flower, among the most striking of all the rock roses. Of leggy, upright habit, it grows to 5ft (1.5m) or more tall and has dark green, sticky leaves. The large flowers have wavy-edged petals and can be pure white or have red blotches at the base. Zone 8 US; 7 Can.

C. laurifolius. One of the hardiest of all rock roses, this species makes a dense bush to 5ft (1.5m) tall or more and has dark gray-green, sticky leaves. The white flowers have a yellow center and are borne in clusters over a long period during summer. Zone 7 US; 6 Can.

C. 'Peggy Sammons'. A bushy, upright hybrid with gray-hairy leaves growing to 3ft (1m) tall. The large, soft pink flowers open in early summer. Zone 8 US; 7 Can.

C. x *purpureus.* Reaching 3ft (1m) tall, this rounded shrub has narrow dark green leaves. The richly colored flowers are among the deepest in color of all the rock roses and are purple-pink spotted with red. Zone 8 US; 7 Can.

C. salviifolius. A common sight in parts of the Mediterranean, this species has dark green, veined, sagelike leaves and reaches 2ft (60cm) tall. The small white flowers, which are borne over a long period, are blotched with yellow at the base of the petals. Zone 8 US; 7b Can.

C. x *skanbergii.* A very compact shrub only 2½ft (75cm) or so tall, with slender gray-green leaves and bearing a profusion of pale pink flowers. Zone 8 US; 7 Can.

Clerodendrum

The 400 or so species in this large genus are mainly tropical with few hardy members. The following is shrubby in warm areas but can be treated as a

Clerodendrum bungei

perennial when it is cut to the ground by frost in winter. It is a valuable border plant for its showy late flowers and needs little pruning apart from the removal of dead wood in spring.

C. bungei. In good conditions this upright semiwoody shrub can spread vigorously by suckers. The purple shoots, growing to 5ft (1.5m) in height, bear bold leaves and are topped in fall by heads of fragrant pink flowers. Zone 7 US; 8 Can.

Clethra

The cultivated members this genus of about 60 species of deciduous and evergreen trees and shrubs, from the Americas, East Asia, and Madeira, are valued for their small, fragrant flowers borne late in the year. Requiring a lime-free soil, they grow in sun or shade as long as the soil is not too dry. They need little pruning.

C. alnifolia. The summersweet is a deciduous shrub growing to 6ft (1.8m) tall or a little more, with dark green leaves that usually turn yellow in autumn. Very fragrant white flowers are borne in slender, upright clusters between midsummer and early fall. 'Hummingbird' is a compact, drought-tolerant form to 4ft (1.2m) with glossy foliage and profuse flowers. 'Pink Spires' has flowers pink in bud before they open to pale pink. 'Rosea' is similar. Zone 3 US; 5 Can.

C. barbinervis. Much more vigorous than *C. alnifolia*, this treelike species can grow to 16ft (5m) tall and has attractive

Clethra alnifolia 'Rosea'

Cleyera japonica 'Fortunei'

peeling bark on the older stems. It also differs in its larger leaves and flower clusters. Zone 5 US; 6 Can.

Cleyera

Related to the camellias, the 18 species in this genus of evergreen trees and shrubs are natives of Central America and East Asia. The only species that is commonly grown requires a not too dry, lime-free soil and will grow in sun or light shade.

C. japonica. This evergreen shrub has spreading to arching shoots and can reach 6ft (1.8m) or more but in cool areas is usually smaller. The glossy green leaves often turn bronze in cold weather, and small fragrant white flowers open along the shoots in summer. 'Fortunei', also known as *C. fortunei*, has dark green leaves edged with creamy white, pink when young. Zone 8 US; 9 Can.

Coleonema

The eight species in this genus of evergreen shrubs are natives of South Africa and are related to *Verbena*. Where winters are mild the following can be grown in a sunny shrub border. It requires an acid or neutral soil and should be trimmed lightly after flowering.

C. pulchrum. Growing to 4ft (1.2m), this evergreen species has narrow pale green leaves. Small, usually pink flowers are clustered at the ends of the shoots in late spring and summer. Zone 9 US; not hardy Can.

Colutea

Pealike flowers and inflated seedpods are the attraction of this genus, with about 25 species of deciduous shrubs native to southern Europe, North Africa, and the Himalaya. Of easy cultivation, they thrive in a sunny position and are useful for dry soils. No regular pruning is required.

C. arborescens. The bladder senna makes a treelike shrub growing to about 13ft (4m) tall. A profusion of yellow flowers during summer are followed by the curious bladders, which burst when squeezed. Zone 5 US and Can.

Comptonia

The single species in this genus, native to eastern North America, is worth growing for its unusual and attractive aromatic foliage. Given a lime-free soil that is reasonably moist, it is relatively easy to grow and is best in a sunny position. The only attention it may need is the removal of some suckers if they become invasive.

C. peregrina. The sweet fern is a deciduous shrub that grows to about 3ft (1m) tall and spreads by suckers. It is easy to recognize by its very distinctive, sharply cut, fernlike leaves, which have an aromatic scent when crushed. The tiny flowers are produced in catkins in spring and are relatively inconspicuous. Zone 2 US and Can.

Convolvulus

Most of the 200 or so species in this widely distributed genus are perennials, but it also contains the following compact shrub, which is a beautiful addition to the gardens where it can be grown. Given a Mediterranean climate, it is of easy cultivation, thriving in hot sun in a dry soil, and can easily be accommodated in a warm border or sunny rock garden.

C. cneorum. This dwarf evergreen shrub reaches only about 2½ft (75cm) tall and is of rounded habit, covered in narrow, silky, silvery gray leaves. The funnel-shaped flowers, borne over a long period during summer, are white flushed pink with a yellow center and contrast well with the foliage. Zone 8 US; 9 Can.

Coprosma

The 90 or so species of evergreen shrubs and trees in this genus are confined mainly to New Zealand. Although some coprosmas are occasionally grown for their berries, the flowers are insignificant, and the showiest are those grown for their foliage. They are ideal for a sunny border or for planting against a wall but will survive only in areas with little frost and will thrive in coastal positions.

C. repens. In its typical form a large shrub growing to 6ft (1.8m) or more, this rich green, glossy-leaved species is most popular for the variegated forms it has given rise to, which are lower growing. 'Marble Queen' has the leaves blotched with white, while 'Variegata' has leaves edged with creamy white. Zone 8 US; 9 Can.

Cornus
Dogwood

With about 50 species of deciduous and evergreen shrubs and trees, as well as some perennials, the dogwoods are a diverse and widely distributed genus with many uses in gardens. The shrubby sorts are particularly valuable for their foliage, with many variegated forms; their brightly-colored ornamental winter shoots; and their fruits. Of easy cultivation, *C. stolonifera* and *C. alba* and their forms are excellent in waterlogged soils and are frequently planted at the water's edge, where their colored winter

Coleonema pulchrum

Comptonia peregrina

Convolvulus cneorum

Cornus mas 'Aureoelegantissima'

Corylopsis pauciflora

Corylus avellana 'Contorta'

shoots are shown to advantage. These sorts are best cut back hard every few years in early spring.

C. alba. This thicket-forming species develops clusters of upright shoots reaching 8ft (2.5m) tall or more, striking in winter when they turn bright red. It bears flattened heads of small white flowers in summer, followed by small white berries flushed with blue. 'Aurea' has bright yellow foliage. 'Elegantissima' has the leaves broadly edged with creamy white. 'Kesselringii' has deep purple, almost black, stems in winter. 'Sibirica' has brilliant red winter stems. 'Spaethii' has broad yellow margins to the leaves. Zone 2 US and Can.

C. alternifolia. Large and treelike in its typical form, this species has given rise to one of the most beautiful of all variegated shrubs. 'Argentea' makes a dense bush to about 10ft (3m) with small leaves conspicuously margined with white. The heads of small white flowers open in summer but are barely noticeable amongst the foliage. Zone 3 US; 4 Can.

C. mas. The cornelian cherry is a vigorous deciduous shrub that can grow to 16ft (5m) tall and across and has dark green leaves that turn to orange, red, and purple in the fall. Its main attraction is the numerous small yellow flowers that are borne on the bare shoots before the leaves open in late winter. In areas with hot summers, these are followed by edible red fruits. 'Aurea' is a form with yellow young leaves that later turn to dark green.

The form 'Aureoelegantissima' is smaller, to 5ft (1.5m) tall, the leaves edged with yellow and pink. 'Golden Glory' flowers very profusely. 'Variegata' is compact, to 8ft (2.5m) tall, the leaves conspicuously margined with white. Zone 4 US and Can.

C. racemosa. This deciduous shrub is of strongly upright habit and can reach 10ft (3m) or more in height. As such it is useful as a specimen shrub or as a "dot plant" in a shrub border. The clusters of creamy white flowers open in summer and are followed by small white berries on red stalks. Zone 4 US; 2b Can.

C. stolonifera. This species, also called *C. sericea*, is very similar to *C. alba* but spreads by stolons. The shoots are normally red in winter. 'Cardinal' has particularly bright red winter shoots while in 'Flaviramea' they are bright yellow-green. 'Isanti' is a compact form with red shoots. 'Kelseyi', also known as 'Kelsey Dwarf', is compact, to 2½ft (75cm) tall, with yellow-green shoots tipped with red in winter. 'Silver and Gold' has the leaves edged with creamy white and yellow-green winter shoots. Zone 2 US and Can.

Corylopsis
Winter hazel

The bright flowers of this small genus of deciduous shrubs are one of the first heralds of spring, opening early in the year just after those of their relatives, the witch hazels *(Hamamelis)*. There are about seven species in eastern Asia. They are generally large shrubs of upright habit

and are ideally positioned in a shrub border or open woodland setting among other plants, in sun or light shade. Little pruning is necessary; any that is should be tackled just after flowering. The leaves will normally turn yellow in the fall.

C. glabrescens. A spreading deciduous shrub growing to 10ft (3m) tall and across or more, with dark green leaves, blue-green beneath. The tassels of fragrant pale yellow flowers open on the bare shoots in early spring. Zone 5 US; 7 Can.

C. pauciflora. The best species for the small garden, reaching only 6ft (1.8m) tall and often less. Clusters of fragrant yellow flowers are profusely borne in early spring. The small leaves are tinged pink when young. Zone 6 US; 7 Can.

C. sinensis. This vigorous species is upright in habit and can reach 13ft (4m) or more in height. The dark green leaves are silky beneath, and tassels of fragrant pale yellow flowers are borne in early spring. 'Spring Purple', also known as *C. willmottiae* 'Spring Purple', has plum-purple young leaves. Zone 6 US; 8 Can.

Corylus
Hazel

With 10 species of deciduous shrubs and trees, in North America, Europe, and Asia, the hazels are best known for their nuts and their early drooping catkins. The ornamental forms grown in gardens make large shrubs and are of easy cultivation. They respond well to hard pruning and can be cut back to restrict size in early spring. *C. avellana* 'Contorta' should be left unpruned, as it develops more character with age.

C. avellana. The European hazel is a large shrub, or a small tree, 16ft (5m) or more tall, with yellow catkins in early spring, followed by edible nuts. The ornamental forms cultivated include 'Aurea' with yellow leaves; 'Contorta' (Harry Lauder's walking stick), with conspicuously twisted shoots, and 'Heterophylla', which has deeply lobed and sharply toothed leaves. Zone 4 US; 5 Can.

C. maxima. Differing from *C. avellana* in its larger, midgreen leaves and larger fruits borne in a long husk, the vigorous, open filbert is cultivated in gardens mainly in the form 'Purpurea', which has deep purple leaves and purple-tinged catkins and fruits. Zone 4 US; 5 Can.

Cotinus

The deciduous shrubs in this small genus, natives of North America, Europe, and Asia, are valued for their foliage, which colors in the fall, and for their striking and long-persistent fruiting plumes. Easy to grow, these shrubs should be given plenty of space, preferably in full sun. Pruning is not essential, but they can be cut back, hard if necessary, in early spring to promote vigorous young growth.

C. coggygria, syn. *Rhus cotinus.* The smoke tree is usually a large shrub of rounded habit 10ft (3m) or more in height and across, with rounded or oval, green to blue-green leaves that turn orange to red in the fall. The small flowers are individually inconspicuous but develop into large fruiting plumes that can be pale brown to deep pink. 'Daydream' has green leaves and large pink fruiting plumes. 'Royal Purple' is similar but with deep purple leaves and deep pink fruiting heads. 'Velvet Cloak' retains its deep purple foliage color for a long time before turning red. Zone 4 US; 5 Can.

C. 'Flame'. This hybrid differs from *C. coggygria* in its more vigorous, upright habit to 20ft (6m) and its larger leaves, which color brilliant orange-red in the fall.

The fruiting heads are pink. 'Grace' is similar but with purple foliage, brilliant red in the fall. Zone 4 US; 5 Can.

Cotoneaster

Of the 200 or more species in this genus of deciduous and evergreen shrubs and trees, natives of Europe, North Africa, and Asia, many have proved themselves invaluable garden plants. Their diversity makes them suitable for many situations, with prostrate species useful for ground cover or rock gardens and others suitable for borders, hedging, growing against walls or as specimen plants. Prostrate species are also excellent for growing on a raised bed, where their branches can be allowed to drape to the ground. They prefer a well-drained soil in sun or partial shade and do not generally require pruning. All have small white- or pink-tinged flowers, usually in late spring to early summer, which are attractive to bees, and berries that range in color from orange and red (sometimes yellow) to nearly black.

C. acutifolius. The Peking cotoneaster is valued for its great hardiness. This fast-growing deciduous shrub grows to 10ft (3m) tall, with arching shoots bearing dark green leaves. The pink-flushed white flowers in late spring are followed by red, later black, berries. Zone 2 US and Can.

C. adpressus. This dense, prostrate deciduous shrub is ideal for ground cover or the rock garden, where it reaches about 8in (20cm) tall, much more across. The leaves turn to scarlet in the fall as the red berries ripen. Zone 4 US and Can.

C. apiculatus. The cranberry cotoneaster is a deciduous, spreading shrub reaching only about 3ft (90cm) tall and excellent for ground cover. The small, rounded, bright glossy green leaves turn

Cotinus coggygria

Cotoneaster franchetii

red in the fall, while pink flowers in late spring and early summer ripen to bright red berries. Zone 4 US and Can.

C. bullatus. A vigorous deciduous species that can grow 13–16ft (4–5m) tall, with arching shoots and deeply veined leaves turning orange-red in the fall. The particularly large red berries ripen early in the season. Zone 4 US; 5b Can.

C. congestus. This miniature evergreen creeper is ideal for a rock garden, where it will drape itself over rocks. Reaching only about 8in (20cm) tall, it is fairly slow growing. The deep green leaves are densely arranged, but fruits are not often borne profusely. Zone 5 US; 5b Can.

C. dammeri. This creeping evergreen is a valuable ground-cover plant. Although reaching no more than about 4in (10cm) in height, it can quickly cover an area several yards (meters) across. It grows well and often fruits more profusely when its shoots are allowed to hang over a wall. The berries are red. Zone 4 US and Can.

C. divaricatus. This fast-growing, dense, bushy deciduous shrub to 8ft (2.5m) makes a particularly good hedge or barrier in the garden. The small, glossy green leaves turn shades of orange and red in fall, when the egg-shaped, deep red berries ripen. Zone 4 US; 5 Can.

C. franchetii. This vigorous evergreen shrub can reach 10ft (3m) tall and has long, arching shoots bearing sage green, later dark green, leaves. It is particularly attractive when bearing its crops of bright orange berries. Zone 6 US; 6b Can.

C. 'Herbstfeuer'. Also known as *C.* 'Autumn Fire', this evergreen shrub varies in habit depending on how it is propagated. Normally low and wide-spreading, it is used as ground cover, although with age it can reach up to 5ft (1.5m) tall. Sometimes it is grafted onto a stem to make a miniature tree with weeping shoots, studded in the fall with orange-red berries. Zone 6 US; 5b Can.

C. horizontalis. This well-known deciduous species is frequently seen trained against a wall, where it can reach 8ft (2.5m) tall or more. As a freestanding shrub it is much smaller, only 3ft (1m) or

so. The spreading branches have a distinct herringbone arrangement, and the glossy leaves turn deep red late in the fall. The berries are bright red. Zone 4 US; 5 Can.

C. lacteus. Also known as *C. parneyi*, this popular evergreen has large, deeply veined leaves and makes a dense bush to 6ft (1.8m) or so tall with arching shoots. It bears broad heads of creamy white flowers in summer and profuse and long-persistent red berries. Zone 6 US; 8 Can.

C. nanshan. Similar to *C. adpressus*, this deciduous species, also called *C. adpressus* var. *praecox*, differs in its larger leaves and fruits. It is more vigorous, reaching 2ft (60cm) or more tall. Zone 3 US and Can.

C. salicifolius. This variable evergreen species has willowlike leaves with deeply impressed veins and bright red berries. It is most commonly seen today in the form of its hybrids and a few selected forms. 'Gnom' is a very compact, spreading form reaching only about 2ft (60cm) tall, good for ground cover. Zone 5 US; 5b Can.

C. simonsii. The distinctly upright habit of this semievergreen shrub makes it a popular choice for hedging. Reaching 10ft (3m) tall, it has glossy dark green leaves and orange-red fruits. Zone 6 US; 7 Can.

C. x suecicus. The evergreen shrubs in this group of hybrids are becoming increasingly popular, as they combine the low habit of *C. dammeri* with the fruiting qualities of *C. conspicuus*. They are all useful for ground cover. 'Coral Beauty' is very dense, with arching shoots to 3ft (1m) tall and glossy dark green leaves. It bears profuse orange-red fruits. 'Skogholm' is lower growing, has smaller leaves, but it does not fruit profusely. Zone 4 US and Can.

Cyrilla

The single variable species in this genus has a wide range of provenances from the southeastern United States to South America and is surprisingly hardy. Grown for its colorful fall foliage, it is an unusual feature in the border or for planting in damp conditions or near water. It requires a moist but well-drained, lime-free soil and is best in a sunny location.

Cotoneaster lacteus

Cyrilla racemiflora

C. racemiflora. The leatherwood is a deciduous to semievergreen or evergreen shrub 6–10ft (1.8–3m) or more tall, with glossy green leaves often turning orange and red late in the fall. The upright spikes of white flowers appear in summer or fall, depending on climate. Mature specimens may spread by suckers and have attractive brown bark. It is lower growing in cooler summers and less evergreen in colder winters. Zone 6 US; 7 Can.

Cytisus
Broom

With about 50 species of usually deciduous shrubs, natives of Europe, North Africa, and western Asia, this genus offers some showy, although not long-lived, flowering plants, well known for their pealike flowers, which are usually borne in late spring. They grow best in a well-drained, not too rich soil in full sun and are suitable for shrub borders or rock gardens, depending on their size. The following, though they lose their leaves in the fall, appear almost evergreen because of their green shoots.

C. x beanii. This deciduous dwarf, sprawling shrub with arching stems is ideal for the rock garden, reaching only about 18in (45cm) in height. In spring it produces large sprays of rich golden yellow flowers. Zone 5 US; 6 Can.

C. x kewensis. Like *C. x beanii*, this is another excellent shrub for the rock garden. It differs in its lower habit to 1ft (30cm) and creamy yellow flowers. Zone 6 US; 7 Can.

C. x praecox. The dense habit to 4ft (1.2m) and numerous upright, green shoots of these hybrids make them popular in gardens, either planted singly or massed for ground cover. The profusely borne flowers that stud the shoots vary in color from white to deep yellow. 'Allgold' has deep yellow flowers. 'Warminster' (Warminster broom) has pale yellow flowers. Zone 7 US; 6 Can.

C. scoparius. The common broom is a vigorous shrub with upright and later arching green shoots, which bear large golden yellow flowers. It can reach 6ft (1.8m) tall and is best on light, acidic soils. A number of cultivars and hybrids are common in gardens. Zone 5 US; 6 Can.

Daboecia

The two species in this genus are dwarf, evergreen, heathlike shrubs related to *Erica* and native to coastal cliffs and mountain heaths in western Europe. They produce showy pitcher-shaped flowers in a variety of colors over a long period during summer and fall. They require similar conditions, so should be given an acidic soil rich in organic matter in full sun, and are especially effective in groups or associated with *Erica* and *Calluna*. A light trimming in spring, before growth starts, will help to retain a compact habit.

D. cantabrica. Popularly known as Connemara or St. Dabeoc's heath, this species forms a mound only about 18–24in (45–60cm) tall and about twice

Cytisus x *praecox*

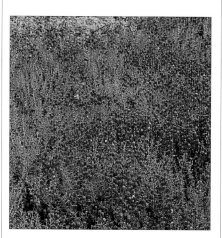

Daboecia cantabrica

Daphne bholua

as much across. The slender, upright shoots are thickly covered with small and narrow glossy dark green leaves. During summer and fall, clusters of purple-pink flowers open above the foliage. 'Alba' has white flowers, 'Praegerae' is low and spreading and bears rich pink flowers. Zone 6 US and Can.

Danae

This genus of a single species native to Southwest Asia is closely related to the butcher's brooms *(Ruscus)*, and as with them, the apparent leaves are really flattened stems. Easy to grow in many situations, it is suitable for sun or shade but perhaps most useful when its bright foliage, stems, and fruit are allowed to brighten a shady spot beneath a tree.

D. racemosa. The Alexandrian laurel is a graceful evergreen shrub with arching shoots making a clump about 3ft (1m) tall or more. The glossy green "leaves" are the main attraction, but it bears tiny green flowers in summer that are often followed by red berries. Zone 8 US; ?9 Can.

Daphne

The cultivated members of this genus of 50 or so species of deciduous and evergreen shrubs from Europe, North Africa, and Asia are among the elite of woody plants, and their often extremely fragrant flowers make them valuable garden plants. Many have a reputation of being difficult to grow, but given the right conditions they will thrive and give pleasure for many years. Most prefer sunny sites with a well-drained soil that is moist underneath. A rock garden provides good conditions, as the soil tends to remain cool and moist at root level. Some, such as *D. bholua*, *D. laureola*, and *D. odora*, will thrive in shady woodland conditions. Usually no pruning is required. The seeds of all species of *Daphne* are poisonous.

D. bholua. This popular, upright, deciduous or semievergreen, winter-flowering shrub reaches about 6ft (1.8m) tall. The very fragrant, purple-pink and white flowers are borne in late winter to early spring. Zone 8 US; 9 Can.

D. blagayana. This sprawling evergreen shrub reaches only about 12in (30cm) tall and is best when its shoots are allowed to root into the soil as they grow. Large clusters of fragrant creamy flowers open at the ends of the branches in spring. Zone 6 US; 7 Can.

D. x burkwoodii. Among the most popular and floriferous of the cultivated daphnes, this semievergreen hybrid is upright at first, later rounded, and reaches about 3–4ft (1–1.2m) tall. The small, very fragrant, pink and white flowers are borne in clusters at the ends of the shoots in late spring and often again in late summer and early fall. 'Carol Mackie' has leaves margined with golden yellow at first, later creamy white. 'Somerset' has profuse pale pink flowers. Zone 4 US; 5 Can.

D. caucasica. This hardy deciduous species makes a rounded bush about 3ft (1m) or a little more tall with narrow, rather light green leaves. The very fragrant flowers are white and open in clusters at the ends of the shoots in late spring and early summer. Zone 6 US and Can.

D. cneorum. The garland flower, or rose daphne, is a dwarf evergreen species to 8in (20cm) for the rock garden, where it makes a mound of trailing shoots. Over a long period during spring it is a mass of fragrant pink flowers. 'Eximia' has particularly large flowers. 'Ruby Glow' has pink flowers, while 'Variegata' has leaves margined with yellow. Zone 2 US; 2b Can.

D. laureola. Although suitable for most situations, the spurge laurel is perhaps most useful for growing in shady places. Growing to about 3ft (1m) tall, it has dark green leaves and pale green, only slightly fragrant flowers in early spring, followed by black berries. Zone 4 US; 8 Can.

D. mezereum. The very hardy mezereon is popular for its fragrant winter flowers. It is a deciduous shrub with upright shoots that bear purple-red, very fragrant flowers along their length in late winter, followed by red berries. Growing to only about 3½ft (1.1m) tall, it is useful in small gardens. Forms with white flowers are also sometimes grown. Zone 3 US; 5 Can.

D. x napolitana. This evergreen hybrid is best suited to a rock garden, where it can be long-lived. A compact bush that reaches only about 3ft (1m) in height, it is upright in habit at first, becoming more rounded, and has small, dark green leaves. Clusters of fragrant rose-pink flowers open over a long period during spring and early summer. Zone 8 US; 9 Can.

D. odora. Although not hardy in colder regions, this evergreen species can, if necessary, be given wall protection. A rounded bush to 5ft (1.5m) or more tall, it has glossy dark green leaves that

Dendromecon rigida

Deutzia gracilis

provide a foil for the fragrant and large pink and white flowers that open in late winter and early spring. It will grow in sun or shade and is among the best species for regions with hot summers. 'Alba' has creamy white flowers, while the very hardy 'Aureomarginata' has leaves edged with yellow. Zone 7 US; 6 Can.

D. tangutica. This evergreen species is easy to grow, being suitable for the shrub border or rock garden and growing in sun or light shade. It makes a rounded bush about 3ft (1m) or a little more and bears clusters of purple-pink and white, fragrant flowers in spring, usually flowering again in summer. Zone 6 US and Can.

Dendromecon
Tree poppy
The single species in this genus, native to California, will make an upright shrub but is most frequently grown against a wall. It prefers a light, well-drained soil in full sun. Train the shoots against a wall and cut out any dead wood in spring.

D. rigida. The upright shoots of this evergreen shrub can reach 13ft (4m) or more against a warm wall and bear blue-green leaves. In good conditions it produces four-petaled flowers like bright yellow poppies. Zone 8 US; 9 Can.

Desfontainia
The single species in this South American genus is an evergreen shrub with striking, unusual flowers. It is at its best in regions that have cool, moist summers and mild winters. With these conditions *Desfontainia* will grow in sun; in drier conditions it needs to be given a cooler position in shade. It needs a lime-free soil.

D. spinosa. This evergreen bush makes a dense mound 6ft (1.8m) or more tall, with green, spiny leaves. The flowers, which are bright red with a yellow mouth, are borne over a long period during summer and in the fall. Zone 8 US; 9 Can.

Deutzia
This genus of some 70 species of mainly deciduous shrubs, natives of East Asia, is related to the better-known mock

oranges (*Philadelphus*). They provide gardens with a range of flowering shrubs that are ideally suited to a mixed shrub border, where they can be combined with other plants to sustain interest. Generally of easy cultivation in any reasonably good soil, they prefer a sunny position. Pruning consists of cutting out some of the older shoots every few years after flowering. This will help promote young growth from the base of the plant and flowers the following year.

D. crenata 'Nikko'. A relatively recent selection that can be used for ground cover or on a rock garden, reaching only 2ft (60cm) or less tall and more across. The slender leaves turn red in the fall, while in late spring it is a mass of pure white flowers. It appears to thrive only given hot summers. Zone 5 US; 5b Can.

D. gracilis. This very hardy species tends to be slow growing but eventually can make a dense mound of upright branches to 5ft (1.5m) tall or more. The white flowers are borne profusely in late spring. It can come into growth very early and in some areas may be damaged by late-spring frosts. Zone 4 US; 5b Can.

D. x *hybrida*. A popular group of hybrids, originally raised by the French nurseryman Lemoine, that usually reach to about 5ft (1.5m) tall with arching branches. 'Magicien' has large flowers, white flushed pink inside, the petals conspicuously banded with deep crimson outside. It is also known as 'Strawberry Fields'. 'Mont Rose' has rose-pink flowers

with wavy-edged petals. 'Pink Pompon' bears large sprays of double, rosettelike, pink flowers. Zone 5 US; 5b Can.

D. longifolia. This elegant and attractive species to 6ft (1.8m) has long, slender leaves and develops peeling bark on the older shoots. The purple-pink flowers open in early to midsummer. Zone 6 US; 7 Can.

D. x *rosea*. This group of hybrids makes small shrubs with arching branches, to about 3ft (1m) tall, bearing clusters of small flowers in shades of pink in late spring and early summer. 'Carminea', the best-known form, has pink flowers, carmine-pink on the outside of the petals. Zone 6 US and Can.

D. scabra. A vigorous species with stout, upright shoots that arch with age, reaching 8ft (2.5m) tall or more. The small white flowers are borne in dense, conical clusters in early to midsummer. 'Codsall Pink' has double pink flowers. 'Plena', also known as 'Flore Pleno', has double white flowers flushed purple-pink outside. 'Pride of Rochester' has double pale pink flowers. Zone 5 US; 6 Can.

Diervilla

Bush honeysuckle

The three similar species in this genus of deciduous shrubs are natives of North America and spread by suckers, forming dense thickets. Although not spectacular in flower, they are useful in gardens for their attractive habit and extreme hardiness. They can be used in borders

or as ground cover. Easy to grow, they prefer a sunny site but will tolerate shade. Pruning is not essential, but old plants can be tidied or rejuvenated by cutting to the ground in spring.

D. sessilifolia. This thicket-forming shrub has arching shoots and dark green leaves and grows to 3ft (1m) tall and more across. Clusters of tubular, yellow flowers open during summer. Zone 4 US and Can.

Dipelta

It is unfortunate that at least some of the four Chinese species in this genus of deciduous shrubs are not more widely available. They are worth growing not only for their imposing habit but also for their showy, fragrant, bell-shaped or tubular flowers; fruit; and peeling bark. Their size makes them suitable not only for the shrub border but also as a specimen planting or amongst other plants in a woodland setting. Cultivation is easy in most soils, in sun or light shade, and pruning is generally unnecessary.

D. floribunda. Growing to 16ft (5m) or more in height, the stout trunk on this treelike shrub develops peeling bark with age. Clusters of large, fragrant pink flowers with a yellow throat open in late spring and are followed by conspicuously winged fruits. Zone 6 US; 7 Can.

Disanthus

This genus of a single species from the mountains and woodlands of East Asia is related to the witch hazels (*Hamamelis*),

Diervilla sessilifolia

Dipelta floribunda

Disanthus cercidifolius

Duranta erecta

Edgeworthia chrysantha

Elaeagnus x *ebbingei* 'Gilt Edge'

and like them, *D. cercidifolius* has excellent color in the fall. Unfortunately, this choice shrub is not particularly easy to grow, as it needs a moist, humus-rich, lime-free soil in a semishady position, preferably sheltered from strong winds.

D. cercidifolius. Certainly one of the most striking plants for fall color, this deciduous spreading shrub reaches about 8ft (2.5m) in height. The smooth, heart-shaped, blue-green leaves change through a range of glorious shades of orange-red and purple in the fall, when the small, purple, rather inconspicuous flowers open. Zone 6 US; 7 Can.

Dodonaea

With about 50–60 species of evergreen trees and shrubs, this genus is widely distributed mainly in tropical regions but particularly Australia. The following is valued mostly for its attractive foliage and fruits. It is useful for growing in hot, dry areas, where it can be planted as a specimen or a hedge, and will grow in sun or partial shade. Prune to restrict growth, or trim hedges in spring before growth starts.

D. viscosa. The hopbush is a fast-growing evergreen shrub reaching 13ft (4m) tall or more, with slender, willow-like, rather wavy-edged leaves. The insignificant flowers in late winter or early spring are followed by often red- or purple-tinged winged seedpods. 'Purpurea' has bronze-purple foliage and pods. Zone 9 US; not hardy Can.

Duranta

The 30 species of *Verbena* relatives in this genus of evergreen shrubs and trees are natives of tropical America. The species listed here is suitable for growing outside only where frosts are minimal. It needs a moist soil in full sun. Cut back long shoots in spring before growth starts.

D. erecta. Also known as *D. repens* and *D. plumieri*, the pigeon berry or sky flower is a fast-growing evergreen, sometimes spiny shrub reaching 16ft (5m) or more tall with long shoots. The blue to purple flowers are borne in spikes in summer, followed by yellow berries. 'Alba' has white flowers. Zone 9 US; not hardy Can.

Edgeworthia

The three species of deciduous or evergreen shrubs in this genus are native to East Asia. The following is an excellent addition to the range of winterflowering shrubs. It is best in a moist soil rich in organic matter in sun or semishade.

E. chrysantha. Reaching about 6ft (1.8m) tall, this deciduous shrub bears its slightly fragrant flowers in dense, nodding, spherical clusters in late winter at the ends of the bare shoots. Each flower has a silky white tube and a contrasting yellow mouth. Zone 8 US; 7 Can.

Elaeagnus
Fall olive

With about 40 species of mainly Asian deciduous and evergreen trees and shrubs, this genus provides gardens with

many plants that are not only highly ornamental but also very useful. The attractive foliage, whether silvery or variegated, makes them valuable for bold plantings. They are also useful for planting in dry soils and for providing shelter in exposed and coastal situations. They are mainly very vigorous and should be pruned as necessary to restrict growth. The variegated sorts often produce green or yellow shoots, which should be cut out when they are seen.

E. angustifolia. The oleaster or Russian olive is a spiny deciduous shrub, sometimes a tree, reaching 15ft (5m) or more in height. It is grown mainly for its slender, silvery leaves but produces small, silvery, fragrant flowers in late spring, followed by yellow berries covered in silvery scales. Zone 2 US; 2b Can.

E. commutata. The silver berry is a thicket-forming deciduous shrub to 6ft (1.8m) or more in height, with upright shoots, spreading vigorously by suckers. The leaves are silvery on both sides. Small, silvery-colored, fragrant flowers open in late spring, followed by silvery-colored berries. Zone 2 US and Can.

E. x *ebbingei.* This vigorous and dense evergreen makes a large bush to 10ft (3m) or more tall and is an excellent wind resister. The large leaves are silvery above at first, becoming dark green, silvery beneath. Small, very fragrant, silvery-white flowers open in the fall. 'Gilt Edge' has leaves edged with yellow. Zone 6 US; 8 Can.

E. macrophylla. A striking foliage shrub, this makes an evergreen mound 6ft (1.8m) or so tall and more across. The broad leaves are very silvery above when young, becoming glossy green, silvery beneath. Profuse, fragrant, small silvery flowers open in fall. Zone 8 US; 9 Can.

E. multiflora. This deciduous species makes a wide-spreading bush at least 8ft (2.5m) tall and across, with the leaves green above, silvery beneath. The fragrant, silvery flowers hang from the shoots during spring and are followed by edible, red berries in summer. Zone 5 US; 7 Can.

E. pungens. This vigorous, dense, spiny evergreen shrub reaches 13–16ft (4–5m) tall, with dark green leaves, dull white beneath. Small, silvery, fragrant flowers open in fall. 'Frederici' is slow growing, the pale yellow leaves narrowly edged with bright green. 'Fruitlandii' has a regular habit, with rather wavy-edged leaves, silvery beneath. 'Maculata' has leaves boldly blotched in the center with bright yellow. 'Variegata' has leaves narrowly edged with pale yellow. Zone 6 US; 8 Can.

E. umbellata. This fast-growing deciduous species is upright at first but spreads with age, reaching 13–16ft (4–5m) tall and across. It has wavy-edged leaves that are silvery above at first, later green, silvery beneath, and produces small, fragrant, silvery flowers in late spring, followed by red berries. 'Cardinal' is a very free-fruiting form recommended for poor soils. 'Titan' has an upright habit, 6ft (1.8m) across. Zone 4 US; 5 Can.

Eleutherococcus

Few of the 50 or so species of deciduous and evergreen shrubs and trees in this genus, natives of East Asia, are seen in gardens. The following, however, makes an elegant and quite hardy foliage plant. Thriving in even very poor soils, it is suitable for sun or shade and can be pruned as necessary to restrict its growth.

E. sieboldianus. Also known as *Acanthopanax sieboldianus*, this deciduous shrub has arching branches reaching 8ft (2.5m) and bearing green leaves normally

Elsholtzia stauntonii

divided into five leaflets. Spherical clusters of green flowers open in late spring. 'Variegatus' has leaflets edged with creamy white. Zone 4 US; 5 Can.

Elsholtzia

This genus of some 30 species of herbaceous plants and subshrubs from Europe, Asia, and Africa provides gardens with a valuable late-flowering shrub with aromatic foliage. It is fairly hardy and can be treated as a perennial in colder areas where the woody growths are cut to the ground by winter frosts. Grow in any well-drained soil in full sun.

E. stauntonii. A deciduous shrub, sometimes grown as an herbaceous perennial, this reaches about 5ft (1.5m) tall and has taper-pointed, mint-scented leaves. During fall it produces dense cylindrical clusters of small pinkish flowers. Zone 5 US; 6 Can.

Enkianthus

With about 10 species of deciduous and evergreen shrubs and trees native to scrub and woodland in East Asia, the cultivated members of this genus are ideally suited to an open position in a woodland garden. They require a lime-free soil with abundant organic matter to retain moisture and are best in sun or semishade. They are valued for their small, urn-shaped flowers and their rich fall color. Pruning is not normally required.

E. campanulatus. Reaching 10–13ft (3–4m) in height, this spreading deciduous

Enkianthus campanulatus

shrub has whorled branches and can develop a treelike habit. The yellow flowers with red veins hang in drooping clusters beneath the foliage in late spring, and in the fall the leaves turn to shades of yellow, orange, and red. The flowers are creamy white in f. *albiflorus*, while 'Red Bells' is upright in habit with flowers richly streaked with red. Zone 4 US; 5b Can.

E. cernuus f. *rubens.* Reaching about 6ft (1.8m) tall, this deciduous shrub bears clusters of deep red flowers with a finely fringed mouth. The fall color is deep reddish purple. Zone 5 US; 7 Can.

E. perulatus. This compact species is ideal for a small garden and will reach 5ft (1.5m) tall or a little more. The tiny white flowers open in midspring, and the leaves turn brilliant red in fall. Zone 5 US; 7 Can.

Erica
Heath

Most species in this large genus of more than 700 evergreen shrubs, sometimes trees, are tender and native to South Africa. The hardy members, primarily European, however, provide great diversity of flowering time and color as well as foliage color in gardens. While the large tree heaths, such as *E. terminalis*, can be planted as specimens, the smaller ones are best in groups. They are traditionally planted in a heather garden, where an effective variety of foliage and flower color can be provided throughout the year. Only *E. carnea*, *E. x darleyensis*, *E. erigena*, and *E. terminalis* will grow on alkaline soils. They are best in full sun. The dwarf species are best if trimmed lightly in spring.

E. arborea. Reaching 2m (6ft) or more tall, the tree heath is an excellent feature plant in the heather garden. The plume-like shoots are covered in small, fragrant white flowers in early spring. var. *alpina* is a particularly hardy form with bright green foliage. Zone 7 US; 8 Can.

E. carnea. Also sometimes known as *E. herbacea*, the winter heath is a dwarf species making a compact mound to about 10in (25cm) tall and is useful for ground cover. It is one of the best of all winter-flowering plants, its deep pink to red or white flowers densely clothing the shoots over a long period. 'Ann Sparkes' has golden foliage and deep pink flowers. 'Cecilia M. Beale' bears profuse pure white flowers. 'December Red' has dark green foliage and deep pink flowers. 'Foxhollow' has yellow foliage, bronze in winter, and pale pink flowers. 'King George' has rose-pink flowers. 'Loughrigg' bears purple-pink flowers. 'March Seedling' has rich rose-pink flowers and dark green foliage. 'Myretoun Ruby' has profuse, very deep pink flowers. 'Pink Spangles' is vigorous, with deep pink flowers. 'Praecox Rubra' is early flowering with deep pink flowers. 'Ruby Glow' has deep red flowers and dark green foliage, bronze in winter. 'Springwood Pink' has clear pink flowers and a spreading habit. 'Springwood White' bears profuse, pure white flowers. 'Vivellii' has deep carmine-pink flowers and dark green foliage, bronze in winter. Zone 4 US and Can.

E. cinerea. The bell heather is a species that bears its flowers in summer and early autumn. Reaching about 12in (30cm) tall, it has bright green foliage and bright purple flowers in clusters at the ends of the shoots. 'Alba Minor' is compact, with white flowers. 'C.D. Eason' has deep pink flowers. 'Cevennes' is upright, with lavender-pink flowers. 'Eden Valley' has lilac-pink flowers, white at the base. 'Golden Hue' has yellow foliage, red in winter, and pink flowers. 'P.S. Patrick' bears sprays of purple flowers. 'Pink Ice' is compact, with pale pink flowers. 'Velvet Knight' has dark green leaves and blackish purple flowers. Zone 5 US; 6 Can.

E. x darleyensis. Similar to *E. carnea*, this hybrid is more vigorous, usually reaching to about 2ft (60cm) tall. Like *E. carnea*, it is tolerant of alkaline soils and flowers over a long period during winter. 'Ada S. Collings' is compact and has dark green foliage and white flowers. 'Arthur Johnson' has long sprays of lilac-pink flowers. 'Darley Dale' bears pale pink flowers. 'Furzey' is compact, with deep pink flowers. 'George Rendall' has profuse deep pink flowers. 'Ghost Hills' has cream young foliage, becoming green, and has pink flowers. 'Jack H. Brummage' has yellow foliage, tinged red in winter, and deep pink flowers. 'Jenny Porter' bears pink flowers. 'Kramer's Rote' has bronze foliage and pink flowers. 'Silberschmelze' carries its profuse white flowers over a long period. Zone 4 US; 5 Can.

E. erigena. Also known as *E. mediterranea*, this shrub forms a dense, upright bush to 6ft (1.8m) or more tall, with dark green foliage. The fragrant, deep pink flowers are produced over a period between late winter and spring. 'Golden Lady' grows to 12in (30cm) and has yellow foliage and white flowers. 'Irish Dusk' is compact, to 18in (45cm), with dark green foliage and rose-pink flowers. 'W.T. Rackliff' is compact, to 4ft (1.2m), with white flowers. Zone 6 US; 7 Can.

E. x stuartii. This hybrid heath is best known in gardens for its forms with colored foliage. They are compact dwarf shrubs reaching about 8in (20cm) in height and flower between late spring and early summer. 'Irish Lemon' has lemon yellow young foliage and bright pink flowers. Zone 5 US; 7 Can.

E. terminalis. The Corsican heath is a tree heath of upright habit, growing to 6ft (1.8m) or more tall, and is among the hardiest of the taller species. The pink flowers are borne in clusters at the tips of the shoots during late summer. Zone 7 US; 8 Can.

E. tetralix. The cross-leaved heath is a dwarf spreading shrub, usually reaching to about 18in (45cm) tall, with gray-green foliage. The pink flowers are produced in clusters at the ends of the shoots during summer and autumn. 'Alba Mollis' has gray foliage and white flowers.

Erica carnea **'Myretoun Ruby'**

Erica carnea **'Springwood White'**

Escallonia 'Iveyi'

Euonymus alatus

'Con Underwood' is compact, to 10in (25cm), with purple-pink flowers. 'Hookstone Pink' has silvery gray foliage and pale pink flowers. 'L.E. Underwood' is compact, with silvery foliage and pink flowers. 'Pink Star' is low and spreading, to 6in (15cm) tall, with gray-green foliage and upright, deep pink flowers. Zone 4 US; 5 Can.

E. vagans. The Cornish or wandering heath is a vigorous species making a low, spreading mound about 2ft (60cm) tall, with densely arranged leaves and slender spikes of purple-pink flowers during summer and fall. 'Lyonesse' has white flowers with curious protruding brown anthers. 'Mrs. D.F. Maxwell' bears deep rose-pink flowers. 'Saint Keverne' has clear rose-pink flowers. 'Valerie Proudley' has bright yellow foliage and white flowers. Zone 4 US; 5 Can.

Escallonia

This genus of about 40 species consists mainly of evergreen shrubs (occasionally small trees) from South America. Found in the wild in woodland, in scrub, and on mountains, they are valued in gardens for their bold glossy leaves and their flowers, which are usually produced over a long period during summer and fall. Escallonias are at their best in areas with relatively mild winters and are ideal for coastal planting. Excellent in the border or when used for hedging, they can be pruned after flowering to restrict growth. They are easy to grow and prefer a sunny position.

The following are among the most popular of many hybrids and selections. In most situations they will reach between 5 and 6ft (1.5 and 1.8m). 'Apple Blossom' has pretty apple-blossom pink flowers. 'C.F. Ball' is vigorous, with deep crimson flowers. 'Gold Ellen' has red flowers and

leaves variegated with yellow. 'Iveyi' is vigorous and upright, with glossy dark green leaves, bronze in winter, and clusters of white flowers; it reaches 13ft (4m) in height. 'Red Elf' is vigorous, with crimson flowers. *E.* x *exoniensis* 'Frades' has carmine flowers. Zone 7 US; 8 Can.

E. rubra. This vigorous shrub grows to 10ft (3m) or more, with glossy dark green leaves and profuse deep red flowers. var. *macrantha* is the most popular form with large glossy leaves and is excellent for hedging. Zone 7 US; 8 Can.

Euonymus
Spindletree

Although most of the species in this genus of some 175 deciduous and evergreen shrubs, trees, and climbers have inconspicuous flowers, their diversity ensures that many are valuable garden plants. Not only do they provide us with some excellent shrubs for fall color and ornamental fruit, but some can be used for hedging or ground cover. They are easy to grow in any reasonable soil, the deciduous species preferring sun, while the evergreens will grow in sun or shade.

E. alatus. One of the most striking and reliable of all shrubs for fall color, this species can reach 10–13ft (3–4m) or more. 'Compactus' is a more compact form, reaching at least 6ft (1.8m) in height. Zone 4 US; 3 Can.

E. europaeus. The common spindle-tree can become a tree but is usually seen as a multistemmed shrub, reaching about 16ft (5m) tall. In the fall the scarlet fruits reveal orange seeds. 'Red Cascade' fruits profusely on arching shoots as the leaves turn scarlet in the fall. Zone 3 US; 4 Can.

E. fortunei. This creeping evergreen to 2ft (6cm) or more is used in many forms for ground cover, but will climb if planted near a tree or wall. Like ivies *(Hedera)*, the adult growth on which flowers and fruits are borne is bushy, and several forms have been propagated for this characteristic. 'Canadale Gold' has leaves margined with golden yellow. 'Coloratus' has dark green leaves, turning bronze-purple in winter. 'Emerald Gaiety' is bushy, with leaves margined with white, tinged pink in winter. 'Emerald 'n' Gold' with leaves margined golden yellow, tinged with pink in winter. 'Harlequin' has leaves speckled with white. 'Kewensis' has wiry shoots and tiny leaves. 'Minimus' is similar. 'Sarcoxie' is bushy, to 5ft (1.5m), with dark green leaves. 'Sheridan Gold' has young foliage flushed yellow, later turning green. 'Silver Queen' is bushy and upright, the leaves with a silver-white margin. 'Sunspot' is low and spreading, the dark green leaves with a central golden yellow blotch. Zone 4 US; 5 Can.

E. japonicus. In its typical form this species makes a rather somber, dark-leaved evergreen shrub reaching 13–16ft (4–5m) or more tall that will survive almost anywhere, from city centers to coastal positions, in sun or dense shade. It is now grown mainly as variegated forms. Small pinkish fruits open in the fall to reveal orange seeds. 'Aureus', also known as 'Aureopictus', reaches about 6ft (1.8m). The leaves have a golden central blotch, but the plant often reverts, producing green foliage. 'Microphyllus' is very compact and upright, with dark green leaves. Two forms similar to this are 'Microphyllus Albovariegatus', with white-margined leaves, and 'Microphyllus Pulchellus', which has young foliage flushed with yellow. 'Silver King' is upright, the leaves edged with white. Zone 7 US; 5b Can.

Euphorbia
Spurge

This very large and widely distributed genus contains some 2,000 species of annual and perennial herbs and shrubs, many of which are cactuslike succulents. The hardy species are valuable because they come into growth and flower early, remaining ornamental for a long period.. Once the flowers have faded, the stems should be cut down to ground level. They are easy to grow in any soil, *E. amygdaloides* preferring a shady spot, while *E. characias* and *E. mellifera* prefer full sun. Any contact with the rash-producing white sap of all types of *Euphorbia* should be avoided.

E. amygdaloides. More of an herbaceous perennial, this species spreads by suckers and is useful for a shady area, where it will grow to about 3ft (90cm) tall. The pale green flowers are attractive during spring and summer. 'Purpurea', also known as 'Rubra', has purple foliage and is best in sun. var. *robbiae* has rosettes of dark green leaves and is excellent ground cover. Zone 7 US; not hardy Can.

E. characias. This subshrubby species forms a dense clump to 5ft (1.5m) tall, with gray-green leaves and yellow-green flowers with purple centers during spring and summer. Subsp. *wulfenii* is similar, but the flowers have green centers. Zone 10 US; not hardy Can.

E. mellifera. This rather tender species makes an evergreen shrub to 6ft (1.8m) tall or more with bold foliage. The brown flowers that open in late spring are honey scented. Zone 10 US; not hardy Can.

Exochorda
Pearlbush

The five species found in this genus are deciduous shrubs, natives of Central and East Asia, grown for their masses of pure white flowers in late spring. Although most reach a large size, one in particular, *E.* x *macrantha* 'The Bride', has become popular for its small size. The following are easy to grow, but *E. racemosa* requires a lime-free soil. Little pruning is generally needed.

E. giraldii var. *wilsonii.* This vigorous shrub can reach at least 10ft (3m) in height and is of upright habit. The large white flowers are borne in profusion in late spring. Zone 6 US; 4 Can.

E. x *macrantha* 'The Bride'. This makes a dense mound of drooping shoots that arch to the ground. It reaches about 6ft (1.8m) tall, with white flowers during early spring. Zone 4 US; 5 Can.

E. racemosa. Similar to *E. giraldii* var. *wilsonii*, this species differs in its spreading habit and slightly smaller white flowers. Zone 4 US; 5 Can.

Euphorbia amygdaloides **var.** *robbiae*

Exochorda x *macrantha* **'The Bride'**

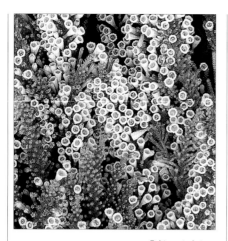

Fabiana imbricata

Fatsia japonica

Forsythia x *intermedia* 'Minigold'

Fabiana

Of the 25 species in this genus of evergreen shrubs from South America, only one is normally seen in gardens. Although easy to grow in most soils, it may require shelter at the limits of hardiness and can be grown with wall protection. It prefers a sunny position and does not normally need to be pruned.

F. imbricata. The tiny leaves densely clothing the upright shoots on this evergreen shrub give it a feathery appearance. Reaching 6½ft (2m) in height, it bears tubular white flowers in early summer. 'Prostrata' forms a spreading mound to 2½ft (75cm) in height and has mauve flowers; f. *violacea* resembles the typical form but has mauve flowers. Zone 9 US; not hardy Can.

Fallugia

The single species in this genus is a native of the southwestern United States. It thrives only in areas with hot dry summers and in cool areas needs the extra heat provided by a sunny wall.

F. paradoxa. The Apache plume is a spreading deciduous shrub, growing to 5ft (1.5m), with peeling bark and small dark green leaves deeply cut into narrow lobes. White flowers in summer are followed by feathery fruit clusters. Zone 6 US; 7 Can.

x Fatshedera

This remarkable evergreen is a hybrid between *Hedera* and *Fatsia japonica* and can be grown either as a freestanding shrub or as a climber against a wall or trellis. Easy to grow in sun or shade, once it is established it can be pruned in spring to restrict growth. The variegated forms are often grown as indoor or greenhouse plants.

x *F. lizei.* This sprawling evergreen shrub can make a loose mound to 5ft (1.5m) in height, more if trained against a wall. It has boldly lobed, dark green leaves and bears rounded clusters of small white flowers in fall. 'Annemieke' has leaves blotched in the center with yellowish green. 'Variegata' has leaves conspicuously edged with white. Zone 7 US; 8 Can.

Fatsia

The term "architectural plant" describes those species with extremely bold foliage, and the only species in this genus, from Japan, is certainly among the finest. It has large leaves that make a striking display in sun or shade. Where it is not hardy it can be grown as a greenhouse plant.

F. japonica. The large, deeply lobed, glossy dark green leaves on this stoutly branched evergreen shrub can reach 1ft (30cm) in width. Growing to 10ft (3m) in height, in fall it produces dense rounded clusters of small white flowers that develop into small black berries. 'Variegata' is slower-growing, with the leaf lobes narrowly edged with creamy white. Zone 7 US; 8 Can.

Forsythia

This small genus of some seven species of deciduous shrubs, from southeastern Europe and eastern Asia, contains some of the best-loved plants for early spring flowers. All have yellow flowers, each with four lobes, borne on the bare shoots before the leaves emerge. Growing and flowering best in a sunny position, they are ideal for the shrub border, for mass planting, or for training against a wall. To prune established plants, cut some of the old shoots to the base after flowering.

F. 'Arnold Dwarf'. This hybrid is grown mostly for its habit. Mass-planted, it makes an effective ground cover, reaching 3ft (1m) in height, with bright green foliage. The pale yellow flowers are not freely borne. Zone 4 US; 5 Can.

F. x intermedia. This hybrid includes some of the most popular of all forsythias. Generally a large shrub reaching up to 10ft (3m) in height, it has arching branches wreathed in late winter and early spring with yellow flowers. 'Beatrix Farrand' is upright, with large soft yellow flowers. 'Karl Sax' is spreading, with large deep yellow flowers. 'Lynwood' has profuse golden yellow flowers. 'Minigold' is compact, with upright shoots and numerous small deep yellow flowers.

'Spectabilis' makes a mass of bright yellow flowers. 'Spring Glory' grows to 6½ft (2m) in height and has sulphur yellow flowers. 'Tremonia' is compact, to 6½ft (2m) in height, with very sharply cut leaves and pale yellow flowers. Zone 5 US; 6 Can.

F. ovata. This species of forsythia is useful for its hardiness in colder regions. Growing to 5ft (1.5m) in height, it is compact and bears bright yellow flowers in early spring. 'Ottawa' is very hardy and flowers profusely. 'Tetragold' is more compact, with large deep yellow flowers borne very early. Other forms and hybrids of this species, selected for their hardiness, are *F.* 'Meadowlark' and *F.* 'Northern Sun'. Zone 4 US; 4b Can.

F. suspensa. The typical form of this species has long arching shoots, which makes it ideal for training against a wall, where the drooping branches will hang to the ground. In such a position it can grow to 16ft (5m) and bears its yellow flowers in early to midspring. Zone 4 US; 5 Can.

F. viridissima 'Bronxensis'. This dwarf forsythia makes a spreading twiggy bush only 1ft (30cm) in height and has small densely arranged leaves and pale yellow flowers in midspring. It is at its best in a warm sunny position. Zone 4 US; 5b Can.

Fothergilla
Witch alder

The two species in this genus of deciduous shrubs from the southeastern United States are ideal choices for those who wish to add something unusual and choice to their plantings. They are easy to grow, given a soil that is lime-free and not too dry, as well as a fairly sunny position. On heavy soils, some organic matter should be incorporated. No pruning is usually necessary.

F. gardenii. This small shrub grows to 3ft (1m) in height and has dark green leaves that turn brilliant shades of yellow, orange, and red in fall. The fragrant white flowers open in upright bottlebrush-like spikes before or as the young leaves emerge in spring. 'Blue Mist' has blue-green leaves on arching shoots.

'Mount Airy' is upright, with dark green foliage; it colors well in fall, and it also flowers profusely. Zone 5 US; 6 Can.

F. major. More vigorous than *F. gardenii*, this species reaches 8ft (2.5m) in height. The bold dark green leaves turn vivid shades of orange, red, and purple in fall. Zone 4 US; 5b Can.

Franklinia

Although originally found in the state of Georgia, this genus of a single species, related to the camellias, is now extinct in the wild. It requires hot summers to thrive and needs a lime-free soil in a sunny position.

F. alatamaha. The Franklin tree is a deciduous large shrub or sometimes a tree, reaching 20ft (6m) in height and more in width under ideal conditions. Fragrant white camellia-like flowers open in late summer. The bold glossy dark green leaves turn brilliant orange and red in fall. Zone 5 US; 6 Can.

Fremontodendron

Given a Mediterranean or California climate, the two species of evergreens in this genus from the southwestern United States and Mexico will make freestanding shrubs or even trees. Normally, however, they are seen trained against a wall, which not only protects them from wind and cold weather but also shows off their striking flowers to best advantage. Grow them in any not-too-rich, well-drained soil in full sun. They are fast-growing, and wall-trained plants often need to be thinned to restrict growth. Tie in long shoots and cut back as necessary in mid- to late summer, avoiding the irritant hairs that clothe all parts of the plant.

F. californicum. Grown against a sunny wall, this vigorous evergreen or semievergreen shrub will reach 20ft (6m). The dark green three-lobed leaves complement large golden yellow flowers over a long period during summer and fall. *F. mexicanum* is similar, with five-lobed leaves and flowers flushed with orange-red

Fothergilla major

Franklinia alatamaha

Fremontodendron 'California Glory'

Fuchsia magellanica **'Variegata'**

Fuchsia 'Tom Thumb'

Fuchsia 'Prosperity'

at the base. Vigorous hybrids between the two species, with large flowers, include *F.* 'California Glory' and *F.* 'Pacific Sunset'. Zone 8 US; 9 Can.

Fuchsia

The well-known fuchsias constitute a genus of some 100 species of shrubs, trees, and climbers and are natives mainly of Central and South America. Innumerable hybrids are grown for greenhouse and indoor decoration, while a smaller number can be grown permanently outside in regions where winters are not too harsh. They can often be treated like herbaceous perennials, for even when the top growth is cut to the ground by frost, they will regrow from the base the following year and will flower over a long period during late summer and fall. Easy to grow in any soil, they prefer a sunny position. The showy parts consist of the tube, sepals, and petals.

F. magellanica. The hardiest species of this deciduous shrub will, in areas where frosts are not too severe, develop a permanent woody stem and reach 6½ft (2m). The slender drooping flowers are red outside with a purple center. var. *molinae*, also known as 'Alba', has pale lilac, nearly white, flowers. 'Sharpitor' is a form of var. *molinae* with leaves margined white. 'Variegata' has leaves edged with creamy white. 'Versicolor', also known as 'Tricolor', has gray-green leaves flushed with pink when young. Zone 6 US; 7 Can.

Fuchsia hybrids. The following hybrids are normally treated like perennials in gardens. Cut back to the ground in spring before new growth commences. They are ideal planted in groups for permanent bedding and shrub borders or for growing in containers. They normally reach 3–5ft (1–1.5m) in height.

F. 'Brutus' has single red flowers with purple centers. 'Chillerton Beauty' has pink sepals and violet-purple petals. 'Corallina' has a low arching habit and bears flowers with bright red sepals and purple petals. 'Dollar Princess' has double flowers with red sepals and

purple petals. 'Garden News' is vigorous, the large double flowers with soft pink sepals and tube and magenta-pink petals. 'Genii' has bright yellow-green foliage and flowers with red sepals and violet petals. 'Lady Thumb' is dwarf and bushy, the semidouble flowers with light red sepals and white petals veined with red. 'Lena' has semidouble flowers, the sepals pale pink with green tips and the petals magenta-pink. 'Margaret' has semidouble flowers with scarlet sepals and violet-purple petals. 'Margaret Brown' is compact and bushy, the flowers with crimson sepals and magenta petals. 'Mrs. Popple' is vigorous and bushy, the large flowers with red sepals and violet petals. 'Phyllis' has semidouble flowers with rose-pink sepals and deeper pink petals. 'Prosperity' has large flowers with deep pink sepals and white petals strongly veined with pink. 'Riccartonii' is very hardy, with red sepals and violet petals; it is useful for hedging. 'Tennessee Waltz' has large double flowers with red sepals and violet petals. 'Tom Thumb' is dwarf, compact, and bushy, the single small flowers with red sepals and purple petals. 'Son of Thumb' resembles 'Tom Thumb' but has lilac petals. Zones 6–7 US; 7–8 Can.

Gardenia

There are some 250 species of evergreen trees and shrubs in this genus, widely distributed in the tropics of the Old World. Where they can be grown outside, they are often used as border shrubs close to buildings, where the fragrance of their flowers can be most appreciated. They need a moist lime-free soil that is rich in organic matter and will grow in sun or semishade. In many areas they are suitable only for the greenhouse, but given prolonged intense summer heat they will withstand considerable frosts.

G. augusta. Also known as *G. jasminoides*, the Cape jasmine makes a compact bush to 5ft (1.5m) in height with dark green leaves. The fragrant large white flowers

Gardenia augusta

Garrya elliptica 'James Roof'

Genista tinctoria 'Flore Pleno'

open over several months during late spring and summer. 'August Beauty' has double flowers borne well into fall. 'Mystery' has large double flowers. 'Radicans' is low and spreading, to 3ft (1m) in height, with small flowers. 'Radicans Variegata' is similar but has leaves margined with white. Zones 9–10 US; not hardy Can.

Garrya

Consisting of 13 species of evergreen shrubs and trees from the western United States and Mexico, this genus provides gardens with some interesting catkin-bearing plants. Male plants are generally more striking in flower and more commonly grown. Garryas are easy to grow in any well-drained soil and in cool areas require only shelter from winds. They grow well against a wall, either sunny or shady.

G. elliptica. The most commonly seen species makes a vigorous large shrub to 16ft (5m) in height with dark green wavy-edged leaves. Slender, pendulous, gray catkins drape the branches during late winter. 'James Roof' is a male selection with catkins that can reach up to 8in (20cm). Zone 7 US; 8 Can.

Gaultheria

This widely distributed genus of 200 species of evergreen shrubs now includes those formerly listed under *Pernettya*. The small urn-shaped flowers and fleshy fruits make the smaller forms charming additions to the shrub border, where they combine well with dwarf rhododendrons, while the larger and more vigorous species make effective ground cover. They need a light, moist, lime-free soil, rich in organic matter, in a semishady or shady position.

G. mucronata. Also known as *Pernettya mucronata*, this is the most popular species in the genus. It makes a thicket of upright shoots clothed with small glossy dark green leaves and will grow to 3–5ft (1–1.5m) in height. Tiny white flowers in late spring and early summer are followed by striking marblelike berries in various

shades. Fruiting is generally best if several forms are planted together. 'Bell's Seedling' is a reliable fruiting form with large deep red berries. 'Cherry Ripe' has large cherry red berries. 'Crimsonia' has large crimson berries. 'Parelmoer', also known as 'Mother of Pearl', has pale pink berries. 'Pink Pearl' has lilac-pink berries. 'Sneeuwwitje', also known as 'Snow White', has white berries spotted with red. 'White Pearl' has large white berries. 'Wintertime' has pure white berries. Zone 6 US; 7 Can.

G. procumbens. The checkerberry, or wintergreen, is an extremely hardy ground cover shrub and makes dense low mats of dark green aromatic leaves that turn red in winter. Growing to only 6in (15cm) in height, it spreads vigorously by underground stems and bears small pinkish flowers in summer, followed by bright red berries. Zone 3 US; 4 Can.

G. shallon. The salal, or shallon, is a vigorous thicket-forming shrub growing to 5ft (1.5m) in height and spreading by underground stems. The red stems bear leathery leaves. Clusters of pinkish flowers in summer are followed by small deep purple berries. Zone 5 US; 6 Can.

G. x wisleyensis. Also known as x *Gaulnettya wisleyensis*, this thicket-forming shrub reaches 4ft (1.2m) in height and spreads by underground stems. 'Pink Pixie' has pale pink flowers in summer and deep purple-red berries. 'Wisley Pearl' has white flowers and oxblood red berries. Zone 5 US; 6 Can.

Genista
Broom

With 80 species of deciduous shrubs in Europe, North Africa, and western Asia, this genus is related to *Cytisus*. The leaves are often inconspicuous or fall early, but most have an evergreen appearance owing to their green shoots. The flowers are pealike and in all the species described here are yellow. Genistas are easy to grow in a well-drained, not-too-rich soil in a sunny position. The smaller forms do best in a rock garden.

G. hispanica. The Spanish gorse makes a dense dark green mound of prickly shoots, 2ft (60cm) in height and width, and is among the best of all small flowering shrubs. Clusters of golden yellow flowers completely smother the bush in late spring. Zone 7 US; 8 Can.

G. lydia. Distinctive for its slender arching blue-green shoots and dwarf habit, this broom, 2ft (60cm) in height, is excellent for massing at the front of a border or for a rock garden. The plant is covered in masses of small golden yellow flowers in late spring and early summer. Zone 4 US; 4b Can.

G. pilosa. This dwarf spreading species forms a dense thicket only 1½ft (45cm) in height and provides ideal ground cover in a rock garden or on a dry bank. Its narrow leaves are silky-haired beneath. In late spring it erupts into a mass of golden yellow flowers. 'Goldilocks', 'Lemon Spreader', and 'Vancouver Gold' all flower profusely. Zone 4 US; 5 Can.

G. sagittalis. This shrub of unusual appearance for a rock garden or a dry wall has creeping stems, edged with broad green wings, that send up leafy flowering shoots to 6in (15cm) in height. The golden yellow flowers open in clusters in early summer. Zone 4 US; 5 Can.

G. tinctoria. The dyer's greenweed is a variable species. Reaching up to 3ft (1m) in height, it bears clusters of golden yellow flowers at the ends of the shoots during summer. 'Flore Pleno' is a dwarf form with double flowers, suitable for a rock garden. 'Royal Gold' reaches 3ft (1m) in height and has profuse golden yellow flowers. Zone 3 US and Can.

Grevillea

Of the 250 or so species of mainly Australasian evergreen shrubs and trees in this genus, many are suitable only for growing as greenhouse plants in all but frost-free areas. There are a number, however, that will withstand a good deal of frost. Their principal attraction is the clusters of tubular flowers, which split as they open. Grow grevilleas in a lime-free soil in full sun, giving wind protection in cool areas. No pruning is generally required. All species zones 9–10 US; not hardy Can.

G. banksii. Growing to 13ft (4m) in height, this species has large leaves cut into long slender lobes. It bears its clusters of red flowers in summer.

G. 'Canberra Gem'. This particularly hardy hybrid makes a rounded shrub to 6½ft (2m) in height with slender dark green leaves. The clusters of deep pink flowers open over a long period during late winter, spring, and summer.

G. juniperina f. *sulphurea.* Also known as *G. sulphurea,* this evergreen shrub will grow to 6½ft (2m) in height and bears densely arranged, bright green, needlelike leaves. The contrasting bright yellow flowers open in dense clusters during late spring and summer.

G. rosmarinifolia. Slender dark green leaves give this shrub the appearance of rosemary (*Rosmarinus officinalis*) when not in flower. Growing to 5ft (1.5m), it bears clusters of deep red flowers over a long period during spring and summer.

Griselinia

The best-known species in this genus of six evergreen shrubs and trees from New Zealand and South America is often used for hedging. Although the flowers are inconspicuous, the distinctive leaves make it an attractive evergreen. It thrives in mild, particularly coastal, areas, where it will take considerable exposure. It is easy to grow in any soil in sun or partial shade and can be pruned as necessary.

G. littoralis. Making a densely leafy shrub to 16ft (5m) in height, this evergreen can, in areas that are virtually frost-free, become a large tree. The attractive broad leathery leaves are a distinctive pale green. 'Dixon's Cream' is slow-growing and has leaves blotched in the center with creamy white. 'Variegata' has leaves edged with creamy white. Zone 9 US; not hardy Can.

x *Halimiocistus*

The plants in this genus of rock roses are evergreen shrubs, hybrids between *Cistus* and *Halimium.* Cultivation is as for *Cistus.* They generally make a spreading mound 1½ft (45cm) in height and more in width.

x *H.* 'Ingwersenii' and x *H. sahucii* have dark green leaves and white flowers. x *H. wintonensis* has gray-green leaves and white flowers, marked at the base of the petals with deep maroon. 'Merrist Wood Cream' has creamy yellow flowers with a maroon base. Zone 9 US; not hardy Can.

Halimium

The seven species in this largely Mediterranean genus of evergreen shrubs are closely related to *Cistus* and *Helianthemum.* They prefer a well-drained, not-too-rich soil in full sun and are suitable for a rock garden or a dry border. Useful for coastal gardens.

Griselinia littoralis **'Dixon's Cream'**

x *Halimiocistus* **'Ingwersenii'**

H. lasianthum. Making a spreading mound to 3ft (1m) in height, this is an evergreen, gray-leaved shrub. The golden yellow flowers, sometimes blotched maroon at the base, open in early summer. Zone 9 US; not hardy Can.

H. ocymoides. Upright in habit, this shrub grows to 2ft (60cm), with golden flowers blotched black and purple at the base. 'Susan' is a compact hybrid to 18in (45cm) with bright yellow, purple-centered flowers. Zone 9 US; not hardy Can.

Hamamelis
Witch hazel
With only five species of deciduous shrubs from North America and eastern Asia, this genus provides some of the best winter-flowering plants. The fragrant flowers, which vary from yellow through orange and red, have four strap-shaped petals and, with the exception of *H. virginiana,* open on the bare shoots during winter. Witch hazels prefer a slightly acid and not-too-dry soil in sun or partial shade and should not be pruned.

H. x intermedia. These popular hybrids are generally large shrubs reaching 16ft (5m) in height, usually with yellow fall color. 'Arnold Promise' is vigorous and wide-spreading, with yellow flowers. 'Diana' has red flowers and orange to red and purple fall color. 'Jelena' has orange flowers and orange, red, and purple fall color. 'Pallida' has sulphur yellow flowers. 'Ruby Glow' has bronze-red flowers and red to purple fall color. 'Vesna' has orange-yellow flowers. Zone 5 US; 6b Can.

H. japonica. The Japanese witch hazel, reaching 10ft (3m) in height, is similar to *H. x intermedia* but usually has smaller flowers and more-crinkled petals. The flowers are only slightly fragrant and the fall color is yellow. 'Zuccariniana' has small pale yellow flowers opening in late winter or early spring. Zone 5 US; 6 Can.

H. mollis. The most fragrant of the witch hazels, reaching 10ft (3m) in height, the Chinese witch hazel has large deep yellow flowers. Fall color is yellow. Zone 5 US; 6 Can.

Hamamelis x intermedia 'Jelena'

H. vernalis. This species is hardier than *H. japonica, H. mollis,* or *H. x intermedia.* Variable in habit, it can reach 16ft (5m) in height and has golden yellow fall color. The small fragrant flowers can be yellow or red and open over a long period during winter. 'Sandra' has young leaves flushed with purple, turning orange, red, and purple in fall. Zone 4 US; 5b Can.

H. virginiana. The common witch hazel is a large shrub reaching 16ft (5m) in height. It is distinct from other species in producing its fragrant yellow flowers in fall, as the leaves turn golden yellow. Zone 4 US; 4b Can.

Hebe
Often known as the shrubby veronicas, this genus contains some 100 species of evergreen shrubs and trees, mainly from New Zealand. Showing great diversity in habit, they can be used in rock gardens and borders or for ground cover or hedging. While the main attraction is their flowers, ranging from white to pink, purple, and blue, many have ornamental colored or variegated foliage. Hebes prefer a sunny site in a well-drained soil and thrive in coastal regions. To prune, cut out any dead wood in spring or restrict growth by cutting back lightly after flowering.
Rock-garden and ground-cover hebes
H. albicans. Making a low spreading mound some 2ft (60cm) in height, this species has densely arranged gray-green

Hebe hulkeana

leaves and produces spikes of white flowers during summer. Forms or hybrids of this species include 'Pewter Dome', which is lower-growing and domed, and 'Sussex Carpet', which reaches only 1ft (30cm) and is good for ground cover. Zone 9 US; not hardy Can.

H. 'Baby Marie'. A dwarf hybrid with a rounded habit, this species reaches about 1ft (30cm) in height. It has tiny bright green leaves and bears small spikes of pale lilac flowers in late spring. Zone 9? US; not hardy Can.

H. chathamica. This mat-forming species makes an excellent ground cover in a sunny site. Reaching only 6in (15cm) in height, in early summer it bears short dense spikes of pale violet flowers that fade to white. Zone 9 US; not hardy Can.

H. 'County Park'. This ground cover plant is of low spreading habit and grows to 1ft (30cm) in height, more in width. It has gray-green leaves edged with red and violet flowers that open in short spikes during summer. Zone 8? US; 9? Can.

H. cupressoides. One of a group known as the whipcord hebes, this distinctive evergreen plant grows to 5ft (1.5m) in height and has upright shoots clothed in tiny blue-green leaves. Tiny lilac flowers open at the tips of the shoots during summer. 'Boughton Dome' is a form with a dense rounded habit and dark green foliage. Zone 6 US; 7 Can.

H. 'Margret'. This compact dwarf has small, densely arranged, bright green leaves and grows to 1½ft (45cm) in height.

Hebe 'Midsummer Beauty'

Hebe albicans 'Pewter Dome'

Hebe pimeleoides 'Quicksilver'

Spikes of sky blue flowers that fade to white, open over a long period during late spring and summer. Zone 6 US; 7 Can.

H. ochracea. This whipcord hebe has foliage similar to that of *H. cupressoides* but of a bronzy gold color. An elegant species, it reaches 4ft (1.2m) in height and assumes a windswept appearance with age. Tiny white flowers open at the top of the bush during late summer. 'James Stirling' is a dwarf form only 1ft (30cm) in height. Zone 6 US; 7 Can.

H. pimeleoides. This low-growing species is variable in habit, from sprawling to upright, and generally reaches no more than 1ft (30cm) in height. The most commonly seen form, 'Glaucocaerulea', has dark upright shoots to 1½ft (45cm) in height and blue-green leaves edged red. The short spikes of violet-blue flowers open in summer. 'Quicksilver' is wide spreading, with tiny silvery gray leaves and pale lilac flowers. Zone 7 US; 8 Can.

H. pinguifolia. The best-known form of this species, 'Pagei', is among the best for ground cover. A dwarf spreading shrub reaching only 6in (15cm) in height but more in width, it has small gray-blue leaves and bears short spikes of white flowers in late spring. 'Sutherlandii' makes a dome-shaped bush 2ft (60cm) in height. Zone 6 US; 7 Can.

H. 'Red Edge'. Also known as *H. albicans* 'Red Edge', this dwarf shrub makes a dense mound of upright shoots 1ft (30cm) in height. The gray-blue leaves have a distinct, narrow red margin,

particularly in winter, and short spikes of lilac flowers, fading to white, open in summer. Zone 9 US; not hardy Can.

H. vernicosa. This very ornamental species makes a dense bun-shaped bush up to 1½ft (45cm) in height and has densely arranged, thick, glossy, and very dark green leaves. White or lilac-tinted flowers are borne in short spikes in late spring. Zone 7 US; 8 Can.

H. 'Wingletye'. A dwarf for a rock garden, this species makes a spreading mound of small blue-gray leaves to 6in (15cm) in height. Spikes of deep mauve flowers open on short upright shoots in early summer. Zone 8? US; 9? Can.

H. 'Youngii'. Also known as *H.* 'Carl Teschner', this popular dwarf is ideal for ground cover or a rock garden. Of sprawling habit and reaching 8in (20cm) in height, it has dark shoots and small leaves. The short spikes of violet flowers open during summer. Zone 5 US; 6b Can.

Border and hedging hebes

H. 'Amy'. Reaching up to 4ft (1.2m), this upright shrub has dark green leaves, which are bronze-purple when young. The violet-purple flowers are carried in dense spikes during summer. Zone 7 US; 8 Can.

H. 'Autumn Glory'. This popular shrub reaches 2½ft (75cm) in height and has a spreading habit. The dark green leaves have a red margin, and spikes of deep violet flowers are borne over a long period during late summer and fall. Zone 7 US; 8 Can.

H. 'Bowles' Hybrid'. This small shrub makes a rounded bush to 2ft (60cm) in height and has narrow glossy leaves. It is very attractive during spring and summer, when it is covered in slender spikes of mauve flowers. Zone 7 US; 8 Can.

H. x franciscana 'Blue Gem'. This spreading shrub is popular in coastal areas, where it is often used for bedding or for hedges. Reaching 4ft (1.2m) in height and more in width, it has glossy dark green leaves and dense spikes of relatively large, bright violet-blue flowers over a long period during summer and fall. 'Variegata' has leaves edged with creamy white. Zone 7 US; 8 Can.

H. glaucophylla 'Variegata'. A popular variegated hebe with slender gray-green leaves edged with cream. It makes a rounded bush to 3ft (1m) in height and produces pale lilac flowers in small spikes during summer. Zone 7 US; 8 Can.

H. 'Great Orme'. This attractive hybrid makes an open rounded bush about 4ft (1.2m) in height with glossy green leaves. Long spikes of bright pink flowers, fading to white, open over a long period during late summer and fall. Zone 8? US; 9? Can.

H. hulkeana. A distinctive and very beautiful species that makes a loose open bush with upright shoots to 2ft (60cm) in height. The glossy dark green leaves have toothed red margins, and the tiny lilac flowers are carried in large open clusters during early summer. It is best if deadheaded after flowering. Zone 9 US; not hardy Can.

H. 'La Séduisante'. This shrub is one of several attractive but rather tender hybrids. Reaching 4ft (1.2m) in height, it has bold glossy green leaves flushed purple beneath. The long showy spikes of violet-purple flowers are borne during summer and fall. Zone 7 US; 8 Can.

H. macrantha. A distinctive species making a rounded bush to 2ft (60cm) in height, with small, leathery, bluntly toothed leaves. The large, pure white flowers open in clusters in late spring and early summer. Zone 6 US; 7 Can.

H. 'Marjorie'. Popular because of its comparative hardiness, this small shrub reaches 3–4ft (1–1.2m) in height and is of compact rounded habit. The mauve-blue flowers, which fade to white, are borne in short dense spikes in summer. Zone 5? US; 6? Can.

H. 'Midsummer Beauty'. This hybrid is a very popular, vigorous, and hardy hebe. Growing to 5ft (1.5m) in height, it has dark green leaves, purple beneath when young. Lilac-purple flowers, fading to white, are borne in long spikes during summer and fall. Zone 7? US; 8? Can.

H. 'Mrs. Winder'. This dense rounded bush grows to 3ft (1m) in height and is popular for its dark green leaves that turn bronze-purple in winter. Violet-blue flowers appear in dense spikes in late summer. Zone 7? US; 8? Can.

H. rakaiensis. Among the hardiest hebes, this plant's compact habit, glossy foliage, and profuse flowering make it popular for bedding, borders, and low hedges. Growing to 3ft (1m) in height, it bears masses of white flowers in spikes during late spring and early summer. Zone 6 US; 7 Can.

H. salicifolia. Long narrow willowlike leaves give this shrub an elegant appearance. Reaching 5ft (1.5m) in height, it bears long slender spikes of white flowers in summer. Zone 7 US; 8 Can.

H. 'Simon Delaux'. Reaching 4ft (1.2m) in height, this beautiful but tender hybrid resembles *H. 'La Séduisante'* but with longer spikes of crimson flowers during summer and fall. Zone 7 US; 8 Can.

H. topiaria. This increasingly popular hebe has a dense rounded habit and grows to 3ft (1m) in height. White flowers are borne in very short spikes in summer. Zone 7 US; 8 Can.

Helianthemum
Rock rose

With 100 or more species of widely distributed, mainly evergreen shrubs, these delightful dwarf plants are excellent for adding color to a rock garden. A wide range of colors is available, with both single and double flowers, and many also have attractive gray foliage. They need a sunny site in a well-drained soil and ideally should be trimmed lightly after flowering to keep them compact. The following are among the most popular and will normally grow to 1ft (30cm) in height. All of the following varieties are hardy to Zone 5 US, 6 Canada.

'Amy Baring' is single and deep yellow with an orange center, has gray-green foliage, and is compact and low-growing. 'Beech Park Red' is large, with single scarlet flowers and gray foliage. 'Ben Fhada' is large, single, deep yellow with an orange center, and vigorous. 'Ben Hope' is a single carmine red with an orange center and gray foliage. 'Ben Ledi' is a large scarlet single with a deeper center and green foliage. 'Boughton Double Primrose' is a double pale yellow with dark green foliage. 'Cerise Queen' is a double deep pink with an orange-yellow center and green foliage. 'Georgeham' is large, with single pink blooms and dark green foliage. 'Henfield Brilliant' is large, single, orange-red with gray foliage, and vigorous. 'Jubilee' is a double pale yellow with dark green foliage. 'Mrs. C. W. Earle' is a double scarlet with a yellow base and dark green foliage. 'Mrs. Clay', also known as 'Fire Dragon', is a bright orange-red single, with gray foliage. 'Praecox' is a single, yellow with gray foliage. 'Raspberry Ripple' is a single pink with white-tipped petals and gray foliage. 'Rhodanthe Carneum', also known as 'Wisley Pink', is a large single pink with an orange center and gray foliage. 'Salmon Queen' is a single pink with an orange-yellow base and green foliage. 'The Bride' is a single, white with a yellow center and gray foliage. 'Wisley Primrose' is large, yellow with a deeper center, and has gray foliage. 'Wisley White' is large, white with a yellow center, and has gray foliage.

Helichrysum

Best known for annuals that produce "everlasting flowers," this genus contains some 500 species of annual and perennial herbs and shrubs, mainly from South Africa and Australia. The following are ideal for a dry or gray garden. They are easy to grow in a well-drained soil in full sun.

H. italicum. This evergreen shrub has upright shoots clothed in silvery gray, aromatic leaves and grows to 2ft (60cm)

Helianthemum 'Ben Ledi'   *Helichrysum italicum*

in height. Small yellow flower heads are borne in clusters during summer and fall. Ssp. *serotinum*, the curry plant, has aromatic foliage. Zone 8 US; 9 Can.

H. splendidum. One of the best plants for gray foliage, this upright evergreen shrub will reach 4ft (1.2m) and has small, silver-gray, woolly leaves. Small heads of yellow flowers open in summer and fall. Zone 9 US; not hardy Can.

Heptacodium

The single species in this genus is a native of China. A relative of the honeysuckles (*Lonicera*), it is of relatively recent introduction to cultivation and deserves to be more widely grown. Proving quite hardy, it is of easy cultivation in any well-drained soil in sun or light shade.

H. miconioides. Known as the seven son flower of Zhejiang, this upright deciduous shrub, also known as *H. jasminoides*, reaches 16ft (5m) in height and has bold leaves and pale gray-brown peeling bark. The small white fragrant flowers open in late summer and early fall, followed by red fruits if the weather is warm and sunny. Zone 4 US; 5 Can.

Hibiscus

The 200 or so species of evergreen and deciduous perennials, shrubs, and trees in this genus are confined largely to tropical and subtropical regions. However, the most commonly grown hardy species, *H. syriacus,* provides temperate gardens with some of the most striking of all fall-flowering shrubs. *H. rosa-sinensis* needs a Mediterranean or California climate to do it justice but is commonly grown as an indoor or greenhouse plant. These are ideal border plants needing a well-drained soil in full sun.

H. rosa-sinensis. This well-known but tender species is a rounded evergreen shrub to 10ft (3m) in height with dark green leaves. The showy red flowers are borne throughout the summer. There are many cultivars with flowers varying from single to double and

in color from white and pink to orange and red, as well as those with variegated leaves. Zone 10 US; not hardy Can.

H. syriacus. A hardy deciduous shrub, this has upright shoots growing to 10ft (3m) in height. Large showy flowers open over a long period during late summer and fall. 'Aphrodite' has deep pink flowers with a red eye. 'Ardens' has double violet flowers. 'Blue Bird', also known as 'Oiseau Bleu', has blue flowers with a red center. 'Diana' has white flowers with wavy-edged petals. 'Hamabo' has pale pink flowers with a red center. 'Minerva' has lavender-pink flowers with a red eye. 'Pink Giant' has deep pink flowers with a red center. 'Red Heart' has white flowers with a red center. 'Woodbridge' has pink flowers with a red center. Zone 5 US; 6 Can.

Hippophae

The three species in this genus of deciduous shrubs and trees are widely distributed in Europe and Asia. The following species is sometimes a tree but is often shrubby. It is an excellent choice for mass planting on a bank, with berries that often persist through winter. Male and female flowers occur on separate plants, and both need to be grown to obtain fruit. It will grow in most soils but prefers one that is moist and sandy.

H. rhamnoides. The sea buckthorn is a dense deciduous shrub, reaching 20ft (6m) in height, that will form thickets by suckering. The spiny shoots bear gray-green leaves, and on female plants insignificant flowers in early spring are followed by bright orange berries. 'Sprite' is a compact and upright male, good for hedging. Zone 3 US; 2b Can.

Holodiscus

The eight species of shrubs in this genus, natives of western North America to northern South America, are related to *Spiraea*. The following species is easy to grow and thrives in a sunny border or woodland clearing. Prune after flowering by cutting back some of the older shoots.

Hibiscus syriacus **'Blue Bird'**

Hippophae rhamnoides

Holodiscus discolor

H. discolor. Known in its native California as the ocean spray, this upright deciduous shrub reaches 10ft (3m) in height and has arching shoots. The nodding clusters of small white flowers open from the ends of the shoots in summer. Zone 6 US; 7 Can.

Hydrangea

With 23 species of deciduous and evergreen shrubs and climbers from the Americas and eastern Asia, few other groups of shrubs can match the hydrangeas for their floral effect. Although individual flowers are small, they are borne in large heads. Lacecaps have flattened flower heads with a ring of larger sterile flowers at the margin, while mopheads have dense rounded heads consisting mainly of sterile flowers. They are easy to grow in any good, not-too-dry-soil in sun or partial

Hydrangea involucrata 'Hortensis'

Hydrangea paniculata 'Unique'

shade. *H. arborescens*, *H. macrophylla*, and *H. paniculata* can be cut back, hard if necessary, in spring. The following are all deciduous.

H. arborescens. This fast-growing shrub makes a rounded bush 5ft (1.5m) in height, sometimes spreading by suckers. The broad lacecap heads of white flowers open during late summer and early fall. 'Annabelle' has large white mopheads. 'Grandiflora' is similar but has smaller flower heads. Zone 3 US; 3b Can.

H. aspera. Ideally suited to woodland conditions, this upright species reaches 10ft (3m) in height. The dark green leaves are rough to the touch, and broad lacecap heads of small blue flowers are edged with showy, white to pink or purple, sterile flowers. subsp. *sargentiana* has stout, very bristly shoots and large flower heads with white sterile flowers. Zone 5 US; 6 Can.

H. heteromalla. This variable species grows into a large, upright, sometimes treelike shrub to 13ft (4m) in height with large dark green leaves. The broad white lacecap heads appear in summer, the marginal flowers often turning pink as they age. Zone 6 US; 7 Can.

H. involucrata. This charming species, which grows to 3ft (1m) in height, is suitable for the smaller garden and enjoys a semishaded site. The lacecap heads of small blue flowers are edged with white or pale blue sterile flowers and open during late summer and fall. 'Hortensis' is a beautiful form with double pale pink and white sterile flowers. Zone 7 US; 8 Can.

H. macrophylla. This popular species reaches 6½ft (2m) in good conditions and has glossy green, fleshy leaves. It is grown in a great variety of colors, both lacecaps and mopheads (*see below*), and prefers a moist soil in a sunny site. White forms are always white but blue flowers become pink on alkaline soils. Zone 5 US; 6 Can.

Lacecaps

'Geoffrey Chadbund' is deep red to purple-blue. 'Lanarth White' is pure white. 'Mariesii' is pale blue to white or pale pink. 'Quadricolor' has leaves edged with cream and yellow, and pale lilac to pale pink flowers. 'Veitchii' has very large sterile flowers, white at first, turning red. 'White Wave' has white sterile flowers, becoming flushed green. Zone 5 US; 6 Can.

Mopheads (Hortensias)

'Altona' is deep red to purple-blue, turning brick red in fall. 'Ayesha', also known as 'Silver Slipper', has unusual small cupped flowers that can be pink to white or blue. 'Générale Vicomtesse de Vibraye' has large dense heads of rich blue or pink. 'Hamburg' is deep pink to dark blue. 'King George' is rich pink to deep blue, with large sterile flowers. 'Madame Emile Mouillère' has dense pure white heads that turn greenish or pink in fall. 'Nigra' has dark, nearly black shoots and small heads of lilac-pink to pale blue flowers. 'Nikko Blue' has large heads of rich blue to pink. 'Pia' is a dwarf, to 1ft (30cm) in height, with small deep pink flower heads. Zone 5 US; 6 Can.

H. paniculata. This vigorous and extremely hardy species can grow to a large size, sometimes 16ft (5m). Its large conical flower clusters open white in late summer and turn pink in some forms during fall, and it varies in the proportion of sterile flowers that each cluster bears. 'Grandiflora', known as the peegee hydrangea, bears large heads of mainly sterile flowers that turn pink in fall. 'Kyushu' is upright, with glossy leaves and heads with few sterile flowers. 'Pink Diamond' is vigorous, the heads having mixed fertile and sterile flowers that turn deep pink. 'Praecox' has small heads with few sterile flowers that open in early summer. 'Tardiva' is vigorous and flowers late, in early to midfall; it has mixed fertile and sterile flowers that become tinged with pink. 'Unique' has large heads of mainly sterile flowers that turn deep pink. Zone 3 US; 3b Can.

H. quercifolia. The oakleaf hydrangea is distinct from other common species in its deeply lobed leaves, which turn orange, red, and purple in fall. Making a spreading mound to 6½ft (2m) in height, the conical heads of both fertile and sterile white flowers open in late summer to early fall.

It likes a sunny site and a moist soil. 'Snowflake' has double sterile flowers that turn pink with age. 'Snow Queen' has dense heads of mainly sterile flowers that turn pink in fall. Zone 4 US; 5b Can.

H. serrata. This species is closely related to *H. macrophylla* but is more graceful, with smaller leaves and slenderer shoots. It grows to 5ft (1.5m) in height. The lacecap or mophead flower heads open in mid- to late summer and fall, their color often depending on the acidity or alkalinity of the soil. 'Bluebird' has lacecap heads with pale blue or pale pink sterile flowers that turn white, then deep pink. 'Grayswood' has lacecap heads with white sterile flowers that turn bright red. 'Preziosa' has mophead flower heads with cream flowers that turn to pink, red, or violet. 'Rosalba' has lacecap heads with few white sterile flowers that become spotted with pink and turn deep pink. Zone 5 US; 6 Can.

Hypericum

The plants in this widely distributed genus of some 400 species are herbaceous perennials, shrubs, or even trees and have almost exclusively yellow flowers. Many of the shrubby species will flower in the border in summer and fall, while others are effective as ground cover or in a rock garden. Most prefer a sunny or lightly shaded site in a reasonably good soil, but *H. androsaemum* and *H. calycinum* thrive in shade. They can be cut back hard in spring to restrict growth.

H. androsaemum. The tutsan is a sparsely branched deciduous shrub reaching 3ft (1m) in height with broad leaves. Small yellow flowers open in clusters during summer and early fall, followed by red, then black spherical berries. Zone 6 US; 7 Can.

H. calycinum. This is popular as an evergreen ground-cover plant for sun or shade and forms a dense leafy mound 1½ft (45cm) in height that spreads by underground stems. Very large yellow flowers are produced during summer. Zone 4 US; 5b Can.

Hydrangea serrata 'Preziosa'

Hypericum forrestii

Hypericum x *moserianum* 'Tricolor'

H. forrestii. This deciduous or semievergreen species is a bushy shrub reaching 5ft (1.5m) in height or less, with dark green leaves that turn orange and red in fall. Yellow flowers in summer are followed by fruits that are flushed red when young. Zone 5 US; 6 Can.

H. frondosum. This beautiful deciduous species grows to 3ft (1m) in height and has blue-green leaves and peeling bark on the larger branches. The yellow flowers, with a central boss of stamens, open in summer. 'Sunburst' is more compact and bears large flowers. Zone 5 US; 6 Can.

H. 'Hidcote'. Combining a dense rounded habit with handsome foliage and large flowers, this is a deservedly popular evergreen hybrid. Reaching 5ft (1.5m) in height, it has large golden yellow flowers that open over a long period during summer and fall. Zone 5 US; 6 Can.

H. x inodorum. Like *H. androsaemum*, this hybrid is one of the hypericums that bear berries. An upright deciduous shrub reaching 5ft (1.5m), often with aromatic foliage, during summer it has small yellow flowers that are followed by egg-shaped berries in shades of red or pink. 'Elstead' is a striking form with bright salmon-pink fruits. Zone 6 US; 7 Can.

H. kouytchense. This semievergreen shrub makes a rounded bush 4ft (1.2m) in height. During summer the golden flowers are followed by long tapered fruits that are conspicuously flushed red when young. Zone 5 US; 6 Can.

H. x moserianum. A small, more or less evergreen shrub reaching 2ft (60cm) in height, effective when mass-planted. Golden yellow flowers with red anthers are borne during late summer and fall. 'Tricolor' has leaves edged with creamy white and pink. Zone 4 US; 5b Can.

H. olympicum. This clump-forming dwarf deciduous shrub, reaching 1ft (30cm) in height, is ideal for a rock garden and typically sends up tufts of upright shoots covered in small blue-green leaves. Large yellow flowers are borne in clusters during summer. 'Citrinum' has pale yellow flowers. 'Sulphureum' has very large pale yellow flowers. Zone 4 US; 5b Can.

H. prolificum. Similar to *H. frondosum* in its peeling bark, this deciduous species grows to 4ft (1.2m) in height and has dark green leaves. The yellow flowers, each with a conspicuous boss of stamens, open during summer. Zone 3 US; 4 Can.

H. 'Rowallane'. This semievergreen hybrid, best suited to milder gardens, can reach 6½ft (2m) in height and has dark green foliage. The large cup-shaped flowers are rich yellow and open in summer and early fall. Zone 6 US; 7 Can.

Ilex

Holly

This genus comprises 400 widely distributed species of deciduous and evergreen trees and shrubs, and various forms are well known in gardens. The shrubby hollies not only provide ornamental fruit, but their often attractive foliage and habit make them useful for borders and hedges or as garden specimens. Several forms of *Ilex* x *altaclerensis* and *I.* x *aquifolium,* such as 'Golden King', are also cultivated. *Ilex* are easy to grow in any reasonably fertile soil in sun or partial shade. Both male and female plants are needed to produce fruit.

I. cornuta. The Chinese, or horned, holly is an evergreen shrub or small tree, with dark green leaves. Reaching 10ft (3m) in height, it bears red berries. 'Burfordii' is a female form that fruits freely, with leaves that are normally spined only at the tip. 'D'Or' is like 'Burfordii' but has yellow fruits. 'Dwarf Burford' is a compact female form, less than 6½ft (2m) in height. 'O'Spring' is a female form with gray-green leaves margined with cream. 'Rotunda' is female, but not free-fruiting, and makes a dense mound 3ft (1m) in height with spiny leaves. Zone 7 US; 8 Can.

I. crenata. The Japanese holly is a variable evergreen species, either a shrub or a small tree, reaching 10ft (3m) in height, and grows well in sun or shade. Female plants bear small black berries. 'Compacta' makes a dense rounded mound 6½ft (2m) in height. 'Convexa' is

Ilex x *meserveae* 'Blue Angel'

Ilex cornuta 'Burfordii'

Ilex 'Sparkleberry'

a female form, wide-spreading, to 6½ft (2m) in height, with blackish green convex leaves. 'Golden Gem' has yellow-flushed foliage and is best in sun. 'Green Lustre' is spreading, 5ft (1.5m) in height, with glossy green foliage. 'Helleri' is a dwarf female form making a compact mound 4ft (1.2m) in height with small leaves. 'Hetzii' is a female form similar to 'Convexa' but with larger leaves. 'Mariesii' is a narrow upright female form with tiny rounded leaves. 'Shiro-fukurin' has leaves margined with creamy white. Zone 6 US; 7 Can.

I. glabra. The inkberry is a spreading evergreen shrub forming a dense mound of slender, glossy dark green leaves that can become tinged purple in cold weather. It grows to 6½ft (2m) in height, and female plants bear black berries. Selected forms are sometimes grown with good purple foliage color in winter, a compact habit, or white berries. This species needs a lime-free soil. Zone 4 US; 5b Can.

I. x *meserveae.* The evergreen so-called blue hollies are the result of an attempt to introduce extreme cold-hardiness into the English holly (*Ilex aquifolium*). They reach 6½–10ft (2–3m) in height, have spiny leaves, and show greater hardiness than *I. aquifolium.* 'Blue Angel' is a compact female with large red berries. 'Blue Prince' is a vigorous and very hardy male. 'Blue Princess' is vigorous, with deep red berries. *I.* 'China Boy' and 'China Girl' are similar hybrids that both make dense mounds to 10ft (3m) in height with glossy foliage. The former is male and a good pollinator for the latter, which has profuse red berries. Zone 4 US; 5 Can.

I. pernyi. This spreading evergreen shrub has arching shoots and can reach 10ft (3m) in height. The small leaves are densely arranged and have a long triangular tip. Red berries cover the branches of female plants. Zone 6 US; 7 Can.

I. verticillata. Perhaps the handsomest of all the deciduous species, this shrub, known as the winterberry, grows to 8ft (2.5m) and has dark green leaves that can turn yellow in fall. Though small, the showy berries are a glistening red and are borne profusely on female plants.

'Chrysocarpa' has yellow berries. 'Sparkleberry' is a female hybrid of this species with profuse bright red berries. 'Winter Red' has abundant bright red berries that persist throughout winter. Zone 3 US; 3b Can.

I. vomitoria. The yaupon is a vigorous evergreen shrub that can grow to 16ft (5m) in height and is best in areas with very hot summers. It has small glossy green leaves and small red berries that persist through winter. Selected forms include 'Grey's Little Leaf', with red-purple leaves when young; 'Nana', a dwarf female form reaching 3ft (1m) in height; and 'Pendula', which has weeping shoots and occurs in both male and female forms. 'Stoke's Dwarf' is compact, with bronze young foliage. Zone 7 US; 8 Can.

Illicium
Anise tree
The 40 or so species in this genus of evergreen aromatic shrubs and trees, natives of the southeastern United States, the West Indies, and eastern Asia, are relatives of the magnolias. Their main attractions are their unusual flowers and their aromatic foliage. They need a moist but well-drained lime-free soil and are best given a shaded to semishaded position.

I. anisatum. Upright in habit, this evergreen shrub reaches 10ft (3m) and has glossy green leaves. It is striking in spring, when it bears clustered yellow-green flowers. Zone 8 US; 9 Can.

I. floridanum. The Florida anise tree is a very aromatic shrub that can grow to 8ft (2.5m) in height. The starry red flowers can have up to 30 petals and open in spring to early summer. 'Album' has white flowers. 'Halley's Comet' has redder flowers. Zone 7 US; 8 Can.

I. parviflorum. This species has small yellow-green flowers and is grown mainly for its attractively fragrant foliage. Frequently used in landscape plantings in regions with hot summers, it grows well in sun or shade and forms a dense mass 10ft (3m) in height. Zone 7 US; 8 Can.

Indigofera
This large, mainly tropical genus of some 700 species provides gardens with graceful shrubs whose elegant foliage and small flowers add interest to the border in late summer and fall. Where winters are cold, they can be treated as herbaceous perennials and often benefit from a hard cutting back every few years in spring. They prefer a well-drained soil in full sun.

I. amblyantha. An upright deciduous shrub that can reach 6½ft (2m) in height. The numerous, small, purplish pink flowers are borne in slender upright clusters over a long period from early summer to early fall. Zone 6 US; 7 Can.

I. heterantha. This deciduous shrub is normally seen as a clump of upright shoots reaching 6½ft (2m) in height. The spikes of purple-pink flowers open during summer and fall. Zone 7 US; 8 Can.

Itea
The two most commonly grown plants in this genus of 10 species of deciduous and evergreen shrubs and trees, natives of eastern Asia and North America, are very different. Both are very adaptable and grow well in sun or shade. *I. virginica* needs a moist lime-free soil and can be pruned by cutting back older shoots to ground level in spring.

I. ilicifolia. This open spreading evergreen shrub grows to 10ft (3m) in height and has glossy dark green, hollylike leaves. The tiny greenish flowers are produced in late summer, in hanging catkinlike clusters up to 1ft (30cm) long. It can be grown against a wall in locations where it is not completely hardy. Zone 8 US; 9 Can.

I. virginica. The Virginia sweetspire is a deciduous or semievergreen shrub with upright shoots growing to 5ft (1.5m) in height. Small fragrant white flowers are produced in slender upright clusters in midsummer, and the bright green leaves turn red in fall and winter. 'Henry's Garnet' has bright red-purple fall color. Zone 5 US; 6 Can.

Jasminum
Jasmine
This large genus contains some 200 species of evergreen and deciduous shrubs and climbers, widely distributed in the Old World. The hardy shrubby species all have yellow flowers. They prefer a sunny position in any reasonably

Illicium floridanum

Indigofera heterantha

Itea ilicifolia

Jasminum nudiflorum

Kalmia latifolia 'Ostbo Red'

Kerria japonica 'Picta'

good soil and can be pruned by cutting back some of the older growths to the base in spring.

J. floridum. This is an evergreen or semievergreen shrub growing to 5ft (1.5m) in height that needs a warm climate or sunny wall to thrive. It has dark green leaves with three or five leaflets and bears clusters of small yellow flowers during summer. Zone 8 US; 9 Can.

J. fruticans. Forming a thicket of arching shoots, this semievergreen shrub grows to 5ft (1.5m) in height and has small dark green leaves with three leaflets. Clusters of small yellow flowers open in summer. Zone 8 US; 9 Can.

J. humile. With upright shoots reaching 6½ft (2m) in height, this variable semievergreen shrub has leaves with up to 11 or even more leaflets. Clusters of small yellow flowers open in summer. 'Revolutum' has larger slightly fragrant flowers. Zone 9 US; not hardy Can.

J. mesnyi. Given a Mediterranean climate, the evergreen primrose jasmine makes a mound of arching and scrambling branches 8ft (2.5m) in height, but it is often grown against a wall in colder areas. The large double yellow flowers are borne during spring. Zone 8 US; 9 Can.

J. nudiflorum. The deciduous winter jasmine is one of the best-known winter-flowering plants. Trained against a wall, it can reach 13ft (4m), but it will also trail down a steep bank or wall. The bright yellow flowers open over a long period during winter. On a wall it is best cut back

hard after flowering. 'Aureum' has leaves heavily blotched with yellow, while in 'Mystique' they have a narrow silver margin. Zone 6 US; 7 Can.

J. parkeri. This dwarf evergreen species is best in a rock garden making a dense mound, 1ft (30cm) in height, with very small leaves. The tiny yellow flowers open in summer. Zone 8 US; 9 Can.

Kalmia

Related to the rhododendrons, this genus contains seven species of evergreen shrubs, natives of North America and Cuba. They all need a lime-free soil, rich in humus and moist but well-drained. They flower best in a sunny position but in dry areas need to be given partial shade.

K. angustifolia. The sheep laurel, or lambkill, is a small evergreen shrub forming a low thicket up to 3ft (1m) in height but frequently less, with the leaves often arranged in threes. Pink flowers open in clusters in early summer. 'Rubra' has deep red flowers. Zone 2 US and Can.

K. latifolia. The mountain laurel, or calico bush, is a large rhododendron-like evergreen shrub growing to 10ft (3m) in height, sometimes treelike, with bold dark green leaves. Clusters of saucer-shaped, usually pink flowers open from intricately crimped buds in dense clusters in late spring to early summer. 'Bullseye' has bronze young foliage and white flowers banded with purple-red inside. 'Carousel' has flowers attractively patterned with

red-purple. 'Elf' is compact, with small leaves and white flowers. 'Goodrich' has deep red flowers edged with white. 'Nipmuck' has flowers that are deep red in bud and open nearly white. 'Olympic Fire' has pink flowers opening from red buds. 'Ostbo Red' has bright red buds opening to pink. 'Pink Charm' has red buds opening to rich pink, banded deep maroon inside. 'Richard Jaynes' has pink flowers, flushed silvery white inside, opening from rich red buds. 'Silver Dollar' has very large white flowers. Zone 4 US; 5b Can.

Kerria

The single species in this genus, from China, is a striking flowering plant for a shrub border and is easy to grow in any well-drained soil. Kerria will grow well in sun or shade and can be pruned after flowering by cutting some of the old stems to the base.

K. japonica. This vigorous thicket-forming deciduous shrub reaches 6½ft (2m) in height and has slender green arching shoots. The bright green taper-pointed leaves are attractively veined, and yellow flowers open in mid- to late spring. 'Golden Guinea' has particularly large flowers. 'Kinkan' has shoots striped with yellow. 'Picta', also known as 'Variegata', is less vigorous, with leaves edged with white. 'Pleniflora' is a very vigorous form with upright shoots to 10ft (3m) and large double yellow flowers. Zone 4 US; 5 Can. (cultivars 5b Can.).

Kolkwitzia

Beautybush

Related to the abelias, the one species in this genus, native to China, is easy to grow in any reasonable soil in full sun or partial shade. It is best given space to spread and is well suited to a position among other large shrubs or small trees. Any pruning can be carried out after flowering, by cutting back old or weak shoots.

K. amabilis. The beautybush is a deciduous shrub with arching shoots and can reach 13ft (4m) in height. The bell-shaped flowers are pale pink with a yellow throat and are borne in clusters in late spring and early summer. 'Pink Cloud' has deeper pink flowers. Zone 4 US; 5 Can.

Lagerstroemia

With 50 species of deciduous and evergreen summer-flowering trees and shrubs, native from southeastern Asia to Australia, this genus is mainly represented in gardens by the many forms and hybrids of *L. indica.* While able to withstand a good deal of frost, they will only do so in areas with hot summers. Grown in a moist well-drained soil in sun, they make handsome plants suitable for growing as specimens, for mass planting, or as screens. Cut out any dead wood in spring, or cut the whole plant to the ground and allow it to resprout.

L. indica. The crape myrtle is a fast-growing, deciduous large shrub or rounded tree reaching 20ft (6m) in height, the branches with gray-brown peeling bark. Large clusters of crimped flowers, which vary from white to pink or red, open at the ends of the shoots in summer and early fall. Selections and hybrids include 'Natchez', which is vigorous and upright to 20ft (6m) with mottled bark and white flowers; 'Pecos', rounded and compact, to 10ft (3m) in height, with pink flowers; 'Zuni', similar to 'Pecos', with lavender flowers; and *L. fauriei,* hardier (zone 6 US), growing to 25ft (8m) in height with red-brown peeling bark and white flowers. Zone 7 US; 8 Can.

Kolkwitzia amabilis

Lagerstroemia indica

Lavandula stoechas

Lavandula

Lavender

The lavenders, with 28 species of evergreen shrubs native from the Mediterranean region to India, are well known for their aromatic foliage and flowers. They thrive in a dry, well-drained, not-too-rich soil in sun and are ideal for low hedges and borders. Old plants may become leggy in habit, and lavenders are best trimmed regularly in spring to retain a compact habit.

L. angustifolia. The common or English lavender is an evergreen shrub reaching 3ft (1m) but usually kept lower by pruning. The slender gray-green leaves are aromatic, and the dense aromatic spikes of purple flowers open on long stems in summer. 'Alba' has white flowers. 'Folgate' has lavender-blue flowers. 'Hidcote' has gray foliage and deep purple flowers. 'Hidcote Pink' is compact, with pale pink flowers. 'Munstead' has short spikes of blue-purple flowers and is hardier. Zone 5 US; 6 Can.

L. x intermedia. A group of hybrids, reaching 3ft (1m) in height, that includes the vigorous Dutch lavenders, differing from *L. angustifolia* in their broader leaves, longer stems and more-open flower spikes borne from late summer. 'Grappenhall' has lavender-blue flowers. Zone 6 US and Can.

L. stoechas. The French lavender is a compact, very aromatic shrub growing to 3ft (1m) in height or less, with slender gray-green leaves. The dense spikes of small deep purple flowers are topped with a cluster of purple bracts and are borne on very short stalks. f. *leucantha* has white flowers and bracts. subsp. *pedunculata* has flower spikes on long stalks. *L. viridis* is similar but has greenish white flowers and bracts. Zone 6 US; 7 Can.

Lavatera

Mallow

This genus of mallows contains 25 species of herbaceous and shrubby plants, natives of Europe, western Asia, Australia, and California. The woody members are represented in gardens largely by forms and hybrids of *L. olbia,* which provide large showy flowers over a long period during summer and fall. They should be cut back to the base regularly in spring. Where not fully hardy, they should be grown in a sheltered spot. They are easy to grow in any well-drained soil in full sun.

L. olbia. This deciduous or semievergreen shrub that will quickly reach 8ft (2.5m). The large pink mallow flowers are borne continuously during summer and fall. 'Barnsley' has pale pink flowers with a red eye. 'Burgundy Wine' has deep purple-pink flowers. 'Candy Floss' has pale pink flowers. 'Rosea' has mauve-pink flowers. Zone 4 US; 5 Can.

Ledum

This genus of four species of evergreen shrubs from northern regions of Europe, Asia, and North America is closely related to the rhododendrons. Suited to areas with cool summers, they need a moist, humus-rich, lime-free soil and will grow in sun or semishade. Pruning should not be necessary, but they will benefit from deadheading after flowering.

L. groenlandicum. The Labrador tea is an evergreen shrub forming a mound 3ft (1m) in height with aromatic dark green leaves covered in rusty hairs beneath. The small white flowers are produced in dense clusters in late spring and early summer. 'Compactum' is dense, reaching 2ft (60cm) in height. Zone 2 US and Can.

Leptospermum

The 80 or so species in this genus, related to the myrtles, are mainly Australasian evergreen shrubs and trees with usually white flowers. Thriving in a warm dry climate, they do not do well in humid conditions but are easy to grow in any well-drained soil, preferring full sun. Regular light pruning in spring will help retain a compact habit.

L. lanigerum. This is a vigorous species with upright shoots growing to 16ft (5m) in height, densely covered in gray leaves. The white flowers open in early summer. Zone 9 US; not hardy Can.

L. rupestre. Also known as *L. humifusum*, this species makes a dense mound of spreading and arching shoots 3ft (1m) in height, the dark green leaves bronzing in cold weather. It is studded with small white flowers in early summer. Zone 9 US; not hardy Can.

L. scoparium. The manuka, or tea tree, is an evergreen shrub growing anywhere from 6½ to 16ft (2 to 5m) in height, with aromatic leaves and normally white flowers in early summer. 'Chapmanii' has deep pink flowers and bronze foliage. 'Helen Strybing' has deep pink flowers. 'Kiwi', a dwarf form 1ft (30cm) in height, has deep pink flowers and bronze foliage. 'Nichollsii' has large crimson flowers and bronze young foliage. 'Red Damask' has double red flowers. 'Ruby Glow' has double red flowers and bronze-purple foliage. Zone 9 US; not hardy Can.

Lespedeza

Bush clover

Related to *Indigofera*, and similar in their garden uses, this genus comprises 40 species of herbaceous perennials and shrubs from North America, eastern Asia, and Australia. Suitable for the shrub border, they will grow in any well-drained soil and should be pruned by either cutting out dead wood or cutting to ground level in spring. In cold areas they can be grown as perennials.

L. bicolor. Reaching up to 8ft (2.5m) in height, this deciduous shrub bears masses of tiny, purple-pink pea flowers in clusters during late summer and fall. 'Avalanche' has white flowers. Zone 4 US; 5 Can.

L. thunbergii. Less hardy but showier than *L. bicolor*, this deciduous shrub often dies to the ground in winter. The arching shoots, growing to 8ft (2.5m) in height, bear clusters of purple-pink flowers during the fall. Zone 5 US; 6 Can.

Leucophyllum

Of the 12 species of evergreen shrubs in this genus, native to the southwestern United States, the following thrives in areas with hot dry summers. Suited to

Lavatera olbia 'Barnsley'

Lespedeza thunbergii

a shrub border or for using as a low hedge, it needs a dry well-drained soil in full sun.

L. frutescens. Known as the Texas silverleaf or the Texas ranger, this evergreen shrub makes a dense bush growing to 6½ft (2m) in height. The deep violet-purple flowers in summer contrast with the silvery gray foliage. 'Compactum' is compact, with silvery leaves and pink flowers. 'Green Cloud' is compact, with dark green leaves and deep purple flowers. *L. candidum* is similar but more compact, growing to 4ft (1.2m), with densely arranged silvery leaves. 'Silver Cloud' is a dense form with violet-blue flowers. Zone 8 US; 9 Can.

Leucothoe

The cultivated species in this genus of 40 or so species of deciduous and evergreen shrubs from North America and Japan are ideal for shady places, and *L. fontanesiana* in particular is excellent for ground cover. They require a moist, lime-free, and humus-rich soil in shade or semishade. Prune only when essential by cutting back the oldest shoots after flowering.

L. fontanesiana. Known as the dog-hobble, this evergreen shrub forms a thicket of arching shoots up to 6½ft (2m) in height, bearing dark green tapered leaves. Small white flowers are produced in clusters in late spring. 'Rainbow' has leaves mottled with creamy white, tinged with pink when young. *L. axillaris* is similar but has smaller leaves. Zone 5 US; 6 Can.

Leycesteria

Of the six species of deciduous shrubs in this genus, related to the honeysuckles (*Lonicera*) and natives of the Himalaya and China, only one is commonly cultivated. It is ideally suited to a position in a shrub border, where it will provide attraction over a long period, and is easy to grow in any reasonably fertile soil in sun or partial shade. To prune, cut some of the older shoots to the ground in spring.

L. formosa. Popularly known as the pheasant berry or Himalaya honeysuckle, this deciduous shrub will reach 6½ft (2m) in height and forms a thicket of blue-green shoots. From early summer to fall, the dense clusters of white flowers appear amid purple-red bracts, the red-purple berries ripening while the later flowers are still opening. Zone 7 US; 8 Can.

Ligustrum

Privet

With 50 species of deciduous and evergreen shrubs and trees, native from Europe and Asia to Australia,

Leucothoe fontanesiana 'Rainbow'

Leycesteria formosa

Ligustrum quihoui

the privets provide gardens with some of the most popular and toughest hedging plants. There are also several that are attractive ornamentals in their own right. Easy to grow in any soil, they prefer a sunny or semishaded site. The shrubby species respond well to cutting back and can be pruned as necessary.

L. amurense. The Amur privet is a deciduous upright shrub and will grow to 13ft (4m) in height. It bears clusters of creamy white flowers in late spring to early summer. It is useful for hedging in cold climates. Zone 4 US; 5 Can.

L. delavayanum. This distinctive evergreen species makes a mound of arching shoots 8ft (2.5m) in height with small glossy green leaves. White flowers in summer are followed by dense clusters of blue-black berries. Zone 8 US; 9? Can.

L. japonicum. Sometimes grown as *L. texanum*, this evergreen shrub can reach 13ft (4m) and is best in areas with hot summers, where it makes an effective hedge or specimen plant. It has leathery dark green leaves, and clusters of white flowers in late spring to summer are followed by black berries. 'Silver Star' has leaves edged with creamy white (zone 7 US; 8 Can.). *L. lucidum* is similar but more vigorous, with glossy leaves. It will make a tree to 33ft (10m) but is often grown clipped as a hedge. Zone 8 US; 9 Can.

L. obtusifolium. This species makes a wide-spreading deciduous shrub to 10ft (3m) in height with dark green leaves that are often purple in fall. The small clusters of white flowers are followed by blue-black berries. Zone 4 US; 5b Can.

L. ovalifolium. This vigorous, upright, glossy-leaved semievergreen shrub can reach 16ft (5m) in height but is usually grown as a hedging plant. It has clusters of white flowers in summer and glossy black berries. 'Argenteum' has leaves margined with white. 'Aureum' has leaves edged with golden yellow (zone 4 US; 5 Can.). *L. x ibolium* is similar but with darker foliage. Zone 4 US; 5b Can.

L. quihoui. A graceful deciduous species and one of the more ornamental privets, this makes an arching bush to

10ft (3m) in height. Large clusters of white flowers open at the ends of the shoots in fall. Zone 7 US; 8 Can.

L. sinense. Growing to 16ft (5m), the semievergreen Chinese privet is of spreading habit. It bears clusters of white flowers in summer, followed by purple-black berries. An invasive weed in the U.S. South. Zone 7 US; 8 Can.

L. vulgare. The common privet is a spreading deciduous to semievergreen shrub growing to 10ft (3m), with dark green leaves. The white flowers open in dense clusters in early summer, followed by black berries. 'Cheyenne' is a hardy semievergreen form. 'Lodense' is low and spreading, reaching less than 5ft (1.5m) in height. Zone 4 US; 5b Can.

Lindera

With 80 species of deciduous and evergreen shrubs and trees, natives of eastern Asia and North America, the cultivated linderas are grown mainly for their fall color. They need a not-too-dry lime-free soil and will grow in sun or shade. Fruits are produced only if both male and female plants are grown.

L. benzoin. The spicebush is a deciduous shrub with aromatic foliage that grows to 13ft (4m) in height and has pale green leaves that turn butter yellow in fall. Tiny yellow-green flowers open in spring before the leaves, followed by bright red berries. Zone 4 US; 5b Can.

L. obtusiloba. Among the best shrubs for fall color, this bushy deciduous species reaches 16ft (5m) in height. The often three-lobed green leaves turn butter yellow in fall. In spring it bears yellow flowers on the bare shoots, followed by black fruits. Zone 6 US; 7 Can.

Lithodora

This genus of seven species of evergreen shrubs from Europe and southwestern Asia provides some gems for the rock garden. Given a well-drained soil in full sun, they are easy to grow. *L. diffusa* needs a lime-free soil and benefits from having some of the old shoots and any dead wood cut out after flowering.

Lindera obtusiloba

L. diffusa. Also known as *Lithospermum diffusum,* this species makes a dense mat of bristly leaves less than 1ft (30cm) in height. The blue flowers open in late spring and early summer. Selections include 'Alba', with white flowers, and 'Cambridge Blue', with pale blue flowers. 'Grace Ward' has large flowers. 'Heavenly Blue' has rich blue flowers. Zone 6 US; 7 Can.

L. oleifolia. Lower than *L. diffusa,* to 6in (15cm), with broader, silky hairy leaves. Zone 6 US; 7 Can.

Lonicera
Honeysuckle

While this genus of some 180 species, both deciduous and evergreen, and widely distributed in the Northern Hemisphere, is best known for its climbing members, it also contains numerous shrubs. Mainly very hardy, they are easy to grow, preferring a sunny site, and can be used in the shrub border or for hedging. Pruning consists of cutting out any dead or weak shoots in winter. If necessary, some of the older shoots can be cut to the ground at the same time. Hedges of *L. nitida* can be cut back as necessary or pruned hard in early summer.

Lithodora diffusa 'Heavenly Blue'

L. fragrantissima. Normally semievergreen, this spreading shrub with arching shoots and dark green leaves grows to 6½ft (2m) in height. The fragrant white flowers open during late winter and early spring. Zone 4 US; 5b Can.

L. involucrata. This vigorous deciduous shrub makes a dense bush to about 8ft (2.5m) in height with stout shoots and bright green leaves. The yellow flowers open in early summer and, as the black berries ripen, conspicuous red bracts enlarge around them. Zone 1 US and Can.

L. maackii. This deciduous shrub forms a wide-spreading bush 16ft (5m) in height bearing dark green leaves.

Its fragrant white flowers, which turn yellow as they open along arching shoots in early summer, are followed by small glossy red berries. Zone 2 US; 2b Can.

L. morrowii. This invasive deciduous shrub has an arching habit and makes a mound of dark gray-green leaves, often tinged purple when young, up to 5ft (1.5m) in height. Creamy white flowers in early summer turn yellow, followed by red berries. Zone 3 US; 4 Can.

L. nitida. A popular evergreen hedging plant, this species has glossy green leaves and makes a very dense bush up to about 10ft (3m) in height. As a hedge it needs frequent clipping. The creamy white flowers are inconspicuous in summer. 'Baggesen's Gold' has bright yellow foliage. Zone 7 US; 8 Can.

L. pileata. Closely related to *L. nitida* but hardier and lower-growing, with larger leaves, this evergreen species makes a dense low mound up to 3ft (1m) in height and is a useful ground cover shrub in sun or shade. The spreading shoots are densely covered with glossy green leaves. Zone 6 US; 7 Can.

L. x purpusii 'Winter Beauty'. For its free-flowering habit, this deciduous form is unequalled among winter-flowering honeysuckles and is among the best of all fragrant winter-flowering shrubs. Similar to *L. fragrantissima*, it reaches 8ft (2.5m) in height and produces fragrant white flowers over a long period during winter and early spring. Zone 6 US; 7 Can.

L. standishii. This winter-flowering semievergreen species is upright in habit, growing to 8ft (2.5m) high, with pointed dark green leaves. Fragrant white flowers open during winter and early spring but usually only sparsely. Zone 6 US; 7 Can.

L. syringantha. A charming deciduous shrub with arching shoots and blue-green leaves, this grows to 5ft (1.5m) tall. The fragrant lilac-pink flowers open in pairs along the branches in late spring and early summer. Zone 4 US; 5b Can.

L. tatarica. One of the hardiest of all honeysuckles, this vigorous deciduous species makes a dense bush to 10ft (3m) in height with blue-green leaves. The white or pink flowers are borne in late spring and early summer, followed by red berries. 'Arnold Red' has deep red flowers. 'Hack's Red' has purple-red flowers. 'Zabelii' has pink flowers. Zone 2 US and Can.

L. x xylosteoides. This deciduous hybrid is grown mainly as forms selected for their compact habit. It bears white flowers in late spring, followed by red berries. 'Clavey's Dwarf' is compact, reaching 6½ft (2m) in height. 'Emerald Mound' has blue-green foliage and reaches 3ft (1m) in height. 'Miniglobe' is similar but with green foliage and hardier. Zone 3 US; 4 Can.

Loropetalum

Closely related to the witch hazels, the single species in this genus, from China and Japan, is an interesting winter-flowering plant for a shrub border. It prefers a humus-rich, moist but well-drained, lime-free soil and will grow in sun or shade. It is a success only in areas with hot summers and mild winters. Plants can be pruned as necessary.

L. chinense. This bushy evergreen shrub can reach 10ft (3m) in height and develops peeling bark with age. The fragrant white flowers open in late winter and early spring. 'Blush' has green foliage and magenta flowers. 'Burgundy' has wine-colored foliage and magenta flowers.'Razzleberri' has wine-tinged foliage and magenta flowers. Zone 8 US; 9? Can.

Lycium

Few species in this widely distributed genus of 100 or so deciduous and evergreen, often spiny shrubs are seen in gardens. The following species is sometimes used for naturalizing on a steep bank or for hedging and is particularly good in coastal situations. It may need to be kept under control by cutting back hard during winter.

L. barbarum. The Chinese box thorn, or Duke of Argyll's tea tree, is a thicket-forming, sometimes spiny deciduous shrub, spreading by suckers, with arching shoots to 8ft (2.5m) in height. Purple flowers hang from the branches in summer and are followed by bright orange or red berries. Zone 6 US; 7 Can.

Lonicera fragrantissima

Loropetalum chinense

Lycium barbarum

Magnolia liliiflora 'Nigra'

Mahonia x *media* 'Charity'

Mahonia japonica

Magnolia

With 125 species in the genus, both deciduous and evergreen, natives of the Himalayas, eastern Asia, and North and South America, the tree magnolias are the best known in gardens. There are, however, many species and hybrids that are shrubby and suited to the small garden. They generally require a good soil rich in organic matter and moisture-retentive and will grow in sun or partial shade. Little pruning is usually necessary.

M. liliiflora. The deeply tinted blooms of this deciduous species have frequently been used in hybridization to impart richly colored flowers to the offspring. It grows to 10ft (3m) in height. The upright flowers are purple outside and white within and appear over a period of several months during spring and summer. 'Nigra' is a compact form with large, deeply colored purple flowers. Zone 5 US; 6 Can.

M. liliiflora x *stellata.* Known as the Kosar/de Vos hybrids or the little girl magnolias, these deciduous shrubs combine the qualities of *M. liliiflora* with those of *M. stellata.* Growing to 8ft (2.5m) in height, they bear their richly colored flowers in late spring and early summer. 'Betty' has large flowers red-purple outside and white within. 'Jane' is compact, with fragrant red-purple flowers. 'Susan' is upright, with red-purple flowers paler inside, opening from deeply colored slender buds. Zone 4 US; 5b Can.

M. sieboldii. This beautiful species is a deciduous shrub growing to 10ft (3m) in height. The fragrant white flowers have a pink to crimson center of stamens and open over a long period during late spring and summer, often followed by striking red fruits. Zone 5 US; 6b Can.

M. stellata. The well-known star magnolia is a dense bushy deciduous shrub growing to 10ft (3m) in height. The striking starry fragrant flowers open during spring. 'Centennial' has large white flowers flushed with pink. 'Royal Star' has pink buds opening nearly white. 'Waterlily' has very fragrant white flowers opening from pink buds. Zone 4 US; 5 Can.

M. wilsonii. This wide-spreading deciduous shrub can reach 20ft (6m) and is best appreciated as a mature plant. The large pure white flowers with a center of crimson stamens hang from the shoots in late spring and early summer and are best viewed from beneath. Zone 7 US; 8 Can.

Mahonia

With some 70 species of evergreen shrubs in eastern Asia and North and Central America, this genus provides gardens with splendid foliage as well as flowering plants. The larger forms are best as specimen shrubs or planted in a woodland setting among other shrubs and trees. The dwarf forms make good groundcovers and will grow in sun or shade. *M. aquifolium* can become leggy with age and benefits from a hard cutting back occasionally after flowering.

M. aquifolium. The Oregon grape is a variable shrub reaching up to 5ft (1.5m) and forms low thickets by creeping underground stems. The glossy green leaves can turn purple in cold weather, and large clusters of fragrant bright yellow flowers open in spring, followed by blue-black berries. 'Apollo' is low-growing, with large dense flower clusters. 'Smaragd' is compact and upright. Zone 4 US; 4b Can.

M. fortunei. This small shrub is best suited to regions with warm summers and makes a clump of upright shoots to 3ft (1m) with leaves with slender, only slightly spiny leaflets. Spikes of yellow flowers are borne on the ends of the shoots in late fall or spring. Zone 6 US; 7 Can.

M. japonica. This stiffly branched, spreading shrub will reach 6½ft (2m) in height and has large dark green leaves with very spiny leaflets. Pale yellow, very fragrant flowers open during late fall and winter in slender spreading spikes. 'Bealei' is more upright, with upright flower spikes. Zone 6 US; 7 Can.

M. lomariifolia. A splendid species with a narrowly upright habit, this grows to 10ft (3m). The long bright green leaves have numerous spiny leaflets. Dense upright spikes of bright yellow flowers open from the ends of the shoots in late fall. Zone 9 US; not hardy Can.

M. x *media.* A group of hybrids between *M. japonica* and *M. lomariifolia,* these make imposing shrubs with bold foliage, the leaves having numerous spiny leaflets. The yellow flowers are borne in late fall in long upright or spreading spikes clustered at the ends of the shoots. 'Buckland' has long spreading spikes. 'Charity' has deep yellow flowers in upright, later more spreading spikes. 'Lionel Fortescue' has long upright spikes of bright yellow flowers. 'Winter Sun' has dense upright spikes. Zone 8 US; 9? Can.

M. nervosa. This low-growing species is best in sun, its leaves often turning red or purple in winter. Spikes of yellow flowers open in late spring and early summer, followed by blue-black berries. It reaches 1½ft (45cm) in height and spreads by suckers. Zone 5 US; 6 Can.

M. x wagneri. This hybrid is normally upright, reaching 6½ft (2m) in height. It has dark green to blue-green leaves and clusters of yellow flowers in spring. 'Undulata' has green wavy-edged leaves and yellow flowers. Zone 8 US; 9? Can.

Menziesia

This small genus contains 10 species of deciduous shrubs from North America and eastern Asia. They need a moist, peaty, and well-drained soil and prefer a position in full sun, but they require shade or partial shade in dry areas and are suitable for a peat or rock garden. No pruning is normally necessary.

M. ciliicalyx. This slow-growing deciduous shrub reaches 3ft (1m) in height, its leaves clustered at the shoot tips. In late spring, drooping urn-shaped flowers, which are cream tipped with purple, are borne in clusters. var. *purpurea* has purple flowers. Zone 6 US; 7 Can.

Michelia

With 45 species of evergreen shrubs and trees in southeastern Asia, this genus is related to the magnolias. The following species needs a humus-rich acidic soil in sun or partial shade.

M. figo. The banana shrub is an evergreen relative of the magnolias reaching 10ft (3m) in height. During spring the very fragrant flowers, which are yellow-green flushed with purple, are set among glossy dark green leaves. Zone 9 US; not hardy Can.

Menziesia ciliicalyx var. purpurea

Myrica

Bayberry, Wax myrtle

The cultivated shrubs in this widely distributed genus of 50 or so species of deciduous and evergreen shrubs and trees have little beauty of flower but have aromatic foliage and are useful for screening, for naturalizing, or in the shrub border. Best in sun or partial shade, they require acid soil. All except *M. californica* normally bear male and female catkins on separate plants.

M. californica. The California bayberry is a vigorous upright evergreen shrub, to 16ft (5m) in height, with glossy green, slightly aromatic foliage. Small pealike purple fruits persist on the shoots during fall and winter. Zone 6 US; 7 Can.

M. cerifera. The wax myrtle is an evergreen fast-growing shrub making dense clumps 16ft (5m) in height with slender aromatic leaves. The tiny wax-covered fruits, which densely clothe the shoots, remain ornamental well into spring. This species thrives only in areas with hot summers. Zone 7 US; 8 Can.

M. gale. The bog myrtle is a thicket-forming, deciduous shrub with dark green aromatic leaves, reaching 5ft (1.5m) in height and spreading by suckers. Small pale brown catkins open in spring before the leaves. It is useful for growing in very wet conditions. Zone 1 US and Can.

M. pensylvanica. Similar to *M. cerifera,* the bayberry has broader leaves and is deciduous to semievergreen and much hardier. Variable in height, it can grow to

Myrtus communis

6½–10ft (2–3m) and sometimes spreads by suckers. Female plants are striking in fall with their waxy gray fruits. Zone 2 US and Can.

Myrtus

Of the two species of evergreen shrubs in this genus, from southern Europe and North Africa, the following needs a Mediterranean climate in which to thrive. It can, however, be successfully grown in colder areas, given shelter and a hot sunny position, and can be effectively grown on a sunny wall. Growth can be restricted, if necessary, by cutting back in spring.

M. communis. The common myrtle can grow to 13ft (4m) in height. It has glossy green leaves that are aromatic when crushed, and in late summer it bears fragrant white flowers followed by purple-black berries. 'Compacta' is a dwarf form, growing to 2ft (60cm) in height. subsp. *tarentina* is a compact form, 3ft (1m) in height, with small densely arranged leaves. It can be used as an attractive formal hedge in warm areas. 'Variegata' has gray-green leaves margined with creamy white. Zone 8 US; 9 Can.

Nandina

The single species in this genus, from China and Japan, has a curious appearance and, although related to *Berberis,* is often likened to a bamboo. It is easy to grow in any good soil in sun or shade, although fruiting is better in a sunny position. Fruits are also more freely borne if summers are hot. Old stems can be cut to ground level if desired in spring.

N. domestica. Known as the sacred bamboo, this evergreen shrub produces stout upright unbranched shoots to 6½ft (2m) in height, bearing large leaves divided into numerous slender leaflets. The foliage is bronze-purple when young and can turn red in winter. Large clusters of small white flowers open from the ends of the shoots, followed by bright red berries that persist to spring. 'Alba' has creamy white berries. 'Firepower' is a very compact form 2ft (60cm) in height with broad leaflets, yellow and red in winter. 'Gulf Stream' is compact, with red winter foliage. 'Harbour Dwarf' makes a dense mound to 3ft (1m) in height, red-purple in winter. 'Nana Purpurea' is dwarf, to 2ft (60cm), with foliage purple-red when young and in winter. 'Richmond' bears profuse red fruits. 'Royal Princess' has slender leaflets. 'San Gabriel' is compact, with elegant fernlike foliage. 'Umpqua Warrior' is vigorous, with large berries. 'Wood's Dwarf' is a dwarf form with red winter foliage. Zone 6 US; 7 Can.

Neillia

The following species is one of 10 species of deciduous shrubs in the genus, natives of eastern Asia. It is easy to grow in any good soil in sun or partial shade, and pruning consists of occasionally cutting some of the older stems to the base in spring.

N. thibetica. This vigorous shrub forms thickets of shoots to 8ft (2.5m) and spreads by suckers. The long arching clusters of pink flowers open in late spring and early summer. *N. sinensis* is similar but smaller, to 6ft (1.8m), with shorter flower clusters. Zone 6 US; 7 Can.

Nerium

The single species in this genus, native from southwestern Asia to China, is well known in the Mediterranean or California climates, where it thrives. It is more difficult to grow outside elsewhere, although after abundant summer heat, it will withstand considerable frost. It is adaptable to a wide range of conditions from dry to wet soils, sun and shade, and coastal sites. All parts are very poisonous.

N. oleander. The oleander is a vigorous evergreen shrub reaching 16ft (5m) in height with stout shoots and leathery dark green leaves. The showy fragrant flowers open during summer and fall. It is typically pink, but there are forms available with single or double flowers of almost any shade between white, cream, yellow, apricot, red, and purple. There are also dwarf forms growing to 3ft (1m) and forms with variegated leaves. 'Calypso' has single red flowers. 'Hardy Pink' has single pink flowers. 'Hardy Red' has single red flowers. 'Hawaii' has single pink flowers with a yellow center. 'Little Red', with single scarlet flowers, and 'Little White', with single white flowers, are semi-dwarf forms reaching 6½–8ft (2–2.5m). 'Sister Agnes' is vigorous, with single white flowers. 'Tangier' has single soft pink flowers. Zone 9 US; not hardy Can.

Neviusia

The two species in this genus of deciduous shrubs related to *Spiraea,* and natives of North America, are both uncommon in the wild and in gardens. The following is easy to grow, given a not-too-dry soil in sun or light shade. In good conditions, it will spread by suckers and can be cut back after flowering if necessary.

N. alabamensis. The Alabama snow wreath is, despite its origin, quite hardy. Making thickets up to 5ft (1.5m) in height, it bears white flowers in late spring that consist of clusters of stamens tipped with yellow anthers. The conspicuous green sepals persist after flowering. Zone 4 US; 5b Can.

Oemleria

Name changes have not helped the popularity of this much neglected shrub. The only species in the genus, a native of California, it is valuable for producing its foliage and flowers very early in the year. It is easy to grow in any soil that is not too dry, in sun or light shade. Size can be restricted by cutting some of the older shoots to the ground after flowering. Male and female flowers are on separate plants and both are needed to produce fruit. The male is the more effective in flower.

Nerium oleander

Neviusia alabamensis

Olearia x *scilloniensis*

O. cerasiformis. Also known as *Osmaronia cerasiformis,* the Oso berry is an upright suckering deciduous shrub growing to 8ft (2.5m). Small fragrant white flowers open in drooping clusters in late winter just after the bright green young leaves. Female plants bear purple berries like small plums. Zone 7 US; 8 Can.

Olearia
Daisy bush

This genus of 130 species of Australasian evergreen shrubs and trees contains some highly ornamental members with attractive foliage and flowers. Though mainly at their best in areas with mild winters, some are surprisingly hardy, and all are very tolerant of coastal conditions. Prune in spring if necessary.

O. avicenniifolia. An evergreen species, this makes a rounded bush 8ft (2.5m) high with broad, glossy dark green leaves that are white underneath. Its domed heads of small white flowers open in late summer and early fall. Zone 9 US; not hardy Can.

O. x *haastii.* This hybrid, the toughest daisy bush, makes a dense mound about 6½ft (2m) in height with small dark green

Osmanthus x *burkwoodii*

leaves. It bears heads of fragrant white flowers in summer and is useful for hedging. Zone 9 US; not hardy Can.

O. macrodonta. Sometimes called the New Zealand holly, this splendid large shrub grows to 16ft (5m) in height and stands full coastal exposure. The bold gray-green leaves, white beneath, are remarkably hollylike, and broad heads of small fragrant white flowers open in early summer. Zone 9 US; not hardy Can.

O. x *mollis.* The plant grown under this name is a compact shrub with silvery gray leaves, growing to 3ft (1m) in height. It bears large heads of white flowers in late spring. Zone 9 US; not hardy Can.

O. phlogopappa. Upright in habit and growing to 6½ft (2m) in height, this species has aromatic gray-green leaves. The flower heads are normally white but in some forms are pink or blue. It flowers in spring. Zone 9 US; not hardy Can.

O. x *scilloniensis.* This compact rounded shrub will reach 5ft (1.5m). In late spring the very profuse white daisylike flower heads are borne so freely that they often completely obscure the foliage. Zone 9 US; not hardy Can.

Osmanthus

With 15 species of evergreen trees and shrubs in Asia, the southern United States, and the Pacific Islands, this genus contains some highly ornamental and useful members. Attractive in foliage and with fragrant flowers, they are ideal as specimen plants, for the border, or

for hedging. They are easy to grow in any good and not-too-dry soil in sun or partial shade. Pruning should be carried out in spring for the spring-flowering types after they have flowered.

O. armatus. This large shrub can reach 16ft (5m) in height and is of dense habit. The rigid leaves can be without teeth but often are edged with several spines. Small fragrant white flowers are produced in clusters in fall. Zone 9 US; not hardy Can.

O. x *burkwoodii.* Also known as x *Osmarea burkwoodii,* this hybrid makes a rounded bush up to 10ft (3m) in hieght, with dark green leaves. The very fragrant white flowers are produced abundantly in spring. Zone 7 US; 8 Can.

O. decorus. This stiffly branched shrub grows to 10ft (3m) in height and has large, usually untoothed, very leathery leaves. In spring it produces clusters of fragrant white flowers, which can be followed by blue-black berries. Zone 7 US; 8 Can.

O. delavayi. A dainty species with small toothed dark green leaves, it grows up to 6½ft (2m) in height. Clusters of fragrant white flowers in spring can give rise to blue-black berries. Zone 7 US; 8 Can.

O. x *fortunei.* Treelike in habit, this hybrid can reach 16ft (5m). The glossy dark green leaves are edged with sharp teeth, although on mature plants they often lack teeth. Small fragrant white flowers appear in fall. Zone 7 US; 8 Can.

O. fragrans. This rather tender species can, in suitable conditions, make a large shrub 16ft (5m) in height with glossy dark green leaves. Clusters of small but extremely fragrant white flowers open in fall. f. *aurantiacus* is similar but has orange flowers. Zone 9 US; not hardy Can.

O. heterophyllus. This upright species grows to 16ft (5m) in height, with hollylike, glossy dark green, spiny leaves. Small white fragrant flowers are borne in clusters during fall. 'Aureomarginatus' has leaves edged with yellow. 'Goshiki', also known as 'Tricolor', has bronze leaves when young, becoming mottled with yellow. 'Gulftide' is compact, with very spiny leaves. 'Purpureus' has glossy deep purple young foliage that turns dark green.

'Rotundifolius' has rounded spineless leaves. 'Variegatus' has leaves edged with white. Zone 7 US; 8 Can.

Osteomeles

With three species of evergreen shrubs or trees native from China to the Pacific Islands, this genus is related to *Pyracantha*. Best given a sunny position, it is suitable for growing against a wall. If necessary, some of the older shoots can be cut back in spring.

O. subrotunda. This graceful evergreen shrub, reaching 10ft (3m), has arching shoots bearing glossy green leaves. Clusters of white flowers in early summer are followed by red berries. Zone 9 US; not hardy Can.

Ozothamnus

The 50 or so species of Australasian evergreen shrubs in this genus are sometimes listed under *Helichrysum*. The larger forms make bold plants for a border or against a wall. They all like a sunny position in a well-drained soil and can be cut back lightly in spring.

O. ledifolius. Growing to 5ft (1.5m), this species is distinctive in its narrow dark green leaves, yellowish beneath. The heads of small white flowers open from red buds in summer. Both flower heads and foliage have a strong honeylike scent. Zone 9 US; not hardy Can.

O. rosmarinifolius. The upright shoots of this species are densely covered with dark green leaves. Growing to 6½ft (2m), it produces heads of small fragrant white flowers from deep red buds in summer. Zone 9 US; not hardy Can.

O. selago. A dwarf aromatic shrub 15in (40cm) tall, suitable for the rock garden with slender arching shoots covered in tiny dark green, white-edged leaves. The creamy yellow flower heads open in summer. Zone 9 US; not hardy Can.

Paeonia

There are some 30 species of peony, mainly herbaceous, in Europe, Asia, and western North America. The tree peonies, as the deciduous shrubby species are known, are handsome plants with deeply cut foliage that produce large showy flowers early in the year. They are easy to grow, but the young foliage, particularly in *P. suffruticosa*, is susceptible to late frosts. Little pruning is necessary, but on an established plant some old shoots can be cut to ground level in summer.

P. delavayi. This vigorous species forms dense thickets by suckering, its upright shoots reaching 6½ft (2m) and bearing large deeply cut leaves. The deep red flowers, with a golden center, open in early summer. Zone 7 US and Can.

P. x lemoinei. These hybrids, reaching 5ft (1.5m) in height, are similar to *P. suffruticosa* but combine the coloring of that species with *P. lutea*. Forms grown include 'Alice Harding', with large double white flowers, and 'Souvenir de Maxime Cornu', the double fragrant flowers with golden yellow petals. Zone 5 US; 6 Can.

P. lutea. This vigorous species grows to 6½ft (2m) in height and has bright green, deeply cut leaves. The rich yellow cup-shaped flowers open in late spring to early summer. var. *ludlowii* has very large golden yellow flowers. Zone 6 US; 7 Can.

P. suffruticosa. The Moutan peony produces some of the most spectacular flowers of any hardy shrub. Reaching 6½ft (2m) in height, it is grown in a wide range of colors. The large flowers can be up to 6in (15cm) in width. Young plants may need supporting when in flower. Better-known forms include 'Godaishu', a semidouble white; 'Hana-kisoi', with deep red double flowers; 'Lord Selbourne', salmon-pink flowers; and 'Mrs. William Kelway', white flowers. Zone 4 US; 5 Can.

Parahebe

Closely related to the hebes, this genus contains some 30 species of evergreen Australasian shrubs. Ideally suited to growing in a rock garden, they should be given a well-drained soil in full sun.

P. catarractae. This variable species is typically seen in gardens as a low sprawling shrub 1ft (30cm) in height with small glossy green leaves. Small white flowers veined with pink open on slender upright shoots during summer. 'Delight' has blue flowers. *P. lyallii* is similar to 'Delight' but daintier, with smaller leathery leaves. Zone 7 US; 8 Can.

Paxistima

The two species of evergreen shrubs in this genus, natives of North America, have inconspicuous flowers but are attractive in foliage. The following is best in a soil that is not too dry and will grow in a sunny or shady position, where it can be used for ground cover.

Ozothamnus rosmarinifolius

Paeonia x *lemoinei* 'Souvenir de Maxime Cornu'

P. canbyi. Also known as *Pachistima canbyi,* this is a low spreading evergreen shrub growing to 1ft (30cm) in height and more in width, with stems rooting where they touch the ground. The slender shoots are densely covered with narrow glossy green leaves, which can turn bronze in cold weather. Zone 2 US; 2b Can.

Perovskia

With seven species of deciduous subshrubs, native from southwestern Asia to the Himalayas, the cultivated members of this genus have attractive aromatic foliage and small, but profusely borne, blue flowers. They prefer a well-drained soil in full sun and are best if cut back almost to the base in spring.

P. atriplicifolia. The Russian sage produces clusters of upright shoots to 5ft (1.5m) in height bearing aromatic gray-green leaves. The tall narrow spikes of blue flowers open during late summer. 'Blue Spire' has deeply cut leaves and large spikes of lavender-blue flowers. Zone 4 US; 5 Can.

Philadelphus

Mock orange

Well known in gardens, the mock oranges, with 60 species of deciduous shrubs native to North America and from eastern Europe to eastern Asia, are some of the most popular summer-flowering fragrant shrubs. They will grow in almost any soil but prefer a rich one that is not too dry, and they can be planted in sun or partial shade. Most, except *P. microphyllus,* will benefit from annual pruning when mature. This consists of cutting some of the older shoots to the base after flowering.

P. coronarius. Once the most popular species, now largely replaced by hybrids, this grows to 10ft (3m) in height. The flowers are a distinctive creamy white and very fragrant. 'Aureus' has golden yellow foliage, greening later. The leaves on flowering shoots often burn in full sun. 'Variegatus' is slow-growing, to 6½ft (2m), with leaves edged with white. Zone 4 US; 4b Can.

Philadelphus 'Belle Etoile'

Perovskia atriplicifolia 'Blue Spire'

P. microphyllus. This distinctive species thrives and flowers best in a hot sunny position. Growing to 4ft (1.2m) in height, it has slender shoots bearing small leaves and small but very fragrant white flowers. Zone 6 US; 7 Can.

Philadelphus hybrids

'Avalanche' grows to 5ft (1.5m), with arching shoots and small very fragrant flowers. 'Beauclerk' reaches 6½ft (2m) and has large fragrant flowers, white with a pink flush in the center. 'Belle Etoile' grows to 5ft (1.5m) and is spreading in habit, with large very

fragrant flowers blotched red in the center. 'Buckley's Quill' is compact and upright, to 6ft (1.8m), the double fragrant white flowers with numerous quill-like petals. 'Galahad' is compact, with arching shoots to 5ft (1.5m) and single fragrant white flowers. 'Innocence' has leaves blotched with creamy yellow and bears fragrant white flowers. 'Minnesota Snowflake' has large double white flowers on arching shoots to 8ft (2.5m) and is extremely hardy. 'Natchez' is vigorous and upright, growing to 8ft (2.5m), with large, mainly single white flowers. 'Silberregen', also known as 'Silver Showers', is a small rounded shrub to 3ft (1m) with large fragrant white flowers. 'Snowdwarf' is compact to 2 ½ft (75cm) with clusters of large double white flowers. 'Snowgoose' is upright to 5ft (1.5m), with fragrant double white flowers. 'Sybille' is compact and spreading, to 4ft (1.2m), with fragrant flowers marked with purple-pink at the base. 'Virginal' is vigorous and upright, to 10ft (3m), with large, fragrant double white flowers. All hybrids zones 3–4 US; 3–4b Can.

Phillyrea

With four species, native from the Mediterranean region to southwestern Asia, these evergreen shrubs are closely related to *Osmanthus.* They are best grown as specimen plants but can also be used for screening. Growth can be restricted by pruning after flowering.

P. angustifolia. Reaching 10ft (3m) in height, this species has slender dark green leaves and makes a dense bush. In late spring and early summer it bears clusters of small, fragrant, greenish white flowers. *P. latifolia* is similar but more vigorous, growing to 16ft (5m) and sometimes treelike, with broader glossy dark green leaves. Zone 9 US; not hardy Can.

Phlomis

This genus contains 100 species of herbaceous plants and evergreen shrubs found from the Mediterranean region to eastern Asia. The two-lipped flowers

Photina × *fraseri* 'Birmingham'

Phygelius aequalis 'Yellow Trumpet'

Physocarpus opulifolius 'Dart's Gold'

are borne in whorls along the shoots. They are easy to grow in any good soil in full sun, preferring a soil that is well-drained. Any pruning should be carried out in spring.

P. fruticosa. The Jerusalem sage is a dense evergreen shrub growing to 4ft (1.2m) in height and very effective when mass-planted. It has gray-green leaves and the yellow flowers are borne in numerous whorls in summer. 'Edward Bowles' is similar but subshrubby, with larger leaves and paler flowers. Zone 6 US; 7 Can.

P. italica. Upright in habit, this evergreen grows to 2½ft (75cm) and has gray hairy leaves that contrast well with the lilac-pink flowers in summer. Zone 9 US; not hardy Can.

Photinia

The photinias are a genus of some 40 species of deciduous and evergreen trees and shrubs native to eastern and southeastern Asia. The evergreens are popular both as specimen plants and for screens and hedges and will grow in most soils in sun or light shade. Any pruning should be carried out in spring before growth starts.

P. davidiana. Also known as *Stranvaesia davidiana*, this vigorous evergreen can reach 20ft (6m) in height. The dark green leaves are bronze when young and can turn red in fall and winter. White flowers in summer are followed by red berries. 'Palette' is a slow-growing form, the leaves splashed with white. Zone 8 US; 9? Can.

P. × *fraseri.* The three commonly grown forms of this hybrid are evergreen large shrubs or small trees reaching 20ft (6m) in height, popular for their brightly colored young foliage. In North America 'Birmingham' is common, where, known as the red tip, it is used for hedging, the young foliage emerging bright red in spring. In Europe 'Red Robin', with bright red foliage, and 'Robusta', with coppery red foliage, are grown. All produce small white flowers in spring if not cut as hedges. Zone 7 US; 8 Can.

Phygelius

The two species of evergreen shrubs in this genus are native to South Africa. In gardens they are often treated as perennials and are best if they are cut to the base in spring before growth starts. The tubular flowers come in various shades, all with a yellow throat, and open from summer to fall. They prefer an open soil that is not too dry, in a sunny position, and can spread extensively by suckers.

P. aequalis. This species grows to 3ft (1m) or less and bears pale to dusky pink flowers with a red mouth. 'Trewidden Pink' ('Pink Trumpet') has pale dusky pink flowers. 'Yellow Trumpet' has yellow flowers. Zone 7 US; 8 Can.

P. capensis. More vigorous than *P. aequalis*, this species reaches 5ft (1.5m). The orange flowers are sharply turned back toward the stem and open around the upright shoots. Zone 7 US; 8 Can.

P. × *rectus.* These hybrids between the two species come in many forms. Generally resembling *P. capensis*, they are vigorous, growing to 5ft (1.5m). 'African Queen' has pale red flowers. 'Devil's Tears' has deep reddish pink flowers. 'Moonraker' resembles *P. aequalis* 'Yellow Trumpet' but with flowers borne around the shoots. 'Winchester Fanfare' has reddish pink flowers. Zone 7 US; 8 Can.

Physocarpus

With 10 species of deciduous shrubs in North America and eastern Asia, the plants in this genus are grown mainly in the selected forms described here. Cultivation is easy in any soil, the yellow-leaved forms coloring best in a sunny position. If pruning is required to restrict growth, cut some of the older shoots to ground level in spring.

P. capitatus. In its typical form this vigorous deciduous shrub will reach 8ft (2.5m), with three-lobed leaves and dense heads of small white flowers in early summer. 'Tilden Park' is a low spreading form good for ground cover, growing to 3ft (1m) in height. Zone 6 US; 7 Can.

P. opulifolius. Known as ninebark, this species is similar to *P. capitatus* and has flowers tinged with pink. It is most commonly grown as 'Dart's Gold', a compact form reaching 5ft (1.5m), with bright yellow young foliage. This is an improvement on the older 'Luteus', which is more vigorous and has paler yellow foliage. Zone 2 US; 2b Can.

Pieris

The cultivated members of this genus of some five species of evergreen shrubs, natives of North America and eastern Asia, are unrivaled in gardens. They provide many ornamental features, from their handsome foliage to their small urn-shaped flowers in spring to their flower buds in winter. Pieris require an acid, moist but well-drained soil and flower best in sun or partial shade. They are best grown as specimen shrubs, except for the smaller forms, which can be mass-planted. Little pruning is generally required.

P. floribunda. The hardiest species in the genus makes a dense rounded bush, to 6½ft (2m) in height, with dark green leaves. The upright spikes of white flowers open from greenish white buds. Zone 4 US; 5B Can.

P. formosa. This vigorous species has bold glossy green leaves, bronze to red when young, and can reach 13ft (4m) in height, often spreading by suckers. Large clusters of white flowers are produced in late spring. 'Jermyns' is spreading in habit, to 6½ft (2m), with deep red young foliage and slender drooping spikes of white flowers from red buds. 'Wakehurst' has brilliant red young foliage (zone 7 US; 8 Can.). Hybrids of this species include 'Bert Chandler', with bright pink young foliage turning creamy yellow, white, then green, and rarely flowering; 'Flaming Silver', a slow-growing form to 4ft (1.2m) with bright red foliage, later green edged with silvery white; and 'Forest Flame', which is vigorous, growing to 10ft (3m), with bright red foliage turning pink, then cream to green. Zone 5 US; 6 Can.

P. japonica. Numerous selections have been made of this species, which typically grows to 6½ft (2m) in height and has bronze-tinged young foliage and drooping clusters of urn-shaped white flowers in spring. 'Blush' has pink flower buds opening white tinged pink. 'Christmas Cheer' has pink flowers, darker at the tips, on pink stalks. 'Dorothy Wyckoff' has dark red buds opening pink, with deep red sepals, the dark green leaves bronzing in cold weather. 'Flamingo' has deep red buds opening dark pink. 'Little Heath' is dwarf and compact, to 1½ft (45cm) in height, with small leaves edged with white. 'Mountain Fire' has brilliant red young foliage becoming glossy brown.

'Pink Delight' has pale pink flowers in long drooping clusters. 'Purity' is compact, to 3ft (1m) in height, with pale green young foliage. Zone 4 US; 5b Can.

Pittosporum

The 200 or so species in this genus are evergreen shrubs and trees native to Australasia, eastern Asia, and Africa. While *P. tenuifolium* is typically a tree, it has many variegated, often shrubby forms that are used in the shrub border or for planting against a wall. *P. tobira,* where hardy, is used for hedges and mass plantings.

P. tenuifolum. This columnar evergreen tree can reach 33ft (10m) and has glossy green wavy-edged leaves on deep purple shoots. The small deep purple flowers open in spring and are strongly scented of honey, particularly at night. 'Irene Paterson' is a slow-growing form reaching 6½ft (2m), the young foliage nearly white, becoming speckled with green. 'Purpureum' has deep purple foliage, pale green when young. 'Silver Queen' grows to 8ft (2.5m) and has gray-green leaves edged with white. 'Tom Thumb' is dwarf and compact, to 3ft (1m) in height, with purple foliage, pale green when young. 'Warnham Gold' reaches 10ft (3m) in height, with pale green foliage, yellow in winter. Zone 9 US; not hardy Can.

P. tobira. Given a warm climate, this species makes a large shrub up to 16ft (5m) in height, of dense habit, with glossy

Pieris japonica 'Flamingo'

Pittosporum tobira 'Variegatum'

dark green leaves. It will grow almost anywhere, from dry soils to coastal sites, in sun or shade. The intensely fragrant flowers open in spring and early summer and are white turning creamy yellow. 'Variegatum' has gray-green leaves edged with white. 'Wheeler's Dwarf' makes a dense mound 3ft (1m) in height with smaller leaves. Zone 8 US; 9? Can.

Polygala

This large genus of more than 500 species contains annual and perennial herbs and shrubs, widely distributed. The following prefers a moist but well-drained acidic soil, flowering most freely in a sunny position, although it will also grow in shade, and makes a colorful addition to the rock garden.

P. chamaebuxus. A dwarf evergreen shrub 4in (10cm) in height, this makes a dense mat of narrow leaves. In the typical form, the small flowers are white and yellow, opening in late spring and early summer. var. *grandiflora,* with purple and yellow flowers, is more commonly seen. Zone 7 US; 8 Can.

Poncirus

The single species in this genus, native to Korea and China, is a close relative of the citrus fruits and is sometimes called the hardy citrus. It is an effective flowering plant for the shrub border, with green shoots that make it attractively ornamental in winter. In warm regions it makes a very dense hedge. In a well-drained soil in sun, it is easy to grow. To prune, cut out any dead wood in spring, or clip hedges after flowering.

P. trifoliata. Reaching 16ft (5m) in good conditions, this deciduous shrub has stout green shoots bearing large thorns. The large white orange-blossom-scented flowers appear in spring before the leaves emerge, and often again in fall. The lemonlike fruits can be used to make marmalade. 'Flying Dragon' is a form with contorted shoots and flowers. Zone 5 US; 6b Can.

Potentilla fruticosa 'Princess'

Potentilla
Cinquefoil

The 500 or so species in this genus are mainly perennial herbs widely distributed in the Northern Hemisphere. The commonly cultivated shrubby species will grow in virtually any soil and can be used in a border or rock garden or for hedging. Yellow- and white-flowered types are best in full sun or partial shade; pink, orange, or red-flowered forms develop their best color given a little shade. Trim vigorous plants lightly each year in spring to retain a compact habit. Hedges can be cut at the same time.

P. fruticosa. This deciduous shrub is very variable, some forms reaching 5ft (1.5m), while others are low and spreading. The saucer-shaped flowers, which range in color from white to yellow, orange, pink, and red, are produced over a long period from late spring to fall. 'Abbotswood' has blue-green foliage and large white flowers and grows 3ft (1m) in height. 'Beesii' is dwarf and compact, to 2ft (60cm), with silvery foliage and golden yellow flowers. 'Coronation Triumph' is dense and vigorous, to 3ft (1m) in height, with bright yellow flowers, 3ft (1m). 'Daydawn' has flowers of an unusual peach-pink flushed cream and is 2ft (60cm) high. 'Elizabeth' has large rich yellow flowers and a dense mound-forming habit, to 3ft (1m). 'Gold Drop' is dwarf and bushy, to 2½ft (75cm), with profuse, rather small yellow flowers.

Prostanthera cuneata

'Goldfinger' is compact, 3ft (1m) in height, with large rich yellow flowers. 'Katherine Dykes' is compact and vigorous, with primrose yellow flowers, to 6½ft (2m). 'Klondike' is compact, to 2½ft (75cm), with large golden yellow flowers. 'Manchu' makes a dwarf mound with white flowers to 1ft (30cm). 'Primrose Beauty' is dense, to 4ft (1.2m), with large primrose yellow flowers. 'Princess' has pink flowers, yellow in the center, and a spreading habit, to 2ft (60cm). 'Red Ace' is compact and spreading, to 2½ft (75cm), with orange-red flowers, 'Sunset' has orange-yellow to brick red flowers and reaches 2ft (60cm). 'Tangerine' is spreading, to 2ft (60cm), with yellow-flushed orange flowers. 'Vilmoriniana' is vigorous and upright, to 5ft (1.5m), with silvery foliage and creamy white flowers. Zone 2 US and Can.

Prostanthera
Mint bush

The 50 or so species of evergreen shrubs in this Australian genus provide gardens with some charming small specimens. Although not at all hardy in the colder areas, their small size means that they can easily be accommodated in a sheltered position such as against a warm wall. They can be pruned to restrict size or remove leggy stems or dead wood in spring.

P. cuneata. This bushy spreading species will reach 3ft (90cm) in height and has small, bright green, very aromatic leaves. The bell-shaped flowers are

Prunus laurocerasus 'Castlewellan'

Prunus tenella 'Fire Hill'

white with purple and yellow markings in the throat and open during summer. Zone 9 US; not hardy Can.

P. rotundifolia. The round-leaved mint bush is similar to *P. cuneata* but taller, to 6½ft (2m), with aromatic purple-lavender to purple flowers. Zone 9 US; not hardy Can.

Prunus

The genus that contains the cherries, plums, peaches, and almonds consists of more than 400 species of deciduous and evergreen trees and shrubs found mainly in northern temperate regions of the world. Perhaps best known for its flowering and fruiting trees, it also includes many shrubby species useful in the shrub border, for hedges and screens, or for ground cover.

P. besseyi. This deciduous shrub, known as the Rocky Mountain or sand cherry, grows to 5ft (1.5m) in height, spreading by suckers, and has distinctive gray-green foliage. It thrives best in a hot dry position, where it bears profuse white flowers in late spring, followed by edible purple-black fruits. Zone 2 US; 2b Can.

P. caroliniana. The Carolina cherry laurel, though commonly grown, particularly for hedging, in its native region, the southeastern United States, is not often seen elsewhere. It is a fast-growing evergreen shrub or tree, reaching 33ft (10m), with glossy dark green leaves. The spikes of fragrant small white flowers open in early spring,

followed by black fruits. 'Compacta' is compact and conical with smaller leaves, reaching 20ft (6m). Zone 7 US; 8 Can.

P. x cistena. Frequently used for hedging, this upright-branched deciduous shrub, known as the purple-leaf sand cherry, grows to 8ft (2.5m) in height. The small pale pink or white flowers open in spring as the deep red-purple leaves expand. Zone 3 US and Can.

P. glandulosa. This deciduous shrub is grown mainly as the following forms. They make rounded bushes 4ft (1.2m) in height, bear showy double flowers in late spring, and can be cut back hard after flowering if necessary. 'Alba Plena' has double white flowers. 'Rosea Plena', also known as 'Sinensis', has double pink flowers. Zone 4 US; 5 Can.

P. incisa. The Fuji cherry makes a deciduous shrub, sometimes a tree, up to 16ft (5m) in height. Small white or pink flowers open on the bare shoots in early spring, and the sharply toothed leaves turn orange and red in fall. 'Kojo-no-mai' is a dwarf form with contorted shoots, reaching 5ft (1.5m). Zone 6 US; 7 Can.

P. laurocerasus. The cherry laurel is a fast-growing evergreen shrub, sometimes a tree, that can reach 20ft (6m), with bold glossy green leaves. Small white flowers open in spikes during midspring, followed by cherrylike fruits that ripen from red to black. Very adaptable to sun or shade, it can be grown as a large screen or clipped hedge. Old plants can be cut back hard in spring if necessary. The smaller forms are

useful when mass-planted for ground cover. 'Castlewellan', also known as 'Marbled White', has puckered leaves mottled with cream and gray-green. 'Mt. Vernon' is slow-growing, making a dense mound probably no more than 3ft (1m) in height. 'Otto Luyken' is dense, with upright shoots and slender, very dark green leaves, reaching 5ft (1.5m) in height. 'Schipkaensis' is particularly hardy, growing to 8ft (2.5m) in height. 'Zabeliana' reaches 5ft (1.5m), with wide-spreading branches and very narrow leaves. Zone 6 US; 7b Can.

P. lusitanica. The Portugal laurel, sometimes confused with the cherry laurel (*P. laurocerasus*), forms a plant with smaller red-stalked leaves, producing its white flowers in early summer. A large evergreen shrub up to 20ft (6m) in height, it is useful for screens and hedges and can be trimmed in spring. Zone 7 US; 8 Can.

P. maritima. The beach plum, or sand plum, is a compact deciduous shrub growing to 6½ft (2m) in height and spreading by suckers. The clustered white flowers appear in late spring, followed by edible red or purple plums. It grows well in coastal sites. Zone 3 US; 4 Can.

P. pumila var. *depressa.* This creeping deciduous shrub forms mats of long spreading shoots only 6in (15cm) in height. It is striking in late spring, when masses of white flowers are produced, and again in fall, when the leaves turn bright orange-red. Zone 2 US and Can.

P. spinosa. The blackthorn, or sloe, is a dense bushy deciduous shrub or tree with spiny shoots growing to 10ft (3m). In early spring, before the leaves emerge, it is covered in tiny white flowers. The black edible fruits are covered in a blue bloom and are used in flavoring sloe gin. Zone 4 US; 5b Can.

P. tenella. The deciduous dwarf Russian almond is among the most striking and hardiest shrubs in the genus, making a thicket of upright shoots to 5ft (1.5m) in height bearing glossy green leaves. The pink flowers open in spring before the leaves emerge. 'Fire Hill' has deep pink flowers. Zone 2 US and Can.

P. tomentosa. Known as the downy or Manchu cherry, this very hardy species makes a dense spreading deciduous bush to 6½ft (2m) in height with dark green downy leaves. Small fragrant white flowers open early in midspring, followed by red fruits like small cherries. 'Leucocarpa' has white fruits. Zone 2 US and Can.

P. triloba. Grown in the open, this deciduous species can reach 10ft (3m) and has a rather ungainly habit. It is most often trained against a warm wall where it will receive the hot sun it needs to thrive. Pale pink flowers open in early to midspring. 'Multiplex' has larger, rosettelike, double pink flowers. It is best cut back after flowering. Zone 2 US; 2b Can.

Pyracantha
Firethorn

The seven species in this genus, natives of southeastern Europe and eastern Asia, are spiny evergreens that bear clusters of small white flowers in late spring to early summer. Their main attraction is colorful berries, which often persist into winter. Grow firethorns as specimens, in the shrub border, trained against a wall, or as a screen or hedge. Any stray branches can be cut back to the center of the bush in spring. Firethorns prefer a fairly good soil in sun or partial shade.

P. angustifolia. This species is unusual in its narrow dark green leaves covered in gray wool beneath and makes a dense bush to 10ft (3m) in height. The orange-yellow berries ripen late and are showy well into winter. Zone 4 US; 5b Can.

P. atalantioides. A very vigorous species reaching 16ft (5m), this grows well against a wall. The long-lasting, small orange-red berries are borne in large dense clusters and persist through winter. Zone 7 US; 8 Can.

P. coccinea. This species is a dense bushy shrub, sometimes treelike, growing to 16ft (5m). It is particularly useful for training against a wall or as a screen or hedge. The berries are bright red. 'Lalandei' is dense and bushy, to 10ft (3m) in height, with long-persistent orange-red

berries. 'Rutgers' is a low-growing form reaching 4ft (1.2m), with orange berries. Zone 5 US; 6 Can.

P. koidzumii. The best species for areas with hot summer, this vigorous shrub grows to 10ft (3m) and has glossy green leaves. Red berries in fall persist until early spring. Zone 8 US; 9 Can.

Pyracantha hybrids

'Cherri Berri' is vigorous, growing to 13ft (4m) with dark cherry red berries. 'Fiery Cascade' is compact, to 4ft (1.2m), with small leaves and orange berries ripening to bright red. 'Golden Charmer' is vigorous, to 16ft (5m), with glossy bright green leaves and profuse large orange-yellow berries. 'Mohave' is bushy, vigorous, and spreading, to 13ft (4m) in height, with glossy dark green leaves and dense clusters of orange-red berries. 'Orange Glow' is vigorous, dense, and upright, to 13ft (4m), with large orange berries. 'Santa Cruz' is low and spreading, to 3ft (1m), with profuse large red berries. 'Soleil d'Or' is upright, to 10ft (3m) in height, with large pale yellow berries ripening early. 'Teton' is upright, to 13ft (4m) in height, with red shoots, small glossy leaves, and small orange-yellow berries. 'Tiny Tim' is slow-growing and dense, to 3ft (1m) in height, with small glossy leaves and bright red berries. Zones 5–7 US; 6–8 Can., depending on variety.

Rhamnus
Buckthorn

With about 150 species of deciduous and evergreen trees and shrubs, the buckthorns are widely distributed, mainly in the Northern Hemisphere. They are easy to grow in most soils in sun or shade. *R. alaternus* likes a sunny position.

R. alaternus. The Italian buckthorn is a variable evergreen shrub growing up to 13ft (4m) or more in height, with glossy dark green leaves. The tiny greenish flowers in summer are followed by red berries that ripen to black. It is most commonly grown as 'Argenteovariegata', which has gray-green leaves edged with white. Zone 9 US; not hardy Can.

Pyracantha 'Golden Charmer'

Rhamnus alaternus 'Argenteovariegata'

R. frangula. The alder buckthorn is a large, very hardy, spreading deciduous shrub that can reach 16ft (5m) or more. It has glossy green leaves, which can turn red or yellow in fall. The tiny green flowers are attractive to bees during the summer and are followed by clusters of red berries ripening to black in the fall. 'Aspleniifolia' has long, narrow, threadlike leaves. 'Columnaris', also known as 'Tallhedge', is upright and is useful for hedging. Zone 3 US; 3b Can.

Rhaphiolepis

With about 15 species of evergreen shrubs and trees in eastern Asia, the cultivated members of this genus are sometimes known as Indian hawthorns. They should be planted in a well-drained soil in full sun, and they grow well in coastal areas or against a sunny wall. No pruning is normally needed.

Rhododendron luteum

Rhododendron dauricum

R. indica. This makes a mound to 3ft (1m) or more in height, with narrow glossy green leaves. Clusters of white flowers tinged with pink, with pink stamens, open in spring and summer. Zone 9 US; not hardy Can.

R. umbellata. Hardier than *R. indica*, with oval or rounded leaves, this grows to 5ft (1.5m) or more. Clusters of fragrant white flowers open in spring and summer. Forms and hybrids of these species include 'Ballerina,' with rose-pink flowers; 'Coates' Crimson,' with crimson-pink flowers; 'Indian Princess,' with pink flowers fading to white; and the vigorous 'Majestic Beauty', growing to 6½ft (2m) or more, with clusters of fragrant pale pink flowers. Zone 9 US; not hardy Can.

Rhododendron

The rhododendrons, including the azaleas, make up a large genus of more than 500 species widely distributed in the Northern Hemisphere, largely in China and the Himalayas but extending through Southeast Asia to Australia. Their great variation in size gives them many uses in the garden, from dwarf forms in a rock garden to large-leaved shrubs for woodland. All require a lime-free moist soil rich in humus, the large-leaved forms preferring light shade, the smaller-leaved forms preferring sun except where soils are dry. All benefit from dead-heading after flowering, when dead wood or misplaced shoots can be cut back.

The following rhododendron species, including azaleas, are evergreen and flower in late spring unless otherwise stated.

Hardy to Zone 3 US; 4 Can:

R. viscosum is a deciduous azalea reaching 8ft (2.5m), with fragrant white, pink-flushed flowers opening in summer.

Hardy to Zone 4 US; 4b Can:

R. catawbiense is dense and very hardy, to 10ft (3m), with lilac-purple flowers in early summer, white in 'Album.' *R. luteum* is a deciduous azalea reaching 10ft (3m), with fragrant yellow flowers and yellow to orange and red fall color. *R. mucronulatum* is deciduous, to 6½ft (2m), with slender upright shoots and bright rose-purple flowers in late winter.

Hardy to Zone 4 US; 5 Can:

R. arborescens is a deciduous azalea reaching 10ft (3m) or more and valued for its late fragrant white or pale pink flowers that open in early summer. *R. dauricum* is semievergreen or deciduous, to 8ft (2.5m), with rose-purple flowers in late winter. *R. ferrugineum* makes a mound to 3ft (1m) and has glossy green leaves and deep pink tubular flowers in early summer. *R. impeditum* is dwarf, to 2ft (60cm), with small aromatic leaves and purple flowers. *R. nakaharae* is an evergreen azalea of dwarf spreading habit, to 1ft (30cm), with small leaves and orange-red flowers in summer. *R. schlippenbachii* is a deciduous azalea, to 10ft (3m), with bronze young leaves, yellow/orange/red in fall, and white to pale pink flowers in early to midspring. *R. vaseyi* is a deciduous azalea, to 16ft (5m), with glossy green leaves, red in fall, and pale pink flowers preceding them.

Hardy to Zone 5 US; 5b Can:

R. keiskei is compact, to 3ft (1m), with yellow flowers in spring. *R. yakushimanum* is compact, to 5ft (1.5m), with white-felted young foliage and beautiful apple-blossom pink flowers.

Rhododendron vaseyi

Hardy to Zone 5 US; 6 Can:

R. atlanticum is a deciduous azalea, to 3ft (1m), with fragrant white or pink-tinged flowers. *R. calendulaceum* is a deciduous azalea, 10ft (3m), with yellow to bright orange or red flowers. *R. campylogynum* is dwarf, to 2ft (60cm), with small glossy leaves and bell-shaped purple-pink flowers. *R. hippophaeoides* is upright, to 5ft (1.5m), with narrow, gray-green, aromatic leaves and saucer-shaped purple flowers in early spring. *R. kiusianum* is a semievergreen azalea, to 3ft (1m), with small glossy leaves and purple or pink flowers. *R. pemakoense* is dwarf, to 2ft (60cm), spreading by underground stems, with small dark green leaves and funnel-shaped purple-pink flowers in early spring. *R. russatum* makes a compact mound, to 3ft (1m), with dark green leaves and purple-blue flowers in mid- to late spring.

Hardy to Zone 6 US; 7 Can:

R. augustinii grows to 10ft (3m) or more and has blue flowers spotted green. *R. calostrotum* is compact, to 4ft (1.2m), with blue-green leaves and open purple-pink flowers. *R. campanulatum* grows to 10ft (3m) and has peeling bark, felted young leaves, and lilac-purple flowers. *R. carolinianum* reaches 6½ft (2m) and bears dense clusters of purple-pink flowers in late spring and early summer. *R. cinnabarinum* is upright, to 10ft (3m), with gray-green to blue-green leaves and tubular, red or orange flowers. *R. davidsonianum* reaches 10ft (3m) and has glossy leaves and funnel-shaped purple or pink flowers. *R. fastigiatum* is dwarf and compact, to 3ft (1m), with tiny blue-green leaves and purple flowers. *R. fortunei* is vigorous and treelike, to 10ft (3m) or more, with large leaves and fragrant pale pink flowers. *R. hanceanum* is dwarf and mound-forming, to 3ft (1m), with funnel-shaped yellow flowers. *R. lepidostylum* makes a mound to 3ft (1m) with bristly shoots, small blue-green leaves, and pale yellow flowers. *R. lepidotum* is dwarf, to 3ft (1m), with small scaly leaves and usually pink to purple flowers in late spring to early summer. *R. maximum* is vigorous, to 20ft (6m) or more, with large

leaves and large clusters of purple-pink flowers in midsummer. *R. minus*, also known as *R. carolinianum,* is an early-flowering species growing to 3ft (1m) with white to pink, funnel-shaped flowers opening in late winter to early spring. *R. mucronatum* is an evergreen azalea reaching 4ft (1.2m), with fragrant white flowers in late spring. *R. ponticum* is largely represented in gardens by hybrids that make vigorous shrubs to 20ft (6m) with dark green leaves and dense clusters of mauve to purple-pink flowers in late spring and early summer. *R. racemosum* grows to 6½ft (2m) and has pink flowers densely borne along the rigid shoots in early to midspring. *R. saluenense* is dwarf, to 3ft (1m), with bristly shoots and small, glossy green, aromatic leaves and bell-shaped purple-red flowers. *R. williamsianum* makes a dense mound to 4ft (1.2m) with heart-shaped leaves, bronze when young, and bell-shaped soft pink flowers in midspring.

Hardy to Zone 7 US; 8 Can:

R. forrestii is mat-forming, to 1ft (30cm), with creeping shoots, deeply veined leaves, and bell-shaped scarlet flowers. *R. leucaspis* reaches 3ft (1m) and bears its relatively large, saucer-shaped white flowers with brown anthers in late winter. *R. lutescens* grows to 6½ft (2m) and has bronzy young foliage and lemon yellow flowers in early spring. *R. macabeanum* is treelike, to 16ft (5m), with large glossy dark green leaves and large clusters of yellow flowers spotted inside with purple in midspring. *R. wardii* can reach 16ft (5m) but is usually less tall and has rounded leaves and cup-shaped clear yellow flowers sometimes blotched red inside. *R. yunnanense* reaches 10ft (3m) and is vigorous and semievergreen, with narrow leaves and funnel-shaped pink flowers.

Evergreen rhododendron hybrids
The following flower in late spring to early summer unless otherwise stated.

Hardy to Zone 3 US; 4 Can:

' P.J.M.', also known as 'Peter John Mezit' and 'P.J. Mezit', grows to 4ft (1.2m), with dark green leaves, bronze in winter, and clusters of lilac flowers in early spring.

Rhododendron yakushimanum

Rhododendron atlanticum

Rhododendron williamsianum

Rhododendron **'Dora Amateis'**

Rhododendron **'Fastuosum Flore Pleno'**

Rhododendron **'Elizabeth'**

Hardy to Zone 4 US; 4b Can:

'English Roseum' is compact and upright with pale pink flowers. 'Nova Zembla', to 6½ft (2m), has deep red flowers with darker spots. 'Ramapo' is dwarf and compact, to 2ft (60cm), and very hardy, with small leaves gray-blue when young and small violet-purple flowers. 'Yaku Princess' is compact, to 5ft (1.5m), the pale pink flowers deeper inside.

Hardy to Zone 4 US; 5 Can:

'America' has bright red flowers. 'Anna H. Hall' is semidwarf, with pale pink and white flowers. 'Besse Howells' is compact, to 5ft (1.5m), the deep red flowers with a darker blotch. 'Boule de Neige' is compact, to 5ft (1.5m), with glossy foliage and large white flowers. 'Lee's Dark Purple' is compact, to 6½ft (2m), with dense rounded clusters of deep purple flowers.

Hardy to Zone 5 US; 5b Can:

'Doc' is compact, to 4ft (1.2m), with rounded clusters of wavy-edged rose-pink flowers. 'Dora Amateis' is compact, to 3ft (1m), with small scaly leaves and funnel-shaped white flowers, spotted yellow, from pink buds in midspring. 'Fastuosum Flore Pleno' is vigorous, to 13ft (4m), with large clusters of funnel-shaped double mauve-blue flowers. 'Furnivall's Daughter' is vigorous and compact, to 10ft (3m), with dense clusters of funnel-shaped, red-flushed pale pink flowers. 'Lord Roberts' is upright, to 5ft (1.5m), with black-spotted deep crimson flowers in dense clusters.

Hardy to Zone 5 US; 6 Can:

'Carmen' is dwarf and spreading, to 3ft (1m), with deep waxy crimson, bell-shaped flowers. 'Cunningham's White' is compact, to 10ft (3m), with white flowers from mauve buds. 'Ginny Gee' is dwarf and spreading, to 2ft (60cm), with small dark green leaves and pale pink flowers in midspring. 'Gomer Waterer' is tough and dense, to 6½ft (2m), with clusters of fragrant white flowers flushed mauve and blotched deep yellow. 'Holden' is compact, with red flowers turning to pink. 'Moerheim' is dwarf and compact, to 2ft (60cm), with

small glossy leaves, red in winter, and violet-blue flowers in midspring. 'Scarlet Wonder' makes a dense mound of dark green foliage to 4ft (1.2m), with bright red bell-shaped, wavy-edged flowers in midspring.

Hardy to Zone 6 US; 7 Can:

'Baden-Baden' is mound-forming, to 2ft (60cm), with waxy red flowers. 'Bashful' is spreading, to 6½ft (2m), with silvery young foliage and pale pink flowers. 'Blue Diamond' is compact and upright, to 5ft (1.5m), with small leaves and dense clusters of lavender-blue flowers in midspring. 'Blue Peter' is vigorous, to 10ft (3m), and bears compact clusters of violet-blue flowers, white in the center. 'Bow Bells' makes a dense mound to 6½ft (2m), with bronze young leaves and bell-shaped bright pink flowers. 'Christmas Cheer' is compact, to 6½ft (2m), with flowers pink in bud and opening white in late winter but rarely at Christmas. 'Crest' is vigorous, to 10ft (3m), with glossy leaves and very large bell-shaped, pale yellow flowers from orange buds. 'Cynthia' (hardy hybrid) is very vigorous, to 20ft (6m) or more, with large clusters of funnel-shaped crimson-pink flowers. 'Dopey' is compact, to 6½ft (2m), with rounded clusters of bell-shaped, bright orange-red flowers. 'Egret' is dwarf and compact, to 2ft (60cm), with small glossy leaves and relatively large white flowers tinged green. 'Elizabeth' is compact, to 3ft (1m), with dark green leaves and profuse, funnel-shaped, bright red flowers. 'Grumpy' is compact and spreading, to 5ft (1.5m), with rounded clusters of cream flowers edged pale pink and spotted orange-yellow. 'Halfdan Lem' is vigorous, to 8ft (2.5m), with dark green leaves and large clusters of bright red flowers with deeper spots. 'Kluis Sensation' is very hardy, to 6½ft (2m), and has dense clusters of bright scarlet flowers with deeper spots. 'Moonstone' is dome-shaped, to 3ft (1m), with pale yellow bell-shaped flowers from deep pink buds. 'Mrs. Charles E. Pearson' is vigorous, to 6½ft (2m), with clusters of large mauve-pink flowers eventually fading

Rhododendron 'Patty Bee'

Rhododendron 'Pink Pearl'

Rhododendron 'Bric-a-brac'

to white. 'Oudijk's Sensation' forms a dense mound, to 5ft (1.5m), with bronze young foliage and bright pink bell-shaped flowers. 'Patty Bee' is compact and dwarf, to 2½ft (75cm), with dark green leaves, bronze in winter, and pale yellow flowers in early spring. 'Percy Wiseman' is compact, to 5ft (1.5m), and bears rounded clusters of creamy flowers flushed with pink. 'Pink Drift' is compact and dwarf, to 1½ft (45cm), with small aromatic leaves and profuse pale mauve-pink flowers. 'Pink Pearl' is vigorous, to 10ft (3m) or more, with large clusters of broadly funnel-shaped wavy-edged pink flowers from deep pink buds. 'President Roosevelt' is an unusual variegated hybrid growing to 6½ft (2m), the dark green leaves blotched with yellow in the center, and producing clusters of bright red flowers with white throats in midspring. 'Purple Splendor' is compact and vigorous, to 10ft (3m), with large clusters of wavy-edged deep purple flowers marked with black inside, borne in late spring and early summer. 'Sapphire' is dwarf and rounded, to 2ft (60cm), with small leaves and purple-blue flowers in midspring. 'Sappho' is vigorous, to 10ft (3m), with large clusters of white flowers, spotted with purple, from mauve buds. 'Sneezy' is compact, to 3ft (1m), with soft pink flowers, blotched red with deeper margins, from red buds. 'Songbird' is compact, to 4ft (1.2m), with small leaves and dense clusters of deep violet-blue flowers in midspring. 'Unique' is dense and rounded, to 5ft (1.5m), with compact clusters of cream flowers, spotted red, from pink buds in mid- to late spring.

Hardy to Zone 7 US; 8 Can:

'Anna Rose Whitney' is vigorous, to 13ft (4m), with large deep pink flowers. 'Blue Tit' is compact and spreading, to 4ft (1.2m), with small leaves and lavender-blue flowers. 'Chikor' is dwarf and compact, to 2ft (60cm), with pale yellow flowers. 'Cilpinense' is rounded, to 3ft (1m), with white flowers flushed pink, from pink buds, in early spring. 'Creeping Jenny', also known as 'Jenny', is low and spreading, growing to 3ft (1m) in height and is good for ground cover, has funnel-shaped deep

red flowers. 'Golden Torch' is compact, to 5ft (1.5m), with dense clusters of pale yellow bell-shaped flowers from salmon-pink buds. 'Hotei' is dense, to 6½ft (2m), with deep yellow bell-shaped flowers. 'Mrs. G.W. Leak' is vigorous and compact, to 10ft (3m), with large clusters of pale pink flowers, each conspicuously blotched with a ray of black and brown marks. 'Seta' is upright, to 5ft (1.5m), with tubular pink flowers, white at the base, opening in early to midspring. 'Winsome' reaches 5ft (1.5m) and has bronze young foliage, later dark green, and funnel-shaped deep pink flowers from scarlet buds.

Hardy to Zone 8 US; 9 Can:

'Alison Johnstone,' to 6½ft (2m), has small leaves and tubular pale yellow flowers flushed orange and pink. 'Bo-peep' grows to 4ft (1.2m) and has pale yellow flowers profusely borne in early spring. 'Bric-a-brac' reaches 3ft (1m) and has large white flowers in early spring.

Azaleas (deciduous)

Deciduous azaleas usually thrive best in a sunny or semishaded site. The following will grow to about 6½–8ft (2–2.5m) and flower in late spring to early summer.

Hardy to Zone 3 US; 4 Can:

'Golden Lights' has fragrant yellow flowers. 'Orchid Lights' is compact, to 5ft (1.5m), with lilac yellow flowers. 'White Lights' has large fragrant white flowers with a yellow center.

Hardy to Zone 4 US; 5 Can:

'Gibraltar' has clusters of bright orange-red frilled flowers from deeper buds. 'Homebush' has double deep pink flowers in dense rounded clusters. 'Persil' has white flowers with a deep yellow flare, in compact clusters. 'Strawberry Ice' has deep pink buds opening to pale pink with a deeper flush and golden yellow flare.

Hardy to Zone 5 US; 6 Can:

'Berryrose' has bright rose-pink flowers and bronze young foliage. 'Fireball' has deep orange-red flowers and coppery red young foliage. 'Irene Koster' has very fragrant white flowers flushed pink with a yellow flare.

Azaleas (evergreen)

Most evergreen azaleas grow to about 3ft (1m) in height and are most effective when mass-planted. Best planted in partial shade, many have foliage that turns bronze or red during cold weather. They normally flower in late spring to early summer.

Hardy to Zone 5 US; 6 Can:

'Stewartsonianum' has small brick red flowers and red winter foliage.

Hardy to Zone 6 US; 7 Can:

'Hershy's Red' has large red flowers.

Hardy to Zone 7 US; 8 Can:

'Addy Wery' has deep red flowers. 'Blaauw's Pink' has salmon-pink flowers. 'Blue Danube' has violet-purple flowers. 'Delaware Valley White' has large white flowers. 'Fedora' has deep purple-pink flowers. 'Gumpo Pink' is compact with large, wavy-edged pink flowers. 'Gumpo Red' is compact with large, wavy-edged red flowers. 'Hino-crimson' has bright red flowers. 'Hinode-giri' has crimson flowers. 'Johanna' has deep red flowers. 'John Cairns' has deep orange-red flowers. 'Leo' has bright orange flowers. 'Mother's Day' has deep rose-red double flowers. 'Palestrina' has white flowers marked with green. 'Rosebud' has double rose-pink

flowers. 'Vuyk's Rosyred' has deep satin pink flowers. 'Vuyk's Scarlet' has deep scarlet flowers with wavy petals.

Rhodotypos

The single species in this genus is native to Japan and China. It is easy to grow in almost any situation, in sun or shade. Established plants can spread by suckers and their size can be controlled by cutting back, to ground level if necessary, after flowering.

R. scandens. This thicket-forming deciduous shrub can grow to 5–6½ft (1.5–2m) in height and has arching shoots that bear deeply veined leaves. Large white four-petaled flowers open at the ends of the shoots in late spring and early summer, followed by clusters of glossy black berries. Zone 4 US; 5b Can.

Rhus
Sumac

This large genus of some 200 species is widely distributed throughout the world, occurring in tropical and temperate regions and containing deciduous and evergreen shrubs, trees, and climbers. The cultivated species are grown for

their fall color and fruits and are easy to grow in most well-drained soils, coloring best in full sun. Male and female flowers normally occur on separate plants, only females bearing fruit.

R. aromatica. The fragrant sumac is a spreading deciduous shrub that can reach 6½ft (2m) in height. The aromatic leaves consist of three leaflets and turn orange-red and purple in fall. Clusters of small yellow flowers in spring are followed by red fruits. 'Gro-low' is wide-spreading and low-growing, reaching less than 3ft (1m) in height. Zone 3 US and Can.

R. glabra. Known as the smooth sumac, this deciduous shrub reaches at least 8ft (2.5m) in height and spreads by suckers. The bloomy shoots bear leaves with numerous leaflets that turn red in fall. Small yellowish flowers are followed on female plants by large clusters of red fruits. 'Laciniata' has finely cut leaflets and has been confused with *R. x pulvinata* 'Red Autumn Lace,' which has non-bloomy, slightly hairy shoots and more congested fruit clusters. Zone 2 US; 2b Can.

R. typhina. The staghorn sumac is a vigorous deciduous shrub, sometimes a tree, reaching 20ft (6m) or more, with densely velvety young shoots. The bold leaves, with numerous leaflets, turn orange to red in fall and female plants bear large congested clusters of red fruits. 'Dissecta,' sometimes grown as 'Laciniata,' is a fruiting selection that has finely cut leaflets. Zone 3 US and Can.

Rhododendron **'Mother's Day'**

Rhus typhina **'Dissecta'**

Ribes odoratum

Ribes sanguineum

Robinia hispida

Ribes

Currant and Gooseberry

The 150 or so species of deciduous and evergreen, sometimes spiny shrubs in this genus are widely distributed, mainly in north temperate regions but extending to South America. While generally preferring a sunny position in the shrub border, *R. laurifolium* will also grow in shade, where it will make a good ground cover. *R. speciosum* grows well trained against a sunny wall. To restrict growth, cut back after flowering.

R. alpinum. The alpine currant is a dense bushy deciduous shrub growing to 6½ft (2m) in height. The bright green leaves open very early in spring, and tiny yellow-green flowers appear soon after. It is extremely hardy and can be used for hedging. 'Aureum' is lower-growing and has bright yellow young foliage. 'Green Mound' is one of several dwarf forms making a compact dome about 3ft (1m) in height. Zone 2 US and Can.

R. x gordonianum. This spreading deciduous shrub will grow to 6½ft (2m) in height and combines the flower colors of the flowering currant (*R. sanguineum*) and the buffalo currant (*R. odoratum*). In midspring it bears nodding clusters of small flowers that are a mixture of deep pink and yellow. Zone 6 US; 7 Can.

R. laurifolium. This unusual evergreen species has dark green leathery leaves. The pale greenish white flowers open in showy drooping clusters in early spring. If both male and female plants are grown,

red berries, followed by black, can be borne. It grows to 2ft (60cm) in height and more in width. Zone 9 US; not hardy Can.

R. odoratum. The buffalo currant is an upright deciduous shrub that reaches 6½ft (2m) or more in height, with glossy green lobed leaves that in fall turn attractive shades of orange-red and yellow. Clusters of small aromatic flowers open in midspring. Zone 2 US and Can.

R. sanguineum. The popular flowering currant is a vigorous deciduous shrub that will reach 10ft (3m) or more in height and has aromatic foliage. The small flowers, which open in drooping clusters in midspring soon after the leaves, are in various shades of pink and red and are followed by black berries covered in a blue-white bloom. 'Brocklebankii' has yellow foliage and pink flowers. 'King Edward VII' has deep crimson flowers. 'Pulborough Scarlet' has deep red flowers. 'Tydeman's White' has white flowers. Zone 5 US; 6 Can.

R. speciosum. This showy semievergreen shrub can grow to 10ft (3m) in height, or more against a wall, and has red bristly shoots and glossy leaves. The showy red flowers, like tiny fuchsias, hang in small clusters in late spring. Zone 7 US; 8 Can.

Robinia

The 10 or so deciduous species in this genus are natives of North America and provide gardens with some striking flowering trees. Of the shrubby species,

the following is the best known and is useful for growing in dry sunny sites. Grows in any soil that is not waterlogged.

R. hispida. The rose acacia, or bristly locust, is a deciduous upright shrub, spreading by suckers, that can reach 10ft (3m) in height. Pink pea flowers hang in clusters from bristly shoots in late spring to early summer. Zone 4 US; 5 Can.

Rosa

Rose

With some 150 species widely distributed in the Northern Hemisphere, roses will always have a special place in gardens. They come in such a variety of forms that there are roses to suit every taste, from the grace of the wild roses to the flamboyance of the large-flowered hybrids. Their diversity gives them many uses in the garden: as specimen shrubs; in shrub borders; as wall, bedding, or ground cover plants; or for growing in containers. Roses generally prefer a humus-rich well-drained soil in full sun.

Rose species and their hybrids

The wild roses and their immediate hybrids have a charm that is perhaps not found in many of the more highly derived hybrids, and they include some of the best roses for fruit. Normally little pruning is required except to thin out established plants by cutting some of the older shoots to the base after either flowering or fruiting.

R. x alba. The long-cultivated white rose of York is best known today in its

Rosa banksiae 'Lutea'

Rosa filipes **'Kiftsgate'**

various forms and hybrids, which reach 5ft (1.5m) and have gray-green foliage and fragrant flowers. These include 'Céleste', with double pink flowers; 'Königen von Dänemark', with densely double and fragrant deep pink flowers; and 'Maiden's Blush', with double, very pale pink flowers. Zone 3 US and Can.

R. banksiae. The Banksian rose is an evergreen species suited to Mediterranean conditions but grows well on a sunny wall in cooler areas. The slender shoots are almost thornless and can reach 33ft (10m) in height. 'Lutea' has double yellow flowers. Zone 7 US; 8 Can.

R. x *centifolia.* The old Provence rose grows to about 5ft (1.5m) and has fragrant double pink flowers. Today it is best known as 'Cristata', the crested moss rose, with conspicuous mosslike crests on the sepals, and 'Muscosa', the moss rose, with shoots densely covered in moss-like bristles. Zone 3 US; 4 Can.

R. eglanteria. Also known as *R. rubiginosa*, the eglantine, or sweet brier, is a vigorous prickly bush reaching 8ft (2.5m) in height. Single fragrant pink flowers are followed by long-persistent red fruits. Zone 5 US; 6 Can.

R. filipes. This vigorous rambler can reach 33ft (10m) on a suitable support such as a tree. 'Kiftsgate' is the best-known form, with masses of small white fragrant flowers followed by red fruits. Zone 5 US; 6 Can.

R. gallica. This small shrub is an ancestor of many garden hybrids. Reaching about 3ft (1m) in height, it is best known as var. *officinalis*, the apothecaries' rose, with fragrant semidouble deep pink flowers, and 'Versicolor', the rosa mundi, with semidouble pale pink flowers striped with deep pink. Zone 3 US; 4 Can.

R. glauca. Also known as *R. rubrifolia*, this vigorous species has arching red shoots reaching 6½ft (2m) or more in height and purple young foliage. Single rich pink flowers are followed by red fruits. Zone 2 US; 2b Can.

R. moyesii. This vigorous Chinese species grows to 10ft (3m). Its arching shoots bear single deep red flowers, followed by showy flagon-shaped red fruits. 'Geranium' is a compact form with bright red flowers and larger fruits. Zone 5 US; 6 Can.

R. x *odorata* 'Mutabilis'. Growing to about 6½ft (2m) in height, this

slender-branched shrub enjoys a sunny spot. The single fragrant flowers open pale yellow, changing to a deep coppery red. It will continue in flower until the first hard frosts. Zone 5 US; 6 Can.

R. pimpinellifolia. Also known as *R. spinosissima*, the Scotch or burnet rose makes a dense thicket of bristly shoots to 3ft (1m), spreading by suckers. The white or pink flowers open from late spring and are followed by small glossy black fruits. In its many forms and hybrids it is useful for mass planting and ground cover. 'Frühlingsgold' reaches 8ft (2.5m), with semidouble yellow flowers. 'Frühlingsmorgen' has single pink flowers, yellow in the center. Zone 4 US; 5b Can.

R. rugosa. This valuable species makes a dense bush to 6½ft (2m) in height, with stout bristly upright shoots. The large white to purple-pink flowers are fragrant and open over a long period, followed by red fruits. It spreads by suckers and is useful for hedging. 'Agnes' has double pale yellow flowers. 'Blanc Double de Coubert' has double white flowers. 'Fru Dagmar Hastrup' has single pink flowers. 'Sarah van Fleet' has semidouble pink flowers. Zone 2 US; 2b Can.

R. sericea. This vigorous species, which grows to 16ft (5m) or more, has long arching shoots and elegant fernlike foliage. The small, usually four-petaled, creamy white flowers are followed by small red or yellow fruits. f. *pteracantha* has large striking red thorns on the shoots. Zone 5 US; 6 Can.

R. xanthina. The arching branches on this dense bush can reach 10ft (3m) in height. Bright yellow semidouble flowers are borne among the ferny foliage, followed by red fruits. 'Canary Bird' has single flowers. Zone 4 US; 4b Can.

Ramblers

These vigorous scrambling roses are ideal for growing over a wall or trellis or into a tree, where the large clusters of relatively small flowers are displayed well. All will usually reach about 16ft (5m) with support. Established plants can have some of the older shoots cut to the base after flowering. Recommended forms are 'Albéric Barbier' with double creamy white flowers; 'Albertine', with double pale pink flowers; 'American Pillar', with single white-centered red flowers; 'Bobbie James', with semidouble creamy white flowers; 'Dorothy Perkins', with double pink flowers; 'Emily Gray', with semidouble pale yellow flowers; 'Félicité Perpétue', with double pale pink flowers; 'Rambling Rector', with semidouble creamy white flowers; 'Sander's White Rambler', with double white flowers; and 'Veilchenblau', with double violet flowers striped with white. Zone 5 US; 6 Can.

Hybrid tea and floribunda roses

Now correctly called large- and cluster-flowered bush roses, these are commonly used in bedding or for hedges. They are upright in habit, producing their large fragrant flowers over a long period: those of the large-flowered bush roses (hybrid teas) singly or in small clusters, those of the cluster-flowered bush roses (floribundas) in small to large clusters. They are best cut back hard to 1–1½ft (30–45cm) in late winter, after which they will generally grow to 3–5ft (1–1.5m) in height. Recommended forms include 'Arthur Bell' (cluster-flowered) with double yellow flowers; 'Chinatown' (cluster-flowered), with double yellow flowers flushed with pink; 'Blessings' (large-flowered) with salmon-pink double flowers; 'Blue Moon' (large-flowered), with double lilac flowers; 'Fragrant Cloud' (large-flowered), with very fragrant double scarlet flowers; 'Iceberg' (cluster-flowered), with double creamy white flowers; 'Just Joey' (large-flowered), with double pink flowers; 'Korresia' (cluster-flowered), with double yellow flowers; 'Margaret Merril' (cluster-flowered), with double pink to white flowers; 'Mountbatten' (cluster-flowered), with double yellow flowers; 'Pascali' (large-flowered), with double white flowers; 'Peace' (large-flowered), with double yellow flowers flushed with pink; 'Polar Star' (large-flowered), with double creamy white flowers; 'Queen Elizabeth' (cluster-flowered), with double pink flowers; 'Remember Me' (large-flowered) with double deep coppery orange flowers; and 'Whisky Mac' (large-flowered), with very fragrant golden amber double flowers. Zone 5 US; 6 Can.

Old shrub roses

The old-fashioned roses have a distinct charm of their own. Normally reaching about 5ft (1.5m) in height, most have double highly fragrant flowers. Included here are bourbon, centifolia, gallica, and moss roses. Prune lightly after flowering. Bourbon and gallica roses hardy to Zone 4 US; 5 Can. Centifolia and moss roses are hardy to zone 3 US and Can. Recommended forms include 'Cardinal de Richelieu' (gallica), compact, with dense double velvety purple flowers; 'Charles de Mills' (gallica), large double deep purple-pink; 'Complicata' (gallica), large silvery pink single flowers with center of yellow stamens; 'Louise Odier' (bourbon), highly scented double rose-pink; 'Madame Pierre Oger' (bourbon), globular fragrant flowers, cream flushed violet-pink; 'Fantin Latour' (centifolia), vigorous with double light pink flowers; 'Souvenir de la Malmaison' (bourbon), double pale pink flowers; 'William Lobb' (moss), vigorous with mossy stems and double gray-purple flowers; and 'Zéphirine Drouhin' (bourbon), vigorous, with thornless stems and loosely double pink flowers—can be grown as a climber.

Modern shrub roses

Modern rose breeding has used many different parents to produce a wide array of hybrids in a range of colors, mainly with fragrant flowers produced over a long period. They can be cut back after flowering. Most will reach as high as 5–6ft (1.5–2m). Recommended forms include 'Abraham Darby', large double apricot-pink flowers; 'Ballerina', profuse small single pale pink flowers with

Rosa rugosa **'Fru Dagmar Hastrup'**

Rosa **'American Pillar'**

Rosa **'Peace'**

a white center; 'Bonica', spreading habit with double pink flowers; 'Cécile Brunner', upright and sparsely thorny, with small double pale pink flowers; 'Constance Spry', double rose-pink flowers and will climb given support; 'Cornelia', double pink flowers with yellow base, very fragrant; 'Felicia', compact, with very fragrant double salmon-pink flowers flushed yellow; 'Fritz Nobis', vigorous, with double pink flowers; 'Golden Wings', compact, with large single yellow flowers; 'Little White Pet', vigorous, with small double white flowers from red buds reaching 2ft (60cm); 'Marguerite Hilling', arching habit, with semidouble deep pink flowers; 'Mary Rose', double pink flowers; 'Nevada', vigorous with large single creamy white flowers; 'Penelope', compact, with semidouble creamy white colored flowers flushed pink; and 'Prosperity', vigorous, with an arching habit and double creamy white flowers. Zone 5 US; 6 Can.

Miniature, patio, and ground cover roses

These small roses, which are suitable for containers, as dwarf edging, or in a rock garden, produce small, usually unscented flowers over a long period. They normally grow to about 1½–2ft (45–60cm) and can be cut back lightly after flowering. Recommended forms include 'Flower Carpet', a ground-cover rose with double deep pink flowers; 'Gentle Touch', a patio rose with semidouble pale pink flowers; 'Nozomi', a vigorous ground cover rose with profuse single pink flowers; 'Pretty Polly', a compact patio rose with double pale pink flowers; 'Surrey', a vigorous ground-cover rose with double rose-pink flowers; 'Sweet Dream', a patio rose with double pale apricot flowers; and 'Sweet Magic', a patio rose with semi-double orange-yellow flowers. Zone 5 US; 6 Can.

Climbers

Ideal for brightening a wall, fence, or pergola, train these against a support, tying in where necessary. As they reach their required size, they can be cut back annually to keep them within bounds. Recommended cultivars include 'Crimson Shower', 8ft (2.5m), with clusters of semidouble deep crimson flowers; 'Danse de Feu', 8ft (2.5m), with large double scarlet flowers; and 'Gloire de Dijon', 15ft (5m), vigorous, with double pink flowers. Zone 5 US; 6 Can.

Rosmarinus

Of the two species of evergreen Mediterranean shrubs in this genus, only one is commonly cultivated. Valuable in the garden for its aromatic foliage and flowers, it prefers a hot sunny position in a well-drained soil. Regular light pruning after flowering will help it to retain a compact habit.

R. officinalis. The common rosemary is an evergreen shrub growing to 6½ft (2m) in height in a suitable position. The small blue and white flowers are produced among the narrow, very aromatic leaves in spring. Grow against a warm wall where not fully hardy, to make a useful hedge. var. *albiflorus* has white flowers. 'Benenden Blue' has rich blue flowers. 'Majorca Pink' has pink flowers. 'McConnel's Blue' is low and arching, with deep blue flowers. 'Prostratus' is creeping, with pale blue flowers, but is rather tender. 'Roseus' has pink flowers. 'Severn Sea' is low-growing, with arching stems. 'Tuscan Blue' is upright, with deep blue flowers. Zone 6 US; 7 Can.

Rubus

This genus of more than 250 species of deciduous and evergreen shrubs and herbaceous perennials contains some familiar plants grown for their edible fruits, such as the raspberries and blackberries. The ornamental species are useful in gardens for their flowers and winter shoots, and for ground cover. They are easy to grow, preferring a sunny or semishaded position; those suitable for ground cover do well in sun or shade.

R. 'Benenden.' This vigorous deciduous shrub produces arching shoots to 8ft (2.5m) in height that bear broad lobed leaves. The large white flowers with yellow centers open in late spring. Zone 7 US; 8 Can.

Rosa 'William Lobb'

Rosa 'Golden Wings'

Rosa 'Sweet Magic'

R. cockburnianus. Among the best of all shrubs for its winter stems, this deciduous species makes a mass of arching shoots to 8ft (2.5m) that are showy in winter, when they are brilliant blue-white. The flowers and fruits are inconspicuous. 'Golden Vale' has golden yellow foliage and is lower-growing. Zone 6 US; 7 Can.

R. odoratus. Forming thickets of thornless stems to 6½ft (2m) or more by suckering, this species bears showy fragrant purple-pink flowers in summer. The deciduous leaves are broad and lobed. Zone 3 US and Can.

R. pentalobus. Also known as *R. calycinoides*, this evergreen ground cover species makes a dense mat of dark green leaves less than 4in (10cm) in height. The white flowers open during summer. Zone 4 US; 5b Can.

R. phoenicolasius. The wineberry is often grown for its edible raspberry-like fruits but is also a useful ornamental. The vigorous shoots grow to 10ft (3m) and are densely covered in red bristles. Zone 6 US; 7 Can.

R. spectabilis. The deciduous salmonberry makes a dense thicket of upright shoots to 6½ft (2m) in height and produces fragrant purple-pink flowers in spring. The most striking form is 'Olympic Double', which has very large double rosettelike flowers. Zone 4 US; 5 Can.

R. thibetanus. Another useful plant for winter effect, this deciduous shrub produces arching shoots that are a striking blue-white in winter. The fernlike gray leaves are also attractive. Zone 6 US; 7 Can.

R. tricolor. A valuable evergreen for ground cover, this vigorous species has arching shoots that reach 2ft (60cm) in height and are covered in glossy leaves. White flowers in summer are followed by edible red fruits. Zone 7 US; 8 Can.

Ruscus

The six species of evergreen shrubs in this genus are found in Europe and western Asia. They are unusual in that what are apparently leaves are in fact flattened stems that bear the tiny flowers. Both male and female plants are normally required to produce fruits. The following is excellent for growing in dry soils in dense shade.

R. aculeatus. The butcher's broom makes a dense thicket of upright shoots to 3ft (90cm) bearing sharp-pointed dark green "leaves". The red berries on female plants are striking over a long period during fall and winter. Zone 7 US; 8 Can.

Ruta

Of the eight species of shrubs and perennials in this genus, which are found mainly in the Mediterranean region, the following is grown in the herb garden. It requires a warm sunny position in a well-drained soil and is best cut back hard in spring. The foliage should be handled with care, as it can cause an allergic reaction.

R. graveolens. Common rue is a clump-forming evergreen shrub reaching about 2ft (60cm) in height. The finely divided gray-green leaves are very aromatic, and heads of small yellow flowers open during summer. Zone 4 US; 5b Can.

Salix
Willow

There are some 300 species of deciduous willows, native mainly to north temperate regions. Apart from the more familiar trees, the shrubby species give a range of ornamental effects in gardens, from attractive foliage and winter shoots to catkins. Each plant usually carries catkins of only one sex. While the large willows can be grown in a shrub border, the dwarf ones are best in a rock garden.

S. x boydii. This unusual dwarf hybrid is ideal for a trough or rock garden, where it will slowly reach 1ft (30cm) in height. It has rounded gray-green leaves and may produce small catkins in spring. Zone 6 US; 7 Can.

S. elaeagnos. This dense bushy shrub can grow to 10ft (3m) in height and is recommended for planting near water. The long slender dark green leaves are white beneath, and upright catkins open in spring. Zone 4 US; 5b Can.

Rosmarinus officinalis **'McConnel's Blue'**

Rubus **'Benenden'**

Rubus phoenicolasius

S. exigua. The coyote willow is a vigorous species reaching 10ft (3m) and spreading quickly by underground stems, particularly in a sandy soil. The slender upright shoots bear narrow leaves that are a striking silvery gray. Zone 3 US; 3b Can.

S. fargesii. This distinctive species can grow to 10ft (3m) in height and has red-brown shoots and prominent red buds. The bold leaves are glossy green, and long slender upright catkins open in spring. Zone 5 US; 6 Can.

S. gracilistyla. A stoutly branched, spreading bush, this species will reach 8ft (2.5m) in height and has attractive gray-hairy young foliage. The male plant is particularly fine when its silky gray catkins open before the leaves. 'Melanostachys' has black catkins with red anthers. Zone 4 US; 4b Can.

S. hastata. This dwarf willow grows to 5ft (1.5m) in height and has stout dark shoots. The most popular form is the male 'Wehrhahnii', which produces an abundance of silvery, later yellow, catkins in early spring just before the leaves. Zone 4 US; 5 Can.

S. helvetica. Ideal for a rock garden, the Swiss willow grows to about 2ft (60cm) in height and has small gray-green leaves. Small silvery catkins open before the leaves in spring. Zone 4 US; 5 Can.

S. irrorata. This vigorous shrub, growing to 13ft (4m) in height, has slender shoots that are purple in winter with a white bloom. Small gray catkins, the males with red anthers, open before the narrow bright green leaves. Zone 5 US; 6 Can.

S. lanata. The wooly willow is a stoutly branched, bushy shrub growing to 3ft (1m) or more, with gray-wooly young shoots. The rounded leaves, which are covered in gray hair at first and then become dark green, open after the large gray catkins. Zone 4 US; 5 Can.

S. purpurea. In its typical form the purple osier is a large shrub or small tree with slender purple-tinged shoots reaching 16ft (5m) or more in height. It is most commonly grown as selected forms, which include 'Nana', a dwarf form

Salix exigua

Salix hastata **'Wehrhahnii'**

Salvia officinalis **'Tricolor'**

suitable for hedging and reaching about 3ft (1m), with gray-green leaves. 'Pendula' reaches about 5ft (1.5m) and has slender arching shoots. Zone 4 US; 4b Can.

S. repens. The creeping willow is a low spreading shrub reaching 2ft (60cm) or more, with usually gray-green leaves. Male plants have gray, later yellow, catkins that appear before the leaves. var. *argentea* has conspicuously silky hairy leaves. Zone 1 US and Can.

S. udensis 'Sekka'. This vigorous large shrub grows to 16ft (5m) or more in height and has slender leaves on red shoots that are often flattened at the ends and bear silky gray catkins in winter. Zone 4 US; 5b Can.

Salvia
Sage

This large genus of some 900 species of often aromatic perennials and shrubs is widely distributed. Of the evergreen, shrubby species, S. *officinalis* is the hardiest and most widely grown, but others can be grown in areas with mild winters or against a warm wall in cooler climates. These include S. *greggii*, growing to 2ft (60cm) in height, with usually red or pink flowers; and S. *leucantha*, reaching 3ft (1m), the white flowers with showy purple sepals.

S. officinalis. The common sage is often grown in the herb garden or border for culinary use, making a mound of gray-green leaves to 2½ft (75cm) in height. The spikes of blue two-lipped flowers open during summer. 'Albiflora' has white flowers. 'Icterina' has variegated green-and-yellow leaves. 'Purpurascens' has purple young foliage. 'Tricolor' has leaves conspicuously marked with creamy white, purple, and pink. Zone 4 US; 5b Can.

Sambucus
Elder

The 25 species in this genus of trees, shrubs, and perennial herbs are widely distributed. Shrubby elders provide bold foliage plants for the shrub border and are easy to grow in most soils. They can be cut back, hard if necessary, in early spring to restrict their size.

S. canadensis. The American elder is a strong-growing deciduous shrub reaching 10ft (3m) or more in height. The large divided leaves show off broad flattened heads of small white flowers in summer, followed by black berries. 'Aurea' has leaves flushed golden yellow and red berries. 'Maxima' has very large leaves and flower heads. Zone 3 US and Can.

S. nigra. The European elder is similar to *S. canadensis* but has smaller leaves and flower heads. In its typical form it can reach 16ft (5m) or more but is normally grown in one of its selected forms. 'Aurea' has yellow foliage. 'Guincho Purple' has purple foliage. 'Laciniata' has very finely cut leaves. 'Pulverulenta' has leaves mottled with white. Zone 3 US; 4 Can.

S. racemosa. This vigorous shrub grows to about 10ft (3m) and bears large conical heads of creamy flowers in spring, followed by red berries. 'Plumosa Aurea' has golden foliage, bronze when young. 'Sutherland Gold' is less likely to burn in full sun. Zone 3 US and Can.

Santolina

This small genus of evergreen Mediterranean shrubs has given gardens some valuable border and rock-garden plants. They have aromatic foliage and buttonlike heads of flowers over a long period during summer. Easy to grow in a well-drained, not-too-rich soil in full sun, they can be cut back hard in spring to retain a compact habit. A light trim after flowering is also beneficial.

S. chamaecyparissus. The lavender cotton makes a dense mound of gray-white foliage to 2ft (60cm) or more, covered in summer with long-stalked yellow flower heads. Zone 6 US; 7 Can.

S. pinnata subsp. *neapolitana.* Similar to *S. chamaecyparissus,* this mound-forming shrub has gray-green feathery foliage and heads of bright yellow flowers in summer. 'Edward Bowles' has creamy white flowers. 'Sulphurea' has pale yellow flowers. Zone 6 US; 7 Can.

S. rosmarinifolia. Also known as *S. virens,* this species makes a dense

Sambucus racemosa **'Plumosa Aurea'**

Santolina chamaecyparissus

Sarcococca ruscifolia

mound of bright green foliage to 2ft (60cm) in height and in summer bears contrasting bright yellow flower heads. 'Primrose Gem' has pale yellow flowers. Zone 7 US; 8 Can.

Sarcococca
Christmas box

With about 14 species in eastern Asia, this genus of evergreen shrubs is valuable in gardens for the plant's fragrant winter flowers and for their ability to thrive and provide ground cover in dense shade. They are at their best in a not-too-dry soil in shade or semishade and rarely need pruning, although stray or damaged shoots can be cut back in spring.

S. confusa. Perhaps the best species for general planting, this is very compact, growing to 3ft (1m) or more, with dark green foliage. Small fragrant creamy flowers in winter are followed by black berries. Zone 6 US; 7 Can.

S. hookeriana. In a good position this species can spread by suckers and makes a dense thicket of upright shoots that can reach 4ft (1.2m) and have taper-pointed leaves. The tiny creamy white flowers are very fragrant in winter and are sometimes followed by black berries. var. *digyna* has slender leaves and tiny, fragrant, pink-tinged flowers. var. *humilis* is dwarf, growing to 2ft (60cm) or less, with tiny pink-tinged flowers, and is excellent ground cover. Zone 6 US; 7 Can.

S. ruscifolia. The arching shoots of this species reach 3ft (1m) in height and bear taper-pointed glossy green leaves. Fragrant creamy flowers in winter are followed by red berries. Zone 6 US; 7 Can.

Shepherdia

The three species in this genus are natives of North America and are related to the more familiar *Elaeagnus.* Grown for their silvery foliage, they have very small flowers. The fruits are more conspicuous, but it takes both male and female plants for them to be produced. Shepherdias are suitable for growing in dry alkaline soils, preferring full sun, and are useful coastal plants. No pruning is normally needed.

S. argentea. The buffaloberry is a deciduous, treelike spiny shrub growing to 10ft (3m) or more, with the foliage covered in silvery scales. The tiny yellowish flowers in spring are followed on female plants by edible red berries. Zone 2 US; 1 Can.

S. canadensis. Similar but smaller, reaching 6½ft (2m) in height, and with gray-green foliage. Zone 2 US; 1 Can.

Sinocalycanthus

The single species in this genus, a relative of *Calycanthus*, is a native of China and only relatively recently cultivated. It is best in a good humus-rich soil in sun or semishade and should not need pruning.

S. chinensis. Reaching about 10ft (3m) in height, this deciduous shrub has broad glossy green leaves that turn yellow in fall. The large flowers are white or pink-tinged, with a yellow and maroon center, and nod from the ends of the shoots in early summer. Zone 8 US; 9 Can.

Skimmia

The four species of evergreen shrubs and trees in this genus are natives of the Himalayas and eastern Asia. They are grown in gardens for their attractive aromatic foliage, winter buds, early flowers, and berries. These species are particularly valuable for the shrub border or woodland garden or for ground cover, and, except for *S.* x *confusa*, prefer a shady position. With the exception of *S. japonica* subsp. *reevesiana*, plants are normally either male or female and both are needed to produce fruit. Pruning is not usually required.

S. x *confusa* 'Kew Green'. This selection makes a broad mound to 3ft (1m) in height, with dark green, very aromatic foliage. It is male and bears large clusters of creamy white fragrant flowers in spring. It is equally happy in sun or shade. Zone 7 US; 8 Can.

S. japonica. This variable species is grown in a range of forms, from sprawling to upright shrubs reaching 6½ft (2m) in height. White flowers open in spring from often red buds, followed on female plants by red berries. 'Bowles' Dwarf' is compact, reaching 6in (15cm) in height, and has red winter buds. Both male and female forms are grown. 'Fragrans' is a compact male form with profuse flowers. 'Nymans' is female, with large red berries. subsp. *reevesiana* has flowers that are both male and female and is most commonly grown as the cultivar 'Robert Fortune', with egg-shaped long-persistent fruits. 'Rubella' is male, with deep red winter buds. 'Veitchii' is an upright female with large red berries. Zone 6 US; 7 Can.

Solanum

This very large genus of perhaps 1,500 species contains mainly herbaceous plants and is widely distributed. The shrubby members are largely tender, but a few are grown outside. They like a good soil in full sun.

S. aviculare. The kangaroo apple, which grows to 10ft (3m) in height, is a vigorous evergreen shrub with stout upright purple shoots bearing large lobed leaves. Clusters of violet flowers with a yellow center open during summer and fall. Zone 9 US; not hardy Can.

S. pseudocapsicum. Often grown as a pot plant, the Christmas or winter cherry can reach 4ft (1.2m) in height. It is an evergreen shrub that bears small white flowers in summer, followed by red or yellow fruits. Zone 9 US; not hardy Can.

Sorbaria

This genus consists of 10 species of deciduous shrubs that are native to eastern Asia. They are related to *Spiraea* but have bold leaves with numerous leaflets. Sorbarias are easy to grow in moist soils in sun or partial shade, and as they usually sucker from the base, some of the older shoots can be cut to the base in early spring.

S. tomentosa. This vigorous species has arching shoots growing to 16ft (5m) in height. The tiny white flowers open in summer, in large conical clusters. *S. sorbifolia* forms thickets of upright shoots to 10ft (3m). Zone 6 US; 7 Can.

Sorbus

The 100 or so species in this genus are largely deciduous trees, but a few are shrubs. Widely distributed in temperate regions of the Northern Hemisphere, the following is grown for its fall color and

Sinocalycanthus chinensis

Skimmia x *confusa* 'Kew Green'

Solanum pseudocapsicum

Sorbus reducta

attractive berries and makes an unusual shrub for use in the shrub border or heather garden.

S. reducta. This dwarf suckering shrub makes a low thicket of upright shoots to 3ft (1m) or more. The glossy green leaves turn red-purple in fall as the pink berries ripen. Zone 4 US; 5 Can.

Spartium

A genus of a single species related to the brooms (*Cytisus* and *Genista*), native to the Mediterranean region and ideally suited to a warm sunny position in a well-drained soil. A light trim every year in spring helps to retain a compact habit, while old straggly plants can be cut back hard.

S. junceum. The Spanish broom, which grows to 10ft (3m), is a vigorous, almost leafless shrub with green rushlike shoots. The large, fragrant, canary-yellow pea flowers are borne profusely over a long period during summer. Zone 7 US; 8 Can.

Spiraea

With about 80 species of deciduous shrubs found in north temperate regions, this genus has contributed an invaluable range of hardy flowering and foliage shrubs to gardens. Though most are suited to the shrub border, the smaller ones are useful for ground cover or even for a rock garden, where they will grow in sun or partial shade. The late-summer-flowering sorts can be cut back hard in spring; with those flowering in spring or early summer it is necessary either to cut back some of

Spiraea japonica **'Shirobana'**

the old shoots in spring or to cut them back hard after flowering.

S. 'Arguta'. The bridal wreath, or foam of May, is a popular spreading shrub growing to 6½ft (2m) in height. The small white flowers are borne very profusely in clusters along the shoots in mid- to late spring. Zone 2 US; 2b Can.

S. x *cinerea* 'Grefsheim'. The arching shoots of this shrub reach 5ft (1.5m) in height that bear narrow gray-green leaves. In midspring it is a mass of white flowers that almost obscure the branches. Zone 4 US; 4b Can.

S. japonica. Also known as *S.* x *bumalda*, this shrub is now available in a wide range of forms selected for flower and foliage color. It normally makes a clump of upright shoots to 5ft (1.5m) in height that bear large flattened heads of small pink flowers in mid- to late summer. 'Albiflora' has white flowers and pale green foliage. 'Anthony Waterer' has very deep pink flowers and leaves often marked with white. 'Bullata' is dwarf and compact, growing to 1½ft (45cm) in height, with small puckered leaves. 'Froebelii' has deep pink flowers. 'Gold Mound' is low-growing, with yellow foliage and pale pink

flowers. 'Goldflame' has red young foliage turning yellow, then green. 'Little Princess' is compact and mound-forming, to 2ft (60cm). 'Nana', also known as 'Alpina', makes a dwarf mound to 1½ft (45cm) in height. 'Shirobana', which grows to 5ft (1.5m), bears both pink and white flower heads. Zone 2 US; 2b Can.

S. nipponica 'Snowmound'. Among the most popular of all flowering shrubs, this vigorous plant makes a dense bush to 5ft (1.5m) with blue-green leaves. Clusters of white flowers clothe the branches in early summer. Zone 3 US and Can.

S. prunifolia. The arching shoots of this shrub, which grows to 6½ft (2m), bear glossy green leaves that turn orange or red in fall. Double white flowers open in small buttonlike clusters in spring. Zone 3 US; 4 Can.

S. thunbergii. The slender arching shoots of this shrub grow to 5ft (1.5m) in height and bear narrow leaves that turn yellow in fall. The white flowers open in small clusters in early spring. Zone 3 US and Can.

S. x *vanhouttei.* This vigorous hybrid reaches 6½ft (2m) or more in height and has arching shoots bearing blue-green leaves. The profuse white flowers open in clusters along the branches in early summer. Zone 3 US and Can.

Stachyurus

The cultivated species of this genus of six species of deciduous shrubs from the Himalayas and eastern Asia provide unusual winter flowers. They are easy to grow in any good soil in sun or partial shade and are suitable for use in the shrub border or for training against a wall.

S. chinensis. This spreading shrub will reach 6½ft (2m) in height and has pointed leaves. Its main appeal is the drooping spikes of pale yellow flowers that open in late winter. 'Magpie' has leaves margined with creamy white, tinged pink. Zone 9 US; not hardy Can.

S. praecox. This is similar to *S. chinensis* but has long, pointed, deep green leaves and flowers slightly earlier. Zone 6 US; 7 Can.

Staphylea
Bladdernut

The 10 or so species in this genus of deciduous shrubs and trees are natives of north temperate regions. The following can be grown as specimen shrubs in a border or woodland setting. Easy to grow in any good soil, they can be restricted in size if some of the older shoots are cut to ground level.

S. colchica. This vigorous shrub forms a thicket of upright shoots to 10ft (3m) bearing bold divided leaves. Upright clusters of fragrant white flowers in late spring are followed by large green bladderlike fruits. Zone 5 US; 6 Can.

S. holocarpa 'Rosea'. This shrub or small tree, which can reach 33ft (10m) in height, has blue-green leaves, bronze when young. It bears its pink flowers in spreading clusters in late spring, followed by pale green fruits. Zone 6 US; 7 Can.

S. trifolia. Reaching 13ft (4m) or more in height, this shrub can sucker from the base. White flowers are produced in nodding clusters during mid- to late spring, followed by green bladderlike fruits. Zone 3 US; 4 Can.

Stachyurus praecox

Stephanandra tanakae

Symphoricarpos x *chenaultii* **'Hancock'**

Stephanandra

The four species of deciduous shrubs in this genus are most closely related to *Spiraea* and are natives of eastern Asia. They are easy to grow in any good soil in sun or partial shade and are best suited to the shrub border. *S. incisa* 'Crispa' can be used for ground cover.

S. incisa. The long arching shoots of this shrub reach 6½ft (2m) in height and are orange-brown in winter. Small greenish white flowers open in early summer amid deeply cut leaves. 'Crispa', a compact low-growing form, reaches 2ft (60cm) in height. Zone 4 US; 5 Can.

S. tanakae. Similar to *S. incisa* but with less deeply cut leaves. Zone 5 US; 6 Can.

Styrax

There are more than 100 species of trees and shrubs in this genus, mainly from warm regions of the Northern Hemisphere. While several popular species are trees, the following shrubby one is sometimes grown and prefers a humus-rich soil in sun or partial shade.

S. americana. The American snowbell is a deciduous shrub growing to 8ft (2.5m), with slender upright shoots. Pendulous white bell-shaped flowers open in summer. Zone 5 US; 6 Can.

Symphoricarpos

This distinctive genus of about 17 species of deciduous shrubs from North America, Mexico, and China is related to the honeysuckles. Although the flowers are rather insignificant, the shrubs often have showy white or colored berries. They are easy to grow in any soil, in sun or partial shade, and are suitable for the shrub border or as a hedge.

S. albus var. *laevigatus*. The snowberry is a dense thicket-forming bush with slender arching shoots growing to 5ft (1.5m) in height. The tiny pink flowers in summer are followed by large showy white berries. Zone 3 US and Can.

S. x chenaultii 'Hancock'. Quite popular as a ground cover plant, this makes a low mound 3ft (1m) or more in height, with wide-spreading shoots. The deep pink berries can be showy during fall and winter. Zone 4 US; 5 Can.

S. x *doorenbosii*. These Dutch-raised hybrids contain some of the most popular garden selections. They are vigorous and compact, generally reaching about 5ft (1.5m). 'Magic Berry' has rose-pink berries. 'Mother of Pearl' has large white berries flushed pink. 'White Hedge' has white berries. Zone 4 US; 5 Can.

S. orbiculatus. The coralberry, or Indian currant, is a compact shrub growing to 6½ft (2m). The purple-pink berries are small but borne in dense clusters. 'Foliis Variegatus' has leaves margined with yellow. 'Taff's White' has leaves edged with white. Zone 2 US; 2b Can.

Symplocos

Only one deciduous species from this large, mainly tropical genus is commonly cultivated. It makes a fine specimen or shrub-border plant for its unusual berries and, provided it is correctly sited, rarely needs pruning.

S. paniculata. The sapphire berry is a large shrub or sometimes a small tree that grows to 16ft (5m) or more in height. Clusters of small fragrant white flowers in summer are followed by bright blue berries. Zone 4 US; 5b Can.

Syringa

Lilac

With about 20 species of deciduous shrubs and trees, found from eastern Europe to eastern Asia, the lilacs are perhaps unrivaled in gardens for their floral effect. The small, usually highly fragrant flowers are often borne in large clusters and come in a wide range of colors. Lilacs prefer a good well-drained soil in full sun.

S. x *hyacinthiflora*. Similar to the more popular *S. vulgaris*, this group of hybrids grows to 16ft (5m) in height and flowers early in midspring. There are many selections, with flowers ranging from white to purple to red, including 'Assessippi', with profuse single lilac flowers that open early.
Zone 2 US; 2b Can.

S. x *josiflexa* 'Bellicent'. This vigorous upright shrub reaches 13ft (4m) in height and bears large clusters of rose-pink flowers in late spring. Zone 4 US; 4b Can.

S. laciniata. This graceful lilac makes a small shrub to about 5ft (1.5m) in height. The profuse lilac-purple flowers open in late spring. Zone 4 US; 4b Can.

S. meyeri 'Palibin'. Sometimes known as *S. velutina*, this lilac makes a dense bush to 5ft (1.5m) in height with small leaves. Dense clusters of lilac-pink flowers are borne in late spring. Zone 3 US and Can.

S. microphylla 'Superba'. This spendid lilac is among the best for smaller gardens. Reaching about 6½ft (2m) in height, it bears its clustered rose-pink flowers profusely in late spring and summer. Zone 3 US and Can.

S. pekinensis. This large shrub can grow to 16ft (5m) or more and develops attractive peeling bark with age. Large clusters of creamy white flowers open in early summer. Zone 3 US and Can.

S. x *persica*. This compact shrub reaches about 6½ft (2m) in height and bears dense clusters of lilac-purple flowers in late spring. 'Alba' has white flowers. Zone 3 US; 3b Can.

S. x *prestoniae*. The Preston lilacs are vigorous and very hardy hybrids reaching 13ft (4m) or more and bearing clusters of flowers in a variety of colors. 'Donald Wyman' is deep red-pink. 'Royalty' is violet-purple. Zone 2 US and Can.

S. reflexa. This distinctive species makes a large shrub to 13ft (4m) in height. Purple-pink flowers are borne in nodding clusters in late spring. Zone 4 US; 5 Can.

S. reticulata. At its best in regions with hot summers, this species can make a small tree to 33ft (10m) in height with cherrylike bark. Small creamy white flowers open in very large clusters in early summer. Zone 2 US and Can.

S. vulgaris. The common lilac is a vigorous shrub reaching 16ft (5m) or more and is sometimes treelike. The large flower clusters open in late spring and early summer. 'Andenken an Ludwig Späth' has deep wine red flowers. 'Aurea' has golden foliage and lilac flowers.

Symplocos paniculata

Syringa meyeri 'Palibin'

Syringa vulgaris

'Belle de Nancy' has lilac-pink double flowers. 'Charles Joly' has deep red-purple double flowers. 'Katherine Havemeyer' has large clusters of pale lilac-pink double flowers. 'Madame Lemoine' has large clusters of double white flowers. 'Michel Buchner' has pale lilac-pink double flowers. 'Miss Ellen Willmott' has long clusters of double white flowers. 'Mrs. Edward Harding' has double purple-red flowers, later pink. 'Président Grévy' has large clusters of double lilac-blue flowers. 'President Lincoln' has purple buds opening blue-violet. 'Primrose' has pale yellow flowers. 'Wedgwood Blue' has blue flowers from lilac-pink buds. 'Yankee Doodle' has purple flowers. Zone 2 US and Can.

Tamarix
Tamarisk

The 50 species in this genus are deciduous shrubs or trees that are native to Europe, North Africa, and Asia. Their beauty lies in their feathery foliage and their large flower clusters, while at the same time they are extremely resistant to coastal winds and dry salty soils. These species benefit from regular pruning, *T. ramosissima* in spring and *T. tetrandra* after it has flowered.

T. ramosissima. Also known as *T. pentandra*, this vigorous shrub will grow quickly to 16ft (5m) in height, with long arching shoots. It is a mass of pink flowers in late summer and fall. 'Summerglow' has pink flowers. Zone 2 US; 2b Can.

T. tetrandra. This species differs from *T. ramosissima* in having dark shoots and flowering in spring. Zone 5 US; 6 Can.

Telopea

The four species of evergreen shrubs and trees in this genus, natives of Australia, are striking plants. The following needs a lime-free, moist but well-drained soil in a sunny position, sheltered from winds in cold areas.

T. truncata. The Tasmanian waratah is a stoutly branched shrub that grows to 16ft (5m) or more in height, and has leathery dark green leaves. The large heads of

Telopea truncata

Teucrium fruticans

Tibouchina urvilleana

crimson flowers open in early summer. 'Essie' has yellow flowers. Zone 9 US; not hardy Can.

Ternstroemia

This mainly tropical genus contains about 85 species of evergreen shrubs and trees. The following is useful in regions with hot summers as a specimen shrub or for hedging and is best in a lime-free, moist but well-drained soil in shade or semishade.

T. gymnanthera. Often grown incorrectly as *Cleyera japonica*, this species will reach 10ft (3m) or more in height. The dark green leaves are bronze when young and often turn purple in winter. Fragrant white flowers are borne in early summer. 'Burnished Gold' has bronze leaves turning yellow. 'Variegata' has leaves edged with white, pink-tinged in winter. Zone 7 US; 8 Can.

Tetrapanax

The single species in this genus is related to *Fatsia* and is native to southern China and Taiwan. It is suitable for a shrub border in full sun in reasonable soil and prefers areas with hot summers. In cooler regions it can be grown against a wall.

T. papyrifer. A bold foliage shrub reaching up to 16ft (5m) in height, this vigorous evergreen has large lobed leaves. The clusters of small white flowers open in fall, followed by black berries. Zone 8 US; 9? Can.

Teucrium

This mainly Mediterranean genus of some 100 species consists of aromatic perennial herbs and shrubs. They require a sunny position in a well-drained soil. *T. chamaedrys* is suitable for a rock garden, while *T. fruticans* can be grown in the border, against a wall, or as hedging. Both can be kept compact by pruning in spring.

T. chamaedrys. The wall germander is an evergreen subshrub growing to about 1ft (30cm) in height, with dark green aromatic leaves. Spikes of deep pink flowers open above the foliage during summer. Zone 5 US; 6 Can.

T. fruticans. The shrubby germander reaches 6½ft (2m) or more in height with gray-green aromatic foliage. Spikes of pale blue flowers open over a long period during summer. Zone 8 US; 9? Can.

Tibouchina

The 350 species of perennials and shrubs in this genus are natives of tropical America. Although the following is not hardy in frost-prone areas, it is a very striking shrub for a sunny border in warm regions. It can be cut back lightly in spring to retain a compact habit.

T. urvilleana. The glory bush is an upright evergreen shrub growing to 10ft (3m) in height, with stout shoots and bold velvety leaves. The large violet flowers open over a long period during summer and fall. Zone 10 US; not hardy Can.

Trochodendron

The single species in this genus is a very distinctive, unusual evergreen shrub or tree. Ideally suited to a woodland setting, it is best in a moist but well-drained lime-free soil in sun or partial shade.

T. aralioides. This evergreen shrub, sometimes a small tree, grows to 25ft (8m) in height. The leathery leaves are bright green, and clusters of unusual bright green flowers open in late spring and early summer. It needs shelter from cold winds. Zone 6 US; 7 Can.

Ulex

Gorse

With about 20 species in Europe and North Africa, these spiny shrubs appear evergreen, as despite being almost leafless they have year-round green stems and thorns. Ideally sited on a dry sandy soil in full sun, they can be cut back, hard if necessary, after flowering to retain a compact habit.

U. europaeus. The common gorse is a very spiny shrub reaching 6½ft (2m) or more. The bright yellow fragrant flowers are produced over a long period in spring, sometimes earlier. 'Flore Pleno' is compact, with double flowers borne very profusely. Zone 6 US; 7 Can.

Ulex europaeus 'Flore Pleno'

Ulmus
Elm

The 45 species of mainly deciduous trees in this genus are distributed throughout north temperate regions. Although the elms have suffered seriously from Dutch elm disease, the following shrub has not succumbed. It is ideal for use in a shrub border in any reasonable soil in full sun.

U. 'Jacqueline Hillier'. This compact, bushy deciduous shrub grows to 8ft (2.5m) in height. The small and sharply toothed leaves are densely arranged and turn yellow in fall. Zone 7? US; 8? Can.

Vaccinium

This widely-distributed genus of some 450 species of deciduous and evergreen shrubs and trees is found mainly in the Northern Hemisphere, with a few species in the Southern Hemisphere. They require a moist but well-drained lime-free soil and are best in sun or semishade.

V. corymbosum. The highbush blueberry, popular for its edible fruits, is a deciduous shrub reaching about 6½ft (2m) in height. Small pink or white flowers in late spring are followed by edible blue-black berries. Zone 3 US and Can.

Vaccinium cylindraceum

V. cylindraceum. This very distinctive semievergreen shrub grows to 6½ft (2m) in height and has glossy green leaves. The green flowers are flushed with red and carried in dense clusters in late summer, followed by blue-black berries. Zone 10 US; not hardy Can.

V. glaucoalbum. Forming a low clump of suckering shoots to 3ft (1m) in height, this evergreen species has green leaves that are blue-white beneath. Small, white pink-tinged flowers open in late spring and early summer, followed by blue-black berries. Zone 9 US; not hardy Can.

V. macrocarpon. Well known for its fruits, the cranberry is an evergreen shrub with slender creeping shoots and small leaves, making a mat less than 6in (15cm) in height. Small pink flowers during summer are followed by the familiar red edible berries. Zone 2 US and Can.

V. vitis-idaea. The cowberry is a prostrate evergreen shrub forming a dense mat of glossy dark green foliage up to 10in (25cm) in height. Small white flowers tinged with pink open in summer, followed by edible bright red berries. 'Koralle' has profuse large red berries. subsp. *minus* has very small leaves. Zone 2 US; 1 Can.

Viburnum

The 150 or so species of deciduous and evergreen shrubs and trees in this genus are found mainly in north temperate regions but also in South America. They are well represented in gardens and are so diverse in their characters, which include ornamental foliage, fall color, flowers (often fragrant), and fruits, that one can be found for almost every situation. Generally suited to a shrub border or for planting between other shrubs and trees,

they are usually best given space to grow and left unpruned. Hedges of *V. tinus* can be cut in spring.

V. betulifolium. A vigorous deciduous shrub, this reaches 13ft (4m) and has wide-spreading branches. Tiny white flowers in summer are followed by long-persistent red fruits. Zone 5 US; 6 Can.

V. x bodnantense. A gem among winter-flowering shrubs, this deciduous upright hybrid grows to 10ft (3m) in height. Clusters of fragrant flowers open over a long period during fall and winter. 'Charles Lamont' has bright pink flowers. 'Dawn' has deep pink flowers, opening white and flushed pink. 'Deben' has nearly white flowers. Zone 6 US; 7 Can.

V. x burkwoodii. This popular evergreen or semievergreen shrub has glossy green leaves, sometimes coloring in fall or winter, and grows to 8ft (2.5m). Fragrant white flowers, tinged pink, open during spring, followed by red then black fruits. Among the recommended forms of this hybrid are 'Anne Russell', and 'Park Farm'. Zone 5 US; 6 Can.

V. x carlcephalum. This robust deciduous shrub reaches 8ft (2.5m) and has leaves that turn orange-red in fall. In

late spring the clusters of fragrant white flowers open from pink buds. 'Cayuga' is compact, with profuse flowers. 'Eskimo' is a semievergreen hybrid with snowball-like flower heads. Zone 5 US; 6 Can.

V. carlesii. This deciduous shrub is among the most popular for its scented flowers. It grows to 6½ft (2m) in height, with gray-green leaves and dense clusters of very fragrant white flowers, flushed pink, that open during mid- to late spring. 'Aurora' has pink flowers from red buds. 'Charis' has fragrant white flowers that open pink from red buds. 'Compactum' is a dwarf form reaching only 3ft (1m) in height. 'Diana' has purple-tinged young foliage and flowers that open red and become pink. Zone 4 US; 5b Can.

V. davidii. A very popular ground cover plant, this evergreen shrub makes a dense mound to 3ft (1m) in height with bold dark green leaves. Clusters of small white flowers in late spring are followed by blue-black berries. Often several different seedlings are needed to produce fruit. Zone 7 US; 8 Can.

V. dentatum. The arrowwood is a vigorous and very tough deciduous shrub with upright, later arching shoots reaching 10ft (3m) or more, with glossy leaves that can turn red or yellow in fall. Clusters of white flowers in late spring and early summer are followed by blue-black fruits. Zone 3 US and Can.

V. dilatatum. This rather upright deciduous shrub reaches 8ft (2.5m) and has dark green leaves that turn bronze or

Viburnum carlesii

Viburnum davidii

Viburnum farreri

Viburnum plicatum

Viburnum tinus

red in fall. It bears clusters of small white flowers in early summer and bright red fruits that often persist into winter. 'Erie' makes a compact mound 6½ft (2m) in height with profuse fruit and orange-red fall color. Zone 4 US; 5 Can.

V. farreri. Growing to 8ft (2.5m) in height, this beautiful deciduous shrub has bronze young leaves. The white flowers, tinged with pink, are very fragrant and open during fall and winter. 'Candidissimum' has pale green leaves and white flowers. 'Nanum' makes a dense mound about 2½ft (75cm) in height. Zone 4 US; 5b Can.

V. x juddii. This rounded bushy shrub, popular for its fragrant blooms, reaches 6½ft (2m) in height. The white flowers, tinged with pink, have a sweet fragrance and open in mid- to late spring. Zone 4 US; 5 Can.

V. lantana. The wayfaring tree is a vigorous deciduous shrub growing to 13ft (4m) or more, with gray-green leaves that can turn red in fall. Heads of creamy white flowers in late spring and early summer are followed by red then black fruits. 'Mohican' is a compact form with orange-red fall color. Zone 3 US; 2b Can.

V. macrocephalum 'Sterile'. Sometimes grown as *V. macrocephalum*, this semievergreen shrub reaches to 16ft (5m) in height and can be trained against a wall. The large snowball-like flower heads open in late spring. Zone 6 US; 7 Can.

V. odoratissimum. This vigorous evergreen is not fully hardy in cold regions but is well adapted to areas with hot

summers. Growing to 16ft (5m) or more, it has bold glossy leaves and bears clusters of fragrant white flowers in late spring, followed by red fruits that turn black. Zone 8 US; 9 Can.

V. opulus. The Guelder rose is a vigorous deciduous shrub reaching 16ft (5m) in height, with boldly lobed leaves turning red in fall. The lacecap-like heads of white flowers in early summer are followed by glossy red fruits. 'Aureum' has yellow leaves. 'Nanum' is a compact form, growing to 3ft (1m) in height, that rarely flowers. 'Roseum', also known as 'Sterile', has snowball-like flower heads and no fruit. 'Xanthocarpum' has golden yellow fruits. Zone 3 US; 2b Can.

V. plicatum. Several forms of this deciduous shrub are popular in gardens. Reaching 10ft (3m) in height, it has a spreading habit with layered branches, and leaves that turn purple-red in fall. Lacecap-like white flower heads open along the shoots in late spring, followed by red fruits. 'Grandiflorum' has snowball-like flower heads. 'Lanarth' is vigorous, with large flower heads. 'Mariesii' has a pronounced layered habit and large flower heads but few fruits. 'Nanum Semperflorens' is compact and upright, to 6½ft (2m) in height, and flowers during summer and fall. 'Pink Beauty' has white flowers that turn pink. 'Rowallane' has large flowers and profuse fruit. 'Shasta' is wide-spreading with large flowers and profuse red fruits. Zone 4 US; 5b Can.

V. x rhytidophylloides. This vigorous shrub can reach 16ft (5m) and has dark green, long-persistent leaves. Clusters of creamy white flowers open in late spring and are followed by red fruits that turn black. 'Alleghany' has leathery, dark green leaves and red fruit. Zone 4 US; 5 Can.

V. rhytidophyllum. This distinctive and vigorous evergreen species grows to 16ft (5m) in height, with long glossy dark green, deeply veined leaves. Large heads of creamy flowers open in late spring, followed by heavy clusters of red fruits, ripening to black. Zone 5 US; 6 Can.

V. sargentii. Similar to *V. opulus*, this deciduous species can grow to 16ft (5m) in height and has lobed leaves, bronze when young and turning yellow or red in fall. Lacecap-like heads of white flowers in late spring are followed by glossy red fruits. 'Onondaga' is a striking form with bronze foliage and red flower buds that contrast with the white outer flowers. Zone 3 US; 3b Can.

V. sieboldii. This is a vigorous and spreading deciduous shrub to 10ft (3m) tall with bold glossy leaves. Small white flowers are profusely borne in large clusters in late spring, followed by showy red fruits. 'Seneca' has large clusters of long-persistent fruits. Zone 4 US; 5 Can.

V. tinus. The laurustinus is a dense evergreen shrub often used for screens and hedges where winters are not too cold. Reaching 10ft (3m), it has dark green leaves and heads of white flowers from pink buds during fall and winter, followed by blue-black fruits. 'Compactum' is a compact form up to 6½ft (2m) in height. 'Eve Price' makes a dense bush that grows to 8ft (2.5m), with profuse flowers from deep pink buds. Zone 7 US; 8 Can.

V. trilobum. This North American species reaches 16ft (5m) and is similar to the European *V. opulus.* It produces dark green leaves, bronze when young but turning yellow to red in fall, and tiny white flowers in late spring. Forms include 'Compactum', which grows to only 6½ft (2m) and fruits freely, and 'Wentworth', which has fruits that turn from yellow to red and red fall color. Zone 2 US and Can.

Vinca

Periwinkle

Of the seven species of perennials and shrubs in this genus, a few are grown in gardens for use as ground-cover plants. They will grow in any reasonable soil and thrive in sun or shade. All can be cut back hard in spring if it is necessary to restrict growth.

V. major. The greater periwinkle is a vigorous shrub with slender arching and trailing shoots, growing to 2ft (60cm) in height and much more in width. Large, bright blue flowers are borne from spring to early fall. 'Maculata' has leaves blotched with bright yellow-green. 'Oxyloba' has deeper blue flowers with narrow pointed lobes. 'Variegata' has bright green leaves edged with creamy white. Zone 5 US; 6 Can.

V. minor. The lesser periwinkle differs from *V. major* in having creeping stems, 6in (15cm) in height, that root as they trail along the ground. The bright blue smaller flowers are produced in spring and also into summer. 'Alba' has white flowers. 'Alba Variegata' has white flowers and yellow-edged leaves. 'Atropurpurea' has deep violet-purple flowers. 'Aureovariegata' has leaves blotched with yellow. 'Gertrude Jekyll' is of dense growth and has small leaves and profuse small white flowers. 'La Grave' has large lavender-blue flowers. 'Multiplex' has double purple flowers. Zone 3 US and Can.

Vinca major 'Oxyloba'

Vitex

This genus of some 250 species of deciduous and evergreen trees and shrubs is mainly tropical in distribution. The following are the most commonly grown in temperate regions and require a hot sunny position in a well-drained soil.

V. agnus-castus. The chaste tree is a deciduous shrub, sometimes a tree, reaching 10ft (3m) or more, with aromatic gray-green foliage. The long spikes of small blue flowers open in summer or fall depending on the amount of summer heat. 'Alba' has white flowers. 'Rosea' has pink flowers. Zone 6 US; 7 Can.

V. negundo. Similar to *V. agnus-castus,* this species, which needs more summer heat, is of slenderer growth, with toothed leaflets and lavender-blue flowers. var. *heterophylla* is a distinctive form with finely cut leaflets. Zone 5 US; 6b Can.

Weigela

The 12 species in this genus are deciduous shrubs, native to eastern Asia, with showy, usually funnel-shaped flowers in late spring to early summer, varying in color from white to yellow or red. They are easy to grow in a shrub border in any

Vitex agnus-castus

Weigela 'Bristol Ruby'

reasonable soil. To prune, cut some of the old shoots to the base after flowering each year, leaving young shoots to flower the following year. Unless otherwise stated, the following reach about 6½ft (2m) in height. 'Abel Carrière' has reddish pink flowers. 'Briant Rubidor', also known as 'Rubigold,' has deep red flowers and yellow foliage and is best in partial shade. 'Bristol Ruby' has deep red flowers. 'Eva Rathke' has crimson flowers. 'Evita' is compact and low-growing, to 3ft (1m), with red flowers. *W. florida* is grown in several forms, such as 'Foliis Purpureus', with bronze foliage and pink flowers; 'Variegata', with leaves edged creamy white and pink flowers; and 'Versicolor', with flowers changing from white to red. 'Looymansii Aurea' has golden foliage and pink flowers. *W. middendorffiana* has pale yellow flowers marked with orange. 'Minuet' is compact, to 2½ft (75cm), with bronze foliage and red flowers with a yellow throat. 'Newport Red', also known as 'Vanicek', has purple-red flowers. 'Pink Delight' is compact, with pink flowers. *W. praecox* 'Variegata' has pink flowers and leaves edged with white. 'Red Prince' has red flowers also borne into summer. Zone 4 US; 5 Can.

Xanthorhiza

This genus consists of a single deciduous species found in North America. Preferring a moist well-drained soil in sun or semishade, it is a useful shrub for ground cover, particularly in shady places.

X. simplicissima. The yellowroot is a deciduous upright shrub reaching 2ft (60cm) and spreading by underground stems. The finely cut leaves open bronze in spring, turning red-purple in fall, and panicles of very small purple flowers are produced in spring. Zone 3 US and Can.

Yucca

The 40 or so species in this genus of evergreen trees, shrubs, and perennial herbs are natives of North and Central America. They have long swordlike leaves and prefer a hot dry position in full sun. Although the stemless species, which have leaves in dense rosettes, are strictly herbaceous, they are often regarded as woody and are included here.

Y. filamentosa. Known as Adam's needle, this stemless species has dark green rigid leaves edged with slender white threads. Panicles of white flowers 6½ft (2m) in height are produced in summer. 'Bright Edge' has leaves edged with yellow. 'Ivory Tower' has a dense rosette of leaves and ivory white flowers. 'Variegata' has leaves edged with white. Zone 4 US; 4b Can.

Y. flaccida. Similar to *Y. filamentosa*, this species differs in its more flexible, often drooping leaves and panicles of flowers reaching 5ft (1.5m). 'Golden Sword' has leaves banded with yellow in the center. 'Ivory' has large white flowers flushed with green. Zone 4 US; 5b Can.

Y. glauca. This short-stemmed species has sharp-pointed, blue-green leaves in a dense rosette. The greenish white flowers are carried on a panicle to 5ft (1.5m) in height in summer. Zone 3 US; 4 Can.

Y. gloriosa. The Spanish bayonet develops a thick stem to 3ft (1m) or so, crowned with a dense rosette of sharp-pointed rigid leaves. Tall panicles of white flowers to 8ft (2.5m) in height open in late summer. 'Variegata' has leaves edged with white. Zone 6 US; 7 Can.

Y. recurvifolia. This species has a short stem and bears drooping leaves that are conspicuously blue-green when young. Creamy white flowers in summer are borne on a panicle to 3ft (1m) in height. Zone 6 US; 7 Can.

Zenobia

The single species in this genus is a deciduous or semievergreen shrub native to North America. It prefers a moist but well-drained, lime-free soil in sun or semi-shade. Remove dead flower clusters before fruit develops.

Z. pulverulenta. Growing to 6½ft (2m) in height, this attractive shrub has blue-green foliage and in early summer produces dense lily-of-the-valley-like clusters of drooping, bell-shaped, fragrant, flowers. Zone 5 US; 6 Can.

Xanthorhiza simplicissima

Yucca glauca

Zenobia pulverulenta

A guide to choosing shrubs

Use this section to identify plants for a specific soil or location in your garden. It also provides an easy way to select plants with particular features, such as variegated foliage or fragrant flowers. All the plants are described in the Plant Directory (pp.130–207), where further information on each one is given.

Clay soils

Abelia, all

Aronia, all

Aucuba, all

Berberis, all

Chaenomeles, all

Colutea, all

Cotinus, all

Cotoneaster, all

Deutzia, all

Elaeagnus, all

Escallonia, all

Forsythia, all

Hamamelis, all

Hibiscus, all

Hypericum, all

Lonicera, all

Magnolia, all

Osmanthus, all

Philadelphus, all

Potentilla fruticosa

Pyracantha, all

Ribes, all

Rosa, all

Spiraea, all

Viburnum, all

Weigela, all

Dry, alkaline soils

Aucuba, all

Berberis, all

Buxus, all

Colutea, all

Cornus mas

Cotoneaster, all

Deutzia, all

Euonymus, all

Forsythia, all

Fuchsia, all

Hebe, all

Hibiscus syriacus

Ligustrum, all

Lonicera, all

Mahonia, all

Olearia, all

Paeonia, all

Philadelphus, all

Potentilla fruticosa

Rosa, most

Rosmarinus officinalis

Sambucus, all

Spiraea, most

Syringa, all

Vinca, all

Weigela, all

Moist soils

Aesculus parviflora

Amelanchier alnifolia

Aronia, all

Cornus alba

Cornus stolonifera

Cyrilla racemiflora

Gaultheria shallon

Hippophae rhamnoides

Myrica, all

Salix purpurea

Vaccinium, all

Dry shade

Aucuba japonica

Buxus sempervirens

Danae racemosa

Euonymus fortunei

Euonymus japonicus

Fatsia japonica

Hypericum calycinum

Lonicera nitida

Lonicera pileata

Osmanthus heterophyllus

Prunus laurocerasus

Rubus tricolor

Ruscus aculeatus

Skimmia, all

Vinca, all

Dry, sunny sites

Acer tataricum subsp.

    ginnala

Caragana, all

Caryopteris × clandonensis

Ceratostigma, all

Cistus, all

Coleonema pulchrum

Convolvulus cneorum

Cytisus, all

Eleutherococcus sieboldianus

Fallugia paradoxa

× Halimiocistus, all

Halimium, all

Helianthemum, all

Helichrysum, all

Leucophyllum frutescens

Lycium barbarum

Perovskia atriplicifolia

Phlomis, all

Rosmarinus officinalis

Salvia officinalis

Santolina, all

Shepherdia argentea

Tamarix, all

Teucrium fruticans

Ulex europaeus

Vitex, all

Yucca, all

Coastal gardens

Artemisia arborescens

Baccharis, all

Ceanothus, all

Coprosma, all

Escallonia, all

Cistus all

Griselinia littoralis

Halimium all

Hebe, all

Hippophae rhamnoides

Lycium barbarum

Nerium oleander

Olearia, all

Pittosporum, all

Rhaphiolepis, all

Shepherdia argentea

Tamarix, all

Ulex europaeus

Wall shrubs

Acacia, all

Azara lanceolata

Callistemon, all

Camellia, most

Carpenteria californica

Ceanothus, most

Cestrum nocturnum

Chaenomeles, most

Chimonanthus praecox

Choisya ternata

Cotoneaster horizontalis

Dendromecon rigida

Forsythia suspensa

Fremontodendron, all

Jasminum mesnyi

Jasminum nudiflorum

Leptospermum scoparium

Osteomeles subrotunda

Pyracantha, most

Rhaphiolepis umbellata

Ribes speciosum

Specimen shrubs

Aralia elata

Arbutus unedo

Asimina triloba

Camellia, many

Cornus alternifolia 'Argentea'

Corylus avellana 'Contorta'

Dipelta floribunda

Fatsia japonica

Heptacodium miconioides

Kolkwitzia amabilis

Lagerstroemia, all

Magnolia, many

Mahonia x media

Michelia figo

Olearia macrodonta

Photinia x fraseri

Robinia hispida

Sinocalycanthus chinensis

Syringa, many

Tetrapanax papyrifer

Trochodendron aralioides

Ulmus 'Jacqueline Hillier'

Ground cover

Abelia x grandiflora

'Prostrata'

Arctostaphylos uva-ursi

Baccharis pilularis

Calluna vulgaris

Ceanothus gloriosus

Ceanothus prostratus

Ceanothus thyrsiflorus

var. repens

Cotoneaster adpressus

Cotoneaster apiculatus

Cotoneaster congestus

Cotoneaster dammeri

Cotoneaster horizontalis

Cotoneaster salicifolius 'Gnom'

Diervilla sessilifolia

Erica, except tree heathers

Euonymus fortunei

Euphorbia amygdaloides

var. robbiae

Forsythia 'Arnold Dwarf'

Gaultheria procumbens

Gaultheria shallon

Hebe, many

Hypericum calycinum

Leptospermum rupestre

Leucothoe fontanesiana

Lonicera pileata

Mahonia aquifolium

Paxistima canbyi

Prunus pumila var. depressa

Ribes laurifolium

Rubus pentalobus

Rubus tricolor

Sarcococca confusa

Skimmia, most

Stephanandra incisa 'Crispa'

Symphoricarpos x chenaultii

'Hancock'

Vinca, all

Xanthorhiza simplicissima

Rock garden shrubs

Arctostaphylos uva-ursi

Berberis wilsoniae

Ceanothus gloriosus

Ceanothus prostratus

Cistus, most

Cotoneaster congestu

Cotoneaster horizontalis

Cytisus, many

Daphne, most

Genista, many

Hebe, many

Helianthemum, all

Hypericum olympicum

Lithodora diffusa

Nandina domestica, dwarf

forms

Parahebe, all

Polygala chamaebuxus

Salix, dwarf forms

Shrubs that flower over a long period

Abelia x grandiflora

Abutilon megapotamicum

Euphorbia characias

Fuchsia, most

Helianthemum, most

Hypericum, most

Lavatera, most

Leycesteria formosa

Magnolia liliiflora 'Nigra'

Nerium oleander

Potentilla fruticosa

Shrubs with two-season ornamental features

Berberis, many

Calluna, many

Chaenomeles, most

Cotoneaster, most

Dipelta floribunda

Erica, most

Fothergilla, all

Gaultheria, all

Hamamelis, all

Leycesteria formosa

Lindera obtusiloba

Pyracantha, all

Rosa, many

Solanum pseudocapsicum

Staphylea, all

Symplocos paniculata

Shrubs that flower in winter or early spring

Abeliophyllum distichum

Corylus, all

Daphne bholua

Daphne mezereum

Daphne odora

Edgeworthia chrysantha

Erica carnea

Erica x darleyensis

Erica erigena

Euphorbia amygdaloides

var. robbiae

Euphorbia characias

Forsythia, all

Garrya elliptica

Hamamelis, most

Jasminum nudiflorum

Lonicera fragrantissima

Lonicera x purpusii 'Winter

Beauty'

Loropetalum chinense

Mahonia aquifolium

Mahonia japonica

Oemleria cerasiformis

Pieris japonica

Prunus tenella

Salix, several

Spiraea 'Arguta'

Spiraea thunbergii

Spiraea x vanhouttei

Stachyurus, all

Viburnum x bodnantense

Viburnum farreri

Late-flowering shrubs

Abelia x grandiflora

Calluna vulgaris

Clerodendrum bungei

Daboecia cantabrica

Erica, several

Fuchsia, all

Heptecodium miconioides

Hibiscus syriacus

Hypericum, most

Mahonia × media

Osmanthus × fortunei

Osmanthus heterophyllus

Vitex agnus-castus

Vitex negundo

Aromatic foliage

Aloysia triphylla

Calycanthus floridus

Choisya 'Aztec Pearl'

Choisya ternata

Comptonia peregrina

Elsholtzia stauntonii

Helichrysum italicum

Illicium floridanum

Lavandula, all

Lindera obtusiloba

Myrica, all

Myrtus communis

Ozothamnus ledifolius

Prostanthera, all

Ribes sanguineum

Rosmarinus officinalis

Ruta graveolens

Salvia officinalis

Santolina chamaecyparissus

Skimmia, all

Fragrant flowers

Calycanthus floridus

Carpenteria californica

Cestrum nocturnum

Chimonanthus praecox

Choisya, all

Clethra alnifolia

Corylopsis, all

Daphne, all

Edgeworthia chrysantha

Elaeagnus, all

Franklinia alatamaha

Gardenia augusta

Hamamelis, all

Heptacodium miconioides

Lavandula, all

Loropetalum chinense

Magnolia, most

Michelia figo

Oemleria cerasiformis

Osmanthus, all

Ozothamnus ledifolius

Philadelphus, all

Phillyrea, all

Pittosporum, all

Rhaphiolepis, all

Rubus odoratus

Sarcococca, all

Spartium junceum

Syringa, all

Viburnum, many

Zenobia pulverulenta

Fall color

Acer palmatum

Acer tataricum subsp. ginnala

Aesculus parviflora

Amelanchier alnifolia

Aralia elata

Aronia, all

Berberis, deciduous sorts

Callicarpa, all

Corylopsis, all

Cotinus, all

Cotoneaster, deciduous sorts

Disanthus cercidifolius

Enkianthus, all

Euonymus alatus

Euonymus europaeus
'Red Cascade'

Fothergilla, all

Hamamelis, all

Hydrangea quercifolia

Itea virginica

Lindera obtusiloba

Prunus pumila var. depressa

Rhus, all

Viburnum × carlcephalum

Viburnum dentatum

Viburnum dilatatum

Viburnum lantana

Viburnum opulus

Viburnum plicatu

Viburnum sargentii

Variegated leaves

Abelia × grandiflora
'Francis Mason'

Abutilon megapotamicum
'Variegatum'

Acer palmatum 'Butterfly'

Aralia elata 'Variegata'

Aucuba japonica, several forms

Berberis thunbergii 'Pink
Queen' and 'Rose Glow'

Buxus sempervirens,
several forms

Cleyera japonica 'Fortunei'

Coprosma repens,
several forms

Cornus alba, several forms

Cornus alternifolia 'Argentea'

Cornus mas 'Variegata'

Cornus stolonifera
'Silver and Gold'

Daphne × burkwoodii
'Carol Mackie'

Daphne cneorum 'Variegata'

Daphne odora 'Aureomarginata'

Elaeagnus × ebbingei
'Gilt Edge'

Elaeagnus pungens,
several forms

Eleutherococcus sieboldianus
'Variegatus'

Escallonia 'Gold Ellen'

Euonymus fortunei,
several forms

Euonymus japonicus,
several forms

× Fatshedera lizei 'Annemieke'
and 'Variegata'

Fatsia japonica 'Variegata'

Fuchsia magellanica,
several forms

Gardenia augusta
'Radicans Variegata'

Griselinia littoralis
'Dixon's Cream' and
'Variegata'

Hebe × franciscana 'Variegata'

Hebe glaucophylla 'Variegata'

Hydrangea macrophylla
'Quadricolor'

Hypericum × moserianum
'Tricolor'

Ilex cornuta 'O'Spring'

Ilex crenata 'Shiro-fukurin'

Jasminum nudiflorum 'Aureum'
and 'Mystique'

Kerria japonica 'Picta'

Leucothoe fontanesiana
'Rainbow'

Ligustrum japonicum
'Silver Star'

Ligustrum ovalifolium
'Argenteum' and
'Aureum'

Myrtus communis 'Variegata'

Osmanthus heterophyllus,
several forms

Philadelphus coronarius
'Variegatus'

Photinia davidiana 'Palette'

Pieris 'Flaming Silver'

Pittosporum tenuifolium,
several forms

Pittosporum tobira 'Variegatum'

Prunus laurocerasus
'Castlewellan'

Rhamnus alaternus
'Argenteovariegata'

Rhododendron
'President Roosevelt'

Salvia officinalis 'Icterina'
and 'Tricolor'

Sambucus nigra 'Pulverulenta'

Spiraea japonica
'Anthony Waterer'

Stachyurus praecox 'Magpie'

Symphoricarpos orbiculatus
'Foliis Variegatus'

Symphoricarpos orbiculatus
'Foliis variegatus' and
'Taff's White'

Ternstroemia gymnanthera
'Variegata'

Vinca, several

Weigela florida 'Variegata'

Weigela praecox 'Variegata'

Yucca filamentosa 'Variegata'

Yucca flaccida 'Golden Sword'

Yucca gloriosa 'Variegata'

Yellow leaves

Berberis thunbergii 'Aurea'

Calluna vulgaris, several forms

Caryopteris × clandonensis
'Worcester Gold'

Choisya ternata 'Sundance'

Cornus alba 'Aurea'

Corylus avellana 'Aurea'

Erica carnea, several forms

Hebe ochracea

Ilex crenata 'Golden Gem'

Lonicera nitida
'Baggesen's Gold'

Philadelphus coronarius
'Aureus'

Philadelphus opulifolius
'Dart's Gold' and 'Luteus'

Pittosporum tenuifolium
'Warnham Gold'

Ribes alpinum 'Aureum'

Ribes sanguineum
'Brocklebankii'

Rubus cockburnianus
'Golden Vale'

Sambucus canadensis 'Aurea'

Sambucus nigra 'Aurea'

Sambucus racemosa
'Sutherland's Gold'

Spiraea japonica
'Gold Mound'

Ternstroemia gymnanthera
'Burnished Gold'

Viburnum opulus 'Aureum'

Weigela 'Briant Rubidor' and
'Looymansii Aurea'

Red or purple leaves

Acer palmatum, several forms

Berberis × ottawensis 'Superba'

Berberis thunbergii
f. atropurpurea

Corylopsis sinensis
'Spring Purple'

Corylus maxima 'Purpurea'

Corylus coggygria 'Purple
Cloak' and 'Royal Purple'

Dodonaea viscosa 'Purpurea'

Euonymus fortunei 'Coloratus'

Loropetalum chinense,
several forms

Nandina domestica

Osmanthus heterophyllus
'Purpureus'

Photinia, several

Pieris, many

Pittosporum tenuifolium
'Purpureum' and
'Tom Thumb'

Salvia officinalis 'Purpurascens'

Sambucus nigra
'Guincho Purple'

Spiraea japonica 'Goldflame'

Viburnum sargentii 'Onondaga'

Weigela florida
'Foliis Purpureus'

Gray or silver leaves

Acacia pravissima

Artemisia arborescens

Atriplex canescens

Atriplex halimus

Calluna vulgaris, several forms

Caryopteris × clandonensis

Cistus, several

Convolvulus cneorum

Dendromecon rigida

Elaeagnus, most

Erica tetralix

Halimium lasianthum

Hebe albicans

Hebe cupressoides

Hebe pinguifolia

Helianthemum, several

Helichrysum, all

Hippophae rhamnoides

Lavandula, most

Leptospermum lanigerum

Leucophyllum frutescens

Phlomis italica

Salix × boydii

Salix exigua

Salix lanata

Salvia officinalis

Santolina chamaecyparissus

Shepherdia argentea

Yucca glauca

Bold foliage

Aralia elata

× Fatshedera lizei

Fatsia japonica

Hydrangea quercifolia

Hydrangea aspera

Mahonia japonica

Mahonia × media

Photinia × fraseri

Rubus odoratus

Sambucus canadensis
'Maxima'

Tetrapanax papyrifer

Viburnum davidii

Viburnum. × rhytidophylloides

Viburnum rhytidophyllum

Viburnum. sieboldii

Yucca, all

Ornamental shoots
or bark

Cornus alba

Cornus stolonifera

Corylus avellana 'Contorta'

Dipelta floribunda

Euonymus alatus

Heptacodium miconioides

Kerria japonica

Kerria japonica 'Kinkan'

Lagerstroemia fauriei

Lagerstroemia indica
and hybrids

Poncirus trifoliata

Rhus typhina

Rubus cockburnianus

Rubus phoenicolasius

Rubus thibetanus

Salix irrorata

Salix udensis 'Sekka'

Spartium junceum

Stephanandra, all

Hedges and screens

Acca sellowiana

Arbutus unedo

Berberis, several

Buxus, several

Camellia, many

Cotoneaster, several

Dodonaea viscosa

Elaeagnus, several

Escallonia, several

Griselinia littoralis

Hebe, several

Hippophae rhamnoides

Hypericum 'Hidcote'

Ilex, several

Lagerstroemia, all

Lavandula, all

Ligustrum, many

Lonicera, several

Olearia × haastii

Photinia × fraseri

Pittosporum tenuifolium

Potentilla fruticosa

Prunus laurocerasus

Prunus lusitanica

Pyracantha, all

Ternstroemia gymnanthera

Ulex europaeus

Viburnum, several

Seasonal reminders

The gardener's year is a continuous cycle of varying tasks and pleasures. There is truly no beginning and end in the literal sense, but rather an ongoing progression from one season to the next. The reminders highlighted below are general tips to spur your memory.

These seasonal reminders are oriented toward Northern Hemisphere, temperate-climate gardener. Depending on whether you garden in a colder or warmer region, you may find that you need to begin different tasks earlier or later in each season. Year-to-year variation in the specific conditions of each season will also be an important factor. A late, cold spring will mean delays in much of the spring work, for example. An early, hot dry spring may mean avoiding doing most of the planned transplanting that particular year. Each year's accumulated experience in your garden will add to your knowledge about timing and managing all your seasonal tasks for the following cycle. One of the most delightful aspects of gardening is the continual change and development of the plants and landscape. The only thing that is certain in gardening is that nothing will ever be quite the same from one year to the next—whatever the weather.

Rosa x *odorata* 'Mutabalis'

Shrub roses like this *Rosa* x *odorata* 'Mutabalis' require a light annual renewal pruning in winter to remove dead, damaged, diseased, or weak wood, leaving the plant healthy for the next season's growth.

Spring

- **Soil preparation and planting.** When the soil is lightly moist, work aged organic matter or compost in new beds. Make sure to leave mulch on beds until the last of the extreme winter weather has passed, and then rake heavy winter mulches away from plants and beds. Clean away any debris, fallen limbs, and the like. Plant all new plantings as early as possible after all danger of frost has passed. Transplant deciduous shrubs either very early before significant new growth has emerged or late in spring after new growth has emerged and begun to firm. Make sure to water consistently and thoroughly both before and after planting and transplanting, especially for late plantings. In cold climates, fertilize lightly with a slow-release fertilizer. Refresh mulch on existing plantings with a light cover of new material. Be careful to keep the mulch several inches away from the main stems to avoid rotting the bark or encouraging pests.
- **Routine care.** Remove all protective winter structures and repot into larger container if required. Remove any protective heavy mulches from containerized shrubs, resume active and regular watering once new growth is visible on containerized shrubs, and fertilize lightly with a slow-release fertilizer.
- **Pruning and training.** In early spring, do all coppicing, hard pruning, and renewal pruning of shrubs that flower on the current year's wood. In late spring, once the first flush of new growth has emerged and hardened off somewhat, give hedges a light shearing. Train and prune espalier and topiary. In late spring, after flowering, prune shrubs that flower on the previous year's wood. After the main pruning, continue to remove all dead and diseased wood whenever you notice it.
- **Propagation.** In early to midspring, root softwood cuttings; in late spring, root semisoftwood cuttings.

Summer

- **Soil preparation and planting.** Keep plantings free of weeds. Refresh mulch lightly where needed and mulch new beds with 2–3in (5–8cm) of mulch. Avoid planting and transplanting in the summer, except for containers and raised beds.
- **Routine care.** Keep newly planted and transplanted plants well watered. Established shrub plantings should be watered if an extended dry period occurs that is unusual for your region.

• **Pruning and training.** Shear hedges lightly as needed, making sure to retain a silhouette with the base wider than the top. Prune summer-blooming shrubs that flower on the previous year's wood after they have finished flowering. Continue pruning and training espalier and topiary as required.

• **Propagation.** Root semihardwood cuttings in early to midsummer and hardwood cuttings in late summer as appropriate. Collect seed of those species that bear early-maturing fruit and clean and process the seed as soon as it has been collected. Layer or divide shrubs as appropriate.

Fall

• **Soil preparation and planting.** Do not fertilize any plantings as that would delay winter acclimation. In early fall, plant and transplant hardy evergreen shrubs, making sure to keep newly-planted plants well watered for a month or so. In late fall, transplant deciduous shrubs and apply thicker, protective winter mulches where needed.

• **Routine care.** Avoid supplemental watering during fall unless your region has been experiencing a very prolonged drought. Keep beds well weeded. In late fall, cover susceptible shrubs with protective winter structures, but make certain to wait until all warm weather is finished for the season.

• **Pruning and training.** Do corrective pruning and shaping of most evergreen and some deciduous shrubs, but avoid pruning shrubs that flower on the previous year's wood if possible. In early fall, do renewal pruning of evergreen shrubs. Continue to remove dead, diseased, and damaged limbs and branches as needed. Train espalier and topiary as required. Plan which shrubs to coppice in late winter.

• **Propagation.** Root hardwood cuttings and root cuttings in early fall from appropriate species and cultivars. Clean and process seed as soon as it is collected. Construct outdoor seedbeds and sow cleaned seed of species to be overwintered outdoors. Apply other seed treatments to other seed as needed. Layer or divide shrubs as appropriate.

Winter

• **Soil preparation and planting.** Plant in late winter in warm climates once the soil is thoroughly free of frost and is not too wet. In warm climates, apply a slow-release fertilizer in very late winter (in cold climates, wait until very early spring).

• **Routine care.** In early winter, cover evergreens such as boxwoods and rhododendrons with any necessary snow-protective structures. Make sure to wait until transitional swings from warm to cold weather have abated, to avoid delaying the onset of cold acclimation in protected plants. Gently brush snow loads off the upper canopies of all medium to large shrubs, particularly sheared hedges. Low-growing shrubs may benefit from the insulating qualities of snow cover and should therefore be left covered for as long as the snow lasts.

Deciduous azalea
Many deciduous shrubs that flower in spring or early summer carry their flowers on wood produced in the previous growing season. These plants should be pruned in summer after flowering.

• **Pruning and training.** Remove all dead, diseased, and broken limbs and branches as you find them. In late winter, do any necessary formative or corrective pruning that was not apparent during the growing season. Late winter is a particularly good time to prune blueberries and grapes.

• **Propagation.** In early winter, root those species/cultivars that root well from winter hardwood cuttings or from root cuttings. Sow seed of shrubs that has undergone stratification as soon as adequate light is available. Some shrubs can be propagated in late winter, although it is advisable to take particular care of most of them at this most inhospitable time of year.

Glossary

Acid soil: Soil with a pH of less than 7; the opposite of **alkaline** soil and **basic soil**.

Alkaline soil: Soil with a pH of more than 7, the opposite of **acid soil** (the same as **basic soil**).

Balled-and-burlapped: Describes trees and shrubs grown in the field with an attached root ball that has been covered and tied in a layer of burlap.

Bare-root: Describes trees and shrubs (such as roses) that have been grown in the field and dug when dormant without a soil ball.

Basic soil: Soil with a pH of more than 7, the opposite of **acid soil**.

Border: A garden style of planting that involves arranging a diversity of ornamental plants in a linear or curvilinear contiguous bed.

Broad-leaved evergreen: An evergreen plant that is not a conifer (and thus does not have needlelike foliage).

Bud: An undeveloped, unexpanded leaf, flower, shoot, or combination of all three, in its dormant state and usually covered with scales.

Clay: A type of soil material made up of very tiny mineral particles that are sticky when wet. Clay soil is generally poorly drained, poorly aerated, and easily compacted when wet, but it may be quite fertile.

Clone: An exact genetic copy of one individual, produced in plants by vegetative propagation.

Cluster: A group of flowers or fruits that have developed together.

Compost: Rotted organic matter.

Container grown: Describes plants that have been grown from cuttings or seed in containers.

Coppicing: Pruning all the stems of a tree or shrub to uniform height to induce newly invigorated regrowth.

Crown: The area of a shrub where the roots and stem meet, near and just above the soil line.

Cultivar: A cultivated variety of a species that has been selected for a particular trait, such as unusual flower color.

Cutting: A piece of stem, leaf, or root, separated from the parent plant and used for propagation to produce a new plant.

Deciduous: Said of plants that lose their leaves at the end of each growing season .

Dieback: The death of the shoots of plants, due either to seasonal response or to disease.

Division: A method of propagation whereby the crown or offshoots, of the parent plant are divided and separated into new plants that retain roots and shoots of their own.

Dormancy: A quiescent period when a plant experiences no active growth or development.

Drainage (of soil): The relative speed at which water and/or other solutions permeate and move through the soil profile. Well-drained soil absorbs moisture readily and does not puddle or remain soaked for extended periods.

Dwarf: An often misused term to describe a selection that is slower growing than the parent species. Dwarf selections may reach mature heights that may or may not seem very small on a human scale.

Espalier: A plant trained to grow flat against a wall or trellis.

Evergreen: Said of plants that retain most of their leaves for more than one yearly growing cycle.

Family: A botanical group of related genera.

Foundation planting: A planting of often low-growing, plants originally used to disguise the foundations of buildings but now used in many ways.

Full sun: Uninterrupted sunshine with no physical barriers to the light for at least six hours a day.

Genus: A botanical group of closely related species (plural genera).

Germination: The emergence of new seedlings from the seed (sprouting).

Graft: A method of **propagation** that combines a shoot of a desired plant (scion) mechanically with the root (understock) of a nurse plant that then grow together as one plant.

Ground cover: A mass planting of usually low-growing plants that covers an area; an alternative to lawn.

Habit: The silhouette and architecture in relation to the shape of a plant.

Hardwood cutting: A stem cutting taken from a plant late in the growing season when the stem has hardened.

Hardy (of cold): Able to survive the cold-season conditions of a region.

Hedge: A barrier planting of many plants, planted in close proximity to each other to create a living wall.

Herbaceous: Said of a plant with little or no woody tissue that dies to the ground after each growing cycle.

Hybrid: The offspring generation of a cross between two species.

Invasive: Overly vigorous; such a plant grows in an uncontrolled manner and cannot be easily removed once it has established itself.

Knot garden: A planting of herbs, flowers, and shrubs in beds of close proximity that gives the illusion of a knot or braid. To appreciate its patterns it is best viewed from above.

Layering: A method of **propagation** where roots are induced to grow on an area of stem that remains intact on the parent plant. It is separated once roots have formed to make a new individual.

Loam: A type of soil with a good balance of clay, sand, and organic matter; the best type of garden soil.

Lime: Finely ground alkaline mineral that may be added to soil to help raise the soil pH.

Margin: The edge of a leaf.

Mass: A group of plants planted in close proximity to each other in an irregular shape.

Microclimate : A term used in reference to the specific conditions found in a small area of a garden.

Muck: A specific type of unusual soil with very high organic matter content.

Mulch: A layer of organic material or gravel applied to the garden surface to help retain moisture and prevent weed growth.

Neutral (of soil): Neither alkaline nor acidic, having a pH of 7.

Node: The site on a stem where leaves or branches emerge.

Organic: Said of material derived from organisms; carbonaceous material.

Parterre: A formal planting that is usually sheared regularly to produce a complex, pleasing pattern.

Peat moss: Partially decomposed moss harvested from boggy areas.

Perennial: A plant that remains alive for more than two growing cycles and that produces seed during its life more than once.

pH: A measure of the relative acidity/alkalinity of soils or solutions as described by the concentration of hydrogen ions present.

Photosynthesis: The process unique to green plants that converts light energy from the sun into sugars.

Pollarding: Cutting all the branches and stems of trees or shrubs back to a single main stem or trunk.

Propagation: Increasing a plant in numbers by various methods.

Provenance: The region of origin of a plant species.

Prune: To trim the branches and stems or roots of a plant.

Pruning saw: A saw specifically designed for pruning plants, usually with a curved blade that may or may not have a long extended handle used to reach upper branches.

Root (or root): The below-ground organ of a plant that absorbs water and nutrients and anchors the plant in the ground.

Sand: A type of soil material made up of relatively large mineral particles that are not sticky when wet. Sand is used in some gardens to improve the drainage of heavy soils.

Scales: The diminutive, modified leaves covering a dormant bud.

Screen: A planting intended to shield part of the garden or landscape from view or from winds.

Seed: A fertilized ovule generally covered with a protective coat and found inside a fruit or cone.

Seedling: A very young plant recently emerged from a seed.

Secateurs: A pair of hand pruners or clippers that fits readily in one hand.

Semievergreen: Said of plants that retain some of their foliage for more than one growing cycle.

Semihardwood cutting (also known as semiripe): A stem cutting taken from a plant midway through the growing season, when the stem has begun to harden only slightly.

Sexual propagation: Propagation using seed in which there has been exchange of genetic material between the parent plants.

Shear: To cut away parts of a plant in a uniform manner to create flat, even surfaces (such as for hedges).

Shoot: An above-ground portion of a plant.

Shrub: A woody perennial plant with multiple main stems that is generally smaller than a tree.

Species: A botanical group of very closely related individual plants that reproduce readily with each other and that are clearly distinguishable from other species.

Specimen: A plant grown as an individual, especially ornamental, feature in the garden.

Stake: To bind a plant to upright sticks in the ground in order to stabilize an especially tall plant, or a plant that is newly planted.

Stem: A nonfoliar aboveground portion of a plant on which buds, leaves, and flowers are borne.

Stratify: To pretreat seed to enhance germination by storing it in moist material in a refrigerator or other cold place above freezing temperatures.

Sucker: A secondary shoot emerging from buds on the underground parts of a plant.

Thin: To prune by removing densely spaced stems on a shrub.

Topiary: A form of pruning that results in plants with highly manipulated shapes (such as animals or geometric forms).

Transpiration: The process whereby water evaporates from the surfaces of the leaves of a plant and is replaced by water moving up from the roots and through the vascular system.

Transplant: To plant a plant in a new location, either by digging it from the ground in one location and planting it in a new one, or by planting a **container** grown or **balled-and-burlapped** plant.

Variegation (of leaves, flowers, or stems): Variably colored, with margins or surfaces that are splashed, spotted, speckled, or striped with a contrasting color.

Variety: A population of plants differing in a minor but consistent way from the parent species; a more informal term than **cultivar**.

Vascular system: The circulatory tissues in a plant (xylem and phloem) that transport water, sugars, nutrients, and other metabolic materials throughout the plant body.

Vegetative propagation: Propagation other than from seed (e.g. from root and stem cuttings), and independent of any exchange of genetic material between plants producing clones of the parent plant (e.g. by root or stem cuttings).

Woody plant: A plant that produces hard stems that remain alive above ground for many seasons and that retain the dormant buds that increase shoot growth from year to year.

Hardiness zones

While there are many factors that will influence a plant's survival in a particular area,

one of the most important is the lowest temperature that a plant is likely to experience

during winter. Plants that survive winters in a particular area are called hardy, while those

that succumb to cold weather are called tender.

The ability of a plant to survive low temperatures is referred to as its hardiness. All plants are hardy somewhere. For example, where a plant occurs in the wild, it is adapted to survive local conditions. However, while many plants can cope with temperatures lower than they would experience in natural conditions, as temperature decreases, a point is reached at which the plant is damaged. For example, the dwarf wooly willow, *Salix lanata*, grows naturally in areas with very cold winters and is unlikely to be killed by frost in almost any garden. On the other hand, the glory bush, *Tibouchina urvilleana,* is hardy only in gardens with very mild winters.

In order to define the areas in which particular plants are hardy or not, a system of hardiness zones was devised by the U.S. Department of Agriculture, originally for North America but later extended to other parts of the world. The 11 zones are based on the average minimum winter temperature in a given area and range from the coldest, Zone 1, with an average minimum winter temperature of below −50° F (−46°C), to the warmest, Zone 11, with an average minimum temperature of above 40°F (4°C). To give you an idea as to whether a plant will be hardy in your area, we have given the hardiness zone of each plant in the Plant Directory (pp.130–207), and the geographical areas to which the zones relate are shown on the maps in the endpapers of this book.

As a rule, a plant designated as hardy in Zone 8 will normally survive winters in Zone 8 and in warmer zones. Although it may survive mild winters or can be given protection in Zone 7, it is much more likely to be killed by winter cold there. Remember that the division between zones is not rigid and that there is considerable overlap between them, particularly at their upper and lower limits. Depending on local conditions, some areas or gardens could be a little warmer or colder in winter than the rest of their zone. For example, a garden that is in a "frost pocket" in one zone could be colder than one where frost drains freely in a neighboring, colder zone. Also, city gardens are generally warmer than those in country areas and could well belong in the next warmest zone, thus allowing many plants not hardy in that zone

to survive. Canadian hardiness zones are described differently. They were devised using winter temperatures and indicator plants. Each zone is divided into two. For example, while a plant hardy to Zone 5 will survive winters in the whole of that zone, one hardy to Zone 5b will survive winters only in the warmer parts.

The importance of summer temperatures

Although hardiness zones are based on winter temperature, other factors, such as summer temperature, are also important. Some plants grow well in an area with high summer temperatures but fail in an area with cooler summers, even though that area may be in a warmer zone. The crape myrtle (*Lagerstroemia indica*) is an example of this. Hardy to Zone 7 in the United States, it fails in milder areas of Britain, not because of winter temperature but because of the lack of summer heat to ripen growth. While it is not surprising that plants from relatively warm areas will often not thrive in areas where winters are cold, some plants that occur naturally in cooler areas may not be able to withstand high summer temperatures. In these areas, high humidity or very dry conditions may also be limiting. In addition, some plants can be excited into growth by warm weather early in the year only to suffer from damage by late-spring frosts. Knowing the hardiness rating of each plant enables the gardener not only to choose plants that will be hardy but also to position them accordingly.

Range of hardiness

The list opposite gives the US/Canadian range of hardiness for each genus described in the Plant Directory. Where a genus is not hardy in Canada, it is shown as NH. This list can be used to find which shrubs can be considered for planting in your garden. For example, if you live in Zone 4, you could grow *Vaccinium, Viburnum,* and *Vinca* since these are species hardy to a colder zone, but not *Vitex*. There may well be some species in a given genus that will not survive for you, but providing the first number in the range is lower than your zone, some certainly will survive.

A
Abelia 5–7/6–7
Abeliophyllum 4/5b
Abutilon 7–8/8–9
Acacia 8/8
Acca 8/8
Acer 2–6/2–6
Aesculus 4/4
Aloysia 8/9
Amelanchier 3/2b–3b
Andromeda 2/2
Aralia 4/NH
Arbutus 7/NH
Arctostaphylos 3/1
Aronia 4/4b
Artemisia 7–8/8–NH
Asminia 4/6
Atriplex 7/8
Aucuba 7/8
Azara 8/9

B
Baccharis 5–8/6–NH
Berberis 3–7/5–7
Buddleja 4–7/4–8
Buxus 4–5/5b–6

C
Callicarpa 5–7/5b–8
Callistemon 9/NH
Calluna 4/3
Calycanthus 4–7/5–7
Camellia 7–8/8
Caragana 2/2–2b
Carpenteria 8/8
Caryopteris 5/6
Ceanothus 4–8/5b–9
Cephalanthus 4/4
Ceratostigma 6–8/8–NH
Cestrum 9/NH
Chaenomeles 4–5/5–5b
Chimonanthus 6/7
Chionanthus 3/5
Choisya 7/8
Cistus 7–8/6–7b.
Clerodendrum 7/8
Clethra 3–5/5–6
Cleyera 8/9
Coleonema 9/NH
Colutea 5/5
Comptonia 2/2
Convolvulus 8/9
Coprosma 8/9
Cornus 2–4/2–4
Corylopsis 5–6/7–8
Corylus 4–5/4–5
Cotinus 4–5/4–5.
Cotoneaster 2–6/2–8.
Cyrilla 6/7.
Cytisus 5–7/6–7

D
Daboecia 6/6
Danae 8/?9
Daphne 2–8/2b–8
Dendromecon 8/9

Desfontainia 8/9
Deutzia 4–6/5b–7
Diervilla 4/4
Dipelta 6/7
Disanthus 6/7
Dodonaea 9/NH
Duranta 9/NH

E
Edgeworthia 8/7
Elaeagnus 2–8/2–9
Eleutherococcus 4/5
Elsholtzia 5/6
Enkianthus 4–5/5b–7
Erica 4–7/4–8
Escallonia 7/8
Euonymus 3–7/3–5b
Euphorbia 7–10/NH
Exochorda 4–6/4–5

F
Fabiana 9/NH
Fallugia 6/7
x *Fatshedera* 7/8
Fatsia 7/8
Forsythia 4–5/4b–6
Fothergilla 4–5/5b–6
Franklinia 5/6
Fremontodendron 8/9
Fuchsia 6–7/7–8

G
Gardenia 9–10/NH
Garrya 7/8
Gaultheria 3–6/4–7
Genista 3–7/3–8
Grevillea 9–10/NH
Griselinia 9/NH

H
x *Halimiocistus* 9/NH
Halimium 9/NH
Hamamelis 4–5/4b–6b
Hebe 5–9/?6–NH
Helianthemum 5/6
Helichrysum 8–9/9–NH
Heptacodium 4/5
Hibiscus 5–10/6–NH.
Hippophae 3/2b.
Holodiscus 6/7
Hydrangea 3–7/3b–8
Hypericum 3–6/4–7

I
Ilex 3–7/3b–8
Illicium 7/8
Indigofera 6–7/7–8
Itea 5–8/6–9

J
Jasminum 6–9/7–NH

K
Kalmia 2–4/2–5b.
Kerria 4/5b
Kolkwitzia 4/5

L
Lagerstroemia 7/8
Lavandula 5–6/6–7
Lavatera 4/5
Ledum 2/2
Leptospermum 9/NH
Lespedeza 4–5/5–6
Leucophyllum 8/9
Leucothoe 5/6
Leycesteria 7/8
Ligustrum 4–8/5–9?
Lindera 4–6/5b–7
Lithodora 6/7
Lonicera 1–7/1–8
Loropetalum 8/9?
Lycium 6/7

M
Magnolia 4–7/5–8
Mahonia 4–9/4b–NH
Menziesia 6/7
Michelia 9/NH
Myrica 1–7/1–8
Myrtus 8/9

N
Nandina 6/7
Neillia 6/7
Nerium 9/NH
Neviusia 4/5b

O
Oemleria 7/8
Olearia 9/NH
Osmanthus 7–9/8–NH
Osteomeles 9/NH
Ozothamnus 9/NH

P
Paeonia 4–7/5–7
Parahebe 7/8
Paxistima 2/2b
Perovskia 4/5
Philadelphus 3–6/4b–7
Phillyrea 9/NH
Phlomis 6–9/7–NH
Photinia 7–8/8–9?
Phygelius 7–8/7–8
Physocarpus 2–6/2b–7.
Pieris 4–5/5b–6
Pittosporum 8–9/9?–NH
Polygala 7/8
Poncirus 5/6b
Potentilla 2/2
Prostanthera 9/NH
Prunus 2–7/2–8
Pyracantha 4–8/5b–9

R
Rhamnus 3/3b
Rhaphiolepis 9/NH
Rhododendron 3–8/4–9
Rhodotypos 4/5b
Rhus 2–3/2b–3
Ribes 2–9/2–NH
Robinia 4/5

L
Rosa 2–7/2b–8
Rosmarinus 6/7
Rubus 3–7/3–8
Ruscus 4–7/5b–8
Ruta 4/5b

S
Salix 1–6/1–7
Salvia 4/5b
Sambucus 3/4
Santolina 6–7/7–8
Sarococca 6/7
Shepherdia 2/1
Sinocalycanthus 8/9
Skimmia 6–7/7–8
Solanum 9/NH
Sorbaria 6/7
Sorbus 4/5
Spartium 7/8
Spiraea 2–4/2b–4b
Stachyurus 6–9/7–NH
Staphylea 37
Stephanandra 4–5/5–6
Styrax 5/6
Symphoricarpos 2–4/2b–5
Symplocos 4/5b
Syringa 2–4/2–5

T
Tamarix 2–5/2b–6
Telopea 9/NH
Ternstroemia 7/8
Tetrapanax 8/9?
Teucrium 5 US; 9?
Tibouchina 10/NH
Trochodendron 6/7

U
Ulex 6/7
Ulmus 7?/8?

V
Vaccinium 2–10/1–NH
Viburnum 2–8/2b–9
Vinca 3–5/3–6
Vitex 5–6/6b–7

W
Weigela 4/5

X
Xanthorhiza 3/3

Y
Yucca 3–6/4–7

Z
Zenobia 5/6

Suppliers

This is by no means a complete list of all the quality nurseries that retail shrubs in North America but is merely a sampling across regions of firms of which the authors are aware. Omission of a particular nursery from this list makes no implication regarding quality or availability of plants sold.

NOTE: Where no telephone number has been provided, either it is not available or proprietors do not wish to receive calls; addresses and phone numbers may be subject to change following publication.

Arborvillage Farm Nursery
PO Box 227
Holt, MO 64048
Tel: 816-264-3911

Blue Meadow Farm
184 Meadow Road
Montague Center, MA 01351
Tel: 413-367-2394

Camellia Forest Nursery
PO Box 291
Chapel Hill, NC 27514

Collector's Nursery
160804 NE 102nd Avenue
Battle Ground, WA 98604
Tel: 360-574-3832

Cummins Garden
22 Robertsville Road
Marlboro, NJ 07746
Tel: 201-536-2591

Eastern Plant Specialties
PO Box 226
Georgetown Island, ME 04548
Tel: 207-371-2888

Fairweather Garden
PO Box 330
Greenwich, NJ 08323
Tel: 609-451-2591

Fjellgarden
PO Box 1111
Lakeside, AZ 85929

Forest Farm
900 Tetherow Road
Williams, OR 97478
Tel: 541-846-7269

Gossler Farms Nursery
1200 Weaver Road
Springfield, OR 97544
Tel: 541-746-3922

Greer Gardens
1280 Goodpasture Island Road
Eugene, OR 97401
Tel: 541-686-8266

Heaths and Heathers
PO Box 850
Elma, WA 98541
Tel: 360-482-3258

Heronswood Nursery
7530 288th Street NE
Kingston, WA 98346
Tel: 360-297-4172

Klehm Nursery
4210 North Duncan Road
Champaign, IL 61821
Tel: 800-553-3715

Logee's Greenhouses
141 North Street
Danielson, CT 06239
Tel: 860-774-8038

Midwest Groundcovers
PO Box 748
St. Charles, IL 60174
Tel: 707-742-1790

Miniature Plant Kingdom
4125 Harrison Grade Road
Sebastopol, CA 95472
Tel: 707-874-2233

Plant Delights Nursery
9241 Sauls Road
Raleigh, NC 27603
Tel: 919-772-4794

Plants of the Southwest
Aqua Fria Road 6, Box 11A
Santa Fe, NM 87501
Tel: 505-471-2212

Rice Creek Gardens
1315 66th Avenue NE
Minneapolis, MN 55432
Tel: 612-754-8090

Rock Spray Nursery, Inc.
Box 693
Truro, MA 02666
Tel: 508-349-6769

Roses of Yesterday and Today, Inc.
802 Brown's Valley Road
Watsonville, CA 95076-0398
Tel: 408-724-3537

Roslyn Nursery
211 Burr Lane
Dix Hills, NY 11746
Tel: 516-643-9347

Siskiyou Rare Plant Nursery
2825 Cummings Road
Medford, OR 97501
Tel: 541-772-6846

Twombly Nursery
163 Barn Hill Road
Monroe, CT 06468
Tel: 203-261-2133

Washington Evergreen Nursery
PO Box 388
Brooks Branch Road
Leicester, NC 28748

Wayside Gardens
1 Garden Lane
Hodges, SC 29695
Tel: 800-845-1124

We-Du Nurseries
Route 5, PO Box 724
Marion, NC 28752
Tel: 704-738-8300

Weston Nurseries
PO Box 186
Hopkington, MA 01748
Tel: 508-435-3414

White Flower Farm
PO Box 50, Route 63
Litchfield,
CT 06759-0050
Tel: 800-503-9624

Woodlander's Nursery
1128 Colleton Avenue
Aiken, SC 29801
Tel: 803-648-7522

Yucca Do Nursery
PO Box 450
Waller, TX 77484

CANADIAN MAIL-ORDER SOURCES

Aubin Nurseries, Ltd.
Box 1089 Carman
Manitoba R0G 0JA
Tel: 204-745-6703

Corn Hill Nursery
R.R.5 Petitcodiac
New Brunswick E05 H20
Tel: 506-756-3635

Hortico Inc.
723 Robson Rd, RR1
Waterdown
Ontario LOR 2HI
Tel: 905-689-6984

Hole's Greenhouses & Gardens
101 Bellerose Drive
St.Albert
Alberta T8N 8N8
Tel: 888-884-6537

Fraser's Thimble Farms
175 Arbutus Rd
Salt Spring Island
British Columbia U8K 1A3
Tel: 250-537-5788

Oslach Nurseries Inc.
R.R.1, Simcoe,
Ontario N39 4J9
Tel: 519-426-9553

Index

Photographic Acknowledgments

Biofotos /Heather Angel 14 bottom, 15
Anne Hyde 8, 14 top, 85 top, 91, 95 top, 108, 111, 137 right, 175 right, 189 center
John Fielding 3, 5, 55 left, 90 right, 122 bottom, 135 center left, 136 left, 146 top, 151 right, 157 top, 161 right, 163 left & right, 167 bottom, 168 left, 171 bottom, 177 top, 180 top, 182 right, 185 top, 188 bottom, 189 top, 197 top, 198 right, 200 top, 204 right, 205 right
Garden Picture Library 21, /Philippe Bonduel 133 top right, 166 top, 174 left, 179 top, /Brian Carter 31 bottom, 112 (Champs Hill, Colwaltham, W Sussex), 126 bottom, 134 center right, 154 left, 177 bottom, /Henk Dijkman 109 (Beth Chatto's Garden, Colchester, Essex), /David England 127 top, /Ron Evans 205 center, /Christopher Fairweather 139 right, 160 right, 175 left, /John Glover 9, 18, 48 bottom, 49 bottom, 59, 79, 81, 89 bottom, 90 left, 101 bottom, 110 bottom, 121 bottom, 157 centre, 160 left, 165 bottom, 167 center, 184 left, 193 right, 195 top, /Sunniva Harte 98 bottom, 148 top, 174 right, 206 center, /Neil Holmes 11, 32 top, 74, 105, 128, 132 top left, 137 left, 156 top, 158 centre, 173 bottom, 180 bottom, 191 center, 191 right, 197 bottom, /Lamontagne 72 (Wisley Rock Garden) 96, 118, 120, 125, 126 top, 172 top, /Jane Legate 190 left, /Mayer/Le Scanff 20, 47, 51, /Marianne Majerus 68 bottom, /Clive Nichols 60 bottom, /Jerry Pavia 82, 93, 123 (Harland Hand Garden, EL Cerrito, USA), 135 bottom left, 144 center & left, 147 bottom, /97 Morley Read (Headlands, Polruran, Cornwall), /Howard Rice 33 bottom, 70 (Cambridge Botanic Garden), 127 bottom (E.J. Rice, Saxlington, Norfolk), 147 top, 169 right, 206 top, /David Russell 168 center, /JS Sira 6 left, 45, 53 top, 85

bottom, 94 top, 99, 104 top, 107 top, 145 center, 150 center, 173 top, 205 left, 207 center, /Friedrich Strauss 87, /Ron Sutherland 84 bottom, 110 top, /Brigitte Thomas 17, 44/5, 67, /Didier Willery 66, 107 bottom, 116 bottom, 207 bottom, /Steven Wooster 77 (Keukenhof, Holland), 83, 117
John Glover 2, 8 (Alan Titchmarsh), 19, 53 bottom (Winkworth Arboretum, Surrey), 84 top (Stream Cottage, Sussex), 86 (The Dillon Garden, Dublin), 88, 89 top, 115 top, 121 top, 122 top, 133 bottom right, 133 center right, 135 top left, 138 right, 141 right, 152 right, 155 top, 157 bottom, 158 bottom, 159 center, 165 top, 171 top, 178 left, 179 bottom
Jerry Harpur 49 top, 61 bottom, 64 (Old Rectory, Sudborough), 103 (Manor House, Bledlow), 114 (The Dingle, Welshpool), 115 bottom (Cambridge Botanic), 124 (Home Farm)
Andrew Lawson Photography 7, 10, 13 top, 32 bottom, 39 top, 46, 57 (The Priory, Oxfordshire), 58, 60 top, 65 (The Garden House), 68 top, 69, 71, 78, 92 (Designed by Rosemary Verey), 94 bottom, 95 bottom, 100, 113 top, 113 bottom (Putsborough Manor), 129, 134 top left, 138 center, 139 left, 140 bottom, 141 top left, 142 right, 143 left, 145 right, 149 top, 155 bottom, 156 center, 159 top, 164 top, 166 bottom, 168 right, 169 left, 170 top, 185 bottom, 192 right, 193 center, 195 center, 195 bottom, 196 bottom, 197 center, 212
S & O Mathews 4/5, 39 bottom, 104 bottom
Clive Nichols Photography 1, 6 center, 9, 61 top (Brook Cottage, Oxfordshire), 101 top (Lakemount, Glanmire, Eire), 102 (RHS Garden, Wisley, Surrey), 141 bottom left, 148 bottom, 150 right, 151

center, 153 bottom, 154 right, 170 bottom, 172 center, 175 center, 186 center, 198 center, 213 (Exbury Gardens, Hampshire)
Photos Horticultural 6 right, 37, 38 bottom, 50 top, 54, 55 right, 56, 62 (Kalmthout Arboretum, Belgium), 63, 80, 98 top, 116 top, 132 bottom left, 132 center left, 134 bottom left, 136 right, 138 left, 140 top, 142 bottom left, 142 top left, 143 bottom right, 143 top right, 144 right, 145 left, 146 bottom, 148 center, 149 bottom, 151 left, 152 left, 153 top, 156 bottom, 158 top, 159 bottom, 161 left, 162, 164 bottom, 164 center, 166 center, 167 top, 169 center, 170 center, 172 bottom, 174 center, 176 left, 176 right, 178 right, 181, 182 left, 183 left, 183 right, 184 right, 186 top, 186 bottom, 187, 188 center, 188 top, 189 bottom, 190 right, 191 left, 193 left, 194 bottom, 194 top, 194 center, 196 center, 196 top, 198 left, 199 left, 199 right, 200 center, 200 bottom, 201, 202, 203, 204 left, 206 bottom, 207 top
Reed International Books Ltd 192 left, /Andrew Lawson 48 top, /Mark Williams 50 top left, 50 top right, 50 far right, 50 bottom left
Saxon Holt 119
Harry Smith Collection 150 left
Curtice Taylor /Virginia Purviance 106 (Rhode Island)

Canadian Hardiness Zones

Zone 1	Zone 2	Zone 3	Zone 4	Zone 5	Zone 6	Zone 7	Zone 8	Zone 9
a b	a b	a b	a b	a b	a b	a b	a b	a b

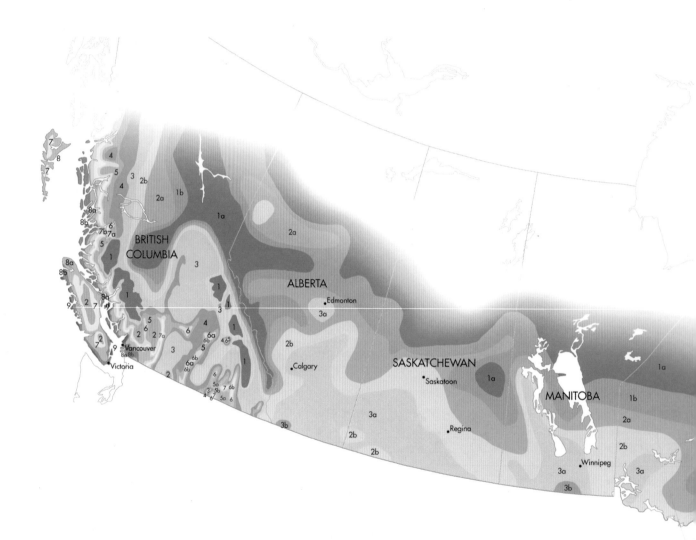